# Clerical Sexual Misconduct

Volume Two

## A Foundational Conversation

Editors

Jane F. Adolphe

Robert L. Fastiggi

En Route Books and Media, LLC
Saint Louis, MO

En Route Books and Media, LLC
5705 Rhodes Avenue
St. Louis, MO 63109

Cover credit: Sebastian Mahfood

ISBN-13: 979-8-88870-033-4
Library of Congress Control Number: 2023932323

Copyright © 2023 Jane F. Adolphe and Robert Fastiggi
All rights reserved.

No part of this booklet may be reproduced, stored in a retrieval system, or transmitted in any form, or by any means, electronic, mechanical, photocopying, or otherwise, without the prior written permission of the author.

For all those women who collaborate
with the hierarchy of the Catholic Church.

# TABLE OF CONTENTS

ACKNOWLEDGMENTS   V

PREFACE
    *REV. CHRISTOPHER POLLARD*   VII

FOREWORD
    *HELEN M. ALVARÉ*   XV

INTRODUCTION
    *JANE F. ADOLPHE AND ROBERT L. FASTIGGI* 1

I.   A MARIAN PERSPECTIVE ON CLERICAL SEXUAL MISCONDUCT WITH WOMEN
    *ROBERT L. FASTIGGI*   9

    RESPONSE: THE ORDAINED PRIEST AS ALTER CHRISTUS: A CHRISTOLOGICAL PERSPECTIVE ON CLERICAL SEXUAL MISCONDUCT WITH WOMEN
    *PAUL GONDREAU*   22

II.   MAN, WOMAN, AND THE REDEMPTION OF THE WORLD
    *DEBORAH SAVAGE*   45

    RESPONSE: CELIBACY AND CONTEMPLATION
    *DEACON JAMES KEATING*   77

III. HUMAN SEXUALITY: THE BATTLE FOR THE HUMAN SOUL
MARIA FEDORYKA                                83

RESPONSE: THE BODY BETRAYED: THE CALL TO INTIMACY AND ITS TRAGIC DISTORTIONS
TIMOTHY FORTIN                                98

IV. THE TREATMENT OF PORNOGRAPHY ADDICTION IN CLERGY AND SEMINARIANS
PETER C. KLEPONIS                             111

RESPONSE: A VIEW OF PORNOGRAPHY THROUGH THE LENS OF ENCYCLICAL LETTER *DEUS CARITAS EST*
JANE F. ADOLPHE                               143

V. EQUALITY OF DIFFERENCE: LEADING TO A MOST PROFOUND INTIMACY AND FRIENDSHIP
PIA DE SOLENNI                                159

RESPONSE: UNDERSTANDING DIFFERENCE: A THEOLOGICAL REFLECTION
REV. DENNIS J. BILLY, C.SS.R.                 167

| VI. | DISCOVERING THE GAZE OF THE VIRGIN: FACING THE IMPACT OF CLERICAL SEXUAL ABUSE ON WOMEN'S CAPACITY FOR SPIRITUAL AND PHYSICAL MOTHERHOOD |
|---|---|
| | *LISA LICKONA*      175 |
| | RESPONSE: THE WHOLE AND HOLY PRIEST: LIVING SPIRITUAL FATHERHOOD THROUGH THE FOUR MODALITIES OF MATURE MASCULINITY |
| | *BILL DONAGHY*      196 |
| VII. | MALE-FEMALE COMPLEMENTARITY: SEXUALITY AND THE CATHOLIC PRIESTHOOD |
| | *MONICA MIGLIORINO MILLER*      207 |
| | RESPONSE: WOMAN IN THE LIFE OF THE PRIEST ACCORDING TO ST. JOHN PAUL II |
| | *REV MSGR PIOTR MAZURKIEWICZ*      226 |
| VIII. | SEXUAL INTEGRITY, SPIRITUALITY AND PRIESTLY FORMATION |
| | *PATRICIA COONEY HATHAWAY*      247 |
| | RESPONSE: CHRISTIAN ANTHROPOLOGY AND THE VOCATION TO CHASTITY |
| | *EDUARDO J. ECHEVERRIA*      275 |

IX.   AFFECTIVE MATURITY AND ITS IMPORTANCE FOR
      SEMINARY FORMATION
      REV. MSGR. MICHAEL K. MAGEE AND
      SUZANNE MULRAIN                                281

      RESPONSE: AFFECTIVE MATURITY IN RELATION
      TO THE SPIRITUAL LIFE AND THE VIRTUES
      CARMINA CHAPP AND ROBERT L. FASTIGGI
                                                     314

FOOTNOTES                                            323

# ACKNOWLEDGMENTS

This book is borne from the diverse experiences of women (religious and lay) and men (clerics and lay) studying and working in clerical environments, with the backdrop of certain news stories regarding clerical sexual violence against girls and women, including nuns. Instead of discussing these cases in detail, we gathered to engage in a foundational conversation about the collaboration of women and men in the Church. We entrust this discussion to the Sacred Heart of Jesus and the Immaculate Heart of Mary.

We are truly grateful to the Catholic Church for her Magisterium, especially regarding the role of women in the Church and the world. The Magisterium's perspective constitutes a response to the errors of the sexual revolution and radical feminism. The essential role of women as wives and mothers is something to be cherished and promoted. Consecrated women as well as single women committed to living holy lives are spiritual mothers called to enrich their environments. The same is true for competent and faithful women called to collaborate with members of the hierarchy for the good of the Church in positions that do not require the sacrament of orders. Jesus Christ did not permit the ordination of women to the priesthood, and neither can His Church. We thank the many priests and bishops who faithfully care for the salvation of souls.

We wish to thank Mr. Leonard Leo for his support of the work of the International Catholic Jurists Forum (ICJF). We likewise extend our thanks to ICJF Fellow, Marissa Eckelkamp, J.D., for her proof reading of the manuscript, and to the authors, who have patiently waited for the publication of this book.

# PREFACE

## Rev. Christopher J. Pollard

*Pastor, St. John The Beloved Roman Catholic Church,
McLean, Virginia,
Former Attaché with the Permanent Observer Mission
of the Holy See to the United Nations,
New York*

Shortly before His triumphant entry into Jerusalem, while the Apostles were still arguing about who was the greatest in the kingdom of heaven, Jesus Christ warned the Twelve:

> ...Whoever causes one of these little ones who believe in me to sin, it would be better for him to have a great millstone fastened round his neck and to be drowned in the depth of the sea. Woe to the world for temptations to sin! For it is necessary that temptations come, but woe to the man by whom the temptation comes! And if your hand or foot causes you to sin, cut it off and throw it away; it is better for you to enter life maimed or lame than with two hands or two feet to be thrown in the eternal fire (*Matthew* 18:6-8).

Neither did He mince words at the Last Supper in speaking of His apostolic betrayer: "The Son of man goes as it is written of him, but woe to that man by whom the Son of man is betrayed! It would have been better for that man if he had not been born" (*Matthew* 26:24). It would not take long for the Christian Church to need advice from the Apostles about how to deal with accusations against priests:

> "Never admit any charge against an elder except on the evidence of two or three witnesses. As for those who persist in sin, rebuke them in the presence of all, so that the rest may stand in fear. In the presence of God and of Christ Jesus and of the elect angels I

charge you to keep these rules without favor, doing nothing from partiality" (*1 Timothy* 5:19-21).

This appears immediately after St. Paul's advice about how a bishop should correct others, which is the only instance in the New Testament which deals specifically with the interactions of clerics and women: "Do not rebuke an older man but exhort him as you would a father; treat younger men like brothers, older women like mothers, younger women like sisters, in all purity" (*1 Timothy* 5:1-2).

Although bishops and popes have always had the mechanisms of discipline at their disposal, there must be a variety of reasons to account for their occasional hesitance to employ them vigorously. Unchecked moral decay in the Church, however, need not lead souls to despair. In some of the darkest times the Holy Spirit has raised up saintly reformers of the clergy such as St. Benedict of Nursia, St. Bernard of Clairvaux, St. Norbert of Xanten, St. Philip Neri, St. Charles Borromeo, St. Francis de Sales, St. Vincent de Paul, and St. Alphonsus Liguori. Few have written more forthrightly on the topic of clerical unchastity than St. Peter Damian who famously penned *Liber Gomorrhianus* for Pope Leo IX. In modern times we hardly can find a more powerful indictment than the virginal words of St. Therese of Lisieux in *Story of a Soul* about how her pilgrimage to Rome in 1887 at the age of fourteen was the occasion for her to realize why the vocation of the Carmelites is to pray for priests. A hundred years later she would have needed only to read the newspaper.

Blood-curdling revelations of sexual predation by a Catholic priest were national news in America in 1992. A further avalanche of crime stories in 2002 about multiple priests prompted the U.S. Conference of Catholic Bishops to draft a landmark document which was focused on the sexual abuse of children in the Church. New procedures were put into place. Fingerprint cards, background checks and safety training became the evidence that the hierarchy was addressing the issue. Lists of credibly accused priests were made public. The President of the Conference at the time, Bishop Wilton Gregory of Belleville, Illinois, offered a protracted apology which included the memorable statement, "If we bishops have learned anything, it is how devastating are the effects of sexual abuse on the children and young people who suffer it". The John Jay Reports of

2004 and 2011 both assisted and distracted from a thorough analysis of the crisis. 2018 brought a new flood of allegations and prominent episcopal resignations in the United States, Chile, and Honduras with bishops accused of abusing or covering up years of abuse against boys, seminarians, and adult men. *Vox Est Lux Mundi* promulgated by Pope Francis, in 2019, codified for the universal Church procedures to be "adopted to prevent and combat these crimes that betray the trust of the faithful" and notably included "vulnerable person" as a category of victim. Surely, pedophilia within the clerical ranks deserves a special kind of disgust. Eliminating crimes against children, the infirmed, and the physically or mentally deficient can only be a beginning. After almost twenty centuries of confronting the sins of fallen human nature, we cannot credibly claim to have been unaware of the gravity of the problem.

*Clerical Sexual Misconduct: An Interdisciplinary Analysis*, edited by Ronald J. Rychlak and Jane F. Adolphe, in 2020, trod where others fear to tread. It addresses the entire phenomenon as it applies to all victims while drawing attention to the fact that priests and bishops' abuse of children usually targeted adolescent males, that seminarians are among those suffering abuse and that sexually active men with same-sex attraction are being ordained. The sordid topic of unnatural perversions requires greater attention in the governance of the clergy; it should not result in the hierarchy and the faithful failing to address the general crisis of priests who are unfaithful to celibate chastity in more ordinary ways.

This second volume *Clerical Sexual Misconduct II: A Foundational Conversation*, edited by Jane F. Adolphe and Robert L. Fastiggi, tackles issues related to sexual misconduct and violence perpetrated by clerics with and against women. The contributors bring to bear their expertise in law, theology, philosophy, Scripture, and psychology. Their analyses regard man created male and female regardless of time and place according to creation and Original Sin, nature and Grace, Sacraments and the priesthood, sexuality and virginity, equality and difference, eros and agape. They also take account of this unique moment of history.

Any adequate account of every evil must include Original Sin as well as the precondition for the Fall. Prior to the Original Sin of Adam and Eve was the *first* Original Sin of the fallen angels. In contrast to the evil one's declaration *"non serviam"*, the priest must repeat many times daily Our

Lady's rejoinder, "*fiat mihi secundum verbum tuum*" (*Luke* 1,38). He brings the Savior into the world as Our Lady did, his generativity mirroring Our Lady's fruitful virginity. Meanwhile, the same evil one who seduced our first parents still "prowls around like a roaring lion, seeking someone to devour" (*1Peter* 5:8). St. Peter admonishes his readers and us to "resist him, firm in your faith, knowing that the same experience of suffering is required of your brotherhood throughout the world" (*1Peter* 5:9). Every Tuesday when the priest reads that in Night Prayer, he knows that it applies to the brotherhood of all Christians and especially to him and his brothers in the priesthood.

If the priest fails in chastity, the failure is not simply one of doing what was forbidden but in failing to do what he was supposed to do or to be who he was supposed to be. When a husband commits adultery against his wife, long before then he was already guilty of not loving his spouse as he promised. The confessional teaches us that one rarely makes an evil decision on its own. A bad fall is cultivated by many, many little bad decisions. The life of faith, hope, and love is filled with countless little sacrifices. What the priest says to the bride and groom in the classic "Exhortation before Marriage" applies to the priest *mutatis mutandi*:

> And so you begin your [ordained] life by the voluntary and complete surrender of your individual [life] in the interest of that deeper and wider life which you are to have in [the Church]. Henceforth you belong entirely to [her]; you will be one in mind, one in heart, and one in affections. And whatever sacrifices you may hereafter be required to make to preserve this [ecclesial] life, always make them generously. Sacrifice is usually difficult and irksome. Only love can make it easy; and perfect love can make it a joy. We are willing to give in proportion as we love. And when love is perfect, the sacrifice is complete. God so loved the world that He gave His only begotten Son, and the Son so loved us that He gave Himself for our salvation. "Greater love than this no one has, that one lay down his life for his friends."

The wise priest will anticipate temptation. If he has the benefit of good priestly mentors, he will not be surprised when his first stalker appears. As a spiritual father he will not enjoy writing his first cease and desist letter. Some souls he will have to entrust to other priests. He will be stretched to love generously even though his antenna will be even more attuned to those who might develop an inordinate attachment to him as well as those to whom he might grow inordinately attached. When he is lured into flirting with the possibility of a sexual relationship as though it were not a kind of violence, the priest who understands himself always as a spiritual father will dismiss that as a metaphysical impossibility. When he counsels women in horrible marriages, where his availability as a kind listener makes him especially attractive, he will avoid the temptation of thinking that he would be a better husband and father for the family in crisis. He will cultivate a respectful distance but not indifference.

Guarding against narcissism despite a great many priests whose success as preachers and public speakers appears to be fueled by vanity, he will nevertheless permit his personality to be of benefit to the spread of the Kingdom of God. He will remain humble and penitential while growing in strength and confidence. Even if he is not a born leader, he will develop a willingness to set the tone in a gathering and take responsibility for the outcome in a given situation. If he already has the mentality of a warrior, he needs to learn how to be a monk. If his disposition is already contemplative, he must strive to adopt the attitude of a man at arms. Through a regimen of prayer, his isolation will turn into solitude. Immersed in a life of right worship he will keep his thoughts on all that is above. By virtue of trusting in Providence, that "in everything God works for good with those who love him" (*Romans* 8:28), he will welcome further opportunities to forego pleasure and store up "treasures in heaven" (*Matthew* 6:20). Like the watchful slaves, he will keep his "loins… girded and [his] lamps burning" (*Luke* 12:25-30).

The occasional tragedies that befall us ought not to cause us to ignore the beauty of this difficult, short life. If we subject ourselves to the constant stream of bad news from across the globe, we might come to the conclusion that life is nothing but tragedy. A steady diet of "news" can only be sustained by the stout of heart and desperately needs to be counterbalanced by an awareness of the good that happens every day. On the other hand, the occasions we have to celebrate something joyous should not lead us to harbor false expectations for a life filled with happiness.

As essential as the theological virtues of faith and charity are, the world also desperately needs *hope*, "the theological virtue by which we desire the kingdom of heaven and eternal life as our happiness, placing our trust in Christ's promises and relying not on our own strength, but on the help of the grace of the Holy Spirit" (*Catechism of the Catholic Church*, 1817). *Heaven is the wedding feast.* Our Lord's parable of the virgins waiting with lamps lit (*Matthew* 25:1-13) does more than describe servants who are waiting dutifully for the moment of the bridegroom's arrival. They were eager to be *in* the wedding feast. Out of that desire they anticipated hardships and endured short-term sacrifices.

So that humanity would not be forever excluded from the wedding feast, Our Lord obeyed the will of the Father and became man. He suffered, died, rose, and ascended into heaven. Jesus trained the Apostles and prepared them to receive the Holy Spirit, Who established the church. To rescue fallen humanity God calls bishops, priests, and deacons to give up their lives as Christ did for the Church, as husbands do for their wives.

> Husbands, love your wives, as Christ loved the church and gave himself up for her, that he might sanctify her, having cleansed her by the washing of water with the word, that he might present the church to himself in splendor, without spot or wrinkle or any such thing, that she might be holy and without blemish. Even so husbands should love their wives as their own bodies. He who loves his wife loves himself. For no man ever hates his own flesh, but nourishes and cherishes it, as Christ does the church, because we are members of his body. (*Ephesians* 5:25-29)

How man relates to woman is part and parcel of how man relates to his own body.

The priest who perseveres in virginity also avoids sins of the flesh and pays minimum attention to his outward appearance. He will regard himself as the worst sinner in the world, especially so because of the great calling he was given. He knows that he cannot simply do what Jesus would have done because Jesus is God and incapable of sin. He will trust that the virtues are stable dispositions of his soul and yet also know that every moment is a new moment and that the battle must always be engaged. He will be a man of prudence, temperance, and courage.

The priest, who becomes the brother and son of God's holy daughters, as described in Pope St. John Paul II's 1995 "Letter to Priests for Holy Thursday", will be a man of prudence, temperance, courage, virtue, joy, and magnanimity. In brief, he will be a man of eros *and* agape. Without exaggerating a supposed spiritual superiority of women, he will value their insights and learn from them. He will not fear women as objects of danger. He will love them as sisters and mothers in all reverence. He will delight in their very existence, honoring the divine glory imparted to them, suffering all that causes them to suffer, and rejoicing in all that gives them joy.

# FOREWORD

### Helen M. Alvaré

*The Robert A. Levy Professor of Law & Liberty, Antonin Scalia Law School*
*Associate Dean for Academic Affairs*
*George Mason University, Arlington, Virginia*

The gap between the Catholic Church's potential and its current struggling to get relationships between women and clerics right within the Church is maddening for those familiar with Scripture, with Jesus's interactions with women, and with recent decades of papal and magisterial teachings. The potential to be a light for believers and even for the whole world is great, but still far from realized. And not only is the Church in need, but so is the world. We are living through a very particular period of history featuring simultaneously ignorance and intense, divisive and politicized confusion, alongside illuminating and often profound inquiries into the significance of God's decision to create two sexes possessing complementary gifts and needs.

Progress in this arena is essential, not only to alleviate the myriad of sufferings associated with the present maelstrom, but because a two-sexed creation and their interactions is closely tied up with imperatives in Christian and all human lives. For Christians, understanding in this realm is intrinsically tied to glimpsing the identity of God, how He loves us, and how we are to love Him and one another. For every human being, it is tied to the meaning of love itself, and genuine freedom and happiness.

I have worked in the Church for many years, married and raised a family. I have witnessed firsthand the importance of these questions, and the results of getting the answers right and wrong.

The Catholic Church has access to unparalleled resources: the Book of Genesis' creation accounts, Jesus's treatment of women, the early Christian communities' innovations regarding respect for women, and how these sharply distinguished Christians from the Greco-Roman societies in which they lived. There is also a great deal of positive momentum in recent decades in the Church as papal, magisterial, and theological inquiries have come to appreciate the need to pay a great deal of attention to matters such as women's equality, dignity, and gifts, and to the necessity of the collaboration of men and women in the Church and in the world. Of course, there is a great deal more work to do. But without a doubt, the documents of Vatican II; John Paul II's Theology of the Body; the apostolic letter, *Mulieris Dignitatem*; the Congregation of the Doctrine of the Faith's *On the Collaboration of Men and Women*; Pope Benedict XVI's *Deus Caritas Est*—bolstered by myriad statements and actions of Pope Francis—represent great strides. So too the somewhat lesser known work of John Paul II's interactions with the United Nations, and the work of the women's section of Pope Benedict XVI's Pontifical Council for the Laity.

The occasion of the Church's terrible fall—in the form of clerical sexual abuse and subsequent cover-ups and revelations concerning the sometime abusive labor practices and sexual harassment of women working in the Church—has also proved a moment for deep reflection and now some positive movement. We are assiduously asking how clerics are formed in their relationships with women and what changes in our institutions may be necessary.

This book wonderfully advances the conversation and provides real grounds for hope in the progress that has been made and can continue into the future. It is intellectually sophisticated, intensely faithful, and at the same time practical. Catholics and all who can benefit from the witness of rightly done male-female relations owe its authors a debt of gratitude. Its exploration of Genesis' accounts of God's two-sexed creation can help men and women understand themselves and their relationships in a deeper and more freeing way. Its psychological and anthropological accounts are brilliant applications of the Catholic method of interplaying faith and reason. Its reports about newer approaches in seminary and continuing formation inspire hope and reveal a willingness to grapple with "things as they are." The volume covers other important topics: seminarians emerging from our culture's often broken ideologies and families; seminarians suffering pornography addictions and a lack of comfort with and respect for women; and ordained priests struggling with clericalism, narcissism, perfectionism, burnout, and loneliness. For sure this collection of essays is bracing in its demystification of the lives and work of clerics, who come from all backgrounds and are often wounded in the ways so many people are these days. They may have to undergo hard conversions concerning how to respect female classmates, professors, and later collaborators in the work of the Church.

The book's material takes a reader so much farther and deeper than even the most positive aspects of the secular world's advocacy for women. The world rightly speaks about women's strengths and their freedom and dignity and equality. It often champions the synergies that emerge from both sexes joint work toward common goals. The exhortations "You GO GIRL!" and "men are from Venus . . ." are positive, but Christian sources interacting with empirical and experiential material offer a far superior foundation for respecting women and for positive, collaborative male-female. These identify women as *Imago Dei*. They articulate not just the good, but the *necessity* of women in God's plan for humanity. They dare to conclude that men cannot fully realize themselves and the meaning of their lives without a proper understanding of, and living out of relationships with, women. They advise that seminarians and priests cannot reach affective maturity if they cannot learn from women informally and formally as professors, and engage women as equals, worthy of respect, and fruitful collaboration. They illuminate the effects of original sin on our male and female natures and our relationships, as a starting point for progress.

I hope that it is not too much to hope that this book gets into the hands not only of Catholic leaders and institutions where women and clerics work together, but also into the hands of Catholics currently influenced by contemporary messages insisting that the Church has no use for, or is intrinsically sexist toward women, and cannot abide efforts toward recognizing women's equality.

# INTRODUCTION

## Jane F. Adolphe and Robert L. Fastiggi

*Professor of Law, Ave Maria School of Law, Naples, Florida, Adjunct Professor of Law, University of Notre Dame, School of Law, Sydney, Australia*

*and*

*Professor of Dogmatic Theology, Sacred Heart Major Seminary, Detroit, Michigan*

## Background

In the 2004 "Letter to Bishops of the Catholic Church on the Collaboration of Men and Women in the Church and the World" (hereafter "Letter to Bishops"), the Congregation for the Doctrine of the Faith (CDF) commences a discussion.[1] It is a "starting point for further examination in the Church... in a sincere search for the truth and in a common commitment to the development of ever more authentic relationships," between men and women.[2] Concerned with certain ideologies that obstruct the true advancement of women, the CDF offers a biblical vision of the human person, underlining that:

> The human dimension of sexuality is inseparable from the theological dimension. The human creature, in its unity of soul and body, is characterized therefore, from the very beginning, by the relationship with the other-beyond-the-self.[3]

The CDF praises the "fundamental values linked to women's actual lives," which is described as a "capacity for the other."[4] It is a "deep intuition of the goodness" that is linked to "women's physical capacity to give life," and contributes to the "growth and protection of the other."[5] It is contrary to the demands of secular society or the radical feminist to promote oneself, as the general principle of living.

Having said that, the CDF contends that "women should not be considered from the sole perspective of physical procreation," which can elicit "serious distortions" that "extol biological fecundity in purely quantitative terms and are often accompanied by dangerous disrespect for women."[6] Like the CDF, John Paul II emphasizes other forms of full realization of motherhood beyond the physical, which he calls "spiritual motherhood."[7] From this perspective, he promotes "the genius of women," which the CDF describes as that "irreplaceable role of women in all aspects of family and social life involving human relationships and caring for others."[8]

In the 2008 Address to participants at the International Convention "Woman and Man, the Humanum in its Entirety," Pope Benedict XVI remembers the work of Pope John Paul II on women, namely his "Letter to Women,"[9] the Apostolic Letter, *Mulieris Dignitatem* and the above "Letter to Bishops."[10] Benedict goes on to recall his own concern for the "masculine mentality," which ignores that "men and women share equal dignity and responsibility" – the uniqueness of Christianity.[11] Elsewhere, Benedict finds support for this proposition in St. Paul for the baptized: "There is neither Jew nor Greek, there is neither slave nor free, there is neither male nor female; for you are all one in Christ Jesus (Gal 3:28)," to which Benedict adds, "all are united in the same basic dignity, although each with specific functions (cf. 1 Cor 12:27-30)."[12] Indeed, he fleshes this point out in his general audiences from September 1, 2010 to April 6, 2011 devoted to holy women in the Church.[13] Returning to his 2008 Address, he underlines that women are discriminated against and undervalued:

> for the sole fact of being women, where recourse is made even to religious arguments and family, social and cultural pressure in order to maintain the inequality of the sexes, where acts of violence are consummated in regard to women, making them the object of mistreatment and of exploitation in advertising and in the consumer and entertainment industry.[14]

That the above mentality exists in the Church is evidenced by the revelations of clerical sexual abuse of girls and women, including nuns. Such clerical sexual sins, and related offenses, delicts and crimes are depraved actions. They leave deep wounds in the victims, cause much anger in the community, and bring considerable shame to the Catholic Church. That such evil plunges the Church into "the mystery of iniquity," as St. John Paul II called it,[15] has been affirmed by Pope Francis. He underlines that such behavior "is all the more grave and scandalous in the Church, for it is utterly incompatible with her moral authority and ethical credibility." [16] According to Francis, "[c]onsecrated persons, chosen by God to guide souls to salvation, let themselves be dominated by their own frailty or sickness and thus become tools of Satan."[17]

Although Popes John Paul II, Benedict XVI, and Francis have instituted new norms or revised others to ensure priest and bishop accountability,[18] questions of a psychological, spiritual, and theological nature remain.

**Cleric-on-Male Sexual Abuse**

With reference to cleric-on-female sexual misconduct, including crimes, as a backdrop, this book is dedicated to foundational issues pertaining to collaboration between women and the ordained. It follows an earlier volume, in 2020, devoted to cleric-on-male sexual misconduct, including crimes, provoked by the 2018 revelation of cases in Chile, Honduras, and the United States.

In response, the International Catholic Jurists Forum organized an expert meeting of Catholic scholars at Ave Maria School of Law in Naples, Florida. Invitations to participate were sent to the Secretariat of State, which advised us to reach out to the Secretary of the Pontifical Commission for the Protection of Minors, and in response, Monsignor Robert Oliver sent a letter of encouragement to the group. The meeting, in turn, led to the publication of *Clerical Sexual Misconduct: An Interdisciplinary Analysis* (Cluny Media, 2020) edited by Jane F. Adolphe and Ronald J. Rychlak. The essays in that volume consider cleric-on-male sexual violence from a variety of disciplinary perspectives with insights of relevance to that specific problem as well as the topic of sexual violence more generally. The book has received many favorable reviews.[19]

## Cleric-on-Female Sexual Abuse

Taking up a study of cleric-on-male violence, alone, was not meant to suggest that cleric-on-female abuse was somehow "less egregious or worthy of treatment."[20] Rather, "the scope of the meeting was limited due to time constraints. Even more fundamentally, media reports at the time had not disclosed, in any great depth, the trials faced by women in the Church."[21] It expressed hope that the volume would provide "an incentive for female victims and survivors to come forward."[22]

Since the 2018 meeting, cases of cleric-on-female sexual violence have received increased attention.[23] For example, following the publication of one article that condemned clerical labor exploitation of nuns,[24] in the monthly magazine "Women Church World," a supplement to the Holy See's newspaper, *L'Osservatore Romano*, a second article was published. It "denounced the sexual abuse of nuns by clergy and the resulting scandal of religious sisters having abortions or giving birth to children who are not recognized by their fathers."[25] A few days later, during a return flight from the Apostolic Visitation to the United Arab Emirates, Francis acknowledged the cultural problem of viewing women as second class citizens, violence against women, and clerical sexual violence against nuns, in the Church.[26] He confirmed the Church's resolve to stop such violence, and congratulated Benedict for his courage to dissolve a corrupt congregation which had involved the "sexual slavery of nuns" by clerics.[27]

Unfortunately, two months later, the founder and editorial staff of the above women's magazine resigned claiming that the work situation had worsened since the publications concerning abused nuns.[28] The magazine's founder, Lucetta Scaraffia, blamed the editor of the Vatican newspaper *L'Osservatore Romano* for a growing "climate of distrust and progressive delegitimization," something contrary to Francis' approach to the magazine and women, generally.[29] The editor of the newspaper denied the claims.[30]

That situation raises an important issue regarding the spectrum of bad treatment and bullying some women have endured in Church institutions, ranging from indifference, shunning, and exclusion to sexual harassment and sexual violence.

## Book Purpose and Outline

The abuse, harassment, or devaluation of women, in any form by Catholic priests and bishops, raises concerns about: 1) whether clerics have a healthy understanding of their own inherent dignity as male persons and spiritual fathers; 2) whether clerics have a healthy understanding of the inherent dignity of women as female persons and spiritual mothers; and 3) whether seminary formation is adequately preparing future priests to interact with women in a healthy, mature, and holy manner. This volume commences a foundational conversation about certain deficiencies in light of God's plan for men and women, redeemed by His grace. The essays examine the Scriptural, theological, anthropological, and psychological dimensions of the Catholic view of men and women and related issues. They constitute the outcome document of an on-line discussions, held in January 2021, organized by the International Catholic Jurist Forum.

The book, divided into eighteen chapters, involves the contributions of nineteen scholars, men (ordained and lay) and woman. Many of the contributors are professors at seminaries, while others are professors or administrators at secular and Catholic universities and institutes. The discussions vary in length and depth; some are informal in tone, while others are more academic. The chapters are conversational in the sense that one scholar begins the dialogue on a given topic to which one or more scholars respond. Efforts have been made to ensure that women and men are speaking to each other, and on occasion, collaborating in the writing of certain chapters.

**Chapter I** considers clerical sexual misconduct from a Marian perspective followed by a response from a Christological viewpoint. **Chapter II** considers man, woman, and redemption of the world with a reply devoted to celibacy and contemplation. **Chapter III** examines human sexuality and the battle for the human soul with a rejoinder on how the body, called to intimacy, is often betrayed with subsequent tragic distortions. **Chapter IV** reflects upon the treatment of pornography addiction in clergy and seminarians followed by a response on pornography through the lens of Encyclical Letter *Deus Caritas Est*. **Chapter V** reflects upon equality of difference as leading to a most profound intimacy and friendship with a reaction regarding the understanding of difference from a theological perspective. **Chapter VI** considers spiritual and physical motherhood in light of clerical sexual misconduct with women followed by a response on how a priest becomes whole by living spiritual fatherhood through the four modalities of mature masculinity. **Chapter VII** discusses male-female complementarity and the priesthood followed by a reply on the vision of woman and her relationship with priests in the writings of John Paul II. **Chapter VIII** examines sexual integrity, spirituality, and priestly formation followed by a rejoinder on Christian anthropology and the vocation of chastity. **Chapter IX** discusses affective maturity and its importance for seminary formation followed by a reply on affective maturity in relation to the spiritual life and the virtues.

## Conclusion

Clearly, the magisterium of the Church, based as it is on scripture and tradition, does not consider women as second-class citizens, neither are they objects to be used or abused, nor are they subjects to be ignored or silenced. Francis has taken concrete actions congruent with the writings of previous Popes. He has appointed more competent and faithful women to the Roman Curia, in positions that do not require the sacrament of orders,[31] and has embedded the possibility of appointing competent and faithful lay men and woman to certain positions of authority, not requiring the sacrament of orders, in the constitution of the Roman Curia.[32] He has acknowledged the sexual abuse of nuns by certain priests and bishops, and has established a home in Vatican City State for nuns, who have been expelled from congregations for various reasons,[33] including retaliatory action against whistleblowers of clerical sexual violence.[34]

In 2020, Cardinal Marc Ouellet, the Prefect of the Congregation of Bishops, urged bishops to ensure that seminaries involve more women in the work of formation.[35] He has reportedly contended that future priests need the presence of women in their education and training to cultivate proper respect and appreciation of women.[36] It is noteworthy that while such integration has been occurring for years in some seminaries in certain countries, this is not the case in many other seminaries and nations.

In 2022, Ouellet followed up with the Theological Symposium: "Toward a Fundamental Theology of the Priesthood," where bishops met with the ordained, religious, consecrated, and lay faithful, male and female, to deepen their "understanding of vocations and the importance of communion between the different vocations in the Church."[37] At the December 2021, press conference that preceded the symposium, Ouellet emphasized how the Church continued to underlined and specify ways to "establish a fundamental relationship between the priesthood of the baptized"[38] and the sacred priesthood, and that the "rapport [was] not to be taken for granted."[39] On the topic of the harmonization of the different vocations, he stated:

> This priesthood of Love, which is exercised by the entire ecclesial community, is animated and supported by a variety of vocations to love, whose distinct forms and colours complement each other. Between priests and lay people, between men and women religious of different charisms, the Holy Spirit communicates the grace which brings about communion among all, enabling obstacles to be overcome, and through this communion, mysteriously and at least virtually, reaching the whole of humanity. [40]

Such beautiful reflections are in stark contrast to cleric-on-female sexual violence, the antithesis of love. Understanding that the Church has norms and practices in place to protect girls and women from clerical sexual abuse, this volume offers an opportunity to deepen the conversation about remaining psychological, spiritual, and theological matters. Like the first volume, *Clerical Sexual Misconduct: An Interdisciplinary Analysis*, this second volume, subtitled *A Foundational Conversation*, is an answer to the call of Pope Francis for assistance from members of the faithful engaged in higher learning to serve the Church through study of the culture of abuse in its midst.[41] We offer our findings to the Apostolic See.

The discussion is timely. It takes place in history, when, due to the success of gender ideology in the West, the very concept of woman is under attack, having been redefined to include a biological man who subjectively self-identifies as a woman, with obvious negative effects for women.[42] For this reason, the 2008 words of Benedict ring clear: the Christian commitment to truth is "all the more urgent so that everywhere it may promote a culture that recognizes the dignity that belongs to women."[43]

# I

# A Marian Perspective on Clerical Sexual Misconduct with Women

## Robert L. Fastiggi

*Professor of Dogmatic Theology,*
*Sacred Heart Major Seminary, Detroit, Michigan*

## Introduction

The sexual abuse of women is a terrible crime. Men in positions of authority sometimes prey upon women who are vulnerable, and they use their power to elicit sexual favors. When such crimes are committed by members of the clergy, there is an added element of scandal and betrayal of trust. Some Catholic women have been sexually abused by priests in whom they placed their trust. Many of these women were in situations of great emotional need due to marital problems, depression, or spiritual confusion.[1] Religious sisters have also been victims of sexual predations by priests.[2] At times, priests have even used the sacrament of penance as a vehicle for sexual manipulation.[3]

Sexual misconduct by Catholic priests towards women can take different forms. Celibate priests are bound by the obligation of "perfect and perpetual continence for the sake of the kingdom of heaven."[4] In spite of this obligation, some priests pursue relationships with women that involve sexual intimacy. Even if these sexual expressions are consensual, the priest is violating his commitment to continence. Moreover, the priest is not free to marry,[5] and thus he is entering into a relationship with a woman that does not involve a permanent commitment. Very often women who become sexually involved with priests end up feeling used and manipulated.

The sexual abuse of women by priests might likewise involve unwanted touches or sexually suggestive comments. Such actions and words are forms of sexual harassment, and they often involve an unhealthy or degrading attitude towards women.

The most egregious form of sexual abuse is rape or sexual assault. In such cases, there is no consent on the part of the abused woman. The priest takes advantage of his position of authority to prey upon a woman sexually.[6] Sometimes the priest will use a situation of spiritual counseling in which the woman develops an emotional bond of dependency on him. The priest then betrays the trust of the woman and takes advantage of her dependency and initiates sexual contact. The woman might not resist these sexual advances physically at the time, but she later comes to realize that she was manipulated and preyed upon because of her vulnerability. The feelings of hurt, confusion, and betrayal are real and painful. Many times women who are abused in this way take years to process what actually happened. They might even experience guilt for putting themselves in such a vulnerable situation. If they later report what happened and are treated with skepticism or suspicion by Church authorities, their pain is only deepened. In some cases, they lose their faith in the Church and God.

**Reasons for clerical sexual misconduct towards women**

The sexual abuse of women by anyone is gravely wrong. Whether the abuser is another woman or a man, such abuse is sinful and worthy of the strongest possible condemnation. Why, though, does such abuse occur? On a theological level, we can point to concupiscence, which is a result of original sin.[7] We can also point to lust, which is one of the capital vices or sins.[8] Men who abuse women often are motivated by a distorted attitude toward women in general. They might look at pornographic images of women that depict them as objects of sexual lust rather than human persons worthy of respect and dignity.

When celibate priests abuse women, we wonder whether they received proper spiritual formation during their years in the seminary. Living in an all-male environment, they might not have learned how to relate to women in a mature and responsible way. They could also be victims of emotional immaturity, and they are fixated in an adolescent attitude towards women

# I. A Marian Perspective on Clerical Sexual Misconduct with Women

and sexuality. In some cases, they might develop an attitude of clerical entitlement, thinking they are superior to women because of their call to the priesthood. Such an attitude could combine with patterns of narcissism in which they become centered on needs for praise, admiration, and self-aggrandizement. Priests with narcissistic tendencies can exploit the love, respect, and trust the faithful have towards them. Unless priests have a mature spiritual life, they can become prey to the same sins of lust as other men. Their status as priests, confessors, and counselors provide them with opportunities to exploit women who are emotionally wounded and dependent on them for guidance.

## Priests and devotion to the Blessed Virgin Mary

If priests have a true devotion to the Blessed Virgin Mary, it is difficult to imagine them engaging in the sexual abuse of women. In his 1935 encyclical, *Ad Catholici Sacerdotii,* Pius XI states that "the priest even more than the faithful should have devotion to Our Lady, for the relation of the priest to Christ is more deeply and truly like that which Mary bears to her Divine Son."[9] In the same encyclical, Pius XI speaks of the vital importance of chastity for priests:

> It is impossible to treat of the piety of a Catholic priest without being drawn on to speak, too, of another most precious treasure of the Catholic priesthood, that is, of chastity; for from piety springs the meaning and the beauty of chastity. Clerics of the Latin Church in higher Orders are bound by a grave obligation of chastity; so grave is the obligation in them of its perfect and total observance that a transgression involves the added guilt of sacrilege.[10]

Devotion to the Blessed Virgin Mary helps all of the faithful to cultivate chastity according to their state in life. This devotion, though, becomes even more important for priests who are called to perfect and perpetual continence. Pope Pius XII, in his 1954 encyclical, *Sacra Virginitas,* calls upon priests to entrust themselves to the maternal care of Mary in order to grow in chastity:

The eminent way to protect and nourish an unsullied and perfect chastity, as proven by experience time and again throughout the course of centuries, is solid and fervent devotion to the Virgin Mother of God. ... Therefore in a paternal way We exhort all priests, religious men and women, to entrust themselves to the special protection of the holy Mother of God who is the Virgin of virgins and the "teacher of virginity," as Ambrose says, and the most powerful Mother of those in particular who have vowed and consecrated themselves to the service of God.[11]

The Second Vatican Council also recognizes Mary as Mother of priests and seminarians. In its *Decree on the Ministry and Life of* Priests— *Presbyterorum Ordinis*—the Council exhorts priests to "love and venerate with filial devotion and veneration this mother of the Eternal High Priest, Queen of Apostles and Protector of their own ministry."[12] The council's *Decree on Priestly Training, Optatam Totius*, says that seminarians "should love and venerate with a filial trust the most Blessed Virgin Mary, who was given as mother to the disciple by Christ Jesus as He was dying on the cross."[13] The importance of Mary in seminarian training is likewise found in the canon 246§3 of the 1983 *Code of Canon Law*, which states that "the veneration of the Blessed Virgin Mary, including the Marian rosary, mental prayer, and other exercises of piety are to be fostered; through these, students are to acquire a spirit of prayer and gain strength in their vocation."

Documents of the Church after Vatican II likewise highlight the importance of Marian devotion for future priests. The Congregation for Catholic Education [CCE] was responsible for seminary formation until January 16, 2013, when the Congregation for Clergy assumed that role.[14] Since 1980, the CCE has made three important interventions regarding the need for seminaries to give more attention to Marian doctrine and devotion. On January 6, 1980, the CCE issued a *Circular Letter Concerning Some of the More Urgent Aspects of Spiritual Formation in Seminaries*.[15] In this letter, it underlines "four of the most urgent guidelines which the work of spiritual formation for future priests ought to follow." One of these urgent guidelines points to the need for a seminary to be "a school of filial love toward her who is the Mother of Jesus and whom Christ gave to us as our mother." The letter notes that Marian devotion "must not merely be a pietistic and sentimental note attached to spiritual formation" but "an integral part of the formation program of a seminary." The *Letter* also underscores the importance of a proper teaching of Mariology, which is a matter of fidelity to the "Marian mystery." It states that "Christology is also Mariology" and proper devotion to the Blessed Virgin Mary "can and must be a guarantee against everything which would tend to eradicate the historicity of the mystery of Christ." In addition to *Lumen Gentium* of Vatican II, the *Letter* recommends a study of Paul VI's 1974 exhortation, *Marialis Cultus*, and the writings of St. Louis Grignion de Montfort (1673-1716).

On March 25, 1988, the Congregation for Catholic Education issued a letter entitled *The Virgin Mary in Intellectual and Spiritual Formation*. This letter came during the 1987-1988 Marian Year proclaimed by St. John Paul II, and it was addressed to "theological faculties, to seminaries and to other centers of ecclesiastical studies." It notes that its message is not restricted to the Marian Year. Instead, "the promotion of knowledge, research and piety with regard to Mary of Nazareth ... must be permanent since the exemplary value and mission of the Virgin are permanent."[16] The letter insists on the need for the teaching of Mariology in seminaries and theological faculties, and this teaching must be organic, complete, and suited to the type of institution.[17] The letter not only addresses the need for the study of Mariology; it also recognizes the need for seminarians to develop an authentic love for the Virgin Mary:

> With this letter the Congregation for Catholic Education wishes to reaffirm the necessity of furnishing seminarians and students of all centers of ecclesiastical studies with Mariological formation which embraces study, devotion and life-style. They must: a) acquire a complete and exact knowledge of the doctrine of the Church about the Blessed Virgin Mary .... b) nourish an *authentic love* for the Mother of the Savior and Mother of mankind , which expresses itself in genuine forms of devotion and is led to the "imitation of her virtues," above all to a decisive commitment to live according to the commandments of God and to do his will (cf. Mt 7:21; Jn 15:14); c) develop the *capacity to communicate* such

love to the Christian people through speech, writing and example, so that their Marian piety may be promoted and cultivated.[18]

A genuine love and devotion of the Blessed Virgin Mary is a secure path to holiness. St. Louis de Montfort (1673–1716) believed that devotion to the Virgin Mary "is the safest, easiest, shortest and most perfect way of approaching Jesus."[19] As is well-known, St. John Paul II took his episcopal and papal motto of *Tutus Tuus* (entirely yours) from St. Louis de Montfort who exclaimed: "O Mary, I take you for my all; give me your heart." [20] In his 1987 encyclical, *Redemptoris Mater*, John Paul II points to St. Louis de Montfort as one "who proposes consecration to Christ through the hands of Mary, as an effective means for Christians to live faithfully their baptismal commitments."[21]

In his 1992 apostolic exhortation on priestly formation, *Pastores Dabo Vobis*, St. John Paul II highlights the importance of the Blessed Virgin Mary in priestly formation when he writes:

> Every aspect of priestly formation can be referred to Mary, the human being who has responded better than any other to God's call. Mary became both the servant and the disciple of the Word to the point of conceiving, in her heart and in her flesh, the Word made man, so as to give him to mankind. Mary was called to educate the one eternal priest, who became docile and subject to her motherly authority. With her example and intercession the Blessed Virgin keeps vigilant watch over the growth of vocations and priestly life in the Church.[22]

This passage of John Paul II is cited in no. 112 of the *Ratio Fundamentalis Institutionis Sacerdotalis* ("The Gift of the Priestly Vocation") issued by the Sacred Congregation for the Clergy on December 8, 2016. It highlights Mary's role as the educator of priests.

In his address to the International Theological Commission on December 5, 2014, Pope Francis recognizes Mary's role as the teacher of authentic theology:

# I. A Marian Perspective on Clerical Sexual Misconduct with Women

The Immaculate Virgin, as a privileged witness of the great events of salvation history, "kept all these things, pondering them in her heart" (Lk 2:19): A woman of listening, a woman of contemplation, a woman of closeness to the problems of the Church and of the people. Under the guidance of the Holy Spirit, and with all the resources of her feminine genius, she unceasingly entered ever more deeply into "all the truth" (cf. Jn 16:13). Mary is thus the icon of the Church who, eagerly awaiting her Lord, progresses day after day in her understanding of the faith, thanks also to the patient work of men and women theologians. May Our Lady, the teacher of authentic theology, obtain for us through her maternal prayer that our charity "may abound more and more, with knowledge and all discernment" (Phil 1:9).[23]

## Marian devotion supports reverence towards women

The clerical sexual abuse of women is often rooted in a lack of respect towards women. Men who sexually abuse women show they regard women as sexual objects to exploit rather than persons to respect. Seminarians and priests, however, who cultivate true devotion to the Blessed Virgin Mary, will develop a deep reverence towards women. Once they come to understand how the Blessed Virgin Mary is at the very center of salvation history, they will realize that their own salvation in a very real way depends on a woman. St. John Paul II affirms the central role of the Blessed Virgin Mary in salvation history in *Mulieris Dignitatem*:

> The sending of this Son, one in substance with the Father, as a man 'born of woman,' constitutes the culminating and *definitive point of God's self-revelation to humanity* ... A woman is to be found at the *center of this salvific event*. The self-revelation of God, who is the inscrutable unity of the Trinity, is outlined *in the annunciation at Nazareth*.[24]

Jesus and Mary are united by an inseparable bond because God became flesh in her. St. Louis de Montfort (1673–1716) exclaims: "Lord, you are always with Mary, and Mary is always with you."²⁵ St. Teresa of Calcutta put it even more simply: "Without Mary, there is no Jesus."²⁶

The Church also teaches that Mary was predestined from eternity to be the Mother of the Word Incarnate.²⁷ Pope Leo XIII, in his encyclical letter of Sept. 22, 1891, *Octobri mense* (Sept. 22, 1891) writes:

> The Eternal Son of God, about to take upon Him our nature for the saving and ennobling of man, and about to consummate thus a mystical union (*mysticum … conubium*) between Himself and all mankind, did not accomplish His design without adding there the free consent of the elect Mother, who represented in some sort all human kind, according to the illustrious and just opinion of St. Thomas, who says that the Annunciation was effected with the consent of the Virgin standing in the place of humanity.²⁸

St. Thomas Aquinas speaks of "a type of spiritual marriage" (*quoddam spirituale matrimonium*) to express the union between the Son of God and human nature. He also says: "Through the Annunciation the consent of the Virgin, in the place of all human nature (*loco totius humanae naturae*) was awaited."²⁹ This passage from St. Thomas— cited in Leo XIII's encyclical— shows that the Incarnation is a type of mystical union or marriage between God and the human race. Mary, therefore, can be understood as the bridge between God and the human race because she brought God into human history by conceiving the Word of God in her womb. In his January 1, 2021, homily for the Solemnity of Mary, Mother of God, Pope Francis highlighted the role of Mary in uniting us to God:

> She is not only the bridge joining us to God; she is more. She is the road that God travelled in order to reach us, and the road that we must travel in order to reach him. Through Mary, we encounter God the way he wants us to: in tender love, in intimacy, in the flesh. For Jesus is not an abstract idea; he is real and incarnate; he was "born of a woman", and quietly grew. Women know about this kind of quiet growth. We men tend to be abstract and want things right away. Women are concrete and know how to weave

# I. A Marian Perspective on Clerical Sexual Misconduct with Women

life's threads with quiet patience. How many women, how many mothers, thus give birth and rebirth to life, offering the world a future![30]

The Incarnation of the Word in Mary's womb is a sacred covenant between God and the human race. Mary assumes the role of the Bride and she is an icon of the Church. She is the New Eve welcoming the New Adam into human history. In the Gospel of Luke 1:38, Mary responds to the invitation to be the Mother of the Son of God by saying: "Behold I am the handmaiden of the Lord. May it be done to me according to your word." In her yes to the invitation of the angel, Mary played an active role in the history of salvation. Vatican II, in *Lumen Gentium*, 56, puts it this way:

> Thus Mary, a daughter of Adam, consenting to the divine Word, became the mother of Jesus, the one and only Mediator. Embracing God's salvific will with a full heart and impeded by no sin, she devoted herself totally as a handmaid of the Lord to the person and work of her Son, under Him and with Him, by the grace of almighty God, serving the mystery of redemption. Rightly therefore the holy Fathers see her as used by God not merely in a passive way, but as freely cooperating in the work of human salvation through faith and obedience. For, as St. Irenaeus says, she "being obedient, became the cause of salvation for herself and for the whole human race." Hence not a few of the early Fathers gladly assert in their preaching, "The knot of Eve's disobedience was untied by Mary's obedience; what the virgin Eve bound through her unbelief, the Virgin Mary loosened by her faith." Comparing Mary with Eve, they call her "the Mother of the living," and still more often they say: "death through Eve, life through Mary."[31]

Pope Francis has testified to the central role of Mary in salvation history. In his homily for the Solemnity of Mary, Mother of God of January 1, 2020, he states:

[t]he first day of the year, we celebrate this nuptial union between God and mankind, inaugurated in the womb of a woman. In God, there will forever be our humanity and Mary will forever be the Mother of God. She is both woman and mother: this is what is essential. From her, a woman, salvation came forth and thus there is no salvation without the woman. In her, God was united to us, and if we want to unite ourselves to him, we must take the same path: through Mary, woman and mother.[32]

Pope Francis has also pointed to the essential role of Mary in the life of the Church. In a flight press conference of July 28, 2013, he said:

A Church without women is like the college of the Apostles without Mary. The role of women in the Church is not simply that of maternity, being mothers, but much greater: it is precisely to be the icon of the Virgin, of Our Lady; what helps make the Church grow! But think about it, Our Lady is more important than the Apostles! She is more important! The Church is feminine. She is Church, she is bride; she is mother.[33]

Since the Church is feminine, priests must look upon women with great reverence. In the same press conference of July 28, 2013, Pope Francis made it clear that "Our Lady, Mary, was more important than the Apostles, than bishops, deacons, and priests." If priests know the centrality of Mary to salvation history, they should look upon every woman as the reflection of Mary who is blessed among women (Lk 1:42).

## How true devotion to the Blessed Virgin Mary helps protect priests from sexual misconduct towards women

In some cases, priests might have an intellectual devotion to the Blessed Virgin Mary, but they still have lustful thoughts towards women. The virtue of chastity requires "an apprenticeship in self-mastery, which is a training in human freedom."[34] Chastity also is a fruit of the Holy Spirit,[35] which means that it is a fruit of divine grace. St. Louis de Montfort speaks of Mary as "the inseparable associate of the Holy Spirit in all these works

## I. A Marian Perspective on Clerical Sexual Misconduct with Women

of grace."[36] Pope Benedict XVI teaches that '[t]here is no fruit of grace in the history of salvation that does not have as its necessary instrument the mediation of Our Lady."[37] The life of grace, as many popes have affirmed, is supported by Mary as the "Mediatrix of all grace."[38]

In his book, *Mary and the Priestly Ministry*, Fr. Emile Neubert, S.M. notes that priests, in spite of their "solemn commitment to perpetual chastity … are still human creatures, burdened from birth with the consequences of the original sin and the sins of their ancestors."[39] "Union with the Immaculate Virgin Mary," however, is "an infallible road to victory" over concupiscence.[40] Prayer is needed in order to overcome temptations against chastity, but an intimate association with Mary, who is all-pure, enables the priest to grow in modesty and prudence in his ministry towards women. Fr. Neubert believes that:

> The Marian priest will imitate his Mother. All his conversations and mannerisms, his bearing and his eye contacts will bear the stamp of decency and indicate a son of the most chaste of virgins. Chastity is the daughter of humility. A son of Mary is marked by humility because pride and a filial devotion to the Blessed Virgin are psychologically incompatible. Humility teaches self-knowledge. Anyone aware of his weakness will stay out of temptation's way. … But for a priest who regularly consults Mary about his activities and undertakes nothing without her approval, she will help him to easily discern whether these reasons are valid or a pretext for passion. If his duty obliges him to become involved in a precarious matter, he will invoke her help and will undertake it in her presence, keeping in mind the intentions of God who created the human body and shared with humans his power of creating in purity and love.[41]

Mary will help priests look upon women with purity and not as objects of lust. Priests should conform themselves to Christ who looked upon women with eyes of purity, and they should imitate Christ in his love for Mary.

Priests who have an intimate love and devotion to the Blessed Mother also have a constant feminine presence in their lives. Fr. Neubert notes that:

> Feminine influence is needed for the formation of a child and of an adult male as well. A woman is able to cultivate, sometimes even to create in men, a sense of refinement, of tact, of compassion, of forgetfulness of self, of total sacrifice that only the most perfect of mothers can bring about. The priest who has no special devotion to Mary lacks something in his nature. He is less complete, less a man, than someone who enjoys the gentle influence of the Virgin Mary.[42]

Priests should also imitate St. Joseph who was legally married to the Blessed Virgin Mary but observed continence in obedience to the will of God. True devotion to Mary should lead to an imitation of St. Joseph who by his complete self-sacrifice "expressed his generous love for the Mother of God, and gave her a husband's 'gift of self.' …. Joseph obeyed the explicit command of the angel and took Mary into his home, while respecting the fact that she belonged exclusively to God."[43]

The imitation of St. Joseph's chaste, spousal love for love for the Virgin Mary can also take the form of a consecration to the ever-virgin Mother of God. Priests should consecrate themselves to Mary following approved practices of the Church such as: a) the vow of servitude to Jesus and Mary encouraged by Cardinal Pierre Bérulle, Jean-Jacques Olier and other adherents to the French School of spirituality;[44] b) consecration or entrustment to Mary according to St. Louis de Montfort; or c) the spiritual marriage or *alliance* with Mary made by St. John Eudes.[45]

There are other ways priests can grow in chastity by devotion to the Blessed Virgin Mary:

> —Priests should see Mary as the icon of feminine beauty that is completely pure and free from all sin and concupiscence. They should look upon Mary as she who is all beautiful (*tota pulchra, panagia*). In this way, they will see women not as objects of lust.

They will look upon women with pure eyes sensitive to the inner, spiritual beauty that reflects the beauty of Mary.
—Priests should learn from the examples of saints like St. Ignatius of Loyola who was able to overcome lust by a vision of Mary and the Christ Child. Icons and statues of Mary help priests to preserve chastity.[46]
—Priests should turn to Mary as the Mother of Mercy when they experience sexual temptations or thoughts. They should also realize that the Blessed Mother is a *Mediatrix* of divine grace and has been recognized as "all-powerful by grace" (*omnipotens per gratiam*).[47]
—Priests should recognize that Mary is their Mother. Love and devotion to the Mary as Mother helps priests look upon all women with the reverence they deserve. Mary's maternal presence helps priests overcome their need for a woman in their lives because her tenderness and love is experienced daily.
—Priests should look upon Mary as their teacher because she is "the seat of Wisdom" (*sedes sapientiae*). Mary will help form priests into mature men who can minister to women with love and purity.

**Conclusion**

Devotion to the Blessed Virgin Mary is vital for the formation of priests who are to live up to their call of perfect and perpetual continence for the kingdom of heaven. The Magisterium of the Church has stressed the importance of the Virgin Mary in the spiritual and intellectual formation of future priests. Mary is at the center of the story of salvation, and priests who recognize her indissoluble bond with Christ and the Church will develop an authentic love for her and reverence towards women. Mary is the spiritual Mother of priests, and she provides them with the love, support, and strength to follow her divine Son and avoid the near occasions of sin. Priests who are truly devoted to the Virgin Mary will never sexually abuse women. They will live up to their sublime call to be configured to Christ and manifest his purity and chaste love for women.

## RESPONSE

# The Ordained Priest as *Alter Christus*: Christological Perspective on Clerical Sexual Misconduct with Women

### Paul Gondreau

*Professor of Theology, Providence College, Providence, Rhode Island*

**Introduction**

"A young woman who was an altar server told me", recounts Pope Benedict XVI in an essay written on the sex-abuse scandal, "that the chaplain . . . always introduced the sexual abuse he was committing against her with the words, 'This is my body, which will be given up for you.'"[48] Harrowing words. That the priest in question voices the words of Christ at the Last Supper to signify not his confecting the Eucharist—as per his usual sacramental duty and whereby he acts in Christ's very Person—but his intention to commit acts of sexual abuse of the most heinous and perverse sort underscores in its own unforgettably disturbing way how sexually abusive clerics epitomize the very antithesis of Christ. This priest hijacked Christ's own words in order to act not in Christ's very Person, as an *alter Christus*, but in his anti-Person, as an *anti-Christus*. And the antithetical nature of this priest's example, as of clerical sexual misconduct against women more generally considered, extends further, since if it confronts us with conduct befitting an *anti-Christus*, it also confronts us with a model of anti-manhood of the worst sort.

The two are not unrelated. Christ was a man, a male individual, and this fact proves of crucial importance in addressing the model of anti-manhood yielded by the phenomenon of clerical sexual misconduct against women—to say nothing of it addressing the crisis of masculinity and of gender confusion that we find currently befuddling western culture as a whole. In its Pastoral Constitution on the Church in the Modern World, *Gaudium et Spes*, no. 22, the Second Vatican Council announces both that

# I. A Marian Perspective on Clerical Sexual Misconduct with Women

"Christ fully reveals man to himself" and that Christ was "the perfect man." If this is of import for all human beings, for men and women alike, it bears on men—on male individuals—in a particular way as well. Christ the man, the perfect male individual, provides the solution to a warped model of manhood. In Christ, men see what it means to be male, how men should treat women, and how men and women should relate. As regards specifically the ministerial priesthood and the issue of clerical sexual misconduct against women, then, the lesson is obvious: in Christ, priests and bishops, as with all men, find their proper "reset"; a reset of what it means to be a man with a healthy male or masculine identity—and of how to treat and relate to women as a result.

Complementing Robert Fastiggi's Mariological treatment of clerical sexual misconduct against women in this present volume, I aim in what follows to offer a Christological treatment of the same, focusing specifically on the male "reset" that the man Christ provides in the effort at manly sexual self-control. To this end, and building on my earlier essay on Christ's maleness from the companion volume to this present collection, I focus first on Jesus's own example, specifically, on his treatment of and attitude toward women, of which the Gospels supply ample evidence.[49] In a second move, I draw out the important lessons this holds for men who enter into Holy Orders, that is, for men who in a particular and privileged way serve as an *alter Christus*, another Christ, in that they act in his very Person (*in persona Christi*) in their sacramental function and represent him as Head and Bridegroom of the Church.

## Jesus's Counter-Cultural Treatment of Women as Equal in Dignity to Men

In his Apostolic Letter *Mulieris Dignitatem*, On the Dignity and Vocation of Women, Pope St. John Paul II asserts: "In all his behavior, Christ emphasized the dignity and the vocation of women, without conforming to the prevailing customs and to the traditions sanctioned by the legislation of the time."[50] The textual evidence unambiguously bears out the Polish pontiff's claim. To show this, we need first to consider the customs and the legislative traditions—or at least some of them, and that by way of rapid overview—to which John Paul alludes. Many of these are well known.

## "Who has not created me a woman"

Epitomizing the regard for women in the Judaism of Jesus's time is the prayer that Jewish men would commonly recite at the beginning of the day, and which we find recorded in the Talmud (the set of rabbinic teachings and commentaries on the Torah, much of which goes back to the second century A.D., which forms the basis of Jewish law): "Blessed are you, Lord, our God, ruler of the universe, who has not created me a woman."[51] Consistent with this prayer, the Talmud also instructs Jewish men to pray for a male child upon learning that their wives are pregnant.[52]

In the matter of intellectual aptitude, particularly in view of rabbinical instruction, women were deemed unfit for this: "women are of light mind," asserts the Talmud.[53] To be fair, the Talmud does praise the intellectual talents of a certain Beruriah, a rabbi's wife who, as the Talmud puts it, "was so sharp and had such a good memory that she learned three hundred *halakhot* [laws] in one day from three hundred Sages."[54] Yet Beruriah seems to have very much marked the exception than the rule, since women were otherwise prohibited from becoming disciples of Jewish rabbis and were excluded from learning the Torah: "you shall teach Torah . . . to your sons, but not your daughters," the Talmud instructs.[55] Not to study under the rabbis themselves, women should instead support their *husbands'* rabbinical education, as the Talmud details when it enumerates how women bring honor upon themselves:

> Women merit [their reward] . . . for bringing their children to read the Torah in the synagogue, and for sending their husbands to study misha in the study hall [i.e., to study in the schools of the rabbis], and for waiting for their husbands until they return from the study hall [i.e., from the schools of the rabbis].[56]

Consistent with the Talmud's insistence that the female sex occupies a separate human category altogether ("women are a people unto themselves"), women were confined to their own court outside the ancient

Temple in Jerusalem, prohibited from entering the Inner Court (unless bringing a special sacrifice).[57] This extended to the synagogue, where women were required to remain behind a rear barrier *(mehitzah)*, principally to protect men from sexual distraction during prayer ("The voice of a woman is indecent," asserts the Talmud).[58] To be sure, in general the Talmud, looking upon women as objects of sexual temptation, recommends that men have as little contact as possible with women whom they are not married to (as dictated by the laws of *negiah*, which are somewhat loosely based on Leviticus 18:6 and 19), even forbidding that they be alone in a room together (this latter would come to be termed the laws of *yichud*).[59] In this connection, the Talmud also stipulates that women (especially married women) stay indoors as a general rule, that they cover themselves as much as possible, in particular their heads, as in accordance with Numbers 5:18 ("And the priest shall set the woman before the Lord, and unbind the hair of the woman's head"), and that they avoid speaking with men they encounter.[60]

As regards marriage, women were treated as the property of their husbands, enjoying few conjugal rights (Numbers 5:20 reminds women, "you are under your husband's authority"). Hence, the Mosaic permission for divorce was in practice a unilateral male privilege, since, generally speaking, the right to divorce was reserved to Jewish men alone. Basing itself on Deuteronomy 24:1-2, the Talmud, for instance, states that only the husband can initiate a divorce, and that this can be for any reason, including the spoiling of his dinner, or for practically no reason—an ancient form of "no-fault" divorce.[61]

The Talmud goes further. Responding to the view, voiced by one rabbi's son, that "a slave is the same as a woman," the Talmud seeks to temper this position, but only so much, maintaining instead that "a slave is more lowly than a woman," as Rabbi Aha bar Jacob puts it.[62] Though in one respect this Talmudic move marks an effort to lift up women, the fact remains that it assigns women to a second-tier social status. Indeed, that the Talmud reports the opinion that women are no different than slaves indicates how the culture of ancient Judaism could easily breed such an attitude, erroneous though it be.

## Gospel Innovation: Jesus Breaks with This Cultural Tradition

By all the ascertainable evidence, Jesus broke, in nearly every instance, with these customs and legislative traditions, elevating women to a status of equal dignity with men in the process. All four Gospels, especially Luke, offer uniform witness of Jesus's persistent efforts to push social boundaries and restrictions as they impinge upon the social status and dignity of women, even to the point of risking offense or scandal.[63] John Paul II holds that this witness constitutes nothing short of "innovation" particular to the Gospel, an innovation that consists in this: "in all of Jesus' teaching, as well as in his behavior, one can find nothing which reflects the discrimination against women prevalent in his day. On the contrary, *his words and works always express the respect and honor due to women*."[64] We can summarize these words and works, which undoubtedly "preserves [an] essential feature of the original figure of Jesus," to quote Benedict XVI, as follows.[65]

## Conspicuous Encounters with Women

Though women were required to avoid contact with men, or, short of that, conversations with men that they encountered, Jesus, for his part, did not hesitate to initiate such conversations. More than that, he was willing to initiate these conversations even when alone with a woman—a taboo practice—as with the Samaritan woman at Jacob's well in John 4:7-26. That the Samaritan woman herself owned a highly checkered moral past (married five times, and at the time living with another man) only underscores how such an occurrence would have raised eyebrows, to put it mildly. Little wonder that the disciples, upon rejoining Jesus at the well, "marveled that he was talking [alone] with a woman," though none dared to ask the obvious question, "'Why are you talking with her?'" (Jn 4:27). An obvious question for a Jewish rabbi speaking alone with a woman with a checkered moral past, indeed.

For another example of a startling encounter with a woman that Jesus initiated, we can turn to the incident with the crippled woman in the synagogue (Lk 13:10-17). Standing presumably in the rear of the synagogue behind the *mehitzah* (rear barrier), the woman seems otherwise to have been making no effort to attract Jesus's attention. All the same, Jesus notices the

# I. A Marian Perspective on Clerical Sexual Misconduct with Women

woman "bent over and hardly [able to] straighten herself" (v. 11). This leads him, evidently in a kind of outreach of affection and compassion, to call out to her: "when Jesus saw her, he called her and said to her, 'Woman, you are freed from your infirmity" (v. 12). That Jesus notices the woman and does not ignore her, and that, moved it would appear by compassion, he *calls out to her* and then goes over to her behind the *mehitzah* so that he can "lay hands upon her" (v. 13)—and this no matter the cultural strictures severely limiting contact between men and women in public, let alone in synagogue—almost certainly raised eyebrows and generated scandal. This would seem confirmed by the reaction of the ruler of the synagogue, who grew "indignant" with Jesus (v. 14). Though the ruler offers the pretext that Jesus healed (i.e., "worked") on the sabbath as the reason for his indignation, he no doubt also took offense at Jesus's calling out to a woman in synagogue, to say nothing of his touching her.

Perhaps the best-known example of Jesus's willingness to treat women with tender compassion, dignity and respect, no matter how socially improper or checkered a woman's moral past, comes in his encounter with the sinful woman in the house of Simon the Pharisee (Lk 7:36-50). That the uninvited woman kisses Jesus's feet and dries them with her hair—her uncovered hair—was an obvious cause of scandal, compounded by Jesus's refusal to rebuff her. Reacting with indignation, Simon seems willing to use the expected male Jewish reaction as a litmus test for determining the authenticity of Jesus's ministry: "If this man were a prophet, he would have known who and what sort of woman this is who is touching him, for she is a sinner" (v. 39). Undeterred, Jesus audaciously upends the social convention by contrasting Simon's example with the woman's: "You gave me no kiss [Simon], but from the time I came in she has not ceased to kiss my feet" (v. 45).

We should also call attention to the fact that Jesus exhibited special affection for certain women, in particular, Mary and Martha, sisters of Lazarus: "Now Jesus loved Martha and her sister and Lazarus" (Jn 11:5). Though on its face this remark strikes as unremarkable, it stands out in sharp relief if we read it against the backdrop of first-century Jewish culture. It would be difficult to imagine a parallel first-century Jewish account of the ministry of a certain unmarried itinerant rabbi making mention, somewhat gratuitously, of the fact that this rabbi "loved" various particular women. One finds no such similar observation in the Talmud, for instance, despite its many narrative accounts about numerous rabbis.

### Equality in Marriage

When it comes to marriage, and in particular the Mosaic permission for divorce, here, too, Jesus boldly upends social convention in his efforts at lifting up women, part and parcel of his determination to affirm the true meaning of marriage: "For your hardness of heart Moses allowed you to divorce your wives, but from the beginning it was not so" (Mt 19:8). Recall that Jewish law relegated women to the property of their husbands—indeed, to a status just above slaves, as per the Talmud—with few conjugal rights. The right to divorce accordingly belonged to men alone. By rescinding the (male) permission for divorce, Jesus was unambiguously affirming, among other things, the fundamental equality of husband and wife in the marriage covenant, with his express appeal to Genesis 2:24 ("And the two shall become one flesh") and Matthew 19:5.[66]

Not at the disposal of their husbands' mere whim or wish, (recall that husbands could initiate a divorce for any trivial reason, or for "any cause," as the Pharisee puts it in Matthew 19:3, and thus practically for no reason), women enjoy, on Jesus's account, the security of full rights and responsibilities that come with any true partnership. Jesus signals unmistakably that women are not to be regarded or treated as chattel, no matter if Jewish law suggests otherwise. Husbands and wives enjoy, by God's design and Jesus's witness, a "friendship of equality [*aequalis amicitia*]," as Aquinas terms it, since, indeed, friendship always presupposes equality (even the pagan philosopher Aristotle observes as much).[67]

### Female Disciples and Traveling Companions

To return to Jesus's relationship with women, though women were prohibited from being disciples of rabbis and learning under them, Jesus freely accepted female disciples and instructed them alongside his male disciples (he would also hold them up as a model of discipleship, as in Luke 10:42, and feature them prominently in many of his parables, as in Luke 15:8-10). What is more, Jesus allowed some, indeed, "many," of his female

# I. A Marian Perspective on Clerical Sexual Misconduct with Women

disciples to travel with him, and thus to belong to his "more intimate community of believers," as Benedict XVI puts it.[68] Luke 8:1-3 reports:

> Jesus went on through cities and villages, preaching and bringing the good news of the kingdom of God. And the twelve were with him, and also some women who had been healed of evil spirits and infirmities: Mary, called Magdalene, from whom seven demons had gone out, and Joanna, the wife of Chuza, Herod's steward, and Susanna, and many others, who provided for them out of their means.

To say such practices by a first-century rabbi would have provoked scandal would be understating the issue. That Jesus flouts the laws of *negiah*—the laws and customs dictating strict avoidance of physical contact between men and women who are not married to each other—in such an overt manner would certainly have offended and dismayed first-century Jewish sensibilities.

## *Equality, Not Sameness: Jesus Favors the Model of Male Headship*

Before examining in further depth how this flouting of the laws of *negiah* bears on the question of moral boundaries between the sexes—a question of obvious pertinence for the issue of clerical sexual misconduct against women—we must give brief pause to the following seeming incongruity: that, on the one hand, Jesus accepts women as traveling companions and as equal in dignity to men; yet that, on the other hand, he fails to include women among the circle of the Twelve, the group chosen by him to exercise headship in the Church. This latter fact makes one question whether Jesus truly favors the equality of the sexes. Oftentimes, the reason given for his exclusion of women from the Twelve is that he was acting in accord with the customs and patriarchal fetters of first-century Judaism—a seeming reasonable explanation, at least at first sight.[69]

Given the evidence presented above, however, the view that Jesus was simply conforming to the cultural mentality of his day in choosing only male apostles proves facile and unfounded. As we have seen, Jesus dignified women and stood up for them persistently and courageously. He defended them and lifted them up in a way that ran counter to a culture that ranked women just above slaves. In brief, Jesus was undaunted by the cultural roadblocks he faced in seeking to lift up women and was determined, it would appear, to level these roadblocks by affirming that women stand before God as equal to men in personal dignity and status.

Such a pattern would seem strongly to suggest, therefore, that Jesus should have included at least one woman among the Twelve. That he opted not to do this—clearly intentionally—suggests that Jesus holds to a distinction between personal dignity on the one side and social role and function on the other. In a word, for him, equality between the sexes does not mean sameness or interchangeability. To affirm the fundamental equality in personal dignity between men and women, between male and female disciples, does not imply interchangeability between the two in terms of tasks or of the holding of office in the society of his disciples, the Church.[70] As Benedict XVI puts it, "the difference between the discipleship of the Twelve and the discipleship of the women is obvious; the tasks assigned to each group are quite different."[71]

On its surface, then, this decision by Jesus to accept only men as apostles, because stopping short of the path that he readily left open for himself in his lifting up of women, remains somewhat enigmatic. The patriarchal-cultural argument may provide a quick explanation for Jesus's decision, but it proves inadequate in the face of the overwhelming countervailing evidence (John Paul II makes this point in *Ordinatio Sacerdotalis*, no. 2). Given this, Jesus's choice "cannot be dismissed as a historically conditioned decision open to subsequent development," reasons the theologian Sara Butler.[72]

It remains that Jesus favors the model of male headship in the Church, without in any way implying inequality in personal dignity between the sexes—analogous to the way the domestic church, the family, is structured. Though Jesus restricts the office of headship in the Church to men, he at the same time clearly signals that men and women remain equal before God. There can be different roles in the Church, including that of headship, that remain tied to sexual difference, yet without calling into question the fundamental equality of the sexes.

Not hesitant to call Jesus's treatment of women "revolutionary," one New Testament scholar, at the same time, recognizes that Jesus fails to push his revolutionary treatment of women as far as he could have, such as to the point of canceling out a preference for male headship in the structuring of the society of his disciples (the Church). He writes:

> Jesus broke with Jewish tradition in having women disciples and travelling companions, and there is no reason why He could not have continued this revolutionary trend by choosing some women to be among the Twelve. It appears then that male headship as a pattern of leadership, if refined and redefined according to the dictates of discipleship and Jesus' example, was acceptable to him.[73]

## *A Riddle to Be Solved*

To return to Jesus's flouting of the laws of *negiah*—the laws and customs dictating strict avoidance of physical contact between men and women who are not married to each other—admittedly this flouting can strike—still today—as somewhat puzzling, shocking even, and leave us with somewhat of a conundrum. On the one hand, the safeguarding of sexual propriety, accomplished through the imposition of strict boundaries between the sexes, marked the chief aim of the *negiah*. By disregarding the laws of *negiah*—most flagrantly by his allowing women to travel with him and his "intimate community" of male disciples—Jesus, it would appear, was throwing strict sexual propriety to the wind.

On the other hand, countervailing evidence shows that Jesus hardly favored a lax approach to sexual morality. Quite the contrary, Jesus sought to elevate and intensify the rigors of the Torah as they concern sexual morality, and this in rather pronounced terms. That he adverts to the arresting phrase "adultery of the heart" to condemn lustful desires (Mt 5:27-28) or that he revokes the Mosaic permission for divorce on the grounds that it marks a concession to sin ("For your hardness of heart, he [Moses] wrote you this commandment" [Mk 10:5]) amply confirms this.[74] Jesus thus insisted quite forcefully upon proper moral boundaries between the sexes—something the laws of *negiah* did as well. How, then, to make sense of his casting aside these latter?

## A Moral Standard that Directs Internal Acts

The answer emerges when we recognize that, relative to the *negiah*, what Jesus prefers—and introduces—is a new and more perfect standard of sexual propriety, one which has direct bearing on the issue of clerical sexual misconduct with women. By enjoining his disciples to discipline their interior sexual urges and to cease looking upon persons as objects of sexual self-gratification, which his arresting language of "adultery of the heart" only amplifies, Jesus promotes a moral standard that imposes not stringent external constraint, but strict *internal* self-governance—a self-governance that the virtue-ethics tradition terms as chastity. Evidently, Jesus views this standard as sufficient for establishing proper moral boundaries—the strictest of moral boundaries—between his male and female disciples, while at the same time allowing, contra the *negiah*, for their close personal interaction.

Put slightly differently, the practice of the virtue of chastity implies self-mastery over one's interior life (thoughts and desires), the source of outward action, whereas the *negiah* places the focus on external action. Jesus prefers an integrated chastity, a self-governance that pervades or integrates our entire being. It is a self-governance that moves from the inside out, from internal thoughts and desires to external bodily action. "What comes out of the mouth proceeds from the heart, and this is what defiles a man," he says in Matthew 15:18.

In this connection, Scholastic theologians, Thomas Aquinas chief among them, hold up the regulation of internal acts as a defining feature of New Testament morality. Aquinas writes: "The New Law [of the Gospel] surpasses the Old [Mosaic] Law," as well "since the New Law directs our internal acts. . . Hence the saying [by Peter Lombard] that 'the Old Law curbs the hand, but the New Law curbs the soul [*anima*].'"[75] Merely dwelling on external action ("curb the hand"), the *negiah* fails to target the proper source of outward action ("curb the soul"), and thereby proves insufficient. That the *negiah*, predicated on the view that women are a sexual temptation (recall from the Talmud, "the voice of a woman is indecent"), does this in an excessively restrictive and rigid fashion explains why Jesus prefers to break with it.

# I. A Marian Perspective on Clerical Sexual Misconduct with Women

## Removing the Sexual Stigma from Women

It bears insisting that by regarding women as a sexual temptation, ancient Judaism both helped exculpate men as regards their own struggles with lust and encouraged men to objectify women and to look upon them with negative suspicion. Hence, the greater strictures that the *negiah* placed on women which were noted above: women were to stay out of public view as much as possible so as to avoid contact with men; they should avoid speaking with men; they should thoroughly cover themselves, especially their heads; they should remain behind the barrier in synagogue and remain confined to the Women's Outer Court at the Temple in Jerusalem; and the list goes on.

Jesus will have none of this. By insisting upon interior self-mastery, which shifts moral responsibility from without—from an external object or person—to within, he accomplishes two things, both of which render the burdensome strictures of the *negiah* defunct. First, in a culture such as that of first-century Judaism, he demands respect for women, since he enjoins men to cease objectifying women and to cease looking upon them with negative suspicion. Jesus removes the sexual stigma from women, and thereby promotes their dignity as persons and elevates them to a status of equality with men.

Second, and in a more general sense, Jesus demands that men (and women) take moral ownership of their actions, denying both sexes, but especially men, the excuse to blame their struggles with lust on someone else. Why this concerns men especially shall be addressed shortly below, but for the moment it is not by accident, I think, that Jesus appears to direct his injunction against lustful desires primarily at men, given his express naming of women (*gynaika*) as the object of said desire: "Anyone who looks at a woman lustfully has already committed adultery with her in his heart" (Mt 5:28).

Jesus's attitude toward the *negiah* emerges as analogous, then, to his regard for the laws governing sabbath observance (the laws surrounding the third commandment). Jesus will be a slave to the strict letter of neither the *negiah* nor the laws governing sabbath observance: "The *negiah* were made for man, not man for the *negiah*," one might say. Yet, at the same time, hardly does Jesus disregard the "spirit" of these two sets of laws either. As a religious man, he continues to observe the sabbath and to respect the third commandment as expressive of a foundational normative good. As a moral man, indeed, as a man of consummate virtue, he continues to observe the "spirit" of the *negiah*, honoring the moral good that the *negiah* seek to bring about, albeit along the superior lines of an integrated chastity.

## *Jesus as* Exemplum Castitatis

That Jesus imbibed in his own person consummate moral virtue merits further remark. "The virtues were in their highest degree in Christ," writes Thomas Aquinas, for which reason he (Aquinas) designates him the *exemplum virtutis*, the supreme model of virtue.[76] This means that when he enjoins his disciples to strive for moral perfection (Mt 5:48), Jesus knows that he leads the way by his own moral example. He models the way of self-control of one's sexual appetites, that is, the way of integrated chastity. His sex drive was not cut off from his moral agency as an acting person but integrated into it.

Because he was sinless, Jesus was not subject to the internal disorder of the struggle of the spirit against the flesh. Introduced into the human condition by original sin, this struggle, which the theological tradition denotes by the terms concupiscence and the *fomes peccati* (the affective "spark" to sin), results from the disharmony that exists between the higher rational powers and the lower, animal-like inclination to bodily goods. Spared this, Christ enjoyed perfect interior rectitude and self-mastery, similar to Adam before the Fall: "[Christ was] not troubled by the passions of the soul nor the desires of the flesh," professes the Second Council of Constantinople (553).[77]

This would include passions and desires of a sexual nature. Jesus experienced no disordered sex drive; in no way can we attribute lust in any form to him. On the contrary, he enjoyed unmitigated command of his sexual impulses. As *exemplum virtutis*, he was by that fact also *exemplum castitatis*, supreme model of the particular virtue of chastity, or even more specifically, highest model of the virtue of virginity *(exemplum virginitatis)*, the virtue that regulates the perpetual renunciation of all sexual pleasure. Jesus looked upon women with eyes of purity, as Prof. Fastiggi observes in his essay, and enjoyed healthy affective relationships with them. The perfect model of being human, he evinces the fullness of human development and affective maturity, where the emotional dimension of human life, especially in the area of sexuality, is properly integrated with the rational and spiritual dimension of the acting person. Chastity emerges as the most basic measure of affective maturity and of the capacity for delayed bodily gratification, key to men regarding women as intellectual and moral equals (and vice versa). All this Jesus exemplifies to the highest degree.

*Jesus as the "Reset" for Male Sexual Self-Governance*

That Jesus enjoyed perfect command of his sexual impulses bears special significance for men, as lust marks an especially male problem. Recent scientific findings have established a neurobiological foundation for the male struggle with lust. These findings show that the structuring of the male brain orients the male sex drive to physical attraction (or to what researchers term objectification) and to physical pleasure—whereas the female brain owns a different type of structuring, one that orients the female sex drive more particularly to relationships.[78] No doubt, the disordering effects of original sin have compounded this male-specific neurobiological predisposition to physical attraction and to seeking sexual pleasure.

Indeed, I think that beyond the more general *fomes peccati*, the affective "spark" to sin that both sexes inherit from original sin, one can affirm in men a veritable *fomes luxuriae*, an affective spark to lust, characteristic of the male fallen condition. The male neurobiological predisposition to physical attraction (i.e., to objectification) and to seeking sexual pleasure becomes, as a consequence of original sin, a condition of "lying in wait"—thus, a "spark [*fomes*]" to lust that stokes or rouses and thereby exacerbates this male neurobiological predisposition. Recent psychological research would seem to bear this out, as studies indicate that men exhibit a greater willingness to pursue sexual opportunities and to engage in casual sex.[79] Studies also show that a much greater occurrence of sexual pathologies and sexually deviant behavior occur in men as opposed to women.[80]

To be clear, it is paramount that we distinguish original sin's wounding of the male sex drive from the natural wiring of the male brain that is expressive of God's creative design. The latter in itself is neither good nor bad, morally speaking. It forms part of the metaphysical biological makeup of the male human being. And since, as Aquinas puts it, "sin does not belong to human nature, a nature that has God for its cause," with the result that "what is natural to man was neither acquired nor forfeited by sin"; it would be deeply erroneous, heretical even, to deem that men are inclined by design to sin (lust) on account of the wiring of their brain for physical attraction and pleasure.[81] (In his discussion of the sexual design of human nature and its concomitant bodily marital act "by which children are procreated," Aquinas calls out the view that "bodily things were caused by an evil God" as representing "the worst of all heresies [*pessima haeresis*]," since it denies the biblical truth that "bodily nature was instituted by the good God.")[82] As with all biological or animal-like features of human life (such as the passions or emotions), the male neurobiological propensity for physical attraction and pleasure becomes moral only when acted upon by reason and will, that is, only in the measure that reason and will finalize and integrate it into a life of proper human flourishing.[83] Following Aristotle, Aquinas insists that moral virtue accomplishes this task—chastity— in the case of neurobiological design and ordered to sexual desire and pleasure.[84]

Like any man, Jesus owned a male-structured brain, part and parcel of his male-structured body. Even if we can attribute no form of lust to Jesus, we must still affirm in him the typical male neurobiological predisposition to physical attraction and to pleasure. Natural biological design, essential to human nature, demands as much. Heeding the soteriological principle that holds that the whole of human nature was saved only if Christ took on the whole of human nature, the conciliar professions of the early Church robustly affirm that Christ's humanity was in no way compromised or diluted; instead, its integrity and distinct identity were preserved.[85] Leaving little doubt what this spells in terms of Christ's sexuality, Aquinas writes: "Christ had to assume everything following upon human nature, namely, all the properties and parts of human nature, among which is sex."[86] At the same time, since Jesus did not contract original sin, he was spared the *fomes luxuriae*, the disordered affective condition characteristic of men. His neurobiological predisposition to physical attraction and pleasure remained just that, a predisposition.

## *Manly* Imitatio Christi

The moral lesson here is paramount: by his own example Jesus provides the proper "reset" for how men should master their sex drive, and thereby neutralize the *fomes luxuriae*. True, Jesus serves as a model of chastity for both sexes. All the same, he serves as a more particular model of "manly" chastity for those who share a male structuring with him—just as the Virgin Mary serves as a particular model of virtue for women. The theme of *imitatio Christi*, revered throughout Christian tradition and enjoying pride of place in the writings of Aquinas, bears particular relevance for men, it must be said.[87] Enjoying unmitigated interior mastery of his sexuality, Jesus exemplifies an integrated chastity in a male-specific or male-appropriate manner. Though men in their fallen condition might commonly struggle to varying degrees with a disordered sex drive, they can, by practicing a manly *imitatio Christi*, find their proper "reset" in Jesus who, at all points, mastered this drive.

Relating this expressly to the female sex, Jesus provides the proper reset for how men should regard and treat women. Jesus's example makes quite plain that proper respect for women and affirmation of their dignity as equal persons begins with interior control of the male sex drive. Where a man has little or no self-governance of his sexual appetites, where he lacks affective maturity and the capacity for delayed gratification, he cannot properly respect women; he will instead necessarily objectify them. John Paul II, in his Apostolic Exhortation *Familiaris Consortio*, observes how "the first victims of this mentality [whereby a human being is looked upon 'not as a person but as a thing, as an object of trade, at the service of selfish interest and mere pleasure'] are women."[88] In Jesus we see that not only does an integrated chastity go hand-in-hand with respect for women, the two are inextricably causally linked. Proper respect for women can only occur within the framework of virtue, headed most obviously by chastity (or virginity for those vowed to celibacy), but also prudence, justice (rendering to women what is their due on account of their equal dignity), charity, and the other virtues.

It cannot be overstated: healthy male-female relationships directly hinge on virtuous character. Hence, the vexatious nature of male enslavement to a habit of objectification—on display not only in the case of clerical sexual misconduct but also and more broadly in the current epidemic of pornography, largely a male problem where rare is the man who has not been adversely impacted or warped by pornographic use. Habitual objectification in any form, but especially in the form of addiction to pornography, impedes the possibility of genuine growth and formation in virtue, most notably in chastity. Now more than ever, then, the male reset provided by Christ proves crucial, particularly for the sake of healthy male-female relations.

### How Did the Apostles, the First Priests of the New Covenant, Respond to This?

Before leaving the topic of Jesus's treatment of women and of his flouting the laws of the *negiah*, we might wonder what his male traveling companions the twelve apostles—the first "priests of the new covenant," to quote the Council of Trent—made of this conduct.[89] How did these first priests of Jesus Christ, who "were believing and observant Jews" (to cite Benedict), find Jesus's attitude toward women, inclusive of his open disregard for the *negiah*?[90]

Evidently, they acceded and adapted to it. If at first they understandably reacted with surprise and dismay, as seems to have happened when they found Jesus speaking alone with the Samaritan woman at Jacob's well (see Jn 4:27), they appear to have quickly learned to follow Jesus's lead, no matter how perplexing this "mysterious new way," as Benedict terms it, may have struck them.[91] Given that the testimony of the apostles marks the primary source of the Gospel witness, it speaks volumes, I think, that all four Gospels offer detailed accounts of Jesus's conduct toward women and do not attempt to cover over such a controversial feature of his ministry. Among other things, this indicates that on the issue of sexual propriety, the apostles in time came to grasp the new standard of purity set by Jesus and that this standard was meant to be part and parcel of the "mysterious new way" of Christian discipleship—with these first "priests of the new covenant" charting the path. The apostles were the first to practice a manly *imitatio Christi* by exercising an integrated chastity in their own persons, freeing them to enjoy healthy affective relationships with women. Their successors in the priesthood would do well to heed their example.

## Application to Clerical Sexual Misconduct with Women

### *Anti-Christus instead of Alter Christus*

How the foregoing bears on the ordained priest and bishop, that is, on those who follow the apostles in serving in a unique and privileged way as an *alter Christus*, as another Christ, should appear obvious. As noted at the outset, clerical sexual misconduct against women exposes us to the scandalous and shameful reality of priests and bishops who act not as an *alter Christus*, but as an *anti-Christus*, as the moral antithesis of Christ. To see this in its full clarity, let us cull a précis of sorts of the principal lessons offered above that relate in an especially pertinent way to this issue.

First, Jesus insists upon and models in his own person an internal self-governance that moves from the inside out, from internal thoughts and desires to external bodily action—what we have termed as an integrated chastity. He models in both word and action the way of self-mastery over one's sexual appetites, the way of integrated chastity. Second, by insisting upon interior self-mastery, Jesus shifts moral responsibility from without—from an external object or person, especially a woman—to within. Demanding proper respect for women in a culture that relegates them to second-tier social status, Jesus coextensively demands that men cease objectifying women and looking upon them with negative suspicion, as a kind of sexual temptation. He refuses to abet the way in which his Jewish milieu, with its denigrating view of women, helped exculpate men in their own struggles with lust.

Third, since lust marks an especially male problem, it is incumbent upon men to practice a manly *imitatio Christi*, whereby they imbibe the example of Jesus, who enjoyed an interior mastery of his sexuality in a male-specific or male-appropriate manner. Though men in their fallen condition might commonly struggle to varying degrees with a disordered sex drive, they can, by practicing a manly *imitatio Christi*, find their proper "reset" in the male Jesus who at all points mastered this drive. Fourth and as a final culminating lesson, interior control of the male sex drive does not simply correlate with proper respect for women, it is foundational to it, and thus causal of proper sexual comportment with women. Where a man has little or no self-governance of his sexual appetites, where he lacks affective maturity and the capacity for delayed gratification, he cannot properly respect women and can easily mistreat them sexually. Proper respect for and treatment of women can only occur within the framework of virtue, chastity most of all—or virginity for those vowed to celibacy.

### Perverse Parodies of Christ

Sexually abusive priests and bishops, it goes without saying, repudiate all this. They repudiate and invert Jesus's charge and the moral example that he and the apostles after him provide, betraying themselves as perverse parodies of both Christ and the apostles. (The parodic punishment that Dante metes out to simoniacs—those clerics guilty of putting sacred office in the Church up for monetary exchange—in his *Inferno* is apt here: these sinners find themselves stuck headfirst in baptismal font-like pits with only their feet extending out, matching the way they had inverted the sacred office they held.) If Christ charges all men to exercise self-governance over their sexual appetites and to respect women as persons rather than as objects, this duty falls in a special way on those who act sacramentally in his own Person (*in persona Christi*) and who represent him as Head and Bridegroom of the Church.

Like the worst perpetrators of the #MeToo movement, many of whom were vowed to marriage and thus bound to the practice of chastity (Harvey Weinstein, Matt Lauer, Glenn Thrush, to name only three), these priests and bishops, all of whom were vowed to total sexual abstinence (celibacy) and thus bound to imbibe the virtue of virginity, abused their position of authority to prey upon the female sex with impunity and with total disregard for their victims' dignity as persons. Enslaved to their lust and ruled by a concomitant habit of objectification, these men regarded women purely and simply as objects of sexual self-gratification, acting opportunistically and predatorially as a result.

I. A Marian Perspective on Clerical Sexual Misconduct with Women        41

*Sacrilege and the Defilement of Holy Orders*

Let us return to the case of sexual abuse cited at the opening of this essay, the one mentioned by Benedict in which a female altar server was repeatedly violated by a priest who would initiate his abuse by his mimicking the words of consecration, "This is my body, which will be give up for you." Truly, words—perverted, heinous, deviant, depraved, debauched, vile, debased, wicked, sick, diabolical—fail to do justice to this crime that cries to heaven, and, again, nothing epitomizes more how sexually abusive priests and bishops epitomize the very antithesis of Christ. But what this case also shows is that the scandal of clerical sexual misconduct concerns not merely sexual sins (those of a most perverse and wicked sort), but sacrilege: "the perversion of Holy Orders, and the defilement of a person solemnly and publicly consecrated to God in chastity," is how the Dominican Dominic Legge explains sacrilege as regards clerical sexual misconduct.[92] Clerical sexual miscreants degrade the office of the priesthood and reduce it a "pleasure-seeking bachelordom," as the Jesuit Paul Mankowksi puts it.

Unavoidably the sacrilege extends to the sacramental ministry that belongs to the office of Holy Orders, defiling the ordained minister's unique identification with Christ when performing the sacraments *in persona Christi*. We see this not only in regard to the sacrament of reconciliation—recall how many cases of sexual abuse have occurred in the confessional—but most especially and most poignantly as it concerns the Eucharist. When pronouncing the words of consecration at Mass, "This is my body, which will be given up for you," the priest identifies himself in the first person with the male Christ. Taking Christ's words that signify his supreme act of self-emptying sacrificial love, re-presented and memorialized in the Eucharist, the priest in the case cited by Benedict twisted these words to fit acts of predatorial sexual deviancy directed to lustful self-gratification. One can hardly imagine a more depraved and perverse parody of the Eucharistic nature of the ordained priesthood.

Sadly, rival cases emerge all too abundantly. There is, for instance, the recent case of a priest from Louisiana who was caught videotaping himself having sex with two dominatrices on the altar of his parish church—the altar on which this same priest had offered Christ's unblemished body, blood, soul, and divinity countless times, presumably earlier that same day. Sacrilege and *anti-Christus*, indeed. Not coincidentally, one of the dominatrices, an adult film actress, had posted on social media the day prior that she was traveling to New Orleans in order to "defile a house of God." In an act of righteous indignation, the archbishop of New Orleans denounced the episode as "demonic" and proceeded to have the altar burned.[93]

### Celibacy as a Participation in the Sacrifice of the Cross

Let us close on an upward note by recalling what priestly celibacy, noble in its likeness to Christ on the Cross, is meant in truth to signify. Cardinal Robert Sarah insists that celibacy opens a window to the very essence of the ordained priesthood, since celibacy implies the sacrifice of oneself (of one's sexuality in its nuptial meaning and direction) and thus a participation in the sacrifice of the Cross—which the priest makes present at every Mass. The words of the Congregation for the Doctrine of the Faith's 1976 Declaration *Inter Insigniores*, On the Question of the Admission of Women to the Ministerial Priesthood, no. 5, are instructive here:

> The supreme expression of this representation [of Christ by the bishop or priest] is found in the altogether special form it assumes in the celebration of the Eucharist, which is the source and center of the Church's unity, the sacrificial meal in which the People of God are associated in the sacrifice of Christ: the priest, who alone has the power to perform it, then acts not only through the effective power conferred on him by Christ, but *in persona Christi*, taking the role of Christ, to the point of being his very image, when he pronounces the words of consecration.

To be this image and for the sacrifice of celibacy to have its proper meaning, the priest's moral character must be shaped by the virtue of virginity, the virtue whereby he renounces all sexual pleasure "for the sake of the kingdom of heaven" (see Mt 19:12). Aquinas reminds us that "the mind's purpose," that is, the soul's free embrace of perpetual abstinence from all sexual pleasure for the sake of the contemplation of divine things, marks the formal element of the virtue of virginity.[94] Yet virtue carries its own reward, namely, happiness and human flourishing, as virtue aligns our lives with the proper human good. Likewise, virginity, targets the good of the soul in its ordering to God. For the priest or bishop who makes this free embrace of perpetual sexual abstinence, then, he can expect genuine human flourishing, holiness even, as its fruit. "Blessed are the pure in heart, for they shall see God" (Mt 5:8).

Granted, the sexual revolution and today's "new philosophy of sexuality," to use the phrase of Benedict XVI to signify a view of sex as nothing more than "a social role we choose for ourselves," subvert the effort at inculcating virginity at nearly every turn.[95] Nothing strikes the modern spirit as more nonsensical and unnatural (read: anti-human) than the perpetual renunciation of sexual pleasure. That today's parish priest often finds himself alone in his parish assignment and stretched in the discharging of his office hardly makes the celibate life any easier.

Little matter. If the ordained priest and bishop finds himself called to heroism in his perpetual abstinence from all sexual pleasure, so be it. Let him, as an *alter Christus*, embrace the heroism of Christ. Let him embrace the Cross, and so be conformed to his virgin Lord.

## Conclusion

In clerical sexual misconduct against women, we see men who, enslaved to lust and to self-serving interests, epitomize the antithesis of Christ, the antithesis of the ordained priesthood, the antithesis of manhood. Christ alone provides the antidote to the grave moral disease that this scandal represents. For the priest or bishop who strives to know and live what it means to be a man, a priest, and an *alter Christus*, it is imperative that he unite himself to the male Christ, to the Jesus who broke barriers and risked the tarnishing of his own name in order to promote the good of women; to promote their dignity, their equality with men, their right to be treated as persons rather than as sexual objects. The ordained priesthood is no place for men who cannot or will not heed the charge of Jesus to cultivate an interior mastery of their sexuality; it is no place for those who cannot or will not renounce lust. Though priests and bishops might struggle in their fallen condition with mastering their sex drive, they can, by practicing a manly *imitatio Christi*, find their proper reset in the Jesus who, in his male-structured nature and in a male-specific manner, at all points mastered this drive. Let this be their solace and their hope, and so help to cleanse the Church of the filth of clerical sexual misconduct.

# II

# Man, Woman, and the Redemption of the World[1]

## Deborah Savage

*Visiting Professor of Theology, Franciscan University, Steubenville, Ohio*

**Introduction**

The crisis of sexual abuse in the Church seems to have no end. The effort to diagnose its cause has become its own distinct field of study. Theologians, psychologists, canon lawyers, seminary formators, the Vatican and other Church officials – all pursue whatever avenues are available to them within the limits of their disciplines and sphere of authority, seeking an approach that would lead us out of it. But the search for an antidote has proven elusive. We need look no further than the disappointed response to the long awaited McCarrick report to grasp the distance left to travel if we are to put it behind us. As each new revelation comes to light, the ordinary Catholic becomes more and more confused, while the experts redouble their efforts to find the right prescription.

Perhaps it is time to consider the possibility that our diagnostic pursuits have missed the mark because we have not yet arrived at the root of the problem. Perhaps it is time to try something new. With that in mind, my intention here is to offer a distinctly different analysis. I contend that there are two factors lurking just below the surface of this crisis: an inadequate account of the nature of man and woman; and an incomplete understanding of Original Sin and its effects on them both. My thesis is that without a fuller understanding of the nature of the masculine *and* the feminine principles in the Divine plan, our attempts to conform ourselves to God's design for us will never be realized. Whether one's vocation is to the priesthood, the religious life, or marriage, neither man nor woman exist without the other. Indeed, we work out our salvation in communion with the other. Finding our way out of the abuse crisis in any permanent sense will require a deeper understanding of man and woman, their identities, their relationship, and their mission. I hope to offer at least a starting place for man and woman to truly understand each other and to work cooperatively with each other – in and through Our Lord Jesus Christ – in the task of redeeming the world.

In what follows, we will first take up the question of the nature of man and woman, both their equal dignity and what differentiates them, by considering anew the creation accounts in Genesis 1 and 2. We will look at those passages through the lens provided by the metaphysical anthropology of St. Thomas Aquinas, itself refracted through a more properly Hebraic anthropology. I will show that the creation accounts provide the entry point for grasping the meaning of the masculine and feminine principles. And I will argue that the particular charisms given to each can be derived from their place in the order of creation.

We will then turn our attention to the account of the Fall found in Genesis 3. It will become clear that scripture itself reveals that, though Original Sin damages both man and woman equally, its concrete expression manifests in ways distinct to each of them. Their darkened intellects are now blind to the original charism they each possess; what had been their particular "genius" has now also become their curse. Their loss of their friendship with God has damaged the unity and complementarity they were meant to enjoy together. And it is this reality that has plagued human history ever since.

Catholic teaching on Original Sin has a long and enduring legacy, one grounded in both Scripture and Tradition, articulated and affirmed by the Church's magisterium since St. Augustine's dispute with the Pelagians.[2] Its essential elements are not in dispute in this paper. And, a systematic analysis of the Church's established teaching of the topic would be beyond our purposes here. That has been done quite well elsewhere.[3] But I will argue that the received tradition, while doctrinally sound in its contours, simply does not go far enough to unpack the full meaning of Genesis 3. Indeed, it has distracted us from pursuing the deeper meaning of the distinct roles that man and woman played in the Fall. The tradition maintains that, though woman appears to be the chief protagonist of the story – and certainly she bears her share of the responsibility – it is man who

## II. Man, Woman, and the Redemption of the World

holds the primary burden for the rupture it caused. With this I quite agree. And my proposal does not differ from this basic tenet of the faith. But the Church has attributed the primacy of Adam's sin to the further claim that this is because he is somehow "more perfect" than Eve. I will argue that this is to misread Genesis 1 and 2 and to ignore the meaning of Genesis 3:17. I will show that, though man is *first* in the order of creation, this does not make him *superior* in some moral sense. On the contrary, it reveals the depth of his transgression. It is *because* man is first in the order of creation that he bears responsibility for the entire series of events in the Garden. We will come to that demonstration and its implications later in the paper.

It will lead to what will be our final consideration: the significance of all this for an understanding of the mission entrusted to both man and woman in Genesis 1:28, to "be fruitful and multiply; fill the earth and subdue it."

Pope St. John Paul II tells us in his *Letter to Women*, that this task, "to transform the face of the earth," given to both men and women *from the start*, issues from the very complementarity which constitutes their relationship. It is this very "uni-duality," he declares, that gives man and woman their *mission*, for "to this unity of the two God has entrusted not only the work of procreation and family life, but the creation of history itself."[4] Though made more difficult by the fall from grace, we still share equally in realizing this mission. We are to return all things to Christ, together. The aim of this paper is to give some indication of how to go about that task.

## A Brief Excursus

Before proceeding, it will be helpful to give a very brief indication of the history of the Church's interest in this question. Though it has certainly been a topic of interest even since the earliest days of the history of Christianity, perhaps not surprisingly, it appears most explicitly in modern times during the aftermath of promulgation of *Humanae Vitae* by Pope St. Paul VI in 1968.

It is a matter of historical record that the years between *Humanae Vitae* and the pontificate of Pope St. John Paul II in 1978 were marked by controversy. The introduction of the birth control pill in 1965 had served to accelerate the sexual revolution already underway. Betty Friedan's widely read book *The Feminine Mystique,* published two years before, had launched a "second-wave" of feminism and the "women's movement" was rapidly gaining steam. Traditional norms that had governed relationships between men and women for centuries were under attack – and so was the Church. The Catholic understanding of the sacred nature of human sexuality was now thought by many to be simply out-of-date. The faithful and clergy alike began to question its validity. *Humanae Vitae* had affirmed the teaching but seemed to provide only rules against what had been declared a merely natural act, and instinct that should not be suppressed. In retrospect, it seems that Paul VI had not provided a clear or adequate account of the anthropology at the core of the teaching.[5]

It is hard to say whether or not this situation had any influence on Karol Wojtyla's election to the papacy in 1978. His interest in these issues, as well as his pastoral experience with young couples working through them, was surely well known. What is certain is that, immediately upon assuming the Chair of Peter, Pope John Paul II began the series of Wednesday reflections now known as *The Theology of the Body*. And less than a decade later, the Church's recognition of what was at stake surfaced in a dramatically simple form. At the 1987 Synod of Bishops on the Vocation and Mission of the Lay Faithful, the Synod Fathers called for a rigorous investigation of two fundamental questions: how are we to understand the Creator's *purpose* in determining that human beings would always exist as only either a man or a woman?; and what are the consequences of that decision? Among the thirty-four proposals included in the Synod's working document was the recommendation that further study be devoted to the anthropological and theological bases of the "dignity of being a woman and being a man." John Paul's Apostolic Letter, *Mulieris Dignitatem* (August 1988), was one particularly significant response to this recommendation.[6]

The Synod's propositions also provided the basis of his Post-Synodal Apostolic Exhortation *Christifideles laici* (December 1988), where he declared that:

> The condition that will assure the rightful presence of woman in the Church and in society is a more penetrating and accurate consideration of the *anthropological foundation for masculinity and*

*femininity* with the intent of clarifying woman's personal identity in relation to man, that is, a diversity yet mutual complementarity, not only as it concerns roles to be held and functions to be performed, but also, and more deeply, as it concerns her make-up and meaning as a person.[7]

This brief summary provides a proper context for our investigation, placing it squarely within the Magisterium. It clarifies that our larger purpose here is to assist the Church in responding more fully to the call to consider the "anthropological foundation of masculinity and femininity," in light of her interest in understanding God's purpose in creating us man and woman. We are ready now to turn to what can be discovered in the creation accounts found in Genesis 1 and 2.

## The Creation of Man and of Woman

The theological framework I propose takes its point of departure from St. John Paul's own starting place, the two creation accounts found in Genesis 1 and 2. In the opening pages of *The Theology of the Body,* Pope St. John Paul II declares that we can derive an account of the human person from the two distinct creation accounts found in Genesis 1 and 2. He argues that the first creation account reveals the meaning of man in the abstract, man *qua* man, that is, as an objective reality, created in the image of God. The second account reveals this meaning in the aspect of his subjectivity.[8] He states that the "powerful metaphysical content" hidden in Genesis 1 has provided "an incontrovertible point of reference and a solid basis" for metaphysics, anthropology and ethics, as well as a source of reflection throughout the ages for those "who have sought to understand 'being' and 'existing.'"[9] But in Genesis 2, he goes on to say, the depth to be uncovered in this second (though historically earlier) creation account has a different character; it "is above all subjective in nature and thus in some way psychological."[10] Here we find man in the concrete, as a subject of self-understanding and consciousness; here the account of the creation of man refers to him "especially in the aspect of his subjectivity."[11]

John Paul himself did not fully exploit this claim, stating that his intent is not to pursue this more metaphysical account of the soul in union with the body, but to focus instead on the "meaning of one's own body."[12] It is nonetheless an intriguing argument begging for further investigation. And so, in what follows, we will consider this claim by providing a more complete analysis of these texts through the lens provided by two distinct accounts of the person: first, an explicitly biblical anthropology; and second, the metaphysical anthropology of St. Thomas Aquinas. The first will allow for a direct reading of the text in its original language; the second will help us to determine if John Paul's use of more properly philosophical categories as an interpretive device is justified. Our thesis is that both of these approaches, taken together, will allow for a more precise account of the nature of man and of woman as ontologically equally human subjects, who are, at the same time, differentiated in relation to one another.

I have shown elsewhere that a careful analysis of these two creation accounts, when considered in light of Aquinas's metaphysical account of the soul in union with the body, does support John Paul II's proposal; they reveal the meaning of both man in the abstract--that is, man qua man--and man in the concrete, created as male and female. But if we are to be true to the text, we need to take an additional, preliminary step and look at John Paul's claim through the lens of two central principles of Hebraic anthropology: the notion of "corporate personality"; and the Hebraic theory of the soul. We will see that a closer read of the creation accounts through a properly Hebraic anthropology also supports the more philosophical analysis proposed by John Paul II.[13] Since our interests here are more specific, I will provide only a summary of what I have demonstrated more fully in previous research.[14] But the analysis that follows will illuminate the essential "equality" of man and woman, while providing the necessary foundation for an exploration of the charisms of man and of woman.

A few general comments about these two accounts as stand-alone texts are in order before we look at them together.

## Genesis 1

The specific pericope of interest to us first is Genesis 1:26-27. In 1:26, God says "let us make man (*adam*) in our image; in 1:27 we read: "So God created man (*ha'adam*) in his own image, in the image of God he created him (otho); male and female (*zâchâr* and *nikevah*) he created them (otham)."[15]

The starting place for my hypothesis is the use of the terms *adam* in the first passage and *ha'adam* in the second. These will provide us with our point of departure and allow us to claim that the first creation account reveals that man and woman are both instantiations of the same human nature, with all that this implies. My argument begins with a consideration of the meaning of the word *adam*, traditionally translated as "man." It is the full meaning of this term that we need to investigate first. We will start with a consideration of the two principles central to Hebraic anthropology mentioned above: the meaning of "corporate personality" and its relationship to the theory of the soul.

It can be difficult for those invested in modern notions of the person as an autonomous, self-determining individual to grasp how profoundly different is the point of departure for the Hebraic account of the person. Its starting place is the principle of the "corporate personality."[16] It is this concept that provides the first hermeneutical key to interpreting the biblical texts under investigation. It will allow us to unpack the intended meaning of *adam* and *ha'adam*. In the Semitic account of the person, itself derived from scripture, the individual is never, even in his concrete existence, an atomistic self, isolated from the community in which he is imbedded.[17] The individual person is an instantiation of the "organic unity" constituted by an ontologically prior corporate reality, not in a metaphorical or symbolic sense, but in terms of what one scholar refers to as a "single group consciousness."[18] This is the principle of corporate personality; it is a reference to the idea that the "one" represents the "many" and the many are contained in the one.[19] That is, the individual stands as *both* the one and the many. The community is *literally* embodied in the individual whose own existence renders present (in real time and space) both past and future generations.[20]

In this account, the individual is neither absorbed into the community nor ontologically cut off from it. He does not suffer a loss of personal identity; his identity is intimately and organically connected to the community. He is indeed an expression of the "corporate personality." The Semitic worldview thus held the "personal and corporate aspects of the person in a dynamic, positive tension."[21] It is a form of "biblical personalism which proclaims the integrity of the individual person in relation to the group, while at the same time admitting that the individual person can… represent the entire group."[22]

This admittedly brief excursus into Hebraic anthropology prepares us to return to our text and consider the meaning of *adam* and *ha'adam*, in light of these two principles. We will take up the term *adam* first.[23] We find it in Gen 1:26 when God says, "let us make man (*adam*) in our image." We now know that the translation of *adam* as "man" does not adequately capture the actual meaning of the term. Indeed, as we will see in a moment, the only thing that comes close to its meaning in English translation is the signifier "man *as such*" or the familiar "man *per se*." The Hebrew author of Genesis 1 is referring here to *adam* (itself taken from *adama* or earth) as an instantiation of the "corporate personality" referenced above. The creation of *adam* signifies the creation of the whole human race rather than merely an individual. But while *adam* contains all members of the community, it also retains connotations of personhood and concreteness. Here we see the significance of the "oscillation" between the one and the many, so essential to biblical personalism. But unlike the signifier "man *per se*," it is not an abstraction; the Hebraic reference always refers to a concrete existent and therefore includes a bodily existence. And since this moment in the text is a reference to the creation of the first human being (and again, not the abstraction "man *per se*), it must be interpreted to mean that the first human being was male. However, as we have seen, simultaneously contained within that existent, indeed, already present within *adam*, is the first woman. And while the connotation of *adam* extends to all of humanity, this reality can only take on a concrete existence through the creation of the first woman, something made clear in the very next passage.[24]

At Gen 1:27 we read: "So God created man (*ha'adam*) in his own image, in the image of God he created him (*otho*); male and female (*zâchâr* and *nikevah*) he created them (*otham*)."[25] The meaning of *ha'adam* is easily stated;

*ha'* is a definite article and the reference now is to *the* man. The text has introduced a new level of specificity to the creation of *adam* but has now declared *adam's* existence as embodied in manifestly masculine and feminine form. Thus, the priceless dignity afforded the first *adam*, created in the image and likeness of God, is extended to *zachar* and *nikevah*. It is *zachar* and *nikevah* who are instructed then to "be fruitful and multiply, fill the earth and subdue it" in Gen 1:28. Here we can anticipate the differentiation that will become more explicit in the second creation account (Genesis 2:22); Genesis 1 reveals that it issues out of a unity that already existed in the original "one".[26] And so, though there is an order to creation that places man in the position of primacy, this in no way compromises the dignity or ontological status of woman. This order will repeat itself in Genesis 2 where it will become even more clear that woman possesses a value that mirrors that of man.

We are now prepared to consider John Paul's claim that the first creation account is a reference to man in the "objective" sense, that is, man *qua* man, or man in the abstract. Does the text support such an interpretation?

The metaphysical anthropology of St. Thomas Aquinas, though grounded in experience and observation of the human person, his powers, and his acts, employs the method of abstraction, that is, it prescinds from the individuating conditions of matter to arrive at more general, universal principles. All existing things are reflections of two principles: form and matter (if inanimate); soul and body (if living). Man *as such,* though an abstraction, is understood to be a union of these two principles, a union of both body and soul, possessing a rational nature, intellect, will, and freedom. This is "man" in the universal sense and every individual instantiation of a rational soul, both male and female, is an expression of this universal human nature.

We have seen that ancient Semitic thought did not have the concept of a universal human nature or the notion of a "substantial form," that which makes something what it is essentially. These were terms introduced by the Greeks. But given what we now know about the meaning of *adam* as an expression of a "corporate personality" containing all of humanity, we can argue that it is perfectly legitimate to say that if there were a reference to the notion of man *qua* man in Hebrew, it would be *'adam*. In this context, *adam* is clearly a reference to man in the *universal* sense. So, when God says, "let us make *adam* in our image," we can safely say that the reference is an approximate equivalent of our concept of man *per se*. That is, it can serve as an approximation of or reference to the creation of the instantiation of the "substantial form" that constitutes the human creature.[27]

The significance of this conclusion, in light of contemporary concerns for the "equality" of men and women, would be hard to overstate. It shows definitively, now in philosophical terms, that Scripture *itself* reveals man and woman to be equally human. Man and woman, here at the level of the species, are both instantiations of the same substantial form and are therefore equally endowed with intellect, will, and freedom. All men and women who, together, comprise the human species, are equally human in every respect. They are both ontologically absolute subjects, possessing individuality, human agency, and the powers and potencies definitive of the rational soul.

This analysis has shown that John Paul II is justified in arguing that Genesis 1:26-27 is concerned with the creation of man in the objective sense, a formulation that, though it corresponds to the categories employed in the metaphysical anthropology of the Aristotelian-Thomistic tradition, finds a correspondence in the Hebraic account of the person. Both approaches demonstrate from Scripture that man and woman are equally human reflections of the principle of equal dignity. But this is not to say that they are interchangeable. We still need to consider that which differentiates them, a topic we will take up next. But before moving to that question, let us be clear: if this interpretation of Genesis 1 is correct – or at least plausible – we simply cannot declare that man is somehow "more perfect" than woman. Here the received tradition on man's role in Original Sin has been revealed to be manifestly inadequate.

## *Genesis 2*

The first account has established that man and woman are equal in dignity. In the second account, we begin to see what differentiates them. It is here that, according to John Paul II, God creates man and woman in their personal subjectivity. In Genesis 2:7, man (referred to here as

## II. Man, Woman, and the Redemption of the World

*hâ'adam, or the man*) is fashioned from *adama*, from the earth; he is the first human being. We know now that he is a reflection of both the one and the many. Gradually, he realizes that he is alone, that something is missing. And so, in a separate, creative act in Genesis 2:22, woman is *made* or *built (banah)* out of one of the man's ribs *(tsela)*. Here, God brings forth woman from the already existing ha'adam, who is himself made in the divine image. And thus, both become the bearers of that image, both possess absolute value and dignity. The man declares "here at last is bone of my bone, flesh of my flesh." He recognizes woman as a person like himself. Indeed, she is his mirror image and, with her appearance, ha'adam awakens to his own subjective existence. Both God and the man are finally content that a proper helper (ezer) has been found.[28] But what must get our attention immediately is the fact that *it is not until this moment in the text* (Genesis 2:22) that the sacred author refers to man and woman *for the first time* as concrete subjects of existence, as real existing persons. They are *only* now *'ish and ishshâh*: man and woman as *actual*. As John Paul II points out, there is no *'ish* without *ishshâh*, for it is not until *ishshâh* appears that the man, previously referred to as *ha'adam*, is finally referred to as *'ish*. Though man maintains the place of primacy (*ishshâh* is made from *'ish*), the plain meaning of the text is clear: there is no concretely existing man without a concretely existing woman; they appear in the text together, at least in terms of their specific identity. It is ultimately these two persons who will be referred to as Adam and Eve.[29]

In philosophical terms, when viewed through the lens of Aquinas' anthropology, this second account of creation can be seen as a description of the moment when signate matter and the principle of individuation have entered the picture. Man and woman (the *'ish* and the *ishshâh*) of the second creation account are the result of particular matter (earth and rib) being introduced; the substantial form or soul that makes man what he is *absolutely (adam)* illuminated in the first account has now found individuation and differentiation via the designated (common) matter which the form animates in the second. The complementarity that characterizes *the nature as such has now been embodied in two concretely existing beings, differentiated by two distinct but related kinds of matter.*

But the difference between man and woman is not reducible to merely the material element. This requires further explanation. From our analysis so far, we can conclude that both man and woman are equally human since both are an embodiment of a substantial form common to the species *humanum*. But both must be seen to be distinct instantiations of the species, made as they are of different signate matter. They are animated by souls that are "commensurated" or adapted to their individual person.[30] It is the meaning of "commensuration" that lends the clarity we need.

This "commensuration" reflects both the universal structure of male and female and the personal structure of any one particular man or woman: man *per se* is a composite of body and soul; each man or woman is a composite of *this* body and *this* soul. But gender is not reducible to matter; it has an ontological component since gender is the type of accident that is attributed to the subject *qua* subject, that is, to the whole composite of soul and body that constitutes the subject as a unity.[31] And so, here offering woman as our example, though matter is one of the things that differentiates woman from man, since woman is composed of both body and soul, and since the soul of each individual woman is meant for her (that would be commensuration), she is in some essential way, a woman. That is, gender is an accident not merely of the matter, like the color of her hair or her eyes. Her woman-ness does not reside in her merely in the matter of which she is made. It is who *she is*, as John Paul II states, both physically and ontologically. And these same things can be said of man: he is in some essential way, a man. *Men and women are equal, composite creatures and, at the level of the individual person, differentiated by both the matter of which they are made and the soul that animates them. This is true of both of them.* And here we can say that John Paul II's claim that Genesis 2 describes man "in his subjectivity" is justified.

Let us pause here to highlight this important point: this account of the equality and difference that characterizes man and woman reveals that *neither the male nor the female of the species is <u>normative</u> for the species*. How so? Because at the level of man or woman *per se*, we are differentiated *in exactly the same way*. Both woman and man are equally human; the sexual difference that characterizes man and woman is rooted in a particular kind of philosophical "accident" driven by, but not reducible to, the matter of which they are made. Men and women are both composite creatures, a union of body and soul, whose gender is an inseparable accident, (but an accident nonetheless), attributable to the composite itself. They are the same in terms of that which differentiates them from each other.

The implications could not be more significant. For here we have a philosophical demonstration, grounded *in Scripture*, that women do not have to act like men to be considered human any more than men have to act like women to be considered human. There is absolutely no risk to the "equality" of men and women in understanding their nature in this way. Man and woman are equally human but different, a fact immediately discernible in human experience and accessible to scientific analysis.[32] Thus, the historical error is corrected. Woman is redeemed, freed, at least in theory, from Aristotle's claim that woman is a "malformed" male.[33] We need to reconsider the significance of the creation of woman in Genesis 2: 18-34. Here it will be shown that, when considered together, Genesis 1 and 2 illuminates more fully the meaning of the second creation account and its significance for our understanding of the creation of man and woman. In particular, such a reading will dispute the traditional claim that woman is created second because she is "less honorable" than man.[34] In fact, it will dispute the claim that woman is created "second" at all.

## *Genesis 1 and 2 Considered Together*

This somewhat foreshortened analysis of Genesis 1 and 2 does establish both the equality of men and women and their difference. But there is more to be found in these texts. Considered together, they allow us to illuminate more fully the meaning of the second creation account and its significance for our questions here.

Let us return first to the creation account found in Genesis 1. Here the author lays out a particular hierarchical order in which God clearly creates. God begins with the heavens and the earth, and then gradually makes his way up the scale of creation to the moment where it all culminates in the creation of *adam*, embodied in *ha'adam*, containing both the first man and the first woman. This is clearly a hierarchy that is on its way *up*, from lower life forms to higher.

Pausing again over what we discover from the second account, we read in 2:7 that *hâ'adam* is made from the dust of the earth. When, in Genesis 2:18, God sees that the man is alone, God forms every creature and brings them to the man to be named. Then God, realizing that none of the creatures correspond to the man's own being, and that it is not good for him to be alone, decides it is necessary to make a fitting helper (the full text is '*ezer kenegdo*) for him[35] – then puts him into a deep sleep and forms the woman (*'issah*) from man's (*'ish*) rib (*tsela*).[36] Upon awakening, Adam says, "This at last is bone of my bones and flesh of my flesh" (Gen 2:23-24). As John Paul II points out, man recognizes in woman another *person*, a being equal to himself, a someone, not a something – a someone he can love, to whom he can make of himself a gift and who can reciprocate in kind. This seems fairly straightforward.

But there are several additional and important points to glean from considering these two chapters together. First, it is only when we come to the making of Eve that we see the final significance of the order introduced in the first account and brought to completion in the second.[37] Adam is made from the earth (*adama*), but Eve is made from Adam. Though it has troubled feminists forever – and is arguably the root of Philo's historical misinterpretation of this passage– the fact that Eve is created second is not to make her subservient. *For in the hierarchy thus established, woman is not created "second"; she is created last.* She is, in fact, made on the way *up* - the last creature to appear, a creature made, not from earth, but from something that arguably *already* contains a greater actualization than dust or clay.[38] It does seem as though she is made of "finer stuff." In any case, because of the order suggested by reading the accounts together, Eve can be seen as the pinnacle of creation, not as a creature whose place in that order is subservient or somehow less in stature than that of Adam. For it is *only* at the moment of her creation that man realizes who he is. It is her appearance that reveals to man the nature of his own personhood.

This proposition is reinforced when we consider that the Hebrew word usually translated as "helper" is "*ezer*" which does not mean servant or slave.[39] When this word is used elsewhere in Scripture, it <u>has the connotation of Divine aid</u>.[40] Used here to express helper or partner, it indicates someone who is most definitely not a slave or even remotely subservient – there is the sense of an equal, a partner, help sent by God.[41] Thus, Eve is not to be his servant – a different word would have been used if that were the intention – but someone who can help him to live.

But an additional, equally significant insight appears when we consider the full meaning of this moment in the text. Woman is described as *ezer kenegdo; kenegdo* is a preposition that means "in front of," "in the sight of," "before" (in the spatial sense). Thus, we can conclude *from the text* that woman is not "below" man in the order of creation, nor is she above him. She stands in front of him, before him, meeting his gaze as it were and sharing in the responsibility for the preservation of all that precedes them. Woman and man are complementary creatures; both constitute the "other" for each other. And so, another misunderstood element in the tradition – that woman is subservient to man, sent to be merely his servant – is corrected. Woman's significance is revealed in its full meaning. Woman's place in the order of creation reveals her true nature and mission – that of help sent *by God* to man - and by extension, to all of humanity.

The man and the woman, now *'ish and ishshâh*, stand face to face with one another, poised to offer themselves as a gift to each other. They both possess intellect, will, and freedom, as well as the capacity for action and receptivity. But their gift of self is made possible by the very differences that characterize them. And the gifts that each bring to the tasks of human living will be necessary to fulfil their mission, given to both of them in Genesis 1:27: to subdue the earth and fill it.

The Genesis account does reveal that it is man who, in a sense, gives woman her place. Importantly, we have seen that this place is one of "face-to-face" equality. But her significance transcends concerns for equality. For it is woman who reveals man to himself and, with that, the meaning of human life itself. Only with the appearance of woman does man's self-gift become possible. And only with woman's arrival does human community appear for the first time – and enter into human history.

Woman has sovereign importance, not independently of the place man occupies, but apart from it. For the simple fact is that *without woman, man has no future*. As St. Paul declares in 1 Cor 11:12, "For just as woman came from man, so man is born of woman; but all things are from God." It is this cosmic reality that has been over-looked throughout the centuries; it reveals the import of woman's "place." For in fact, without her, *none of us have a future*. She points us toward what is above while we all engage in life here below.

Woman and man now are *both* redeemed and free to serve as partners in the great project of building a truly human civilization, ordered as it is toward eternal life with the God who created them. They accomplish this through the charisms given to each of them in virtue of their place in the order of creation. We will now consider in what those gifts consist of. And we will see that both are necessary in the divine plan; both are called to a profound respect for one another; both have been given the mission to "fill the earth and subdue it."

**The Genius of Man and Woman**[42]

We are ready to turn our attention to what might constitute the particular charism or "genius" of man and of woman.[43] My claim is that both can be derived from the passages in Genesis 2 that describe their creation. Since he is first in the order of creation, I will begin with the genius of man. And since this represents an innovation in the received tradition, I will provide a more extended analysis of my proposal regarding his particular charism. Then I will offer a somewhat briefer analysis of the genius attributable to woman. This will allow us to contrast her genius with that of man and to illuminate the complementary nature of their particular charisms.

### *Man*

To grasp what might constitute the genius of man, we return, once again, to the opening chapters of Genesis, beginning with Genesis 2:7-9 and the creation of man, referred to here as *hā'adam*, literally "the human being," the male of the species, man *qua* male. It reveals that man's (that is, the male person's) proper place is in the midst of creation:

> …then the Lord God formed man of dust from the ground and breathed into his nostrils the breath of life and man became a living being. And the Lord God planted a garden in Eden, in the east; and there he put the man whom he had formed. And out of the ground the Lord God made to grow every tree that is pleasant to sight and good for food…

## II. Man, Woman, and the Redemption of the World

The next passage of significance for our question provides an insight into Adam's personal mission as well as his role in the Fall. In Genesis 2:15-17, we read:

> The Lord God took the man and put him in the garden of Eden to till it and to keep it. And the Lord God commanded the man, saying "You may freely eat of every tree of the garden but of the tree of knowledge of good and evil you shall not eat, for in the day that you eat of it you shall die."

This particular passage has profound meaning for our understanding of human work since, clearly, Adam is placed in the Garden to do exactly that. But it also reveals that the instruction not to eat the fruit of the tree of knowledge is given directly to the man. We will come back to these themes shortly.

Finally, in Genesis 2:18-23, we learn that the man is tasked with naming all the living creatures, including the one made a "helper" (*ezer*) for him:

> Then the Lord God said, "It is not good that the man should be alone; I will make a helper fit for him." So out of the ground the Lord God formed every beast of the field and every bird of the air, and brought them to the man to see what he would call them; and whatever the man called every living creature, that was its name.

Having given names to every beast, yet still not encountering a fitting helper, God puts the man into a deep sleep and fashions the woman (*'issah*) out of the rib of the man. When she is brought before him by the Lord God, the man declares: "This at last is bone of my bones and flesh of my flesh; she shall be called Woman, because she was taken out of Man."

These passages reveal several important things about the masculine genius. First, although we have already established that woman does not occupy a subservient role simply because she comes into existence after him, man is clearly first in the order of creation. He is first to know God and, when woman is brought to him, both the man and the Lord God recognize her for who she is – a person, and his partner. The man's prior relationship with God prepares him in a special way to introduce the woman to God and to the things of creation. The origin of man's role in the family can be traced to this fact, as well as to the revelation that woman is herself created out of man. In a sense, man provides the material for the generation of woman and, it could be said, thus establishes his place as the active or generative principle.

This leads to a second important observation and to the heart of my hypothesis concerning the genius men bring to the world. Worthy of our notice is the fact that man is in the Garden alone with God for some period before the appearance of woman, something that has important implications for the place he occupies in the created order and the traditional understanding of man as the head of the household. But aside from this special relationship with the Creator, it can be said that man's first contact with reality is of a horizon that otherwise contains only lower creatures, what we might call "things" (*res*); this is what leads God to conclude that the man is incomplete and alone, and ultimately leads to the creation of woman.[44] We will see that this provides a point of departure for our understanding of the genius of woman as well.

But first, in Genesis 2: 15-23, we learn that man's place is in the midst of the created order and, further, that his task is to care for it. He is put in the Garden to till it. Though it is not insignificant that, in the first account, both woman and man are instructed to "fill the earth and subdue it," to have dominion over the earth, only man is given a specific task. And his task is to work, to care for the things found in God's creation. This becomes more evident when we consider that, as God searches for a partner for the man, He brings to him all the things of creation to see what *he will name them*. One by one, the man gives each a name, that is, *he takes dominion over them*.[45]

Now, in order to name things well, to take dominion over them, man would have to gain some kind of direct knowledge of them and to possess a certain familiarity and sophistication with things. Indeed, Aquinas argues that Adam must have received an additional preternatural gift, infused knowledge, in order to be able to name all the animals brought before him.[46] And it is here that we come to the core of what I propose is man's genius: he learns that he excels at discovering what things are, how they are to be distinguished from one another, and what they are for. This is his gift.

From this account we are justified in at least proposing that man's capacity to name things, to determine what can be predicated of something and what cannot, and an ability to arrive at a systematic way of judging the matter, might be said to be the gifts men bring to the tasks of human living. This very capacity is the provenance of many of the achievements of Western Civilization. As one scholar describes it, without this genius, "without this literal 'discernment,' there can be nothing so intricate as law, the government of a city, higher learning, a church -- not to mention philosophy and theology."[47] When considered along with the fact that man's mission is to work in the Garden, to care for God's creation, we are able to draw a further conclusion: that the genius of man is found in his capacity to know and to use the goods of the earth in the service of authentic human flourishing.

Two further points must be made in this regard. First, it is equally important to point out that the first man's capacity to know and use things does not mean that he is *only* oriented toward things. In truth, his first contact with reality includes the Lord God. He is, in the first instance, aware of his dependence upon his Creator and he is truly marked by that relationship forever after. It is within this context that he encounters the woman. Until the woman is brought to him, both to name and to love as he can love no other, he has no "other" like himself. He knows immediately that the woman is *not* a thing; she is a person. Without hesitation he declares that she is "flesh of his flesh, and bone of his bones." And, while he can and does name her, he cannot have dominion over her in the same way he has over everything else. She represents for him his highest good, the greatest gift God has given him and, as a consequence, the value of all the rest of creation is reordered. From and through his encounter with the woman, the Lord God reveals to him the nature of the reciprocal relationship of the gift of self. And he must realize as well that his own gift – that of caring for and using the goods of creation – is a gift to be exercised in service to her authentic good. As we shall see next, this gift will become clouded by the effects of the Fall. But in the state of original innocence, man well understood the right ordering of creation and the place he occupied in it.

Last, the rather well documented proclivity of men to attend more to things than to persons is often criticized, in many cases, legitimately so, distorted as it can be by the effects of original sin.[48] Nonetheless, I maintain that we are justified in seeing it as a reflection of man's genius, once it is established that it is in virtue of this gift that man contributes to the good of humankind. However, a further proposition is required to support this claim: we must recall that the goods of creation, like persons, have ontological status also. They are created by God, held in existence by God, endowed with a *telos* that orders them toward a final end according to God's design.[49] Thus, though the constant moral context of all human action is the fact that the highest value is and always will be the authentic good of human persons, the only creatures created for their own sake, man's orientation toward "things" is also an orientation toward creatures. In fact, it is this orientation that makes him most properly their steward.

Rightly understood, the particular genius of man has proven throughout history to be an essential gift in sustaining families and creating social order – indeed, it has been the key to the very building up of civilizations.[50] Of all the creatures in the material world, humans are the only ones who actually have to work to master their environment and create conditions that support human flourishing.[51] Without the specific genius of man, the human species would not have survived.[52] We owe men a debt of gratitude even if we must also remember that all of us – man and woman alike – are forever under the sway of the effects of original sin. It is the logic of sin that confuses us, that "needs to be broken [so that] a way forward can be found that is capable of banishing it from the hearts of sinful humanity."[53] But as our faith reveals, self-knowledge is an important weapon in our constant battle with the forces that seek to defeat us. To understand the masculine genius in this way is to equip man with the knowledge he needs to strengthen his own struggle with the effects of original sin, which now can be seen in a new light.

### Woman

We have established that man's first contact with reality is of a horizon that otherwise contains only lower creatures, what we might call "things" (*res*) and that his place in the created order grounds his charism. It is certainly plausible to claim that this seems to provide a point of departure for the well documented observation that men appear to be more oriented toward things than toward people. In contrast and of special significance is the quite legitimate claim that, since woman comes into existence after man, her first contact with reality is of a horizon that, *from the beginning,* includes man, that is, it includes persons. One can imagine the woman, a person endowed with intellect and free will who, upon seeing the man, would recognize another like her, an equal, while the other creatures and things around her appear only on the periphery of her gaze. The self-evident fact about woman's creation is that she has *never lived in a world uninhabited by persons.* This exegetical insight seems to provide a starting place in Scripture for the equally well documented phenomenon that women have naturally shown already; it is woman who reveals to man who he is – a someone, not a something – that is, a person. Though woman is surely the receptive principle, it is her presence that actualizes man's potency for the gift of self. In her, he also recognizes himself. The unfolding of human history begins only when both man and woman know each other.

In *Mulieris Dignitatem,* John Paul argues that the feminine genius is grounded in the reality that all women have the capacity to be mothers – and that this capacity, whether fulfilled in a physical or spiritual sense – orients her toward the other, toward persons.[54] I do not dispute his claim in any way – for we can surely agree that there is plenty of evidence to demonstrate it. And in every sense, Eve is certainly the mother of all humankind. But, my point is that in addition to her capacity to conceive and nurture human life, indeed *prior to it,* her place in the order of creation reveals that – from the beginning – the horizon of all womankind includes persons, includes the other.[55] This may explain why girls and women seem to know – from the beginning – that they are meant for relationship, while it takes men a bit longer to look up and realize they are lonely for something they only just realized was missing and to look for the one who can complete them.

The genius of woman is found here. While man's first experience of his own existence is of loneliness, woman's horizon is different, right from the start. From the first moment of her own reality, woman sees herself in relation to the other. The Fall will result in a disorder in this inclination;

Eve's desire will now be for relationship with man, even when she knows he is using her as an object. But the preceding analysis has shown that this capacity – to include the other – *is not a lesser quality*. It is not something that only unnecessarily complicates things, diverting us from an otherwise clear line of sight to achieving results. Nor does it compromise woman's fundamental intelligence, her competence, her ability to get things done. Woman's mission is grounded in her particular genius; her task is to serve as the catalyst for the personal becoming of every human being. And she is to keep constantly before us the fact that the existence of living persons, whether in the womb or walking around outside of it, cannot be forgotten while we frantically engage in the tasks of human living. Woman is responsible for reminding us all that *all human activity* is to be ordered toward authentic human flourishing.[56]

And so, in these brief sketches, we see the outline of a starting place for both the genius of man and of woman. Scripture, like science and experience, suggests what differentiates men and women: men seem more oriented toward things; women seem more oriented toward persons.[57] These claims do not in any way preclude men attending to persons – or women having dominion over things.

Interestingly, the account of the Fall offers further evidence of the validity of this hypothesis. In Genesis, we will see that man and woman will suffer particular and distinct forms of alienation as a consequence of the Fall.[58] Adam will now fight with creation; Eve will encounter disorder in her relationship to man. These revelations seem to confirm that, in their original innocence, woman and man were in a right relationship to things (man) and persons (woman). Though, as we know, this state of innocence did not endure. We will now turn to a consideration of the account of the Fall in Genesis 3.

## The Consequences of the Fall

So far, our attention has been focused on what the tradition has generally referred to as the state of Original Justice, that which John Paul II terms: the state of Original Innocence. It is a description of what God *meant* things to be before the Fall. Though a more detailed treatment of the nature of Original Sin itself is beyond the scope of this present study, the

## II. Man, Woman, and the Redemption of the World

analysis above does provide us with a framework within which to consider the significance of the ways it manifests in woman and man.[59] In fact, the account of the Fall in Genesis 3 provides further evidence of the plausibility of the theory we have been investigating and provides a critical point of leverage as we consider the larger aims of this endeavor. A brief excursus into the received tradition on Original Sin will ground this part of the paper.

### *Excursus: A Synopsis of the Doctrine of Original Sin*

According to the perennial teaching of the Church, evil entered into the world with the sin of our first parents, described in the familiar account of the Fall found in Genesis 3.[60] Man's original sin was an act of prideful disobedience against a grave precept of God's law, a precept given so that he "could prove by his action that God is his origin and end."[61] It resulted in the "loss of the original justice" a privation of the "complex of gifts" received in his creation. The gravity of this sin caused a rupture in his friendship with God and, as a consequence, he lost the holiness he originally possessed in virtue of the gift of sanctifying grace.[62] All subsequent sin would be a reflection of the loss of this friendship: "disobedience toward God and a lack of trust in his goodness."[63] And since it resulted in a "privation" – the loss of something that would otherwise have been natural to them –we all know that both woman and man have been left with a permanent sense of something missing, a profound experience of lacking. This has led them to pursue various, often disordered paths to fill that void.

Now, though some in the tradition have argued to the contrary, the Church is very clear that Original Sin was not a sexual sin nor is it due to concupiscence.[64] Adam doesn't come to "know" Eve until Genesis 4:1 and so to imply the cause was a disorder already present in them would indicate that they were lacking the supernatural grace that accompanied them at their creation. Concupiscence was the *consequence* of the Fall.[65] The sin was one of *disobedience*, an act made possible by the fact that both man and woman possessed both the freedom to choose *and* knowledge of God's precept.[66] However, this deadly choice was not made as a result of an internal disorder of this freedom; man felt no difficulty within himself to obey God. Rather it was prompted by a temptation that came, not from within, but from without. Man can be either helped or hindered by other creatures. This moment was the first example of the danger to himself, inherent in his freedom.[67]

Original sin affects all men and women, though it does not have the character of a personal fault. It is a deprivation of original holiness and justice. However, human nature has not been totally corrupted: it is "wounded in the natural powers proper to it, subject to ignorance, suffering and the dominion of death, and inclined to sin."[68] Though Baptism erases it and restores him on a path toward God, its consequences for nature persist, leaving him weakened and inclined to evil, and summoning him to spiritual battle. It ruptures the relationships that constitute his being and his self-understanding, first and primarily, his relationship with God; and secondly, and as a result, his relationship to himself and to others.

The tradition maintains that, though the sin was committed by both and constituted a personal sin for them both, Eve lost justice for herself alone, whereas the personal sin of Adam affects all of mankind. Original Sin is transmitted to subsequent generations through propagation, through the man's seed. It is inherited by his posterity as a habitual sin, present in a natural way in all men, and proper to each individual.[69]

None of what has been stated so far is in dispute in this essay. But several points of divergence do appear as we turn our attention to how the received tradition describes the different roles that Adam and Eve are said to play in the events in the Garden, the nature of the responsibility they each bear for the Fall itself – and why. Here I will highlight three aspects of the tradition that I think call for further scrutiny in anticipation of the fuller treatment we will consider later. To clarify, not every element in the following summaries is under dispute here. But these three areas will be the focus of our critique and provide a point of departure for the proposals on offer in this paper.

First, the teaching locates the particular significance of Adam's sin in the events that precede the moment of decision, declaring that the devil approached Eve (and not Adam) since she was "easier prey." Though both had the gift of integrity, Adam had been given "more abundant grace." And so, Eve was "easier to seduce, weaker in resistance, and as clinging to her

## II. Man, Woman, and the Redemption of the World

man she was more apt to seduce him."[70] In the sin of Eve is found, first and above all, *pride,* but also gluttony and scandal, as she also gave some to her husband.[71] And while we find pride and disobedience in the sin of Adam as well, we find also an "inordinate affection" for his wife. His decision was made out of a kind of "condescension" for her and he accepted the forbidden fruit.[72]

Second, though the sin of the first parents was the most serious of all human sins, because Eve was seduced by a mere external temptation, its malice is diminished. It was a sin of pride which, though grave, is not the most serious of sins. That of the fallen angels was far worse. But in comparing the personal sin of Adam with that of Eve, Adam's was far worse since he possessed "greater perfection." It is in virtue of this greater perfection that Adam bears primary responsibility for the Fall.

Third, though in terms of the species of pride, Eve's sin was the more serious of the two, because "'she was more puffed up than the man,' and she led the man into sin and the sin of the man was less, since it was committed out of a certain friendly good-will."[73]

I find these three claims to be problematic, interpretations that, as I have tried to show, are simply not supported by the texts of the first three chapters of Genesis. I do not dispute that both were at fault, nor do I dispute the place man occupies in the created order vis-à-vis woman. However, in what follows I will argue that man betrayed the role God gave him in creating him, thus, and in doing so, betrayed woman as well. He compromised his place in the order of creation, failing Eve at *the* crucial moment of salvation history.

Let us take these points one at a time. First, we have established that woman and man are both instantiations of the same substantial form – the human soul – and must therefore be acknowledged as *both* equally in possession of those capacities that, also according to the Magisterium, belong to every human person: viz., intellect, will, and freedom. Woman is man's equal in that she is equally human, equal in dignity, and equal in terms of the potencies she brings to her encounter with reality. Certainly, this would contradict the claim that the devil approached Eve first since she was "easier prey." Though I will argue below that Eve was definitely at a disadvantage in the confrontation with the serpent, it was not because she was less in possession of these natural human capacities. Eve was innocent in that moment, but she was not naïve.

Secondly, we have also demonstrated that a proper interpretation of Genesis 2 reveals that, contrary to the received tradition, woman was created, not second, but last – the final act in a hierarchy manifestly on its way up. We clarified that woman is *ezer kenegdo*, help sent to man *from above* by God, yet standing face to face with man in the order of creation. This challenges the notion that man possesses "greater perfection" than woman. Though man is certainly first, both man and woman bear a distinct "pride of place" in the created order that, while different, are equally essential to the future of the human race. And so, we cannot legitimately conclude that Adam possesses a greater perfection and that this is the reason he bears primary responsibility for the Fall. While I will argue that he does, it will not be because of a perfection that he possessed was unmatched by Eve.

Thirdly, there is absolutely no evidence in the Scriptural text for the claim that Eve was "more puffed up than the man," making her sin, therefore, more "serious" than that of Adam. Indeed, to claim that Adam's decision to eat of the fruit was an act of "condescension" for her, an action he took under the coercive influence of his "inordinate affection for his wife" or out of a "friendly good-will" toward her is not only pure conjecture. It is an affront to the dignity that woman possesses in virtue of the personhood she enjoys which, as has been demonstrated, is equal to that of man. In addition, the teaching on Original Sin declares unequivocally that the Fall was not a sexual sin. We have taken notice of the claim that Adam and Eve do not "know" each other until Genesis 4:1 and that, therefore, concupiscence must be understood to be a *result* of the Fall, not its cause. How, then can we reconcile that conclusion with the claim that Eve somehow intended to "seduce" Adam? That would seem to imply that, of the two of them, Eve was already subject to concupiscence, something the teaching (and an honest reading of the text) has already ruled out.

And so, it seems we are justified in pursuing a different interpretation of the meaning embedded in the story of the Fall. We will consider one proposal now. But here I would argue that any coherent reading of the text of Genesis 3 must account for three things, two of which we have already demonstrated: first, the undeniable truth that Genesis 1 reveals man and woman both to be equally human; second, the nature of the differences - in terms of both their identities and their missions - that characterize them, as revealed in Genesis 2; and third, and still to be explored, it would have to illuminate the meaning of the fact that the personal consequences visited upon each of them differ in dramatic ways.

Let us begin with this third element first. It seems that the precise nature of the consequences for man and for woman, as described in Genesis 3: 16-19, demonstrates the plausibility of the theory at work in this paper. First, we can stipulate that man and woman certainly both sinned and are equally burdened with its effects; both lost their friendship with God. But the account of the Fall in Genesis 3: 16-19 makes manifestly clear that their sin results in very different consequences for the two of them. The woman will endure greater pain in childbirth; nonetheless, her yearning will be for her husband who will, in spite of her desire, lord it over her. The man will now struggle with creation; those things he named as his own in Genesis 2 will now only yield their fruits with suffering and toil (Genesis 3:16).

It is evident that sin causes the place both had occupied in the state of original innocence to be turned upside-down. Instead of somehow occupying a place of honor (while nonetheless his equal) woman will now be dominated by the man. As for man, instead of occupying the place of secure and confident steward of God's creation, he will now have to fight with it. The effects of original sin will (and clearly do) manifest quite differently in men and in women. We will consider the contours of this reality here.[74] And we will begin with the moments leading up to the act of disobedience itself.

First, let us take up anew the age-old question of why the serpent approached woman first with his temptation. We have already encountered the traditional view on this – that woman, being weaker and more vulnerable, was the easiest prey. But if I have shown that woman is man's equal in that she is fully human and, therefore, endowed with a rational soul and the powers of intellect, will and freedom, we are no longer able to hold to that position. Woman is most certainly innocent, but she is not without intelligence. However, she is at a disadvantage: she knows little about the world of things, whereas man's relationship to the things of the Garden is much more sophisticated. He had named them; he knew God much more intimately than did woman. And so, yes, woman was easier to persuade.

But woman was sent to man as a kind of divine aid; she is man's equal while somehow occupying pride of place in the created order. This means that, in approaching woman, the serpent is executing a very clever strategy: his intent is to corrupt the entire hierarchy of creation and so he begins, so to speak, at the "top." He knows that if he can get to woman, he will soon have man. As John Paul II tells us, woman is first in the order of love; she was sent to safeguard man's heart.[75] Woman was the greatest point of leverage because it was and still is her primary charism to attend to the other, to keep man focused on the end toward which his work is ordered: the flourishing of human persons. And when woman loses her place, when she is corrupted – so is the family, the culture, the nation, indeed the world.

At the same time, Adam also had a job to do. He was first in the order of creation and on intimate terms with the Creator. His prior relationship with the Lord God and his sophistication with things has revealed that his horizon included a greater grasp of the created order and the way it came to be. In relation to man, woman is rather unsophisticated about "things"; she has heard that they are not to eat of the tree at the center of the Garden, but it was man who heard it directly from God. And it is worth noting that man appears to be more or less at her side at the critical moment of decision (Genesis 3:6). His task is to be the first line of defense against the serpent, to protect Eve from the threats to her person. And he failed her. In fact, it is in this very passage that we see man fail in what will be an essential element of his charism – that of protector. He knows first-hand what God has instructed; he has superior knowledge of things. It was his place to stay the hand of the woman as she reaches for the forbidden fruit. Instead, when God calls to them "in the cool of the day" and asks if they have eaten of the tree, man's response is to blame it on the woman *and* on God. He says: "the woman *you* gave me gave me the fruit of the tree, and I ate." Thus, man's guilt in the Fall is exposed. His mission was to ensure that the goods of creation would be used for woman's *good*. He failed to exercise dominion over creation at a critical moment in salvation history.[76]

So, we must conclude that both are complicit in this act of disobedience. Nonetheless, as we see in Genesis 3: 16-19, the consequences of the fall from grace take very different shape for each of them. In fact,

## II. Man, Woman, and the Redemption of the World

the narrative that describes the aftereffects of the Fall does seem to confirm the validity of the theory presented so far: it results in a distortion of the particular gifts given to each. Man will struggle with creation; woman will struggle with relationships.

Since it was her act that brought them to disgrace, God turns to woman first in Genesis 3:16 and says: "I will greatly multiply your pain in childbearing; in pain you shall bring forth children, yet your desire shall be for you husband, and he shall rule over you."

Woman's sin thus leads to a distortion of her own natural gifts. Her capacity to bear and nurture life will now be a source of physical anguish and suffering. Her capacity for relationship and her natural orientation toward persons will now be a source of confusion and torment. She is told that her desire will be for her husband, even in light of his tendency to dominate her. Here "husband" should not be taken too literally; woman's desire will be for man, even when she knows he is using her, even when she understands that the result of their union could be the pain of childbirth, and even when she recognizes that man may elect to abandon her to raise the child alone.

Our contemporary context certainly reflects these factors. The confusion in relationships between men and women that has manifest over the last fifty years is well documented.[77] Certainly it can be said that women manifest a disordered inclination in relationships. It is often the case for many women that their desire is for "the other" even when he treats her as an object, even when he dominates and uses her. The evidence is all around us; it takes shape in the widespread phenomenon of the unwed mother, though we now call them "single" mothers. It shows up in the form of domestic abuse, prostitution, and sex trafficking.[78] Instead of expressing the natural authority that belongs to woman in the order of creation, she becomes anxious in her pursuit of relationships and love, clingy, needy, and fearful of abandonment.[79]

God turns to man next. In Genesis 3: 17-19, the man is told that *because he listened to his wife*, "...cursed is the ground because of you; in toil you shall eat of it all the days of your life; thorns and thistles it shall bring forth to you; and you shall eat the plants of the field. In the sweat of your face you shall eat bread till you return to the ground..." The nature of man's sin must be made clear. His sin was not precisely that he ate of the forbidden fruit; it was "because he listened to his wife." From this we are not to conclude that men err when they listen to their wives! [80] Its subtext must be understood; God is saying to the man that, *because you listened to your wife – and not to me,* you have lost your place in the order I established. It is a clear indication of Augustine's dictate that all authority *comes from God.* Man may seek to fulfill his role as the head of the family. He loses that place when he forgets that his first act must always be an act of obedience to that which is above him.

But it is clear that the man's sin will now result in the need to struggle to realize the specific feature that characterized him in his original innocence. His natural relationship to the things of creation will now be fraught with difficulty, forever after burdened by confusion and back-breaking work. He is told, specifically, that, as a result of his sin, he will have to struggle with creation, which only confirms the uniqueness of man's relationship to the things of creation. Original sin can be said to affect man, in particular, in his tendency to forget that all is gift, that his first obligation is toward his Creator. Most devastating for human relationships, he forgets what he knew in the first instance of his encounter with the woman: that she is *not* an object. This forgetfulness leads to a disordered relationship to things – for now everything and everyone is an object, something to be dominated and used as he sees fit. This manifests for some men in a quest for power over people and nations – and their possessions – frequently leading to actual war (which are, by the way, almost exclusively started by men), or to hostile corporate take overs, or to plain everyday Machiavellian manipulation in the workplace. It has led men, in particular, to forget that the created order is itself a gift, given to him to "till and to *keep*"; instead, they seek to exploit it and the result has been environmental degradation. It leads to a compulsion for work and acquisition that leads them to forget themselves and the real purpose of human existence.

Here, again in these brief sketches, we can grasp the significance of this account for our understanding of man and woman and the path ahead for both. The Scriptural account reveals that the very things that had been the natural charisms of man and woman are now the source of suffering and struggle. These gifts are, at the same time, both our greatest weaknesses and our path to redemption.

## Conclusion

In sum, the masculine genius is grounded in the Scriptural account of the first man, which reveals that his fundamental gift is to know creation and to discover in it the goods that will permit him to contribute to the good of his family and of all humankind. He thus is oriented toward generative activity that leads him to create things *outside of himself*, things which can be brought to bear on man's highest good, that of human flourishing. But because he is marked by the burden of original sin, he often forgets that his donation of self in the act of making of himself a gift is something that can only be given to another person. One cannot make of oneself a gift to a bottom line or a project, no matter how important; on the other end of the donation of self is *always* another self. His particular blindness, the result of the Fall, leads him constantly to forget this fact.

The feminine genius is grounded in the Scriptural account of the first woman, which reveals her to be, first of all, a gift sent by God to all of humankind. She is, above all, *ezer*, divine aid, and her fundamental gift is an orientation toward the other that ensures that the primacy of persons is never forgotten or denied. She is meant to "keep humanity from *not* falling." Her mission is to remind man that the gift of self can only be made to another person and to keep this fact constantly before us by affirming and expressing what she understands through her own genius: that all human activity must be ordered toward the good of persons.

Though many men fail to live up to the potential found in their own genius, surely an equal number of women fail as well. This is not surprising. Both the masculine and the feminine genius are in fact both natural and supernatural realities that, though they can be partially exhibited on the level of nature, require participation in the life of grace to reach full expression. The men, the fathers in our lives, are quite often engaged in superhuman efforts to lead, protect, and support their families. We should all be grateful for the masculine genius. Though certainly, we can acknowledge that mistakes have been made, unquestionably, it has ensured the well-being of families and cultures for millennia.

On the other hand, we have seen that the genius of woman is an equally evident reality; one that, perhaps, has not yet found full expression in the life of our culture, in spite of the progress of the past 150 years. This is surely due, in part, to a devaluing of the nature of woman *qua* woman in many aspects of our culture, both a vestige of the past and a result of the mistaken anthropology that grounds the radical feminist movement. For many reasons, women often face challenges, even obstacles, in giving voice to the gifts they offer and the wisdom they bring, not only in the home, but in the public arena. But they must persist, for the stakes are very high. As John Paul II tells us in *Evangelium Vitae*:

> In transforming culture so that it supports life, women occupy a place, in thought and action, which is unique and decisive. It depends on them to promote a "new feminism" which rejects the temptation of imitating models of "male domination", in order to acknowledge and affirm the true genius of women in every aspect of the life of society, and overcome all discrimination, violence and exploitation.[81]

Women are thus tasked with a very special mission, something the Church has been aware of for almost a century. As Pius XII said to a group of Catholic Women's organizations in 1945: "The fortunes of the family, the fortunes of human society, are at stake – and they are in your hands."[82] These sentiments are even more clearly stated in the more recent *Compendium of the Social Doctrine of the Church,* where we find the following declaration: "The feminine genius is needed in all expressions of the life of society, therefore, the presence of women in the workplace must also be guaranteed."[83]

It seems clear that if we are to recover our culture, we must take much more seriously St. John Paul II's claim in the *Letter to Women* that it is "to this unity of the two God has entrusted not only the work of procreation and family life, but the creation of history itself."[84] It would be impossible to overstate the importance of the conclusion we are led to by this investigation. The key to our future as a civilization – as well as to the future of the Church - is a deep understanding of the nature of woman and man *in relation to one another,* that is, a robust theology of complementarity, grounded in both Scripture and Tradition, which lifts up and acknowledges the genius that both men and women bring to our mission to return all things to Christ.

## RESPONSE

## Celibacy and Contemplation

### Deacon James Keating

*Member of Formation Staff and Professor of Spiritual Theology,
Kenrick-Glennon Seminary, St. Louis, Missouri*

**Introduction**

In the preceding essay, Deborah Savage pulls back the veil on the book of Genesis in a riveting and attractive analysis. It is a meditation filled with consequences for both our spiritual and cultural lives. In it, she introduces us to the truths that lie hidden in Genesis's language, its explication of Hebrew culture, and its explorations into the identity of man and woman in relation to God the Creator. Such a meditation will bear fruit for many but especially for those who form couples for marriage and for those ministers who serve married couples wishing to give themselves more deeply to one another and to God. But what of the celibate? What of the seminarian? What can he gain by understanding the dignity and mission of the woman even after discerning that she will play no nuptial role in his life?

I have ministered in seminary formation for almost thirty years now. I can confirm what Dr. Savage uncovers in Genesis about the male of the species: we forget that we were made to donate the self to another. In its place, not wholly a bad thing, as Dr. Savage concurs, a man more easily attends to things, projects, and goals:

> But because he is marked by the burden of original sin, he often forgets that his donation of self in the act of making of himself a gift is something that can only be given to another person. One cannot make of oneself a gift to a bottom line or a project, no matter how important; on the other end of the donation of self is

always another self. His particular blindness, the result of the fall, leads him constantly to forget this fact.

Dr. Savage then notes that it is the mission of the woman:

> To remind man that the gift of self can only be made to another person . . . that all human activity must be ordered toward the good of persons.

Who is to remind the celibate about this truth so easily lost in the masculine environment of seminary formation? Who is to tutor the seminarian and properly contextualize "work" or ministry within the necessary matrix of intimacy, or "self-donation to another person"?

It is often said that a priest is espoused to the Church, and so he is. Practically, however, this pastoral truth about celibate priesthood can befuddle seminarians. "How am I supposed to be 'married' to the people in my parish?" Such an orientation can confuse the young deacon in his twenties, for example, assigned to a parish and met with mixed responses to his presence. If he is depending upon parishioners to give him love in such a situation, then how does being "married to the Church" work out for him? Maybe not so well.

The correct orientation toward priestly celibacy and sharing in Christ's love for His Bride, the Church, may best be understood not from the perspective of the "Church" *giving* love to the celibate (although, of course, many individuals are generous toward their parish clergy) but from the perspective of his entering into Christ's own pastoral charity *toward the Church's needs*. In this virtue, pastoral charity, the priest is dedicated to self-donation *toward the Church* in her spiritual needs. As such, he shares in, or is configured to, Christ's own self-donative actions upon the Cross as well as His other ministries. The *giving is toward* the Bride primarily. This giving expresses the affective maturity of the men who populate the priesthood, an expression of their emotional and spiritual integration. What, then, of a man's need *to receive love*?

For celibate clergy, the normal interaction between a man and the woman he loves is absent. No woman is there to give to him the "divine aid" that men need in order to remember their call to holy communion with both God and others. It may be true that a priest's sister or mother or a good female friend, one who loves his priesthood more than she loves him, might exercise this role on occasion. But the wife the priest sacrificed will never be fully his to know; such is the nature of the sacrifice. Even still, the young priest needs to *receive love*. He needs to be loved. Also, he needs to *receive guidance* about the quality of his own human development. Both of these are usually gifted to a man, sometimes painfully, by that man's own wife. Of course, the priest may receive the gift of a feminine presence in the women I mentioned above, and "guidance" may be given by these women as well or by a female spiritual director or even a female administrative assistant in the rectory, if she is bold enough. But crucially, there is no woman to give herself to him in his erotic needs, in his need to simply forget himself and gaze in wonder upon the beauty of she to whom he is committed. On this level, the sacrifice of "the woman" (Gen. 3:12) opens up to the embedded gift hidden within this sacrifice. He is not called to contemplate the woman as "bone of my bone and flesh of my flesh" but instead to contemplate her very place of origin, God Himself. Orienting us toward this reality is St. Paul in a passage Dr. Savage alludes to in her comments about women being the divine aid men need, pointing them to what "is above."

"For just as woman came from man, so man is born of woman; but *all things are from God*." (1 Cor 11:12)

Those who are called to consort with the Source of love without the mediation of a spouse are, by necessity, called to deep contemplative prayer. That is where love is to be received. This locus of receiving love is not universally accepted by all who minister. Diocesan priests are not contemplatives, we are told by some. Instead, they are men of pastoral charity, men of action. I would say this is one of the most profound category errors in Church history. These same critics who reject the contemplative dimension of diocesan priestly life want contemplation to remain within its exclusive domicile, the monastery. But contemplation is not exclusively FOR monks; it is for any and all celibates. Without such a depth of prayer, the celibate's need to receive love is not fully met. Here, I am referring to the male who has truly sacrificed the woman in response to an invitation to be sacramentally configured to Christ. I am not talking about men who have low sex drives or personality configurations that leave them at peace in "being single" or the men who simply do not like women and find the male environment of priesthood attractive. For such men, a life of celibacy may not be a sacrifice at all but simply amenable. But for the one who desires to be with the beauty of woman and yet also glimpses a deeper beauty in God, celibacy remains a clear sacrifice. This sacrifice, however, for the truly called is not a negative burden birthing resentment; it is an invitation to something other, more, and adventurous. Can God really satisfy? Is God that real? For such a man who hears the call away from the woman, THAT man needs to become a contemplative.

What is contemplative prayer for the diocesan priest?

I will begin an answer by quoting Pope Emeritus Benedict XVI on Christ Himself:

> "To understand correctly the meaning of chastity, we must start with its positive content... We find this only by looking to Christ. Jesus's life had a twofold direction: he lived for the Father and for others... We see Jesus as a man of prayer, one who spends entire nights in dialogue with the Father... Sacred scripture shows that at no moment of his life did he betray even the *slightest trace of self-interest in his relationship with others.* Jesus loved others IN THE FATHER starting from the Father... Chastity means an INTENSE relationship with Christ and the Father."

This is the life of a celibate: the twofold direction. The turn toward God satisfies the deep need to BE LOVED; the turn toward the other bears to them, the fruit of such trusting vulnerability: pastoral charity. Most seminarians have a difficult time believing God CAN satisfy their heart and body. That is not so different than husbands who, instead of turning toward their wives for consolation and wisdom, seek immediate gratification elsewhere. Both God and the woman are making themselves available to men for deep communion, not "quick hits," serving immediate self-involved gratification. The conversion challenge for the American male who enters seminary is clear: can he move beyond simply intermittent jolts of pleasure to treating the holy as one more fount of self-involvement and trust that God is laboring to love him over time and progressively imparting peace (Phil 4:7)?

If priests are ever to lead the laity to salvation, they themselves must suffer the intimacy of contemplative prayer, a prayer that delivers holy communion. Seminarians looking for transitory experiences in prayer may be basing this expectation upon what engaged them previously in popular culture. Ironically, it was, in part, that culture and its demand for immediate gratification that exhausted them and drove them to consider priestly formation. But such a culture, while superficial in truth is deeply formative in experience. Even if abandoned, it still calls out to seminarians like St. Augustine's sins in his *Confessions,* "Do you think you can live without us?" Hopefully, over the course of true engagement with the relationships found in seminary formation, a man can live without "this passing age" (Rom 12:3).

St. John Paul II pointed the celibate to a correct understanding of such a life. Although the sainted pope is writing about St Joseph below, who can doubt that this way of knowing God was St. John Paul's as well?

> Joseph, in obedience to the Spirit, found *in the Spirit the source of love, the conjugal love which he experienced as a man.* And this love proved to be greater than this 'just man' could ever have expected within the limits of his human heart.

**Conclusion**

Contemplation is gazing upon God Himself. It is a gazing upon the beauty of the actions of the Incarnate God, especially His actions upon the Cross and in the Resurrection, now extended in the Eucharistic Liturgy. To gaze is to receive. Contemplation opens a man to be vulnerable before these Christological mysteries, allowing them to deeply affect him, marking him as one who is loved. It is this love that sustains the celibate. May seminaries begin or continue to form future priests in knowing that such love can be found. This love will reward their trusting act of surrender to be celibate for the sake of the Kingdom. What "the woman" could have given to a man as spouse is, indeed, sacrificed; but all the good that is in feminine love courses from its Source into the celibate's open heart, a Source the New Eve herself points all men toward: "Do whatever He tells you" (John 2:5). Peace follows when one is vulnerable to the Source of love itself.

# III

# Human Sexuality: The Battle for the Human Soul

## Maria Fedoryka

*Professor of Philosophy, Ave Maria University, Ave Maria, Florida*

> *The wounded surgeon plies the steel*
> *That questions the distempered part;*
> *Beneath the bleeding hands we feel*
> *The sharp compassion of the healer's art*
> *Resolving the enigma of the fever chart.*
> *Our only health is the disease*
> *If we obey the dying nurse*
> *Whose constant care is not to please*
> *But to remind of our, and Adam's curse,*
> *And that, to be restored, our sickness must grow worse.*
>
> - T. S. Eliot, *East Coker, The Four Quartets*

*For our struggle is not with flesh and blood but with the principalities, with the powers, with the world rulers of this present darkness, with the evil spirits in the heavens.*

- Ephesians 6:12

## Introduction

The crisis in the Church is a crisis of betrayal: those who freely accepted the charge of safeguarding Christ's teachings, of being minsters of his sacraments, and of guiding his flock to salvation broke faith with both Christ and his flock. The betrayal consists of cover-ups, of the protection and enabling of the criminals, and of the subsequent failure of the bishops to repent of these. But the full extent of the crisis can be grasped only in light of the sacred character of human sexuality and its consequent centrality in the meaning and vocation of the human person. The special character of human sexuality, in turn, reveals why the intimate sphere is a unique locus of battle between God and his enemy for the human soul.

The calling of the human person is of a most transcendent and spiritual nature: that of living in a response to and a communion with the true, the good, and the beautiful, and in a communion of love with other persons, and ultimately in a communion of love with God. In the vocation to transcendence and communion, the human person is like the angels. But this being possessed of a spirit so essential to the fulfillment of its calling finds itself—unlike the angels—wedded to the world of matter; indeed, it's very being is composed of the bodily as well as of the spiritual. We are confronted here by a natural mystery. How can these two orders of being meet, merge, and meld together in this way, without either of them losing its own characteristics? It is perhaps not surprising that the history of this question is riddled with errors that come from giving in to the temptation of rejecting or short-changing one or the other of the pair. But the unity-in-duality of the human person has always been preserved in safety in the heart of the Church's understanding of the human person and reflected in her teachings.

Matter by itself contains a minimum of meaning. But, through the union of matter with form, the visible world is no longer "merely" material but wonderfully participates in, and so reveals to us, the true, the good, and the beautiful, becoming a kind of natural sacrament, a "herald" of what is contained in its fullness in the interior unicity of God. The destiny of the visible world is to play an integral role in the person's vocation to transcendence.

In the human person, the union of the bodily and the spiritual is even more wonderful. Through its union with the rational soul, the animal body is raised immeasurably higher than in nonpersonal beings: through their mutual interpenetration, in which each enters into the other, a body becomes personal-ized even as the personal soul is em-bodied. This is truly a marvel: body becomes "enlivened" *from within* by a *rational soul* and truly takes on a *personal character*. The body, however, returns the favor, as it were.

## III. Human Sexuality: The Battle for the Human Soul

At first glance, it may look as though the bodily limits spirit—and in certain ways it does. But I believe that overall, it is the other way around: having been "lifted" into a personal way of being by its intimate union with the soul, the body is in turn able to enlarge the life of the spirit, enriching the spirit's sphere of experience and activity. By the plan of God, a wonderful mutuality takes place. In the words of Benedict XVI in *Deus caritas est*, "the human person is a unity in duality, in which spirit and matter compenetrate, and [in which] each is brought to a new nobility." Thus, the body, too, is able to participate in the person's vocation to transcendence, and indeed to enrich that vocation.

For the Christian, the embodiment of the human person received a new meaning and a new dignity in the Incarnation of Christ. By means of Mary's faith in and her fiat to God, the second person of the Trinity was united with human nature and "became flesh." In *Gaudium et spes* 22, we read this well-known passage:

> The truth is that only in the mystery of the incarnate Word does the mystery of man take on light. For Adam, the first man, was a figure of Him Who was to come, namely Christ the Lord. Christ, the final Adam, by the revelation of the mystery of the Father and His love, fully reveals man to man himself and makes his supreme calling clear . . . For, by his Incarnation, he, the son of God, *in a certain way united himself with each man.* He worked with human hands, he thought with a human mind. He acted with a human will, and with a human heart he loved. Born of the Virgin Mary, he has truly been made one of us, like to us in all things except sin.

From all eternity, the Son lives in a communion with the Father. When the Son enters time, "uniting himself with human nature," it is the sacred body of Our Lord that is at the center of this communion with the Father. Christ's sacred body is the special locus of his obedience to his father, and through this obedience it becomes the direct means of our salvation. We find in Hebrews 10:5:

> Sacrifice and offering you did not desire,
> but a body you prepared for me;
> holocausts and sin offerings you took no delight in.
> Then I said, "As is written of me in the scroll,
> Behold, I come to do your will, O God."

From the time of his sacrificial death until the end of time, the Lord remains with us on earth in the Eucharist, in his body, blood, soul and divinity, as our nourishment for eternal life. And since the Ascension, by virtue of the Word's union with human nature, there is some real sense in which a human body is present in heaven in the glorified Christ.

In Christ, the meaning of *bodily existence* is revealed to us with full clarity. The Christian now has an infallible roadmap by which to travel the journey of life; in and through the body, in imitation of Christ's gift of himself to the Father and to us, the Christian is to make a gift of himself to God and to others. Through bodily discipline and self-denial, we emancipate ourselves from our fallen flesh so as to come to possess ourselves, as the body is reintegrated into an intimate unity with the spiritual soul; in the process, we gain the freedom to make a gift of ourselves to others. Without minimizing the spiritual works of mercy, or the seriousness of the purely spiritual sin of pride, it is nevertheless true that the body is the special theater or medium for the working out of our salvation. At the end of time, we are told by Christ that we will hear the King say:

> Come, you who are blessed by my Father, inherit the kingdom prepared for you from the foundation of the world. For I was hungry and you gave me food, I was thirsty and you gave me drink, I was a stranger and you welcomed me, I was naked and you clothed me, I was sick and you visited me, I was in prison and you came to me.[1]

The supernatural act of laying down one's own bodily life for another modeled for us by Christ is a complete *gift of self* that surpasses all other ways of making a gift of ourselves in our embodied existence. Because of the centrality of bodily life to the human condition, to give up one's *bodily*

## III. Human Sexuality: The Battle for the Human Soul

life is to give one's *very self*, in one's depth and entirely. Theologians tell us that the shedding of a mere drop of Christ's divine blood would have been sufficient to save us. But they also tell us that, given God's plan for us, it was fitting that our salvation should have come about through Christ's giving up of his bodily life. God's plan was to establish with us the most *intimate* relationship possible, a spousal relationship, and it is on the cross, through his death, that Christ gave himself entirely, and thus *espoused* the Church to himself and in it, its members.

Now, this ultimate form of self-giving in laying down one's life for another out of love has a natural analogue in the *spousal self-giving of man and woman in marriage*. By a mysterious design of God, the bodily sphere of gendered sexuality makes possible a complete mutual giving and receiving of the self of one human person in relation to another that in this life cannot be accomplished without the body. By token of this same design, the reality of human sexuality is also the basis of the most intimate form of union possible between the human soul and God, namely, the state of virginity. This capacity of gendered-bodily-being to be the condition for a spousal union between persons is also the foundation of a uniquely intimate cooperation between God and man, in enabling the fruitfulness ("gen"-erosity) of human love to achieve unimaginable proportions, namely, the engendering of a new immortal soul. In and through engendered bodily complementarity, in its integration with the personal soul and its act of spousal love, God invites human love into a partnership with his own creative love, granting husband and wife a share in his own fatherhood, in which God makes a gift of himself to each person.

On all these counts, it becomes clear that, while all things belong to God, the sphere of human gendered sexuality belongs to God in a unique way and is therefore sacred. It also begins to emerge why it is the special place of battle between God and his enemy, the devil—the *diabolos*, the one who divides by means of the lie. In this essay, I will consider the features of this sphere of bodily existence that account for its sacred character and allow it to figure so centrally in the drama of earthly life. A small but seminal work by Dietrich on Hildebrand titled *In Defense of Purity* will serve as the foundation for these reflections.[2]

Sex as a bodily experience, writes Hildebrand, is unlike any other bodily experience, in that it is *deep* by its very nature. He means by this, first, that in this sphere, the body awakens in its vital depths; there is something in the quality of these experiences that "penetrates to the very root of man's physical being."[3] Other bodily experiences take on this character only when a person's life is at stake, but the domain of sexuality has this deep quality by its very nature, and thus in every instance of its use or awakening. Second, this experience of depth is evidence that the body and the soul "meet in a unique fashion."[4] It is as if here body and soul come to a point of intersection: as the body is awakened in its depth, so the soul is also touched in its depth. This means that in the domain of sexuality, the sphere of the bodily touches and is bound up with the person's *Self* in its depth. This is why Hildebrand writes that sex "occupies a central position in the personality."

We must elaborate on this decisive point, and I do so using the language of Karol Wojtyla when he explains that the sexual sphere touches on and is bound up with the depth within us where we *possess ourselves from within*, in that place where each of us *experiences himself as being "his own."* In *Love and Responsibility*, Wojtyla points out that this connection between sexuality and selfhood is both *objective* and *experiential* (*ontological* and *existential*): "There certainly exists a very special connection between sex and the person in the objective order, which at the level of consciousness has its counterpart in a special awareness of the right of personal property in one's 'I.'"[5] This connection between the self-possessing Self and the sexual sphere as experienced has its metaphysical roots in the structural parallel between them. Just as in our personal selfhood we "have" ourselves from within, there is a parallel way in which we "have" ourselves from within in our bodily being in the sphere of bodily sexuality.

This fact about the structure of human sexuality brings us to the heart of the matter, which is contained in two points. First, by the freely chosen design of God, the self-possessing center of the Self is inseparable from bodily sexuality. Second, this fact explains how it can be that, again, by God's design, the sexual sphere enters into the total surrender of the human person that is proper to spousal love. But this leads to a final metaphysical point regarding the structure of the spousal act itself. In the spousal act, the bodily and spiritual come together in a *mutual integration*, forming one reality in two dimensions. This is found first in the reality that the bodily act of sex is fashioned *on the analogy of the spiritual reality of love*; in particular, one can discern in the bodily gestures, the bodily experiences, and their corresponding experiences in the psyche constituting the act (and, in another dimension, its procreative fruitfulness) an "image" of the features of love. But this would not yet account for the mutual interiority of body and soul in the spousal act. In addition to this analogical relationship between bodily sex and the spiritual reality of spousal love, there is the further relationship of embodiment and ensoulment. The spiritual reality of spousal love itself enters into the sphere of the bodily, which it can do because the bodily act contains an interior metaphysical space fashioned precisely to be "filled" or "animated from within" by spousal love. That is, the sexual act "is itself" only in a *mutual integration* with the self-possessing person *in its act of gendered, spousal self-giving* and is thus by nature a "spousal act."

In a 1972 document in which he considers the indissolubility of marriage, Joseph Ratzinger writes of the depth at which the self-giving of marriage takes place:

> Marriage is one of those fundamental decisions of human existence that can only be made completely or not at all, precisely because therein man as a whole is involved, as his very self, unto that depth where he, touched by Christ, transformed, is taken into his 'I' opened on the cross and open for us all.[6]

Now, the teaching of the Church says that the union of marriage is not entirely accomplished in the vows, solemn as they are, but is *consummated*—that is, *brought to completion* and *made definitive*—only in the bodily act of mutual self-giving. We can see why this is so on the basis of our reflections. Sexuality is bound up with the self-possessing center of the person and is therefore "material" to the act in which the person gives himself from this center. The following lengthy passage from Hildebrand's *Purity* captures eloquently this truth about human existence:

> in a certain sense sex is the secret of every human being [such that] the disclosure of this secret to another creature and the delivery of it to that other in [marriage] constitutes a self-surrender and self-donation of a wholly unique kind. Even the supreme and most complete surrender of the soul to some other human being who is dearer than life itself and in whose soul we plunge our own by a profound mutual discovery and understanding in Jesus, is, nevertheless, not equivalent to that mysterious external self-delivery which takes place in the act of marriage. This may seem a hard saying, since the surrender of the heart to another is something higher and more valuable than the surrender of the body . . . [Nevertheless, on] earth it is not in our power without the cooperation of the body to give our heart to another creature in the same way as when the body plays its part. In eternity alone will it be possible.[7]

Hildebrand then compares the spousal bodily self-giving with the sacrifice of one's life, saying that this sacrifice alone achieves the completeness of self-giving comparable to the completeness of self-giving in the conjugal act.

This act that accomplishes and embodies complete mutual self-giving between husband and wife is also the place in which new human life comes into existence. How fitting that it should be so! Far from being merely the bodily event of the coming together of two gametes, the conception of the child is the "outflow" and crowning of a *concrete act of love* between the parents. In fact, just as the sexual union is an embodiment of the *unitive* dimension of love, so the child is the embodiment of the *fruitfulness* of love that along with union, and flowing from it, makes up the very essence of love. And just as the two dimensions of union and fruit are inseparable in the spiritual reality of love, so they are not to be directly separated in the embodiment of that love in the spousal act. As Paul VI tells us in *Humanae vitae*, the two dimensions of the conjugal act do not just "happen" to be placed together but are meaningfully united. Thus, their separation necessarily dismantles the act as an act of love.

### III. Human Sexuality: The Battle for the Human Soul

And here, if we are allowed to guess at such things, we have perhaps found the highest meaning of the body in the order of nature and the ultimate reason why God made *embodied* persons: because of the body, and because it is bound up with the person's self-possession in the way outlined above, creaturely love is able to be caught up into and cooperate with the divine creative love. In the giving of their bodies for the creation of new human life, the spouses truly give of themselves, truly "loving into existence" the new human life. Angels, having no bodies, cannot be partners with God in the creation of new angels. The soul is indeed "brought to a new nobility," in the words of Benedict, in this pro-creative capacity made possible by the soul's union with the body. In short, spousal intimacy in its unitive and fruitful dimensions together affords the creature a close mirroring of the life of the Trinity.

Hildebrand's book on spousal intimacy ends with a philosophical reflection on consecrated virginity (or celibacy), which he calls "the mystery of supernatural love." The "marriage" with Christ in virginity comes about through the person's vowing of the intimate sphere to God. To truly understand virginity as an espousal of the soul with God, Hildebrand finds that one must have understood the deep and central place occupied by sexuality within the human person, its intimacy and its mystery, its unique capacity to serve the deepest kind of surrender possible of one human person to another. Parallel to the way that the sexual sphere is the means of the entire and irrevocable self-giving of one human being to another, it enters in a similar way into establishing a spiritual marriage between the soul and Christ. In what follows, I again quote some lengthy passages that convey this role of the intimate sphere in establishing a uniquely intimate communion of the human person with Christ:

> The act which places this sexual secret in the hands of Jesus inviolate and sealed forever denotes a self-surrender to Him and marriage with Him which corresponds with the matrimonial self-surrender to a creature. Since Jesus is a heavenly bridegroom, marriage with Him must be completely different from earthly wedlock, a purely spiritual union. Nevertheless, there is a fundamental feature really common to both. That supreme self-surrender of the

entire person—analogous to the surrender of life for another—which can be given to a fellow-creature by marriage alone, is here made to Jesus by the vow never to disclose the secret to anyone, by the radical and final renunciation for his love of all exercise of sex, and by cutting oneself off from the world to live for him alone.[8]

By the consecration of this domain that is so central to human personality, the virgin's psychological center of gravity shifts from this world to the next and is centered on "Him whom [her] soul loves," in the words of the Song of Songs. "By that renunciation [the consecrated virgin] dies to the world and partakes of something that otherwise would be possible only in eternity. A center within herself is, in a sense, set 'free,' which she discloses to Christ alone and whose surrender to a fellow-creature is indissolubly bound up with the disclosure of sex." Hildebrand quotes a beautiful passage from *Methodius of Olympus* with respect to the special purity proper to the virginal state: "'A garden enclosed art thou, my sister, my bride; a garden enclosed, a fountain sealed.' Such is the praise which Christ pronounces on those who have attained the goal of virginity, and He sums all up in the single word 'bride.' For the bride must be espoused to her Bridegroom and bear His name; she must abide spotless and inviolate, like a sealed garden, wherein every scent of heavenly perfume is shed abroad, where Christ alone may enter and gather what grows therein of incorporeal seed." [9]

From these reflections, the Christian, especially, can gain a deeper understanding that human sexuality is *sacred*, as something that belongs to God in a special way. Its sacredness has to do, first, with its role as being in the service of engendering new human life. Here, God becomes present in a unique way, bringing into existence out of nothing the new human soul to en-soul the body conceived by the mutual self-gift of the parents. If we knew nothing else about the spousal act, this should be enough for us to fear appropriating this sphere for any illegitimate use.

Its sacredness, second, is grounded in the fact that God intended to insert the sexual domain as a gift into the very center of the person, from within which the person owns himself; that interior space in which God

## III. Human Sexuality: The Battle for the Human Soul

encounters the person, the interiority out of which he is called to give himself in love to God and neighbor. This truth about the intimate sphere as a sacred space belonging to God should engender reverence and awe in the Christian; it should make him shrink in fear from entering this sphere in any way other than making a gift of himself to another in spousal love, within the bounds of marriage. Further, the fact that the depth of the person is at issue is why there is an intuitive sense in the Christian that it is only with God's sanction that he may enter into the sexual sphere. As co-owner of his being, and the being of the other, God must authorize—and be a partner in—the total self-giving of one person to another.

Centered on the theme of a created person's ownership of his own being at the very depth level in which he necessarily belongs to God, we can gain a new and deeper understanding of the sexual domain as one of the most important interior battlegrounds in the war against God by his enemy for the ownership of human souls. Though it is certainly not the only place of spiritual battle within the human person, it is unique in the opportunities it affords God's enemy because of its special character, as outlined above. It is clear that something of such central importance to God, and of such centrality to human existence, should be targeted for corruption and wounding by the enemy. To strike at this dimension of human life is to strike a blow at the heart of the most meaningful realities of life on earth, a blow that has its full repercussions in eternity. I offer here only a sketch that would require filling in.

It is, in the first place, an easy target. Because it is bound up with that place within the person that is made to love and to be loved, it is particularly vulnerable to temptation and to misuse, and wounds of whatever kind incurred in the depth of the person—whether related to the sphere of sexuality itself or not—tend to make the person susceptible to manipulation in this domain.

Connected to this is the fact that to be wounded in the sexual sphere—especially prior to the period of natural sexual awakening in puberty, though this is true at any time of life—is to be wounded in one's depth. Poetical and mystical language speaks truly of the experience of being "pierced" and "wounded" by love, as the beloved in his beauty enters into the depth of one's being and is offered to one as a gift to be freely received.

This experience is expansive and life-giving. A negative mirror image of this occurs when a person suffers the violent entry of another into this most intimate sphere in which the person belongs to himself. In this entry, the perpetrator seeks by force to "take possession" of the other in his intimate depth and appropriate him for himself in a disregard of the other's dignity and freedom. The person receives an injury both ontological and experiential that, because of its depth level, affects life as a whole for the one so injured, but that, at the same time, is often eclipsed from consciousness because of its intensity. This is too delicate a topic to enter into in this context, but it is a reality of which too many are tragically aware.

It is also an easy target because of the moral separation between body and soul that is present within the human person as the inheritance of original sin, such that the union between them must now be won back by a difficult struggle. In this regard, it is especially in the sphere of sexuality that the Christian must arm himself with the virtues of courage and fortitude and is in need of God's grace. The power and depth of the sexual sphere as a *bodily* experience were originally fashioned by God to correspond to and be in the service of the power and depth of the *spousal love* that they are meant to embody. I agree with John Paul II that in its original structure there is no element of animality to the human sexual sphere, no element of the "instinct" that drives the animal as a being with no power of self-possession. Because of this disintegration resulting from the Fall, however, the body tends to seek its own satisfaction, and then it appears within our consciousness as having a life of its own, and a powerful one. And because the sexual sphere is the point of intimate contact between body and soul, when the body is separated from its proper place as integrated with the soul, it pulls the soul after it, not only making the soul its captive, but also eclipsing its spiritual character. The soul then loses its power of transcendence, and a unique loss of self-possession occurs. The body is no longer animated from within by love, entering into the service of love, but falls and degrades, becoming an empty shell, now a mere instrument to achieving pleasure or some other end, subordinating the person(s) into the position of use and, in fact, of abuse.

We are told that corruption in the domain of sexuality opens the door to other kinds of corruption in a more notable way than other kinds of

## III. Human Sexuality: The Battle for the Human Soul

vices; these reflections help us to see why. Because bodily sexuality intersects with the ontological and existential center within the person, to possess the person in the sexual sphere is to possess him in his personal depth in some mysterious way, as the enemy of God well knows. This is why, according to Aurel Kolnai, "an absence of sexual restraint fairly regularly becomes the soil and focus of other kinds of weakness and vice."[10] The centrality of the sexual sphere means that, even aside from moral considerations, the loss of self, involved in the misuse of the sexual sphere, entails a disintegration of the personality as a whole in a way that is not true of the misuse of other spheres of human action and life.

Up to this point we-have seen how the devil targets sexuality in his attempt to corrupt the human person because of its importance in God's plan. But there is another, more direct connection between the misuse of this sphere and the demonic. The sacred character of sexuality entails an especially intimate presence of God in this dimension of human existence, a greater proximity of the divine to this sphere. In a parallel way, precisely on the basis of this sacredness, the abuse of this sphere involves more directly the presence of the demonic than the misuse or abuse of other spheres of life. Developing this lies beyond the scope of this paper, but to omit mention of it would be to omit an important element in the discussion. Hildebrand makes a valuable contribution in this regard in describing the way in which misused sex does not retain any of its original qualities but takes on diametrically opposed ones. Hildebrand speaks of misuses that range from "treating the pleasure of sex as an end" all the way to its being used as a "vehicle of diabolically evil lust."[11] When sex is exercised in its originally and intrinsically ordained integration with spousal love, it possesses the qualities of the "sublime joy of ultimate surrender, touching, chaste, intimate, sacred and mysterious"; it is "awe-inspiring . . . noble, chaste, and free"; it effects a "liberating surrender" and can therefore be "the medium of the most profound union" between husband and wife. [12] When it is misused, these qualities are not simply diminished but rather are "reversed." The quality that in its chaste use "constitutes the joy and attraction of sex as the medium of the most profound union with another" is replaced by a "fascinating, exciting, and befuddling charm which excludes anything beyond it." Rather than liberating the person from his self-centeredness, it becomes "intoxicating and befogging," "close, bemusing, eerie." Rather than expanding the soul, it contracts it; the God-ordained extraordinary and mysterious nature of sex is replaced by "the twilight of magic, sinister and devilish"[13] and oppresses and corrodes the soul. While it is true that all sexual sin includes concupiscence and entails the instrumentalization of the person (either of oneself or another), I believe that Hildebrand's reflections give expression to an element that goes beyond these—a diabolical element that is added to sexual sin precisely because of the sacredness of sex, and its belonging to God. Without here spelling out the exact connection between them, I suggest that the qualities characterizing the misuse and abuse of sex are those that characterize the world of the demonic and therefore reveal its special presence in sexual sin. And thus, while all sin puts the soul to one extent or another into the power of God's enemy, sexual sin—to differing degrees, depending on the nature of the abuse—affords the enemy a more direct control over the soul.

## Conclusion

The enemy of God is well acquainted with all these features of sexuality, and he makes good use of them in his quest to expropriate the soul, to divide it from itself and from God. The devil parodies God, and the paradoxical laws so characteristic of genuine spiritual life have their parodied version when the human person fails to live according to his transcendent vocation—whether this defection has moral or psychological roots. The life-generating act of dying-to-self, which requires the chaste and generous (life-generating) integration of sexuality into spousal love, is replaced in its unchaste use by the lethal (death-dealing) turn into and against the self and opens up a wound to the diabolical. We are called to make a gift of ourselves in our sexuality, and in the "gathering up of ourselves" in our free spiritual center that takes place in genuine self-giving, we come to possess ourselves, even as we come to belong to the other who receives us. In yielding to the bodily dynamism of sexuality in its misuse, we lose possession of ourselves in our free spiritual center—and become the powerless prey of the enemy. There is a "hound of hell" as well as of heaven, though it would be more fitting to refer to him as the roaring lion who prowls about seeking someone to devour—someone who belongs neither to himself nor to another human person in love nor to God, and thus one who is ready for the taking by God's adversary.

Meditating on the profound nature of the intimate sphere, its meaning, and the role it plays in human life, the Catholic Christian can only feel profound gratitude for the Church's teaching on sexuality, on chastity, on purity, on modesty, and on protecting the innocence of the young—especially the teaching we have received over the last hundred years. The "holy fear" and deep reverence with which the Church teaches us to approach this sphere has nothing to do with finding sexuality in of itself illegitimate or problematical. On the contrary, it has to do with its sacred character, exalted place in the vocation of the human person, and the consequent vulnerabilities to which it is subject. As the custodian of our souls on earth, the Church sees through the trappings of earthly affairs into the true nature of the battle, which is a spiritual one, a battle for man's very soul; and we are able to go to her for the wisdom and the grace necessary to win the battle. Above all, we look to the Mother of God, who never fails to intercede for us before her Son.

*Mother most pure,*
*Mother most chaste,*
*Mother inviolate,*
*Mother undefiled, pray for us.*

## RESPONSE

## The Body Betrayed: The Call to Intimacy and Its Tragic Distortions

### Timothy Fortin

*Associate Professor and Chair of Philosophical Theology, Seton Hall University, South Orange, New Jersey*

*Do not let me hear*
*Of the wisdom of old men, but rather of their folly,*
*Their fear of fear and frenzy, their fear of possession,*
*Of belonging to another, or to others, or to God.*
*The only wisdom we can hope to acquire*
*Is the Wisdom of humility: humility is endless.*[1]

*Then I heard what seemed to be the voice of a great multitude, like the sound of many waters and like the sound of mighty thunderpeals, crying, "Hallelujah! For the Lord our God the Almighty reigns. Let us rejoice and exult and give him the glory, for the marriage of the Lamb has come, and his Bride has made herself ready; it was granted her to be clothed with fine linen, bright and pure..." (Rev. 19: 6-8).*

### Introduction

The destiny of every human person lies in marriage. That message is heralded with thunder and the sound of mighty waters, phenomena that shake man to his core, filling him with both awe and terror. Man's destiny lies in intimacy, in the mutual self-gift, a shared being of one person for and with another. The marriage of the Lamb, once slain, now risen, is a marriage of the Lamb with the human person — the whole human person, soul and body, form and matter. It is a union that radiates with the brilliance of fine linen, bright and pure in its shining (Mk. 9: 2-3), as the harmony of the union of the soul with the Lamb is rejoiced in by and manifest in the body — the body that the soul maintains in being.[2] This union is fruitful, is generative; the light that is the fruit of the union begets yet more light. It is a communion that begets yet more communion.[3] The Lamb once slain takes the Bride whom He has won at the price of the blood and water flowing from His side; she reciprocates and radiates the love she is given.

The destiny of the human person is mirrored in the living sign that is the sacrament of marriage, which, in turn is undergird by the sacramental reality of the sexed body. The reality of human sexual difference destines the human person to the self-surrender of marriage in the natural order — an order elevated by the grace of the sacrament and so made to exceed itself — but further draws the human person to that ultimate marriage in which destiny lies. Every person — cleric, religious, married, single — must navigate and integrate these two intertwining orders of nature and grace, bound as they are to each other, one being an image pointing dimly to the other, and both being written into our very flesh.

Building on the work of Dr. Maria Fedoryka, I hope to lay out the beginnings of a vision of how the orders of nature and grace in realm of sexual difference must be integrated in the life of the seminarian and the priest. This implies full recognition of the beauty, power, and mystery of both grace and nature — and hence the awe and terror that each can evoke. The depth of the sexual sphere in the life of the person, which Dr. Fedoryka so beautifully expresses, points to the necessity of its profound integration in the life of the priest. She adroitly observes how this realm is, as it were, walled off, hidden, the secret garden in which the person who has vowed his virginity to the Lord, meets the true and Eternal Bridegroom of his soul. The priest, however, in setting apart this sphere, must take heed neither to ignore it nor to allow the orders of nature and grace to become confused. Most of all, he must not abuse both orders by twisting them into inversions of what they are meant both to be and signify.

Full exploration of the themes into which we are now wading would be a vast work.[4] I will attempt only to add a little to the work of Dr. Fedoryka. I will begin by looking at the "natural"[5] call to marriage and how that call is quite literally incarnated in the maleness and femaleness of the substantial union of form *and matter* that is the human person. This ordering of man to woman and woman to man in mutual, personal self-gift is first in the order of human experience, even while the ordering of the human person to God in the marriage feast of the Lamb is first in the order of being. It is, in part, this primacy of the "natural" in human experience and its ordering to the higher dispensation of grace that demands that it go neither unheeded nor unintegrated. Because this call resides by nature in his heart, like all men, the priest must properly honor his natural call to espousal and to fatherhood. He must recognize and integrate his natural desire to be a father and the accompanying desire to participate in the spiritual and bodily union that is inseparable from that generativity in the order of nature. Such integration implies lived awareness of how these desires are fulfilled — not sublimated — in the order of grace in his priestly life. Thus, I will also briefly look to the completion of man's natural ordering in the priest's supernatural call to both fatherhood and espousal. Instead of hiding from or repressing his desire for espousal and fatherhood,[6] the priest must find his natural desires as resolved both in the supernatural end to which all are destined, and in the unique way in which he, as priest of Jesus Christ, participates in the salvific mysteries by which the Bridegroom takes the Bride into His home: the heavenly Jerusalem. Thus, his embrace of celibacy is neither renunciation nor repudiation; it is an act of love, an anticipatory embracing of the destiny of every person and a sacramental participation in the divine mysteries through which that destiny is won. And the body is not absent from this supernatural call and gift: The Lamb is the Lamb once slain. He lays down not only his will, but also his body, sacrificing it in love for His Bride on the cross. So, the priest also lays his own body on the altar of sacrifice.

**The Call to Fatherhood & Espousal**

All that is not God is ordered by God to Himself through what St. Thomas refers to as the eternal law.[7] The dynamism of the cosmos is thus governed by its ordering to God as the ultimate meaning of its existence. In this sense, all things "love" God and are ordered to Him as both their origin and end. "In my beginning is my end."[8] The human person

## III. Human Sexuality: The Battle for the Human Soul

participates in this eternal law in a unique way, as an intellectual and hence spiritual being who thus is free and has dominion over his action — in short, as a person. St. Thomas refers to this mode of governance of a rational being by the eternal law as natural law.[9] This law is infused into the human heart; the most fundamental inclination that flows from it moves man in a manner shared with all creation. This foundational ordering is centered upon the recognition of the goodness of being. It is an echo of God's speech at the end of each day of creation when He looks at His work and acclaims its goodness (Gen. 1:4). Through the natural law, man's heart repeats the chorus of this affirmation of the goodness of being, which resolves in the recognition of the goodness of God, and hence in love of God. Thus, by this most fundamental awareness and ordering of reason, man is inclined to the preservation of his own existence and finally to love of the Giver for the gift of his existence. Lawrence Dewan, notes that part of this fundamental movement, however, is also the ordering to generativity, to the praise of the glory of God and the goodness of being through the sharing of the being that has been given.[10] The ordering to fatherhood and motherhood are thus an aspect of the deepest movements of the human heart toward the recognition of the goodness of being, which resolves in the treasuring of God above all else. All men, by nature, are thus "called" to fatherhood, though its expression can vary.[11]

In the natural order, the call to fecundity — fatherhood for men, motherhood for women — is inseparable from the call to espousal and hence to sexual intimacy. The answers to man's deepest desire for fruitfulness and the dissonance of his loneliness are inexorably bound; they are resolved in the same movement. Thus, Aristotle recognizes that, to be truly "human," man must be man and woman together; for, without each other, each lacks the complete power of generation;[12] they lack the power to prolong the goodness of the existence that is the human person. Fatherhood is thus bound to be espousal. To become a father, a man is first to become a husband. He must give himself wholly to another, body and soul: the giving of his whole self in his substance to another in the act of generation — the coming to be of new human person — must be accompanied by the giving of his whole self to another, his wife, in the act of self-surrender that is marriage. This is a mode of giving that is possible only between two persons as it involves the mutual interiority that only spirit affords. It is further only possible among two persons who differ precisely with sexual difference. Thus, this mode of intimacy involves the depth of human existence as it encompasses not just spirit but, body; not only two souls, but two bodies must become one in order for the mutual creative work of God and man to generate a new human person, charged with all the richness of his or her divine origin and destiny. Thus, in the heart of man lies two inseparable imperatives that manifest as longing: the imperative of intimacy and the imperative of generativity.

There is a point here made by Dr. Fedoryka that must be underscored.[13] Though angels are evidently ontologically nobler than human beings, there are two ways in which human persons reflect God as angels cannot: the manner in which the soul contains the body; and the manner in which the human person is able to participate in the generation of one like in kind to himself. The soul is that through which the body exists. Absent the soul, there is no body. Thus, the body exists in the soul in a way similar to that in which all things exist in God. God is in all things as the principle of their being and essence. And also, it is this same body — man's material reality — that permits physical generativity. Because of his existence in matter, man can produce another like in kind unto himself, something which an angel is unable to do. The Father, however, also generates another Person like unto Himself, the Son, from Whom, together with the Father, also proceeds the Holy Spirit. There is a perfect gift of self within the Trinity. This gift is spiritual, personal, and complete. To be like God in generativity — to generate another like himself — he must be like God in self-gift. He must give himself to another in the fullness of his person. But, because he is a human person, this personal gift implies his body and his spirit. Hence, his gift of self in substantial generation is accompanied by a spiritual gift of himself in love that implies his body. Generation is bound to a union of persons and the bodily union that their essential composition of form and matter demands. Thus, Dr. Fedoryka emphasizes the depth at which sexuality involves the human person.

Obviously, the mystery of sexual difference enters here: for it is not just any other for whom the man longs. In order to fulfill himself in the gift of self that is generation, he must give himself in love to another who is unlike him precisely with sexual difference, with that other who possesses the power of generation precisely as he does not. This sexual difference

## III. Human Sexuality: The Battle for the Human Soul

manifests the dynamic of gift, the reciprocity of giving and receiving so beautifully elucidated by St John Paul II.[14] This dance between man and woman is an image of a romance that exists between God and His Bride, the Church and even, with a certain analogy, exists within the Godhead itself. But, before speaking of that, we must examine more closely the glories and perils of union.

Fabrice Hadjadj follows Emmanuel Levinas in describing what I refer to as the paradox of intimacy.[15] It is a paradox perhaps best seen by noting the errors that mimic it. In seeking the union that responds to both his hunger for self-gift in intimacy and for generativity, he may perpetrate or be subject to two fatal errors that accompany union: fusion or dominance. When two become one there is a risk of fusion in which the identity of one is irrecoverably lost in the immensity of the other — as a drop of water is lost in the sea — or where each of those united are both lost in some one new thing — as hydrogen and oxygen each yield their identity to the new being of water. This is the peril of fusion. But there is also the almost equally destructive possibility of domination in which one becomes the vassal and tool of the other. In this "union," one is abuser, the other abused. The relationship is destructive, for different reasons, for both abused and abuser, though, obviously, the oppressed is the direct recipient of harm. However, what Levinas calls the "pathos of love"[16] is the paradox of true intimacy: when two become one, rather than losing their alterity in the other, their otherness is increased. In losing their selves in the intimacy of love, their otherness is increased. The other is not, then, possessed, but rather, as Levinas puts it, recedes into mystery. True intimacy thus does not diminish alterity; it paradoxically increases it as each of those united become more individual. To this increased alterity, however, is added yet more; as Hadjadj observes, the alterity is yet further increased by the coming to be of another other in the child.

So, by nature, man is called to the praise of God's glory in the affirmation of being that is generativity. Alone, however, he cannot be generative. He must find another who is other than he precisely with the otherness of sexual difference if he is to be generative in the order of nature. And to this other he must give himself in spirit and body in an act of self-gift, and he must receive that other in her self-gift. It is in this act of mutual self-gift that God will visit them in the bringing to be of new human person, whose soul will never cease to be. These desires — for fatherhood and for espousal — are planted in the foundational levels of his self. Yet, they point beyond the natural world, beyond the natural order; they point to his ultimate destiny. As such, they can be terrifying in their beauty — both because of the transcendence of that to which they point, and because of the devastation wrought when the reality of true intimacy is replaced with one of its counterfeits.

Perhaps we are now thus able to make our first return to the words of Eliot with which we began these reflections. The human person is inexorably drawn to belonging; but that belonging can be a source of existential terror as one fears to lose one's being, either as it dissolves into another, or faces the slavery of domination. We are also pointed to a mystery which we instinctively know is beyond us: We are pointed to a God whose brilliance blinds us even in its refracted and reflected glimmers. "Belonging to another, or to others, or to God" should not be, but can be a source of terror for us. We can fear that such belonging demands a loss of self. Dr. Fedoryka also provides another key to the fear that accompanies communion: we are called to a fullness of self-gift. The fullness of the gift requires a self-possession that permits the fullness of self-surrender and self-sacrifice. Perhaps, on some level, we all know that, in and of ourselves, we are incapable of the depth of self-possession and self-surrender that our destiny implies. Hence, we fear not only that we might ourselves might be destroyed and or dominated in the realm of intimacy, but also that we might play the role of destroyer or oppressor. We fear our incapacity to be what we are destined to be. We fear the monster we might become. "Wretched man that I am! Who will deliver me from this body of death? (Rom. 7:24)"

## The Order of Grace, the Order of Sacrament

We have already spoken of how marriage is an icon of the ultimate destiny of the human person in union with God. We can also see how the mystery of sexual difference and sexual union are dim reflections of God's interior life in the Trinity. It is to these sacramental considerations of sexual difference that we must now turn our attention. For we must briefly consider the integration of the imperatives to both intimacy and

## III. Human Sexuality: The Battle for the Human Soul

generativity into the life of the priest, called as he is simultaneously to celibacy, espousal, and fatherhood. Here, as indicated earlier, I wish to build on the point made by Dr. Fedoryka: the priest must take the part of himself that is, as it were, destined for spousal love in the natural dispensation, and devote that completely to the Bridegroom of the soul.

We have been speaking of multiple orders in which the priest dwells: the order of nature and the order of grace. However, within the order of grace, we can further distinguish at least two further considerations: an eschatological order — to which Jesus refers when noting that, in the resurrection, they will neither marry nor be given in marriage (Mt. 22:30); and what could be called the salvific order, pertaining to the state of man touched by presence of Christ, the action of the Spirit in history, and the salvation that flows from Their presence. Obviously, both of these orders are relevant to the integration and fulfillment of a man's natural desire for self-gift in espousal and fatherhood, but I shall focus on the salvific mission of the Lord Jesus; for the priest, precisely in his sacramental priesthood, uniquely participates in Jesus' one act of salvation. And, it could be argued, that it is precisely in that salvific act that Jesus Himself fulfills his own *natural* desire for self-gift and fatherhood — a desire that followed from His human nature.[17]

The priest must look to the human nature of Jesus for the keys to that which will fulfill his own deepest desires. It is in that nature that we see the acts of Jesus the bridegroom and Jesus the father. To unveil these titles — bridegroom and father — I will return to an image I have reflected on before:[18] what Christopher West refers to as the nuptial cross.[19] For it is on the cross that Jesus, as it were, consummates his union with His Bride, the Church; in the total gift of Himself, in the radiance of the Father's fatherhood, He becomes father of all those washed clean in His blood.

In this artistic depiction of the sacrifice on Calvary, as Jesus hangs on the cross, and blood and water flow from His side, Mary, the mother of Jesus, holds a chalice below the Lord and gathers that blood and water. West refers to a reflection by Venerable Fulton Sheen.[20] Sheen in turn invokes St. Augustine in referring to the blood and water flowing from Christ's side as His seed that generates those redeemed in that blood and water. Christ is the Bridegroom. He is the new Adam; father of those reborn of His total emptying of Himself. But, at the foot of the cross, there is also the new Eve, the mother of all the living. She stands in place of the Church, the spotless Bride. Her co-generativity is heralded in the words to the young priest, John, who had been ordained to this priesthood only the night before: "Behold your mother (Jn. 19: 27)." On this mountain summit, we find the new Adam and the new Eve; their fruitfulness is immediate: "This day you will be with me in paradise (Lk. 23:43)."

But we must turn our attention now to the young priest also there at the foot of the cross. For our claim is that that which transpired in front of his eyes (that in which he partook as did no other of the newly ordained priests) was also the answer to his (and every priest's) deepest desires for espousal and fatherhood. Our claim has been that sexual difference writes in the morphology of the male and female bodies a symbol of man's ultimate destiny in the wedding feast of the Lamb. The nature of that union is manifest on the cross: The Bridegroom gives all, throws His body upon the cross for the sake of His Bride. It is a chaste love the costs all, that gives all, and that fructifies in the entry of the Bride into the heavenly Jerusalem. The high priest offers sacrifice, and the sacrifice is Himself. John is ordained into the priesthood of Jesus. By this ordination, his espousal and his fatherhood will likewise be of the same order as that of Christ. He will now participate in the fatherhood of Jesus, initiated on Calvary. He will now take the Church as his spouse. He will chastely lay down his life for her and so participate in the generation of the new life always being born within her. Sexual difference has always pointed to this mystery. In the priest, sexual difference not only points to the mystery, it finds its fulfillment in the paternal generativity of Christ on the cross in the act of chaste self-gift to His Bride. Thus, the priest lays down his body in self-sacrifice for his Bride, the Church. He lives that of which sexual difference has always been a sign. In his unique participation in the saving mysteries of Christ, he finds the fulfillment of the imperatives for self-gift and generativity in that of which they have always been an image.

## Betrayal

Dr. Fedoryka incisively observed that we will understand the full depth of the crisis of clerical sexual abuse only if we understand the sacred character of human sexuality and its unique place in the vocation of the human person. The depth of the betrayal can only be understood if the sacrality of that which is violated is understood. Sexuality and its expression in conjugal union reaches to the center of the human person — body and soul. Sex demands an integration of the self, body and soul, for it implies a gift of the self, body and soul. The abuse of another sexually — regardless of by whom it is perpetrated — is thus a violation that reaches to the center of the person; it is a violation of the sacred. When the abuser, however, is a priest, this violation is amplified into new modes of betrayal. Sexual difference is sacramental in that it points to something beyond itself. It resolves in the sacrament of marriage, in which the spouses are meant to incarnate the love that Christ has for the Church and the Church for Christ. The priesthood is also sacramental. It signifies the same love, but in a different way: the priest re-offers the self-same sacrifice of Jesus on Calvary. He is thus called to sacrifice his whole self for the sake of His Bride, as did Jesus on Calvary. To his flock, he must represent the self-emptying love of Christ. He is called to make present the love of God for His sons and daughters precisely in the mysteries through which God chose to redeem His people. It is only in light of this sacramental role that the depth of the offense of sexual abuse can be understood. Certainly, sexual abuse by priests is an abuse of power. But, added to this is an utter betrayal and inversion of that which he is ordained to be and to represent to the people. He is ordained to signify and bring into being the love of God for His people as made present in the sacrifice of Jesus on Calvary. In his sexual abuse, he turns signs into anti-signs; he turns that which should bring new spiritual life into corruption.

And, while any abuse by the priest is a betrayal of his sacramental presence, abuse precisely in the sexual sphere is uniquely devastating. Dr. Fedoryka has pointed to the destruction wrought by all sexual abuse – for, bound as it his to the imperatives for self-gift and generativity– sexuality uniquely touches upon the core of the person as both spirit and flesh. We must, however, also look to that which sex signifies and then to the nodal points of signification between sexual difference and the priesthood. As we have said many times, sexual difference and the right rapport between the sexes signifies human destiny as divine comedy, resolving in a marriage. The priest is adorned with titles charged with this destiny: He is called "father" as he participates in the fatherhood of Christ. He takes the church as his bride and so participates in the spousal identity of Christ the Bridegroom. These realities exist in the order of grace. The natural order, in itself and as elevated by grace, points to this higher order. In sexual abuse, the priest precisely perverts this order. The sexual act — which by its very nature is meant to signify the love that God is and the love that He has for His Bride, and the love His Bride returns to Him — as it were implodes; it is now made to signify abuse, betrayal, and the reduction of the innocent to tools and targets of lust and pathology. As Christopher West so aptly states, that which is meant to be icon is turned into idol.[21] The image of love is inverted into a weapon, a tool of destruction. Thus, he who is supposed to represent to the woman the self-sacrificial love of Christ, who is called to love her with the chaste heroism of Christ, who is to be her father in the order of grace through participation in the fatherhood of Jesus on the Cross, now brings only devastation instead of the life that arises from the Spirit.

The wounds left in wreckage of such abuse run deeper than we can know: The human psyche understands the sacramental order on an intuitive level — that is why the sacramental order exists, because it is understood. Dr. Fedoryka spoke of the depth of the wounds that accompany any sexual abuse. To that depth is added the distortion and sundering of that which is meant to image God and His embrace of His sons and daughters in self-emptying love. What is intended by God to be an image of love becomes an image of betrayal. What is meant to bring life, brings destruction. And this devastation strikes at the heart of that which for which we all most yearn: Our salvation as lying in the embrace of God. In this corruption, the abused woman is symbolically "told" that her destiny in the embrace of God is a lie. For the one given to her as an image of this transcendent love wears the disguise of God but brings only ruin. This betrayal thus has the power to shake the soul at its very core for it strikes a blow at the very heart of human destiny and mangles the images that most powerfully sing of the undying love that the Lord has for His Bride.

# III. Human Sexuality: The Battle for the Human Soul

## Conclusion

> *Know that the Lord is God, he made us,*
> *we belong to him, we are his people,*
> *the flock he shepherds (Ps. 100: 3).*

Our destiny lies in belonging, to God and to each other. Sex, when allowed to be what it is, is both a sign of this ultimate destiny and a foretaste of the communion to which we are called. All sexual abuse strikes at the heart of this destiny in intimacy. There is already fear of such belonging, as Eliot observed; we fear the loss or laceration of ourselves. Sexual abuse confirms the lie at the heart of this fear and magnifies it to terrifying proportions. Often, its effects are not directly seen, but it wreaks secret destruction in the psyche. The abused is taught that belonging is betrayal; intimacy can seem a form of self-destruction bordering on suicide. Because of its sacramental connection to the relationship of the human person to God (and God to her), any sexual abuse potentially wounds the abused in the very internal place where the person meets God. When the abuser is a priest, this most sacred of interior spaces is defiled, desecrated. Or perhaps it is better to say that the victim is made to believe that sanctuary is defiled. The place of belonging to God in self-surrender is transformed from a secret garden — the "holy of holies," where one retreats to meet God — into a place of terror, of fear of this belonging, of betrayal.

Perhaps the priest-perpetrator acts from this very place of fear and betrayal within himself. (This is a topic for another work.) But, when destruction is found where love, security, and rest should abide, the blade cuts all the deeper – in this case, it cuts to the heart of the soul's union with God. Who can free us from these fears, these wounds, these lacerations? The only wisdom is the the wisdom of humility. Humility is endless. It is a healing beyond our power. But "destroy this temple and in three days I will raise it up," says the Lord (Jn. 2:19).

# IV

# The Treatment of Pornography Addiction in Clergy and Seminarians

## Peter C. Kleponis

*Licensed Clinical Therapist and Director of Dr. Peter C. Kleponis & Associates Counseling, Bryn Mawr, Pennsylvania*

## Introduction

Fr. Gabriel was visibly upset when he sought my help; he was a 30-year-old priest, who had only been ordained a few years. His addiction to pornography had begun in his teens. By the time he spoke with me, he was falling several times a week, viewing internet pornography and masturbating. He was filled with great guilt and shame over his sins, understood that he was out of control, and wanted help to recover from his addiction. Fr. Gabriel's story is similar to many priests and seminarians who I have treated over the years. They are living proof that priests and seminarians are not immune from the epidemic of internet pornography in America.

I have been in practice as a therapist for almost 25 years and have specialized over the past 11 years in pornography and sexual addiction. People often ask me why I chose this field of specialization. The short answer is that someone had to do something. Back in 2010, I had noticed a shift in my clientele when more men were coming to my office struggling with internet pornography addiction. Upon further investigation of this trend, I was shocked to learn that there was an epidemic of internet pornography addiction and that no one was willing to talk about it, especially those in the Church. Since the problem existed and people needed help, I went back to school to become certified in the diagnosis and treatment of sexual addiction.

To date, after completing four such certification programs and acquiring certification for treatment in sexual addiction, I have authored books and articles that have informed this chapter.[1] With this knowledge, I have created the first comprehensive Catholic recovery program for pornography addiction, have assisted thousands of men (and now women) find freedom from pornography addiction, and continue to travel extensively in the United States and abroad to lecture on the topic.

This chapter discusses the treatment of pornography addictions in clergy and seminarians. To this end, it offers a definition of pornography and provides statistics proving that it is an epidemic in the United States; considers how pornography addiction attacks masculinity; studies pornography addictions with case studies involving root causes related to family origin of general significance and specific causes pertaining to seminarians; and offers an overview of issues relating to treatment, such as obstacles, programs, and recommendations. For the purposes of this chapter, I am assuming that the pornography addiction does not involve children, which are crimes in civil law, and delicts in canon law, requiring a set of protocols to be followed involving state and Church authorities. Surely, everyone should be treated with respect due to their inherent dignity of persons, but since criminal convictions of clerics, usually result in their laicization, they become participants in the state system and relative recovery protocols.

### Defining Pornography and Understanding the Epidemic

To discuss pornography, we must define the term. This is difficult. Debates over the definition of pornography go back decades. In 1964, during the trial of *Jacobellis vs. Ohio*, Supreme Court Justice Potter Stewart was asked to define hardcore pornography. In a concurring opinion, he wrote: "I shall not today attempt further to define the kinds of material I understand to be embraced within that shorthand description ["hardcore pornography"]; and perhaps I could never succeed in intelligibly doing so. But *I know it when I see it*, and the motion picture involved in this case is not that."[2] Many people agree.

The term "pornography" comes from the Greek, *pornographia* (pornoi= "fornicators"; graphia= "pictures"). While there are many definitions of pornography, I present two working definitions: my clinical definition of pornography; and the definition presented by the Catechism of the Catholic Church. Both definitions complement each other.

## Clinical Definition of Pornography

> Any image that leads a person to use another person for his or her own sexual pleasure. It is devoid of love, intimacy, relationship or responsibility. It can be highly addictive. [3]

The key word in this definition is "use" and consequently, an image can be pornographic and show no nudity at all. What matters is that the individual use the person in the image for his own sexual pleasure. In *The Theology of the Body* and *Love and Responsibility*, Pope St. John Paul II wrote that the opposite of love is not hate, but "use." [4] God never created his children to use one another.

Based on this definition, pornography does not simply consist of naked images of people, or people engaging in sexual activity. It can come in many forms: women at the beach, lingerie catalogs, beer commercials, sexually explicit romance novels, etc.

## Catechism of the Catholic Church Definition of Pornography

> Pornography consists of removing real or simulated sexual acts from the intimacy of the partners, in order to display them deliberately to third parties. It offends against chastity because it perverts the conjugal act, the intimate giving of spouses to each other. It does grave injury to the dignity of its participants, since each one becomes an object of base pleasure and illicit profit for others. It immerses all who are involved in the illusion of a fantasy world. It is a grave offense. Civil authorities should prevent the production and distribution of pornographic materials (CCC, 2354).

This definition focuses more on the damage caused by pornography for both the consumer and the producers. Pornography has transformed sexual intimacy from a holy expression of love between a husband and wife, which is open to new life, into a recreational activity where people are selfishly used.

In both definitions, we can see how pornography leads people to "use" others. When a man views pornography, he is not thinking that the woman before him is a person with thoughts and feelings, nor does he appreciate that she is somebody's daughter, who has likely endured terrible circumstances that pushed her into pornography. His immediate thoughts involve using her for his own pleasure. He is only thinking of himself out of extreme selfishness with no appreciation for the addictive nature of pornography.

In addition to the Catechism of the Catholic Church, individual bishops have written pastoral letters on pornography. Bishop Robert W. Finn, for example, in 2007, paraphrases Pope St. John Paul II:

> The problem with pornography is not that it reveals too much of the person (exposed in the image), but that it reveals too little of the person. The person in the image is reduced to their sexual organs and sexual faculties and is thereby de-personalized.[5]

Bishop Paul S. Loverde, in 2006, writes:

> This plague stalks the souls of men, women and children, ravages the bonds of marriage and victimizes the most innocent among us. It obscures and destroys people's ability to see one another as unique and beautiful expressions of God's creation, instead darkening their vision, causing them to view others as objects to be used and manipulated. Those who engage in such activity deprive themselves of sanctifying grace and destroy the life of Christ in their souls.[6]

To understand the scope of this epidemic, here I provide some statistics on pornography used among Protestant Christians, as compiled by The Barna Group (2016). While no such data has been compiled for Catholics, these statistics might also apply to Catholics.

- Percentages of People who View Internet Porn by Age
  1. Teens 13-17: 85%
  2. Young Adults 18-24: 85%
  3. Older Millennials 25-30: 79%
  4. Gen-Xers 31-50: 77%
  5. Boomers 51-69: 56%
- Percentage of Practicing Christians seek out Porn Weekly
  1. Married Men: 10%
  2. Single Men: 15%
  3. Teenage Boys: 20%
- Statistics on Males 13 and Older who View Porn
  1. View porn daily: 10%
  2. View it monthly: 51%
  3. Claim they never seek out porn: 31%
  4. Consider viewing porn wrong: 44%
  5. Comfortable with how much they view: 68%
- Statistics on Pastors who view Porn
  1. Daily: 1%
  2. Multiple times per week: 15%
  3. A few times per month: 35%
  4. Every few months: 26%
  5. Less often: 21%

**Pornography's Attack on Masculinity**

Men and women are equal, but God calls them to different roles and gives them unique gifts to fulfill those roles. He calls men to be leaders, providers, as well as protectors of marriages, families, parishes, communities, and society. This calling applies to all men whether they are single, married, a priest, or a religious. When men choose to live out these roles with virtue, they become the men God has called them to be. They are embracing their full masculinity. A man cannot fulfill these roles if he is enslaved to anything, including pornography. Let us consider each of these roles in relation to the effects of pornography.

## Leader

God calls men to be leaders in their actions, by their examples. A good leader understands what a great privilege and responsibility it is to guide others. He leads by living a virtuous life and avoiding vice. I am reminded of the Boy Scout Law, which essentially is a list of virtues by which all scouts must live. It states, "A scout is trustworthy, loyal, helpful, friendly, courteous, kind, obedient, cheerful, thrifty, brave, clean, and reverent." There are many other virtues included, such as humility, honesty, and purity. A virtuous man can easily persuade others to follow him because they know he is trustworthy. A good leader avoids anything that would harm himself or others. He is not afraid to speak up for what is good and denounce what is harmful. One such example is Pope St. John Paul II, who strove to live a virtuous life, including daily confession, and to be merciful to him who shot him, to be unafraid in denouncing the "culture of death," and promoting the "gospel of life." A man who uses pornography cannot be a good leader because he cannot be trusted. Who would want to follow a man who uses women for his own sexual pleasure or condones it in others?

## Provider

A man is a provider materially, morally, and spiritually. Through his example of living a virtuous life, he becomes a role model for his children, peers, and colleagues. He sets the standard for moral living. He loves and respects his wife, deals with people with honesty and respect, offers an honest day's work, never cheats his employer, and completes his tasks and assignments. This example helps others to live virtuous lives. John Paul II, for example, was a great provider in the way he lived his life and completed his work. Through encyclicals, pastoral letters, and writings, such as *The Theology of the Body*[7] and *Love and Responsibility* (Wojtyla, 1993), he provided tangible ways for people to live virtuous lives. The man who uses pornography cannot be a good provider, especially morally, and spiritually, since he is not a good role model for others, especially his children.

## IV. The Treatment of Pornography Addiction in Clergy and Seminarians

*Protector*

A virtuous man knows the dangers of the world and strives to protect his wife, family, parish, community, and society. Regarding pornography, he is called to protect his marriage and family by ensuring that it never enters his home. He protects his wife's heart by ensuring that he never views it. He defends his family by monitoring all media that enters the home and removing anything that is offensive. He safeguards his parish by educating parishioners on the dangers of pornography and how they can protect themselves and their families. He defends society by ensuring that porn shops are not established in his community. Through *The Theology of the Body* and *Love and Responsibility*, John Paul II protected the Church by offering a way to enjoy the holy gift of sexuality that protects people and honors God. The man who uses pornography is not protecting anyone and is offending God, his wife, children, parish, community, and society. He hurts women by supporting an industry that harms them. He hurts his wife by committing adultery through viewing pornography and by allowing it into his home. He fails to protect his children, who could discover his pornography.

In sum, the man who embraces the call to be a virtuous leader, provider and protector is embracing his full masculinity. Pornography robs him of this and leaves him in a very weak and selfish state. Since pornography prohibits men from having healthy relationships with women and prevents them from being the leaders, providers, and protectors that God has called them to be, the questions arise: How do we correct the damage caused by pornography? How can men embrace authentic masculinity?

For our society to heal from this damage, men must change their views on pornography, relationships, and sex. They need to realize the selfishness of pornography and the harm it causes. Men must confront their own selfishness and work on growing in virtue, especially humility, in response to God's call. They must learn about healthy relationships and accept the fact that the sexual drive is an appetite, not a need, nor a right to be exercised at any time, in any manner, with any person. This is not impossible. Men can live happy and virtuous lives that respect God and others, especially women, and embrace their true masculinity.

## Defining and Understanding Pornography Addiction

To understand pornography addiction, we must first define it. While there are many definitions for sex/pornography addiction, I prefer the one by Dr. Mark Laaser:

> Pornography Addiction: Any persistent and escalating use of erotic media. It is compulsive in nature and used to avoid or change feelings, despite destructive consequences to self and others.[8]

### *Criteria for Pornography Addiction*

According to Dr. Kevin Skinner, there are ten criteria for pornography addiction:[9]

1. Recurrent failure to resist impulses to view pornography.
2. More extensive/longer viewing of pornography than intended.
3. Ongoing, but unsuccessful, efforts to stop, reduce, or control behavior.
4. Inordinate amount of time spent obtaining pornography, viewing pornography, and/or being sexual – either through masturbation, or with another person or object, or recovering from sexual experiences.
5. Feeling preoccupied with fantasy, sexualized thoughts and/or preparatory activities.
6. Viewing pornography takes significant time away from obligations: occupational, academic, or social.
7. Continuation of behavior despite consequences.
8. Tolerance – more frequent or intense pornography is needed over time to obtain the desired result.
9. Deliberately limiting social, occupational, or recreational activities in order to keep time open for finding and viewing pornography.
10. Distress, restlessness, or irritability if unable to view pornography (withdrawal):
    a. Dizziness

b. Body aches
c. Headaches
d. Sleeplessness
e. Restlessness
f. Anxiety
g. Mood swings
h. Depression

## *Levels of Pornography Addiction*

Dr. Skinner has also divided pornography addiction into seven levels:[10]

**Level I:** People have recently been exposed to pornography and generally have little access to it. Their thoughts and everyday actions are not focused on pornography.

**Level II:** While there is no compulsion to act out with pornography, people continue to have access to it, and may experience a growing curiosity about it.

**Level III:** People are straddling the borderline between a growing problem and an addiction. They may try to restrain themselves, but use pornography about once a month. Quitting may become more difficult because they have been exposed to harder forms of pornography and may fantasize about it.

**Level IV:** Pornography use is impacting more aspects of a person's life: their focus on tasks for work, family, social life. Their fantasies have increased and much effort is needed to fight off strong urges to view pornography.

**Level V:** Pornography use is impacting daily life. Individuals are viewing pornography several times a week. Much time is spent thinking about pornography, a significant amount of time is spent fantasizing about pornography and sex. Individuals begin to feel overwhelmed by their level of involvement. Withdrawal symptoms are more intense.

**Level VI:** Pornography now seems to dominate a person's life. A significant amount of time is spent thinking about pornography and sex. Pornography use is almost a daily occurrence. It has become a compulsive addiction and users are likely to feel out of control, and may lie about their pornography use and take significant risks to view it. They may feel hopeless and depressed about their addiction.

**Level VII:** By now, viewing pornography and acting out sexually is a daily occurrence. There is a deep-seated compulsion to act out, and the type of pornography sought becomes more hardcore and even deviant. They feel out of control. Their mind is dominated by thoughts of pornography and sex. The individual is now fully addicted to pornography.

## *Diagnosing Pornography Addiction*

An addiction to pornography can most accurately be diagnosed by a trained mental health professional. This involves in-depth clinical interviews along with psychological testing. One test, the Sexual Dependence Inventory (SDI) is one of the most comprehensive tests for sexual addiction. It is only offered by Certified Sex Addiction Therapists (CSATs). Another test that can be administered by lay people is the Internet Sex Screening Test (ISST) by David L. Delmonico (2000). Below is a copy of the test, which I have updated for new technology. While it cannot definitely diagnose an addiction to pornography, it can assess one's risk of being addicted.

## *Internet Sex Screening Test*

Read each statement carefully in this *Internet Sex Screening Test*. If a statement is mostly TRUE, as it is applied to one, place a checkmark in the box next to the item number. If the statement is mostly FALSE, as applied to one, skip the item and place nothing in the box next to the item number.[11]

## IV. The Treatment of Pornography Addiction in Clergy and Seminarians

1. ☐ I have some sexual sites bookmarked.
2. ☐ I spend more than five hours per week using my computer/cell phone/tablet for sexual pursuits.
3. ☐ I have joined sexual sites to gain access to online sexual material.
4. ☐ I have purchased sexual products online.
5. ☐ I have searched for sexual material through an Internet search tool.
6. ☐ I have spent more money for online sexual material than I planned.
7. ☐ Internet/social media sex has sometimes interfered with certain aspects of my life.
8. ☐ I have participated in sexually related chats.
9. ☐ I have a sexualized username or nickname that I use on the Internet or in social media.
10. ☐ I have masturbated while on the Internet/in social media.
11. ☐ I have access to sexual sites/social media from computers/cell phones/tablets in locations other than my home.
12. ☐ No one knows I use my computer/cell phone/tablet for sexual purposes.
13. ☐ I have tried to hide what is on my computer/cell phone/tablet so others cannot see it.
14. ☐ I have stayed up after midnight to access sexual material online or in social media.
15. ☐ I use the Internet/social media to experiment with different aspects of sexuality, such as bondage, homosexuality, or anal sex.
16. ☐ I have my own website/social media account(s) that contain some sexual material.
17. ☐ I have made promises to myself to stop using the Internet/social media for sexual purposes.
18. ☐ I sometimes use cybersex as a reward for accomplishing something such as finishing a project or enduring a stressful day.

19. ☐ When I am unable to access sexual information online or in social media, I feel anxious, angry, or disappointed.
20. ☐ I have increased the risks I take online or in social media, such as giving out my name and phone number or meeting people offline.
21. ☐ I have punished myself when I use the Internet/social media for sexual purposes, such as arranging a time-out from my computer/cell phone/tablet or canceling Internet/social media accounts.
22. ☐ I have met face-to-face with someone I met online or in social media for romantic purposes.
23. ☐ I use sexual humor and innuendo with others while online/in social media.
24. ☐ I have run across illegal sexual material while on the Internet or in social media.
25. ☐ I believe I am an Internet sex addict.

Now add up the number of items that one indicated were TRUE for one and record the total below.

Total: _____

Use the chart below to determine if Internet sex may be problematic for one.

### 1 to 8 items marked True = Low Risk:

You may or may not have a problem with your sexual behavior on the Internet or in social media. You are in the low-risk group, but if the Internet/social media is causing problems in your life seek a professional who can conduct further assessments.

### 9 to 18 items marked True = Moderate Risk:

You are at risk for sexual behavior to interfere with significant areas of your life. If you are concerned about your sexual behavior online/in social media and have noticed consequences as a result of your behavior, you should seek a professional who can further assess and help you with your concerns.

**20 or more items marked True = High Risk:**

You are at the highest risk for your online/social media behavior to interfere with and jeopardize important areas of your life (for example, social, occupational, and educational). You should discuss your sexual behaviors with a professional who can further assess and assist you

In addition to trained therapists, the ISST can be administered by seminary formators and spiritual directors. I also firmly believe it should be used by evaluators of candidates for seminary. If an individual appears to be struggling with an addiction to pornography, he can then be referred for professional help.

## Understanding Addiction to Pornography in Clerics (priest or religious) and Seminarians

In 2010, a priest in Massachusetts was accused of stealing over $80,000 from his parish. Most of this was taken from parish collections. He admitted that he was addicted to pornography, and much of the money he stole went to support his addiction. The priest's credit card had a balance of $25,000 that he used to purchase online pornography. A review of his cable bills revealed that he spent over $4,000 on "adult" movies. As a result of his conviction, this priest was placed on probation for three years and was required to perform community service during that time. He was also sent to a psychiatric treatment facility for priests for six months to begin his recovery.[12] Getting caught was a blessing in disguise for this priest because it helped him to realize his sickness. Thankfully, he was able to get help.

While this true story is an extreme case, it does illustrate that clergy are not immune to pornography addiction. I did not treat this priest; however, in my practice, I have worked with countless priests and seminarians who struggle with pornography use. I have even facilitated a phone support group for priests. Today, priests face numerous challenges in their vocation. Many are isolated in remote areas of the country and are working long hours with little time off. Because of their position as moral leaders, they have difficulty asking for help when they struggle.

Currently, there is little research published on Catholic priests, religious, and seminarians who struggle with pornography addiction. However, in addition to the studies listed above, there are several good studies on this disease in Protestant clergy. According to Dr. Lynn Anne Joiner:

> Surveys of Protestant evangelical clergy in the United Stated reported that 33% to 43% admitted to viewing Internet pornography. Of these numbers, approximately 6% to 18% viewed pornography multiple times per month and one survey cited 37% of clergy who described Internet pornography as a current temptation.[13]

Moreover, the National Coalition for the Protection of Children and Families reports: "In an informal survey of pastors in Seattle, WA, 11% of the 58 pastors surveyed intentionally had accessed a sexually explicit website; 9% viewed by choice and felt that it may be a problem for them."[14] Five thousand pastors were questioned through the website with 55% indicating they had visited a pornographic site within the last year; 33% had visited a sexually explicit site within the previous three weeks.[15]

According to national surveys by *Christianity Today* and *Leadership Journal* (2001), "four in ten pastors with Internet access reported they have visited a pornographic website . . . and more than one third have done so in the past year. Slightly over half of the pastors (51%) say Internet pornography is a temptation for them; 37% admit it is a current struggle. Among the laity, 11% report at least occasionally viewing pornography."[16]

In a more recent study, The Barna Group (2016) found that 14% of Protestant Senior Pastors struggle with pornography use, and 33% of these users believe they are addicted. Of the senior pastors surveyed, 43% claim they have struggled with it in the past.[17] In addition, 21% of Protestant Youth Pastors claim using pornography is a current struggle, and 56% of these users believe they are addicted. 43% of Youth pastors also claim they have struggled with it in the past.[18]

This epidemic among Protestant clergy is probably much worse than the statistics show. Moreover, if this is a problem among Protestant clergy, it could be just as severe among Catholic clergy. My personal experience counseling Catholic priests, religious, and seminarians leads me to believe this is so.

These studies among Protestant clergy also shed valuable light on priestly celibacy. Many people believe that Catholic clergy turn to pornography because they cannot marry and therefore substitute pornography for a wife. However, most Protestant clergy are married, and they still struggle with pornography, leading us to deduce that celibacy is not a major issue in sexual addiction. There are much deeper root causes.

## *Root Causes*

As with any addiction, remember that we need to view pornography use as a form of self-medication. Many of these clergy struggle with deep emotional wounds which can lead to addiction. Often, they are not even aware of these wounds, and then one day they discover pornography and realize how good it makes them feel. It eases their pain, but because the effects are only temporary, they continue to go back time and again. They become addicted. It becomes a form of self-medication. Below are some of the root causes. The case studies are those of actual priests that I have treated whose names have been changed to protect confidentiality.

The underlying assumption for many people is that a man who becomes a priest must have come from a loving Catholic family. Unfortunately, this is a stereotype. There are priests who come from very tragic family backgrounds, having had to contend with divorce, death, rejection, abandonment, addiction, and abuse in their families. Many priests have recovered from these wounds and use their experiences to effectively minister to those suffering from similar one; however, there are those who have not healed and have turned to pornography to ease their pain.

**Divorce.** Ever since the sexual revolution of the late 1960s, the divorce rate in America has steadily risen. Many priests today come from families that have been torn apart by divorce, something painful for all parties, especially children. One of the deepest wounds is the inability to trust others, which makes it difficult to develop healthy relationships. The result is deep loneliness. Children of divorce often struggle with a deep guilt; they blame themselves for the breakup of their parents' marriage. And in many divorces, when the father moves out, he rarely visits his children, which, in turn, leaves children feeling rejected and abandoned. They may carry these wounds into adulthood.

Fr. Bill is a forty-five-year-old diocesan priest whose parents divorced when he was ten years old. His father had been serially unfaithful to his mother, and she was deeply wounded and bitter. Subsequently, Fr. Bill learned not to trust people. After the divorce, he rarely saw his father and felt rejected by him. During high school, Fr. Bill joined his parish youth group and had a religious conversion. While his experience of God's love was very comforting, Fr. Bill was still sorely wounded. He became a loner because of his inability to trust others. This continued into seminary. He never thought the divorce wounded him so deeply. In fact, he saw himself as successful despite his upbringing. However, after a few years of priesthood, the stresses of ministry brought to the surface his wounds of guilt, mistrust, and loneliness, and he turned to pornography for comfort. Soon he was addicted, viewing porn almost every day.

**Abuse.** There are also priests who have grown up in abusive homes and have turned to pornography for relief. According to Research by Dr. Patrick Carnes (1989) on sex addicts, 97% were emotionally abused, 74% were physically abused, and 81% were sexually abused. Based on stereotypical views of priests' families, many do not understand that some priests have been abused as children.

When Fr. Ed was seven years old, he was repeatedly sexually abused by his grandfather, who used fear and extorsion to ensure silence. The abuse went on for three years and ended when his grandfather died. While Fr. Ed never told his family about the abuse, he carried guilt, fear, and shame into adulthood, and his silence left him feeling alone and isolated. After several years of priesthood, Fr. Ed became an alcoholic to ease his pain, blaming his drinking on the stresses of ministry. With the help of Alcoholics Anonymous he was able to stop drinking. However, he was still hurting inside from the abuse and turned to pornography, which led to a new addiction.

## IV. The Treatment of Pornography Addiction in Clergy and Seminarians

**Addiction.** I have treated many priests who came from families with addictions. A common theme is the need to appear to the public as "perfect, faithful Catholics." To the outside world, they are model families, but behind closed doors, it's total chaos. This leaves the families of addicts suffering in silence.

Fr. Lou grew up in such a family. His father was an angry alcoholic who would get drunk and violently terrorize the family at night. Pressured into maintaining the façade of the perfect family, Fr. Lou remained silent. He felt alone and helpless. He vowed to never drink, but as an adult he turned to pornography to ease his pain. Thirty years later, his family still had not acknowledged his father's alcoholism problem and its negative effects on them, and one Fr. Lou, in particular.

**Loneliness.** This is a trigger for pornography use. Many believe that a person addicted to pornography is searching for a romantic or sexual relationship, but this is not necessarily true. Recall that pornography addiction is also a serious problem among Protestant clergy, and most of them are married and not seeking a romantic or sexual relationships. The real need is intimacy. They are seeking a deep emotional connection. Sex and romance are just one way to experience intimacy. It can also be experienced in close friendships, among family members, and with God. One might be surprised to learn that many priests do not experience intimacy with God. They have a deep faith in God, but it is intellectual (of the mind) rather than emotional (of the heart). This results in profound spiritual loneliness that many priests struggle with due to a lack of good friendships.

People tend to connect most with others who share the same vocation. Married couples tend to have more friends who are married. Single people tend to have more single friends. Thus, a priest's closest friends should be other priests. Priests can also have good friends who are laypeople, as long as these relationships does not compromise his role as spiritual father. Unfortunately, because of the shortage of priests and the busy lives they lead, many priests do not have time to work on developing healthy friendships. Others may have difficulty making friends, in general, because they lack self-confidence.

Fr. Nick became addicted to pornography shortly after he was ordained. He was assigned as parochial vicar of a large suburban parish with a wonderful pastor, but they were both so busy they rarely saw each other. Parish work kept Fr. Nick from getting together with priests from other parishes, and he had little time to socialize with any laypeople. After a long day, he would retire to his room and surf the net to relax. Before he knew it, he was spending several hours a night viewing pornography. He did not want a wife. He wanted to connect with some genuine friends. Pornography was used to ease the pain of his loneliness.

**Isolation.** This is a unique form of loneliness. Many priests find themselves ministering to Catholics in rural areas or remote areas, such as the desert or deep in the mountains. They don't have priest brothers nearby and only have limited contact with laypeople.

Fr. Ron is pastor of three parishes in the rural Midwest where the parishes are roughly seventy miles apart. Fr. Ron spends much of his time in his car traveling from parish to parish. Each parish has one employee, a part-time secretary, and several lay volunteers. Aside from the secretaries, the only times he sees the volunteers and his parishioners are on Sundays, and the occasional funeral. He spends most of the week alone working around the parishes. Because he was not raised in a rural community, Fr. Ron had great difficulty adjusting to the remoteness and isolation of his pastorate. This led him to turn to pornography for comfort and online chatting to experience human interaction. Before long, he was addicted.

**Ministry Stress.** Many priests are asked to do a lot more because of the shortage of priests. Like Fr. Ron, they are pastors of multiple parishes. Others are also ministering in hospitals, nursing homes, prisons, schools, colleges, homeless shelters, soup kitchens, and food pantries. Due to their heavy workload, many are unable to take a regular day off, which leaves them struggling under mountains of stress. Some of this stress is self-imposed. These priests feel overly responsible to minister to people and have difficulty saying no. They tend to take on excessive amounts of responsibility, even jobs that a layperson could easily handle. If they do say no, they feel guilty, as if they were neglecting their vocation.

Fr. Ben was a pastor of two small inner-city parishes with innumerable needs. Along with his regular pastoral duties, he started a food pantry, literacy program, and a youth group. He liked the excitement of his ministry, but soon the responsibility was wearing on him. He would work up to eighteen hours a day, and despite having every Tuesday off, he always found some work that needed to be done that day. The responsibilities of ministry also took time away from prayer. The stress became overwhelming; he was physically and emotionally drained by the time he got back to his room late at night. He would surf the net to relax, and this soon led to a pornography addiction.

**Ministry Burnout.** Many priests and religious neglect healthy self-care because of the demands of ministry. They forgo days off to relax and rarely take a vacation. Some priests feel pressured to meet all their parishioners' needs and feel guilty if they say no. Others are given more responsibilities than one man can handle. These priests are put in charge of large parishes that should be staffed by two or more priests, and they are often given additional assignments, such as hospital ministry. Then, there are priests who truly love an exciting fast-paced ministry but take on more responsibility than is necessary or healthy. The result in all cases is burnout.

Fr. Stan was a pastor of two parishes because of the shortage of priests in his diocese. Although both parishes had good lay staffs, the workload for Fr. Stan was exhausting. Canon law and bishops mandate that priests take vacations and retreats each year; however, because of the tremendous sense of responsibility, it had been years since he took a restful period. This left him angry and burnt out. He began neglecting his pastoral duties, doing only the bare minimum, and escaped by viewing pornography. Of course, this led to addiction.

**Anger.** A key trigger for many addictions is anger. Often when a person is mistreated, one becomes bitter and resentful. For a priest, the anger can be directed toward the parishioners, staff, bishop, or even God, and pornography can ease his emotional pain. Pornography use can also be a form of rebellion for a priest, a way of getting back at those who hurt him. Some priests may not even be aware they are angry.

Fr. Peter sought treatment for pornography addiction when his secretary discovered pornography on the parish computer. After the staff would go home at night, Fr. Peter would spend hours surfing for porn on the office computer. He had originally been in the navy, and after an honorable discharge he entered the seminary with the hope of becoming a navy chaplain. However, after he was ordained, his bishop assigned him to a parish, instead. Fr. Peter loved being a priest and serving his parishioners, but he was angry with God and very angry with his bishop, something he admitted. He used pornography to ease his pain, but also as a form of rebellion against his bishop. He knew he was defying God, but he was too angry to care. Fr. Peter's use of pornography soon escalated into a full-blown addiction.

**Lack of Confidence.** Some priests use pornography to ease the pain of having little self-confidence. They may have done well in seminary, but the real world of ministry frightens them and they feel inadequate. When comparing themselves to other priests, they are insecure about their abilities and deeply fear that people might consider them incompetent.

Fr. Jude has been a religious priest for fifteen years, and in all that time he has been an assistant pastor of several parishes. He never felt confident enough to be a pastor, so whenever the opportunity arose, he managed to convince his superior that another priest would be a better choice. Deep down, Fr. Jude felt like a failure. He did not think he would ever amount to anything as a priest. He turned to pornography to ease his guilt and pain. He knew viewing pornography was wrong but felt better when he imagined himself as the men in the pornographic images. To Fr. Jude, male porn stars were fearless, strong, take-charge men. He saw them as "real men." This gave Fr. Jude a false (and temporary) sense of confidence that led him to become addicted to pornography. He soon began engaging in online chatting and even made plans to meet a woman from a chat room. Fortunately, he did not have the courage to keep the rendezvous. That was his wakeup call, he immediately sought help.

**The Five A's.** The Five A's of pornography have made it the new drug of choice in our culture, and this is true for priests and religious as well. Its affordable, accessible, anonymous, accepted, and aggressive. Thirty years ago, it was not uncommon to find a priest self-medicating his emotional pain with alcohol, and the media would often poke fun at the "drunken priest." Pornography has changed this panorama. While alcohol must be purchased, pornography is free and just a click away. While a priest must be careful not to be seen intoxicated in public, pornography has become the new drug of choice for many priests, something that can be done in private. While viewing it has become acceptable, especially among young people, pornography is aggressively addictive.

## Specific Causes

Many seminarians who struggle with pornography addiction were addicted before they entered seminary. For others, the stress of seminary triggers deep emotional wounds that can lead to pornography addiction. While all of the root causes cited above apply to seminarians, there are some that affect seminarians in a unique way, due to age and cultural aspects. The case studies are of seminarians who I have treated, whose names have been changed to protect confidentiality.

**Narcissism.** This is not a new phenomenon in ministry. History is riddled with selfish clergy. In 2010, I conducted a study of narcissism in seminarians and found that about 16% are highly narcissistic.[19] Catholic seminarians, most of whom are young adults, are not immune to this, and many of them are raised in small families and overindulged by their parents. Despite their deep faith and desire to serve the Lord, this treatment can lead to a strong sense of entitlement, which, in turn, is fueled during the time in seminary. Imagine a young man who announces to his family and parish that he will be entering seminary. From that moment on, his family and parish treat him like a celebrity, which leads him to believe he is a special person, who has been chosen by God to do great things. During times of high stress, this sense of entitlement can lead a seminarian to seek relief by using pornography.

Kyle is a second-year theology student at a prominent Catholic seminary and is well known in his parish. He enjoys helping in his parish during breaks from school because everyone treats him like a rock star. Parishioners invite him to their homes and offer him gifts, and while he knows he needs to work on remaining humble, Kyle admits he likes this treatment. This led him to expect special treatment all the time. As his narcissism grew, Kyle began to feel entitled to "some relief" after a long day at school, and he subconsciously used this to justify viewing pornography. As his studies became more challenging, Kyle began to view pornography and developed an addiction.

**Perfectionism.** The stress of their state in life can be very intense for many seminarians. As future priests, they are held to a higher standard of moral behavior. Here is where celebrity status has its downside. Many seminarians feel as if their lives are being examined by the public under a microscope. This can lead to a struggle with perfectionism, which, in turn, results in failure and disappointment because they constantly set the bar too high. To deal with this constant sense of failure, many turn to pornography for comfort.

As a young college seminarian, one of Justin's apostolates was to work with a local parish youth group. He realized how tough it was to be a teenager today and wanted to show the teens that they could live a chaste life and be very happy. In wanting to appear perfect before the teens, he set standards for himself that no one could meet. For example, he decided that he should never get angry or show any kind of temper. So as not to appear a hypocrite, he decided to practice this in all of his relationships and not just with the youth group. Soon the stress of being perfect was too much for him to bear. When Justin would return to his room late at night, he would be extremely exhausted and the desire to rebel was intense. He was primed for getting caught in the web of pornography and its addiction.

**The Five A's.** As stated above, the Five A's have a special impact on seminarians. Technology is an integral part of the lives of young people. Most seminarians have grown up with computers, cell phones, and the internet, which has made the affordability, accessibility, and anonymity of pornography more prevalent. Many have been exposed to internet pornography at a young age. To their generation, pornography use is acceptable. The point is not to justify pornography use, but rather to underline how easy it is for young adults and seminarians to become addicted.

Mark is a true tech guru. Growing up, he always had the latest technological gadgets, whether it was a computer, cell phone, or video game system. His parents encouraged him, believing that this knowledge would lead to success in the 21st century. However, his parents did not realize the negative consequences. Buying him the gadgets, spoiled him and engendered in him a sense of entitlement. They were also unaware of the danger in giving him unrestricted access to the internet. Mark began viewing internet pornography when he was thirteen. Easy access and peer acceptance of pornography reaffirmed his own use. Mark knew his parents would not approve, so hid his use. His activities went unchecked for several years. In college, when Mark had a conversion experience and was discerning a call to a priesthood, he desired to stop using pornography, but realized he could not stop. He was an addict.

**Opportunity Induced Addiction.** In studying those who struggle with pornography addiction, researchers have found that many, especially young people, have become addicted not due to deep emotional family-of-origin wounds or other major traumas in their lives. Rather, they have been consistently exposed to pornography from age eight to their young adulthood.[20]

Kevin was first exposed to pornography on a friend's phone at age 10 and had daily access on his unmonitored smartphone. After his parents placed parental controls on his phone, Kevin bought an inexpensive tablet. He then tapped into the wi-fi at home and viewed pornography without his parents' knowledge. That early and consistent exposure hardwired his child brain to become addicted to the rush of dopamine. As the brain became dependent on the neurochemical stimulation caused by pornography, it required more and more to function.

We call this "opportunity induced addiction," which is evident in other addictions to video games, social media, and online gambling. While many addicted people struggle with a deep shame from past emotional wounds which fuels their addiction, opportunity induced addiction struggle with deep shame for the resultant pornography use. Kevin knew he was hooked on porn but was too ashamed to seek help. He feared what his parents would think, and this kept him from turning to his parents for help, which fueled his addiction even more. In this case, the shame leads to the inability to seek help, which in itself becomes an emotional wound.

## *Getting Help: Obstacles*

As with all addictions, receiving assistance can be very difficult. There is much fear, guilt, and shame associated with admitting that one has an addiction. In addition, there is the challenge of finding adequate help, be it support groups, counselors, accountability partners, and others. Lastly, priests, religious, and seminarians have five basic challenges.

**Shame.** While all addicts struggle with shame, I believe clergy struggle with it to a much greater degree because they are public figures whom society holds to much stricter standards of moral living. Shame is the emotion that leads us to believe we are terrible people because of the bad things we have done. Discovering that a priest is struggling with pornography addiction can create a large scandal in the Church, especially if he is well known. There is great fear about what others will think of them, so to preserve their reputation and protect the Church from scandal, many priests remain silent.

Fr. Bill is the pastor of a large suburban parish that prides itself in its many ministries. He is loved by his parishioners who see him as a holy priest. The love and esteem of his parishioners made seeking help for his pornography addiction almost impossible. Fr. Bill feared what they would think if they found out about this dark side of his life. He couldn't bear how disappointed everyone would be in him. It was not until his assistant pastor discovered him viewing pornography that he was compelled to seek treatment. Fr. Bill is now grateful. Had he not been discovered; his shame might have prevented him from ever seeking help.

**Fear of Scandal.** The sexual abuse crisis in the Catholic Church has kept many priests from seeking help for pornography addiction. If anyone discovers their addiction, they fear they will be labeled a pervert or a sexual predator. They also fear the public knowledge of their addiction will cause scandal in the Church.

That is why it took Fr. Howard many months to muster up the courage to seek help. He feared that public knowledge of his illness would cause a scandal and his reputation would be ruined. Several priests in his diocese had been placed on administrative leave because of sexual issues, and a few were deemed unfit for ministry. Fr. Howard feared that his bishop would also find him unfit for ministry. He feared losing his vocation and being laicized if he sought help. Finally, he realized how much his guilt and shame were preventing him from being an effective priest. In the end, due to his sense of responsibility to his parishioners, he sought help.

**Fear of Treatment.** Some clerics refuse to seek assistance, fearing the treatment they must undergo; for example, special psychiatric treatment centers for clerics. Unfortunately, I have found that these treatment centers often over-diagnose or misdiagnose these men. The promotion of treatment for four to eight months of inpatient treatment with extensive outpatient follow up may violate current standards in the mental health profession. Such treatment programs are also extremely expensive for dioceses and religious communities. In my view, most pornography and sex addicts can be successfully treated in outpatient programs. For those who need inpatient treatment, the best programs, in America, usually require stays for thirty to ninety days, followed by outpatient treatment.

Fr. Brian, a religious, struggled with pornography addiction for several years before seeking help. He confessed this to his superior who responded with much care and compassion. He assured Fr. Brian that he would help him find a good recovery program and referred him to a treatment center for clerics. Fr. Brian's evaluation lasted three weeks. He was diagnosed with pornography addiction and the ambiguous diagnosis of "unintegrated sexuality," something not explained to Fr. Brian or his superior. The treatment recommendation was six months of inpatient treatment. Two months into the program, Fr. Brian felt like a prisoner. He was unable to leave the treatment center without being accompanied by a staff-member, had limited communication with people outside of the center, and could not wear his religious garb. He formed the opinion that the program was unhelpful and a waste of money. After three months, he left the treatment center and entered an outpatient recovery program where he achieved and maintained sexual sobriety. The outpatient program was far more effective and cost efficient than the inpatient program. Dioceses and religious communities need to rethink treatment options for priests.

**Denial.** Although a priest might admit his addiction, he could deny the need for outside help, choosing increased prayer, access to the sacraments and spiritual direction, along with an improvement of will power. Such an approach can be fueled by unhealthy shame, fear, perfectionism, and pride; because he is a priest, he should be able to cope with sexual temptations. This type of pride only leads a man deeper into addiction. With continued failures, he becomes more depressed and discouraged, which, in turn, leads him back to pornography to ease the pain.

Frank is a second-year seminarian who struggles with pornography addiction. The rector of his seminary referred him to me for assistance, yet he was resistant to treatment. Although he has been presented with all the facts about pornography addiction and proper treatment, he was determined to overcome it on his own. Reading between the lines, he seemed to be saying: "Don't confuse me with the facts when my mind is already made up." Unsurprisingly, we only had a few sessions. Fortunately, God intervenes in the lives of such men and places them in situations that compel humility whereby assistance is sought and received. For men like Frank, we can only pray that God will intervene soon.

**Family Loyalty.** This is a unique obstacle to recovery in many priests, religious, and seminarians that I have counselled. Family-of-origin wounds are a key factor in the development of any addiction, and a successful recovery requires a man to face these wounds and work on healing them. However, because priests are supposed to come from "good Catholic families," some clerics and seminarians have difficulty admitting that their families are human and flawed. To them, making such an admission is an act of disloyalty to the family. This was the case for Fr. Lou.

Throughout his childhood, his family covered up his father's alcoholism and presented to the public an image of the perfect Catholic family. Maintaining that image was the number one rule in the family. Fr. Lou would be breaking that rule if he admitted to others that he grew up in an alcoholic home. It would be a sign of disloyalty bringing shame to his family and crushing the image they spent years maintaining. Through counseling, Fr. Lou came to understand the damaging nature of the unspoken rule; it gave him the courage to understand how his father's alcoholism deeply wounded him. This realization was key to his healing and recovery.

**Assistance.** For clergy and seminarians struggling with pornography addiction, getting help means letting go of unhealthy shame, fear, denial, and family loyalty. It means facing the truth that they are struggling with a disease that requires treatment. This entails much humility and honesty, due to the pride and shame involved. Priests represent Christ and are supposed to be models of virtuous living, yet they are also human. They deserve respect for their inherent dignity, and the opportunity to acquire dignity through right action, which is the seeking of assistance for recovery from pornography addiction.

Bishops, vicars for clergy, religious superiors, seminary rectors, and vocation directors should treat those struggling with pornography addiction lovingly and compassionately. They should empathize with these men, recognizing how difficult it is to ask for help. Addicted men, in turn, should never fear seeking help. Avoidance, most assuredly, might lead to negatively grave consequences. If a man knows he will be treated with love and compassion, he is more likely to seek help earlier.

Perhaps dioceses can be proactive in reaching out by fostering a genuine atmosphere of compassion and concern. One practical way to do that could be an open letter from the Bishop to each of his priests, something along these lines: "Brothers, it is no secret that a large percentage of the male population of our country struggles with pornography addiction. If one shares in this struggle, please know that help is available." Remember, God often uses the most wounded among us to do great things, and I believe that God has special plans for addicted persons. Once in recovery, God can use them to reach other people, to see the suffering Christ in others, and to be Christ for others.

Another reason why clerics fear seeking help is due to the anticipated type of treatment available – the 1950's paradigm, where a typical stay in a Catholic psychiatric treatment center can cost about one thousand dollars per day, which the insurance company rarely covers. Thereby leaving a diocese or religious community with a huge bill. Simply because a treatment center specializes in assisting a specific population (clerics), does not mean it is the best form of treatment. Were a cleric to have a heart condition, should he be treated in a general hospital that is Catholic or a secular hospital that specializes in treating heart conditions?

Newer treatment programs are effective, shorter in duration, and much less expensive. Most pornography and sex addicts can be effectively treated in outpatient programs, which include counseling, support groups, accountability partners, education, and spiritual assistance. Effective Catholic outpatient programs include the "Integrity Starts Here Recovery Program" and "Catholic in Recovery." For clerics, who require inpatient treatment, the best programs in America are usually thirty to ninety days, with outpatient treatment to follow. There are excellent inpatient treatment centers such as "Gentle Path in Hattiesburg," MS; "Keystone Center ECU" in Chester, PA; "Santé Center for Healing in Dallas," TX; "The Meadows in Wickenburg," AZ; "The Ranch in Nunnelly," TN, and "The Pinegrove Gratitude Program in Hattiesburg," MS.

No one is immune to the pornography epidemic in America, including clerics and seminarians. They need to be educated about the dangers of pornography and taught ways to protect themselves and their parishioners. Effective recovery programs should be available, and no one should fear seeking help. Bishops, vicars for clergy, and religious superiors need to deal with the issue with transparency, encouraging all to seek help. Seminary rectors and vocation directors should do the same with seminarians. These efforts would ensure a healthy priesthood now and in the future.

## Getting Help: Outpatient Recovery Programs

There are many effective outpatient recovery programs available. Programs offered by the "International Institute for Trauma and Addiction Professionals" (IITAP) include those offered by Certified Sex Addiction Therapists (CSAT).[21] Dr. Todd Bowman's "Neuroaffective Program" is offered by "Sex Addiction Treatment Professionals" (SATP) and the "Catholic in Recovery" support groups.[22] Currently, however, the only comprehensive recovery program for Catholics is the "Integrity Starts Here!" recovery program for pornography addiction.[23] This program is based on seven points that are needed for healthy effective recovery. Each point is of equal importance, so all are integrated; the resources are commonly known to be most effective in the treatment of pornography addiction. Moreover, the points incorporate Catholic spirituality, which can increase a person's recovery success. Here is a diagram and a brief overview of the points:

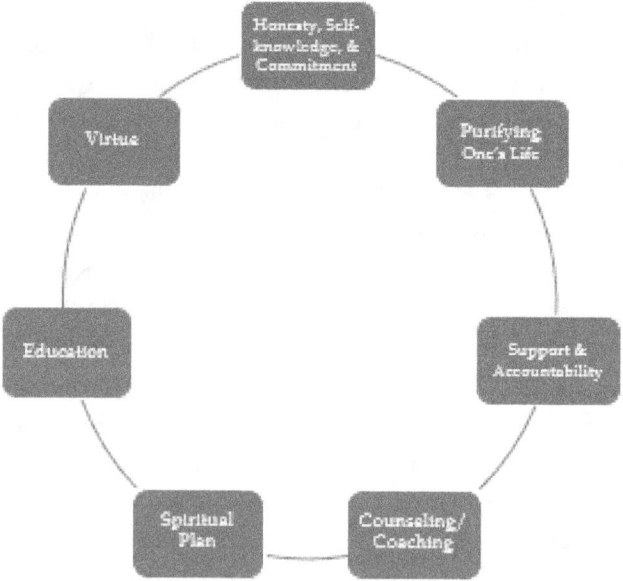

**Honesty, Self-knowledge, and Commitment.** This point focuses on being honest with oneself, others, and God about one's addiction. There can be no denial in recovery. This point includes taking responsibility for the addiction, for the consequences of it, and for one's recovery.[24] Self-knowledge means acknowledging one's weaknesses, which requires monitoring one's emotions and behaviors, as well as identifying one's triggers that provoke acting out. It also means identifying one's danger zones, where one is more likely to be triggered. Finally, it means developing the strategies needed to avoid acting out. Above all, successful recovery requires a total commitment to the process.

**Purifying Your Life.** One must rid his life of all pornography and anything else that might tempt him to act out sexually. For most people this means monitoring all technology and setting clear boundaries. Purification also applies to one's heart and mind. This does not require an immediate change of how one feels about pornography, but rather understanding that the conduct uses and exploits other people. One should appreciate how the women (and men) in pornography are victims (e.g., trafficked, exploited, poor choices) and that, by viewing porn, one is contributing to their victimization. The ultimate goal is for the addict to be repulsed by pornography, both intellectually and emotionally.

**Support and Accountability.** To be successful in recovery one needs support from those who understand the struggle to assist in adherence to the program and support in times of failure. Such teamwork and fellowship can keep a person from using pornography. The approach has been successful in recovery groups such as "Sexaholics Anonymous" and "Catholic in Recovery."[25]

**Counseling.** Following the above three points of the program should bring a person to sobriety; however, more is needed, otherwise they remain in a "white-knuckling" state. In "Alcoholics Anonymous," this condition is known as "dry drunk," because they have not identified and resolved the root cause(s) of the addiction. Here is where counseling is important. Returning to the notion of "self-medicating," that is, when a person uses a substance such as sex or pornography to ease pain. The goal of counseling is to help the addict deal with negative emotions and shame more effectively with a view to identify and heal the root wounds. Once they have identified them and healed, lasting sobriety can be achieved, which is true recovery.[26]

**Spiritual Plan.** A close, intimate relationship with God is important for successful recovery.[27] Here, in that relationship with God, one finds the strength and grace to persevere. Unfortunately, many addicted people do not have a healthy relationship with God. Because of their shame, they believe that God could never love them, or they might be angry with God because of certain tragedies in their lives. Others may have an unhealthy image of God because of struggles with their own fathers. By developing a healthy relationship with God, one can truly experience his great love. One will also find it easier to discern God's will for one's life, which can provide greater hope, strength, and determination to persevere in recovery. Use of prayer, sacraments, scripture, saints, and spiritual direction are integral parts of the program.

**Education.** To recover from an addiction, one must truly understand the nature of the addiction. It is important to know how a person becomes addicted to pornography physically and emotionally and how the recovery process works. One must understand how addictions affect personal lives and relationships and how to protect oneself and one's family. Many people also need to learn about healthy sexuality and relationships and even acquire healthy life skills.[28] Education, therefore, plays a crucial role in recovery.

**Virtue.** Along with a spiritual plan, development of virtue makes this program uniquely Catholic. The essence of a Christian life is virtue. When we strive to live virtuously, we can avoid sin, conquer selfishness, love others as God loves, and truly serve the Lord. Moreover, one of the best ways to fight a vice is with virtue. In this program, one will be challenged daily to grow in virtue. They will be given exercises to help practice virtue in daily life. Performing the exercises will help one become the person God intended he or she to be. When people make virtuous life a mission, it becomes easy to avoid sin. It is also easy to discern God's will for one's life, which can in turn, provoke excitement about one's life and recovery. It is about moving forward, toward becoming true men of God, not running away from pornography.

## IV. The Treatment of Pornography Addiction in Clergy and Seminarians

### *Recommendations*

To help priests who struggle with pornography addiction, I recommend bishops and vicars for clergy to create an environment where priests can talk about such issues without fear. Bishops and vicars for clergy should be compassionate with these men. They should be ready to refer these men to the proper resources for recovery. A diocesan social services agency can help find the proper resources.

The same policy holds true for seminarians. Rather than hiding this problem in the internal forum, seminarians should be able to discuss this problem with their formators without fear. Resources should be provided for recovery, some of which can be provided in-house, such as counseling and support groups. What resources cannot be provided locally can be obtained virtually. Many therapists and support groups now use technology for meetings. Most of all, bishops, clergy and seminarians need to be educated on pornography addiction. Once they are aware of this addiction, its consequences, and recovery process, they can create an environment where any man who struggles can find the help he needs to recovery.

### Conclusion

Research has shown that pornography addiction is an epidemic in America. Priests and seminarians are not immune. Today, many are addicted even before they enter seminary. It is important for the Church to recognize this fact. Instead of penalizing priests and seminarians who are addicted, the Church needs to obtain proper help for them. Priests must be assured that they will not be immediately sent away for six months of treatment, or worse. Seminarians must be assured that they will not be immediately expelled from seminary for being addicted. Priests and seminarians who are addicted can successfully recover. While some may need in-patient services, most can recover in an out-patient program. Through counseling, support groups, education, a strong spiritual plan, and growth in virtue, these men can achieve sobriety, heal the wounds that have fueled their addiction, experience the full transformation of recovery, and embrace their true masculinity. While it can take up to 18 months to achieve full sobriety and three to five years to achieve complete recovery, healthy recovery is possible. I believe that priests who achieve this will be stronger priests. They will truly understand struggle, suffering and compassion. I believe this will make them more effective in ministry.

## RESPONSE

## A View of Pornography through the Lens of Encyclical Letter *Deus Caritas Est*

### Jane F. Adolphe

*Professor of Law, Ave Maria School of Law, Adjunct Professor of Law, Adjunct Professor of Law, University of Notre Dame, School of Law, Sydney, Australia*

**Introduction**

Dr. Kleponis has addressed pornography use in the Church with an emphasis on its addictive properties and views the problem as part of a larger societal crisis in masculinity. He advocates for increased education in the Church about the addictive nature of internet pornography, and, in particular, more instruction for bishops, spiritual directors, and human formators. He underlines the need, in seminarian formation, for an accurate diagnosis through proper assessment and transparency protocols which would bridge the gap between the internal forum (pornography as a private sin) and external forum (pornography as an addiction). To this end, he recommends that spiritual directors urge penitents to seek help so that they can take advantage of support programs, understanding of course that possession and distribution of child pornography is a crime. It is noteworthy that it also constitutes a human rights violation in international law, for example, the 2000 Optional Protocol to the Convention on the Rights of the Child on the Sale of Children, Child Prostitution and Child Pornography.

The purpose of my reflections is to flesh out the perspective of pornography consumption as a sin, a rejection of God as love, and a gateway to the demonic. This chapter seeks to do this through the lens of Pope Benedict XVI in Encyclical Letter *Deus Caritas Est*. To this end, the thesis is fleshed out under the following topics: 1) the problem of digital pornography consumption; 2) sin in the Catechism of the Catholic Church;

3) the Encyclical Letter *Deus Caritas Est*: an overview; 4) *eros is* an overpowering of reason; 5) *eros* requires growth in maturity; 6) mature relations between men and women in the ecclesial workplace; 7) *eros* requires growth in affective maturity; 8) *eros* requires renunciation and sacrifice; 9) eros and agape: two different dimensions of love; and 10) pornography is the rejection of God as Love and gateway to the demonic.

**The Problem**

In October 2022, during his meeting with seminarians and priests who study in Rome, Pope Francis rightly emphasized the diabolical element of pornography consumption. When responding to a question about the digital world and social media, Francis highlighted the temptation of internet pornography, and stated:

> It is a vice that has so many people, so many lay men, so many lay women, and also priests and nuns. The devil enters from there. And I'm not just talking about criminal pornography like child abuse, where you see live cases of abuse-that's already degeneracy. But of somewhat more "normal" pornography. Dear brothers, be careful about this. The pure heart, the heart that receives Jesus every day, cannot receive this pornographic information. That today is so commonplace. And if from your cell phone you can delete this, delete it, so you won't have temptation in your hand. And if you can't delete it, defend yourself well not to get into this. I tell you, it is something that weakens the soul. It weakens the soul. The devil enters from there: it weakens the priestly soul.[29]

About a month later, Father Hermann Backhaus, a Catholic priest of the Diocese of Münster, Germany, who also works as a psychologist, disagreed with Pope Francis. Backhaus offered the common narrative, namely that pornography consumption is benign; it "can have a relieving effect" for celibate people and serve a couple in a sexual relationship – "making their love life become more alive."[30]

Many experts disagree with the common narrative. More than twenty years ago, experts of various religious backgrounds (atheism, agnosticism,

## IV. The Treatment of Pornography Addiction in Clergy and Seminarians

Christianity, Judaism, Islam) gathered to study the problem of internet pornography, under the auspices of the Witherspoon Institute. 31 They produced the 2010 "Social Costs of Pornography: A Statement of Findings and Recommendations" (the Statement). 32 The findings are supported by a scholarly analysis of the data from a broad range of disciplines (e.g., economics, law, neuroscience, philosophy, psychiatry, psychology, sociology). The evidential basis remains available in summary form under each individual finding in the volume of collected papers and in a six-hour video of presentations.[33] The Statement disagrees with the propositions that pornography consumption is harmless entertainment or benign sexual expression, justified as a marital aid or stress reliever.[34]

The Statement notes that the number of pornography consumers is "staggering"[35] and that billions of dollars are spent on pornography in the United States, "more than on football, baseball, and basketball." Indeed, men view "pornography online more than they look at any other subject;" and "66% of 18-34-year-old [boys/] men visit a pornographic site every month."[36] The results of the study, among other things, expose a sharp increase in consumption of internet pornography, including criminal sex abuse images of infants, toddlers, prepubescent children, and teens. In brief, the vast majority of pornography is hard-core (of the graphically violent or sadistic sort), increasingly realistic, highly addictive, easily accessible to all, and harmful to individuals and society at large.[37] The Statement concludes that a "growing body of research strongly suggests that for some users pornography can be psychologically addictive,[38] which, in turn, has a negative effect on "the quality of interpersonal relationships, sexual health and performance, and social expectations about sexual behavior."[39]

Viewing hardcore pornography may escalate and lead to violent acting out of certain fantasies. Consider, for example, convicted felon Thomas Bruce, a former Christian pastor, whose computer "included queries for child pornography and violent, forced sex acts."[40] He confined three women at gun point, commanded them to do intimate acts, and killed the third, when she refused.[41] Moreover, in the case of child pornography, studies demonstrate that "those who collect and disseminate child pornography are likely to molest an actual child;" for example, "in a 2000 study by the Federal Bureau of Prisons, 76 % of offenders convicted of internet related crimes against children admitted to contact sex crimes with children previously undetected by law enforcement and had an average of 30.5 child sex victims each."[42]

These incidents confirm the problem of escalation that was discussed at length in a chapter penned by Father Sean Kilcawley in volume I of this series: "Clerical Sexual Misconduct: An Interdisciplinary Analysis."[43] These incidents also confirm the risk of opening oneself to the diabolical through pornography consumption.

**Sin in the Catechism of the Catholic Church (CCC)**

According to CCC 2354, pornography consists in "removing real or simulated sexual acts from the intimacy of the partners, in order to display them deliberately to third parties." It "perverts the conjugal act, the intimate giving of spouses to each other," and does "grave injury to the dignity of its participants (actors, vendors, the public), since each one becomes an object of base pleasure and illicit profit for others." It is listed as an offense against chastity under the sixth commandment (thou shalt not commit adultery: Ex 20:14; Deut 5:18; Mt 5:27-28), alongside lust, masturbation, fornication, prostitution, and rape.

Pursuant to CCC 1849, pornography is a sin, "an utterance, a deed, or a desire contrary to eternal law" constituting an offense against "reason, truth and right conscience, it is a failure in genuine love of God and neighbor." It is also "an offense against God" since it "sets itself against God's love," and turns inward with "love of oneself even to the contempt of God," something "diametrically opposed to the [loving] obedience of Jesus Christ" (CCC 1850).

Pornography is a mortal sin "whose object is grave matter" (specified by the ten commandments) committed with "full knowledge and deliberate consent;" sin is the gravest when it is committed through "malice, by deliberate choice of evil" (CCC 1857). Mortal sin results in the "loss of charity" and the "privation of the state of grace," and if not redeemed by "repentance and God's forgiveness, it causes exclusion from Christ's kingdom and the eternal death of hell" (CCC 1861).

Imputability of the offense of pornography can be diminished or removed in cases of "unintentional ignorance," "promptings of feelings and passions," and "external pressures or pathological disorders" that negatively affect the "voluntary and free character of the offense." It is noteworthy that no man is "deemed to be ignorant of the principles of the moral law, which are written in the conscience of every man" (CCC 1860).

The sinful social ramifications of pornography are tied to the "proclivity to sin," when it reproduces and reinforces itself, resulting in "perverse inclinations which cloud conscience and corrupt the concrete judgment of good and evil," making "men accomplices of one another and causes concupiscence, violence, and injustice to reign among them," which, in turn, gives rise to sinful "social situations and institutions" (CCC 1865).

## Encyclical Letter *Deus Caritas Est*: An Overview

In his reflections on the understanding and practice of love, Pope Benedict XVI indirectly affirms that pornography is a rejection of the heart of the Christian message: Triune God as Love and the inherent dignity of the human person, made in His image and likeness (DCE, 2). In his Encyclical Letter *Deus Caritas Est,* Benedict considers the meaning of love in philosophy (Ancient Greece), Sacred Scripture, and Tradition in Part I "The Unity of Love in Creation and Salvation History," which is divided into the following subthemes: a problem in language; *eros* and *agape* – difference and unity; the newness of biblical faith; Jesus Christ – the incarnate love of God; love of God and love of neighbor (DCE 2-18). While the topic of pornography is not the core theme, Benedict's discussion proves that it is the antithesis of love.

After noting the "multiplicity of meanings" of the word love, Benedict sets the stage to focus on what he describes as the "epitome of love," where all others "fade in comparison" (DCE 2). It is the "love between man and woman, where body and soul are inseparably joined and human beings glimpse an apparently irresistible promise of happiness" (DCE 2). The question posed is whether love is a single reality comprised of different dimensions or the same word to designate different realities?

In fleshing out a response, he considers the terms: *eros* (ascending, possessive, insecure, indeterminate, worldly, love); and *agape* (descending, oblative, secure, determinate, faith-filled love). He laments that the "distinctions have often been radicalized to the point of establishing a clear antithesis between them" (DCE 7). To bring unity to the two terms, he discusses the meaning of *eros* in ancient Greece, then moves to the term *agape (ahabà)* in the Law and the Prophets in the Old Testament, and ends with the New Testament, where the unity of love (both *eros* and *agape*) is manifested in the twofold commandment of love of God and neighbor in the death and resurrection of "Jesus Christ – the incarnate love of God" (DCE 12).

### Eros *is an overpowering of reason*

Benedict underlines that the Greeks considered *eros* as a "kind of intoxication," a "supreme happiness" and "fellowship with the Divine" (DCE 4). It found expression in the fertility cults involving "sacred" prostitution in the temples, where the "prostitutes were not treated as human beings and persons, but simply used as a means of arousing 'divine madness.'" (DCE 4). Unsurprisingly, the Old Testament opposes the Greek's "perversity of religiosity," and the "counterfeit divinization of *eros*," deeming the "intoxicated and undisciplined *eros*" not as an ascent in 'ecstasy' towards the Divine, but "a fall into the degradation of man" (DCE 4).

Consider the similarity of this vision with that of the person, who sins using pornography and engaging in solitary sins. Since man is a unity of body and soul, man loses his greatness when he denies the spirit as a reality and exalts the flesh or when he denies the flesh as a reality and exalts the spirit (DCE 5). Benedict explains:

> *Eros*, reduced to pure "sex", has become a commodity, a mere "thing" to be bought and sold, or rather, man himself becomes a commodity. This is hardly man's great "yes" to the body. On the contrary, he now considers his body and his sexuality as the purely material part of himself, to be used and exploited at will" (DCE 5).

He continues:

> Nor does he see it as an arena for the exercise of his freedom, but as a mere object that he attempts, as he pleases, to make both enjoyable and harmless. Here we are actually dealing with a debasement of the human body: no longer is it integrated into our overall existential freedom; no longer is it a vital expression of our whole being, but it is more or less relegated to the purely biological sphere. The apparent exaltation of the body can quickly turn into a hatred of bodiliness (DCE 5).

### Eros *requires growth in maturity*

Since love promises eternity, there is a certain relationship between love and the Divine (DCE 5). Benedict contends that *eros* requires discipline, renunciation, purification, and growth in maturity to restore it to its "true grandeur" (DCE 5). On this point, the Catechism speaks of integrity of the person with reference to the chaste person, who has successfully integrated the "powers of life and love" in a unified way through "self-mastery" ordered to the "gift of self" where the good object and morally appropriate means are freely and consciously chosen, something in stark contrast to disordered human freedom driven by "blind impulses" (CCC 2338, 2339, 2340). The integrity of the person does not permit a "double life nor duplicity in speech" (CCC 2338). This has been a matter of much concern for Pope Francis, who has frequently emphasized the evil of "duplicity."[44]

Chastity, a moral virtue, is also "a gift from God, a grace, a fruit of spiritual effort';" under the influence of charity it becomes a twofold witness of love of God and neighbor, through the gift of self (CCC 2340, 2346). Regarding the possibility of a genuine friendship between men and women, ordained and lay, which many may deny, the following section of the Catechism is worth citing in full:

> 2347 The virtue of chastity blossoms in *friendship*. It shows the disciple how to follow and imitate him who has chosen us as his friends, who has given himself totally to us and allows us to

participate in his divine estate. Chastity is a promise of immortality. Chastity is expressed notably in *friendship with one's neighbor*. Whether it develops between persons of the same or opposite sex, friendship represents a great good for all. It leads to spiritual communion.

The love of friendship *(philia)* is part and parcel of man's need for love as articulated by Saint John Paul II in his Encyclical Letter *Redemptor Hominis* at 44: "'Man cannot live without love. He remains a being that is incomprehensible for himself; his life is meaningless, if love is not revealed to him, if he does not encounter love, if he does not experience it and make it his own, if he does not participate intimately in it.'"[45]

### Eros *Requires growth in affective maturity*

Given the above, it is not surprising that the "affective maturity" of seminarians and priests has become an important topic amongst psychologists, including Dr. Kelponis, in his chapter as well as other seminarian formators, administrators and professors in this volume (Monsignor McGee, Suzanne Mulrain, Carmina Chapp, Robert Fastiggi) and others in a previous volume on the topic of clerical sexual misconduct (Rev. Sean Kilcawley,[46] Dale O'Leary).[47] The theme of "affective maturity" is beyond the scope of this chapter, suffice it to say, affective maturity may be understood as the capacity to live out chaste celibacy as part of one's "vocation to love Christ and his Church."[48]

In his Apostolic Exhortation, *Pastores Dabo Vobis*, Saint John Paul II underlines that "[a]ffective maturity presupposes an awareness that love has a central role in human life." [49] It is an integrated love that involves "the entire person, in all his or her aspects - physical, psychic and spiritual." [50] It requires education in the truth and excellence of human love through the cultivation of virtue and healthy human relationships with both men and woman, where a love for Jesus Christ "overflows into a dedication to everyone."[51] It is summed up in the words of St. Paul (Phil. 4:8): "Whatever is true, whatever is honorable, whatever is just, whatever is pure, whatever is lovely, whatever is gracious, if there is any excellence, if there is anything worthy of praise, think about these things."

## IV. The Treatment of Pornography Addiction in Clergy and Seminarians

Healthy relations between women and men and growth in affective maturity begin in the home with appreciation and respect for female persons. Certainly, persons should be respected for their inherent dignity, made in the image and likeness of God, but also for their acquired dignity, in virtuous living and love of God. Studying alongside female students in the seminary, for example, can offer an opportunity for further human development, so can studying under women in positions of authority (professors and administrators), which do not require the sacrament of orders. Interaction with these women requires seminarians to engage with "confident, virtuous, and spiritually mature" females, something that might prove challenging for the misogynist, insecure, effeminate, same-sex attracted or unchaste male.[52] The presence of the female student can be important for discerning troublesome behaviors in candidates (unable or unwilling to express greetings, make eye contact or engage in polite conversation), while the female professors and administrators can detect effeminacy issues, insecurities and "'machismo' or misogynistic attitudes in seminarians, which exacerbate any tendency toward clericalism."[53]

For those living chaste lives, building genuine collegiality or holy friendships with the opposite sex is not something to fear; it is the fruit of Christian freedom. It can be a concern, however, for those who are not living chaste lives or struggling to live one. These persons might view all relationships through the lens of a disordered human sexuality. Still other clerics might intervene to underline some general rule that women and men cannot be friends, despite the fact, that in the history of the Church, numerous examples exist such as St. Francis and St. Clare, St. John of the Cross and St. Teresa of Avila, or St. Francis de Sales and St. Jane de Chantal.

A few clerics might believe in holy friendships, but only with certain women (e.g., nuns). In some quarters, there might be an underlying presumption that most lay Catholics have rejected Church teachings on human sexuality and marriage; so, some clerics might look for cues from how the woman dresses and so forth, buttressed by stereotypes about women. Certainly, professional dress codes should be in place. Yet, beyond the professional dress code, certain clerics might believe they have a residual duty and right to make comments about a woman's personal appearance, something that is prohibited under sexual harassment laws in most Western countries. With this attitude, they might be adopting an approach more akin to the Muslim model that obliges women to adhere to a strict dress code supervised by morality police.

On the issue of judging by appearances and love of neighbor, Benedict XVI in Encyclical Letter *Deus Caritas Est* (December 25, 2005) at no. 18 underlines the following:

> Love of neighbour …consists in the very fact that, in God and with God, I love even the person whom I do not like or even know. This can only take place on the basis of an intimate encounter with God…I learn to look on this other person not simply with my eyes and my feelings, but from the perspective of Jesus Christ. His friend is my friend. *Going beyond exterior appearances*, I perceive in others an interior desire for a sign of love, of concern…If I have no contact whatsoever with God in my life, then I cannot see in the other anything more than the other, and I am incapable of seeing in him the image of God. (my emphasis)

He continues:

> [I]f in my life I fail completely to heed others, solely out of a desire to be "devout" and to perform my "religious duties", then my relationship with God will also grow arid. It becomes merely "proper", but loveless. Only my readiness to encounter my neighbour and to show him love makes me sensitive to God as well. Only if I serve my neighbour can my eyes be opened to what God does for me and how much he loves me.

### Eros *requires renunciation and sacrifice*

The purification of *eros* requires a "real discovery of the other, moving beyond the selfish character"; it must become renunciation but also a readiness and willingness for sacrifice (DCE, 6). According to Benedict, purification is twofold: exclusive (a particular person alone) and forever. Since *eros* "looks to the eternal," love is indeed "ecstasy," but not a self-seeking intoxication (DCE, 6). It is an intentional and deliberate seeking of the beloved's good; it is a "journey, an ongoing exodus out of the closed inward-looking self" toward self-giving, authentic self-discovery and discovery of God; it is a shared journey with Jesus Christ, who likened his own death and Resurrection to the "grain of wheat that falls to the ground and dies, and in this way bears much fruit." (Jn. 12:24) (DCE, 6).

Now consider the base and filthy image of the overfed and sloven cleric in soft clothes, sunk in his comfortable chair, sitting alone in front of his computer, totally absorbed in his lustful pleasures. It is a portrait of inner dissolution. It is in stark contrast to the crucifixion. Christ—beaten, sweaty, and blood— is nailed to a cross standing between heaven and earth. The bottom portion of the vertical beam is sturdily pounded into the ground, while the top portion ascends toward God the Father, and the horizontal beams extend to the ends of the earth. The divine face is disfigured; it stares upward hopefully with ascending love for the Eternal Father, while at other times, looks downward painfully with descending love for sinners. His body is mangled in an agonizing posture of total vulnerability - stripped naked with arms wide. Benedict describes Christ's death on the cross as "love in its most radical form"; it is "the culmination of that turning of God against himself in which he gives himself in order to raise man up and save him" (DCE 12). It is the point, where truth should be contemplated, and love understood (DCE 12).

## Eros *and agape are different dimensions of love*

Love is one reality within the dimensions of eros and agape (DCE 7). The Christian understanding of love is new and distinct in its embrace of the "unbreakable bond between love of God and love of neighbor" in the person of Jesus Christ, as continually present in Sacrament of Charity, the Holy Eucharist, "the gift that Jesus Christ makes of himself, thus revealing to us God's infinite love for every man and woman."[54]

Benedict, in discussing the unity of love (*eros* and *agape*), refers to the account of Jacob's ladder, long understood in tradition as representing the "inseparable connection between ascending and descending love", where *eros* "seeks God" and *agape* "passes on the gift received" (cf. Gen. 28:12; Jn 1:51) (DEC 7). The account of Jacob's ladder is important for the purposes of formation in that seminarians and priests need to understand the need for contemplative prayer in order to give to others (DCE 7).

In the body and blood of Jesus Christ, one finds the new manna, man's real food, "the Logos, eternal wisdom: this same Logos now truly becomes food for us – as love" with a social character (DCE, 14). "Communion draws [one] out of [one]self towards him, and thus also towards unity with all Christians. We become 'one body', completely joined in a single existence. Love of God and love of neighbor are now truly united" (DCE 14). In this way:

> [w]orship itself, Eucharistic communion, includes the reality of both being loved and of loving others in turn. A Eucharist which does not pass over into the concrete practice of love is intrinsically fragmented (DCE, 14).

The concept of neighbor includes every man. There are no longer limitations tied to one's own community or nation; love is the definitive criterion for evaluating the worth of one's life or the lack thereof (DCE 15). Contrast the above with the image of a man who ravenously consumes images of a degraded body of a man, woman, or child. It is an abomination. The human body is devoid of its "nuptial meaning;" the fundamental nature and purpose of eros, "rooted in man's very nature," has been denied. Benedict explains: "Adam is a seeker, who 'abandons his mother and father,' in order to find woman; only together do the two represent complete humanity and become 'one flesh'" (DCE 11). He continues: *"eros* directs man towards marriage, to a bond which is unique and definitive; thus, and only thus, does it fulfill its deepest purpose" (DCE 11). "Marriage based on exclusive and definitive love becomes the icon of the relationship between God and his people and vice versa" (DCE 11).

Regarding what the integration process of *eros* and *agape* looks like, Benedict explains:

> Even if *eros* is at first mainly covetous and ascending, a fascination for the great promise of happiness, in drawing near to the other, it is less and less concerned with itself, increasingly seeks the happiness of the other, is concerned

# IV. The Treatment of Pornography Addiction in Clergy and Seminarians

> more and more with the beloved, bestows itself and wants to "be there for" the other. The element of *agape* thus enters into this love, for otherwise *eros* is impoverished and even loses its own nature.

He continues:

> On the other hand, man cannot live by oblative, descending love alone. He cannot always give, he must also receive. Anyone who wishes to give love must also receive love as a gift."

This second observation is particularly relevant for the seminarian and cleric, who are obliged to live chaste celibacy. Their source of ascending love is that of the Lord, the font of living water (cf. Jn 7:37-38), from which one must "constantly drink anew" (cf. Jn 19:34). It is for this reason that Benedict, citing Pope Gregory the Great, underlines that the "good pastor must be rooted in contemplation. Only in this way will he be able to take upon himself the needs of others and make them his own" (DCE 7).

## *Pornography is a rejection of God as Love and the gateway to the demonic*

Given the alarming statistics on pornography use, reported claims of an equally alarming increase in demonic activity are unsurprising.[55] Apparently, more exorcists are needed to deal with rising demands regarding infestation (places and things), oppression (external events), obsession (thoughts), and possession (the person).[56] According to Father Vincent Lampert, Pastor and Exorcist for the Archdiocese of Indianapolis, "[t]he problem isn't that the devil has upped his game, but more people are willing to play it." [57] Similarly, Monsignor John Esseff, President of the Board of Director of Pope Leo XIII Institute, which provides spiritual formation for exorcists, states: "[a]s the acceptance of sin has increased, so, too, demonic activity."[58] Father Chad Ripperger, an exorcist with the Archdiocese of Denver, attributes the rise of pornography consumption, in all its forms, to increasing cases of obsession, the demonic bombarding of a person's thoughts with lustful images and degrading thoughts.[59]

Exorcism is a sacramental or sacred sign instituted by the Church, employed "[w]hen the Church asks publicly and authoritatively in the name of Jesus Christ that a person or object be protected against the power of the Evil One and withdrawn from his dominion" (CCC 1673). It has two forms: simple or major; the former is performed, for example, at Baptism in the rejection of Satan and all his works. The major exorcism is performed in cases of demonic possession "only by a priest and with permission of the bishop…the spiritual authority which Jesus entrusted to his Church" (CCC 1673; CIC, can. 1172).

The exorcist must be able to distinguish between "[i]llnesses, especially psychological illness," a medical matter requiring medical treatment, on the one hand, and demonic oppression, obsession or possession, a spiritual issue requiring an exorcism, on the other hand. Making the distinction can be difficult. Father Gabriele Amorth, the former Chief Exorcist of Rome, states:

> an expert exorcist will be able to detect the difference more easily than a psychiatrist because the exorcist will keep his mind open to all possibilities and will be able to identify the distinguishing elements. The psychiatrist, in the majority of cases, does not believe in demonic possession.[60]

Amorth has great esteem for those psychiatrists who are "professionally competent and know the limitations of their science" and recognize "when one of their patients exhibit symptoms that go beyond any known disease."[61] In the end, the two fields of expertise need to cooperate.

## Conclusion

When reading *Deus Caritas Est* with mortal sin in mind, it is easy to understand how pornography strikes at the heart of the Christian faith. It is a rejection of the image of the Triune God, a communion of Persons (Father-Son-Holy Spirit) distinguished by their relations with each other, and the resulting image and destiny of man: "a unified creature body and

## IV. The Treatment of Pornography Addiction in Clergy and Seminarians

soul," created by God to love and serve Him and neighbor and to return to Him, in love. (DCE 1, 5). It is a rejection of Love itself, understanding that "God's *eros* for man is also totally *agape*." (DCE 10). It is a rejection of the Person of Jesus Christ, with his death and resurrection, who "united into a single precept" the commandment to love God (Deut. 6:4-5) and the commandment to love one's neighbor (Lev. 19:18; cf. Mk 12:29-31). Consequently, it would be prudent for those addressing the psychological aspects of pornography to consider referring the person to an exorcist to assess the possibility of a diabolical aspect to his pornography use.

# V

## Equality of Difference: Leading to a Most Profound Intimacy and Friendship

### Pia de Solenni

*Global Institute of Church Management*

*Relationships between women and men have long been the source of countless jokes and works of satire. Many are quick to make some equivalent of the "ball and chain" or "Mars and Venus" jokes. Yet, both Aristotle and Aquinas teach that a husband and wife may enjoy together the highest level of friendship, namely that of virtue. Notwithstanding the challenges of marriage, this brief essay seeks to look at the Catholic tradition, specifically that rooted in the thought of St. Thomas Aquinas, to examine the complementarity between woman and man that can lead to a most profound type of friendship.*

For many reasons, we struggle with the concept of difference, particularly difference among human persons. If someone is different (Indeed, if we ourselves are different!), we are quick to make a judgement, sometimes without even wondering why. We are also quick to conform, as most easily noted in fashion trends. Somewhat ironically, trendsetters make great efforts to set themselves apart, knowing full well that their talent will lead others to emulate them, thus eliminating the differences. Despite our preconceptions, such trends are equal opportunity for both sexes. It's only a decade or so ago, with millennials driving the trend, that professional men broke out of the light blue oxford shirt and khaki pants, the so-called business casual look, only to pave the way for...new trends. The *Wall Street Journal* published an article on the new lengths – no pun intended – that men will go to in order to grow a better beard.[1]

When we experience difference, we are quick to assume some type of otherness. In some circumstances, the otherness could be desirable; for example, a unique person that one desires as a spouse, a one-of-a-kind jewel, a beautiful work of art, a rare talent, etc. Generally, though, I would argue that differences tend to lead us to see otherness in persons in a negative light. Racism and various forms of political thought come to mind. We see in these examples the negative implications of seeing otherness as something undesirable. And perhaps one of the most cliché understandings of otherness can be found in the differences between women and men, particularly those in the married state. There are countless variations of the ball-and-chain jokes, the women–are–from–Venus–men–are–from–Mars genre, as well as many others. Every culture has them, indicating that it's a common human experience. Since we use humor to explore them, it is also my hope that we don't take ourselves too seriously all of the time. Yet, looking at the discord that exists between the sexes, in and out of marriage, we know that we do. I would offer that the precise challenge lies in understanding difference constructively.

St. John Paul II offered an important distinction, noting that the differences between women and men existed before the Fall.[2] Therefore, they should be constructive. God created woman and man both in his image and likeness, giving them a shared work to do together.[3] All of this was done before the Fall.[4] The differences, the saint maintains, are not the problem. Rather, the tensions that arise because of original sin create the battle of the sexes we now experience.

Despite being in the Garden of Eden, what we generally understand to have been a paradise of sorts, there came to be unrest between Adam and Eve, made evident by the serpent who convinces them to eat of the fruit of the tree of knowledge. In other words, despite the perfection of their surroundings and existence, despite their habit of walking with God, they were open to breaking the one condition that was required to maintain this perfection. Biblical scholar Scott Hahn highlights the complexity of this scenario.[5] The English translation uses the word "serpent" which doesn't match the seriousness conveyed in the original Hebrew text. Tracing several Scripture references, it is clear that the serpent is in fact Satan in the form of a deadly dragon. In other words, this was not some garden variety snake, nor was it even the cobra that your college friends kept in a bathroom. Hahn writes, "…Adam faced a life-threatening force." And yet the text of Genesis is almost blasé. Adam's wife Eve, the "flesh of his flesh" and "bone of his bone" is talking with this deadly force, but there's no indication that Adam is even mildly concerned. When God confronts them after their transgression, Eve owns that she did as the serpent suggested. The serpent tempted her; she chose to eat of the fruit. Adam, however, passes the blame onto Eve, saying, "The woman whom you put here with me—she gave me fruit from the tree, so I ate it."[6] Even in blaming Eve, Adam first blames God: "The woman whom *you* put here with me…"[7]

I have to wonder if things in paradise were amiss before the serpent showed up. One need not be a perfect husband to know that one's wife is probably not in a safe space if she's conversing with a veritable monster. Nevertheless, that is the definitive point at which we see the consensual rupture of the relationship between God and his first human creatures. The original unity of man and woman now needs restoring.

Thus, the narrative of salvation history commences. The Old Testament details God's relationship with his people to try and restore them to that original state, even preparing them for a better state as fulfilled in the New Testament with the incarnation and death of his only son.

With this in mind, I'd like to propose that we enter into a brief conversation of the relationship that should exist either in spite of the differences or precisely because of the differences. Before looking at Aquinas, I should like first to look at Aristotle, a non-Christian philosopher who was able to articulate the nature about truths in our world in such a way that they are not dependent on time and culture. In fact, an example of this is in his treatment of women. On the one hand, he is insistent that woman is *mas occasionata*, a misbegotten male. In other words, because he attributed generative power solely to the male, he considered a resulting female child to be imperfect because she lacked what would make her male. Yet, in his discourses on friendship, he is clear that women can be virtuous and can exist in friendships of virtue with men.

In the works of Aristotle, the friendship of virtue is typically ascribed to the friendship between two men because the contemplative life was an essential aspect of the virtuous life in Aristotle's account of human flourishing, and the contemplative life was directly related to the intellectual life. Most women did not pursue the intellectual life and, hence, could not have this friendship of virtue in Aristotle's account of human perfection. On the other hand, most men did not reach this level of formation either. It was a friendship which was reserved for the intellectually or philosophically elite.

Yet, Aristotle allows for degrees of friendship in marriage, including even the highest. In the *Nichomachean Ethics*, for example, he teaches:

> Between man and wife friendship seems to exist by nature.... With the other animals the union extends only to this point [reproduction], but human beings live together not only for the sake of reproduction but also for the various purposes of life; for from the start the functions are divided, and those of men and women are different; so they help each other by throwing their peculiar gifts into the common stock. It is for these reasons that both utility and pleasure seem to be bound in this kind of friendship. *But this friendship may be based also on virtue, if the parties are good*; for each has its own virtue and they will delight in the fact.[8]

Also in the *Ethics*, "The friendship of man and wife again is the same that is found in an aristocracy for it in in accord with virtue – the better gets more of what is good, and each gets what befits him; and so, too, with the justice in these relations."[9]

Undoubtedly, Aristotle's notions of aristocracy are idealized and not realistic. Aristocracy does not delineate character as he suggests. Nevertheless, this text demonstrates his regard for some marriages, understanding that they could be very noble and, thereby, confirming the fundamental equality of spouses.

I have argued elsewhere[10] that the notion of female inferiority in the thought of Aristotle rests primarily in his biology and secondarily in his experience of the limited activities of women. Nevertheless, in his own words, he identifies that a friendship of virtue can exist between husband and wife. They are rendered equal and achieve virtue perhaps precisely because of their differences.

Now Aquinas is known for many things, but especially for introducing Aristotle to Christian environs. Typically, Aquinas would be what we call a

## V. Equality of Difference: Leading to a Most Profound Intimacy

solid Aristotelian, someone who follows Aristotle's thought carefully. Nevertheless – and despite the misinformed reputation that he has as a misogynist – he parts from Aristotle's teaching that woman is *mas occasionata* at least five times[11], insisting that even if woman was *mas occasionata* on a biological level – keep in mind that he's working with the same antiquated biology that Aristotle had – she was most certainly intended by God and not malformed in any way. In fact, in one instance of addressing the question, he puts Aristotle in the role of the objector, someone whose view he is contesting.[12]

In the *Summa Theologiae*, Prima Pars, q. 93, 4, ad 1, Aquinas explicitly states that the *imago Dei* is found equally in woman and man and that this is reflected in their intellectual nature. In other texts, he clearly maintains that woman was not created simply for the purposes of reproduction. Rather she shares the same end as man, ultimately to know God.[13]

Earlier in q. 92, article three, Aquinas addresses the question of whether it was fitting that woman should be created from the side of man. Relying on an old Jewish proverb, he first answers that it was not fitting that she should be created from the head of man to rule *over* him, nor from his foot to be ruled *by him*, but from his side to rule *with* him. Aquinas maintains that woman has a role united with that of man: *socialis coniunctio*, a social union of sorts. To strengthen this image, he proposes— also in q. 92, a. 3— that woman was created from the side of man as the Church was created from the side of Christ crucified, in the blood and water which poured forth upon the piercing of his side.

The equality, taken together with the differences of woman and man, serve as a basis for their complementarity and an understanding of woman that was probably countercultural. In fact, such is still the case today in many parts of the world, including the developed nations. Previously, I have argued that Aquinas does not tie women to social norms or other constraints.[14] In fact, I think that his consideration can be used to free the concept of woman from cultural prejudice, recognizing her equal to man in humanity, while respecting the differences as qualities and not defects.

This reading of Aquinas, as arguing fundamentally for the equality of women, is underscored in his treatment of marriage in the *Summa Contra Gentiles* where he discusses whether marriage ought to be monogamous.[15] He develops the idea that between husband and wife there should exist a friendship and that friendship requires a type of equality. If there is more than one wife (or more than one husband), there could not exist a friendship of free individuals. In fact, it would be more of a servile relationship. He points to the example of men who have many wives; they end up treating them as one might treat a servant rather than treating them as an equal. Of course, this is not particular to polygamy or polyamory and can be a defect in monogamous marriages. But the multiplicity of partners means that there cannot be a close, intimate friendship of equals. Here he returns to the thought of Aristotle's idea of friendship in marriage.

Aquinas goes on to argue against marriages involving incest and child brides because precisely because of the fundamental inequality which would render the close friendship, especially one of virtue, impossible.

At this point in this brief overview, I would like to interject Ephesians 5: 21-33, which is perhaps one of the most controversial biblical texts on women. Unfortunately, the modern ear fixates on 5: 22, some version of "wives be submissive/subordinate" to your husbands. In other works, again with the help of Aquinas, I have offered that this is not a servile type of submission where one gives up one's will as a slave is required to do. Rather, it is an economic submission, one which respects the rights and dignity of all parties involved. We freely, even willingly, engage in such submissions every day. Read carefully, St. Paul puts the onus on husbands more than on wives even though he starts out, "Be subordinate to one another out of reverence for Christ." In some ways, I wonder if this passage isn't a correction of Genesis 3. Nowhere does Paul tell wives to love their husbands. But he repeatedly tells husbands to love their wives and that they should love their wives as Christ loved the Church, laying down his life for her. Wives, instead, are admonished to be subordinate to their husbands as to the Lord. Obviously, one can argue that love is implied there, but it is not explicit. Further, the text is clear that this is all in the context of the husband rising to the example of Our Lord. In other words, no woman is expected to be subject to an abusive husband simply because he is a man. The spousal relationship between Christ and the Church shows us what marriage should be like. Nevertheless, as humans we only live that type of self-gift, union, and intimacy in an analogous manner. Christ and the Church live it perfectly.

## V. Equality of Difference: Leading to a Most Profound Intimacy

Further, in the discourses of the Last Supper, Jesus tells his disciples, "This is my commandment: love one another as I love you. No one has greater love than this, to lay down one's life for one's friends. You are my friends if you do what I command you."[16]

I don't think it's a stretch to say that in marriage, where the husband is called to lay down his life for his wife as Christ did, there should exist a deep friendship as should exist between each soul and Christ, and between Christ and the Church.

Augustine calls original sin the *felix culpa*, the happy fault, because through the incarnation we have the potential to be restored to a state higher than that experienced by Adam and Eve before the Fall. We are invited to become not only sons and daughters of God but friends of God. Aquinas implies that in this capacity, humans are greater than the angels even though the angels are higher in the order of being.[17]

While the Church is dependent on Christ for her existence, Christ has raised humanity in the Church to the level of his equal. This raising also involves very much the movement of Christ. He becomes man, one of us, in order to go beyond restoring us to humanity's original state before the Fall. Indeed, his love is a radical love, but it is only possible in the context of a radical equality where he becomes like us so that we may become like him.

Proverb 27:17 echoes this theme, "Iron sharpens iron and one man sharpens another."[18] Interestingly, Ronald Knox, a 20th century priest, biblical scholar, and author, in his English translation of the Bible, uses the word "friend" in place of "one man," again indicating the intimacy of good and true friends.[19]

Knox, in one of his reflections on the Eucharist, observes that we tend to think that He instituted the Eucharist with bread and wine because they reminded Him of the grace that comes from the Eucharist. However, Knox offers that it's the opposite order. Instead, God gave us bread and wine so that we would eventually understand the Eucharist. Knox writes, "He did not design the Sacred Host to be something like bread. He designed bread to be something like the Sacred Host."[20]

If I may borrow from this, I would offer that the deep friendship that can exist between husband and wife should in fact exist because our experience of marriage informs our understanding of the spousal relationship between Christ and his Church. Put another way, Aquinas taught that grace builds upon nature. If we do not understand something on the natural level, it makes it far more difficult to understand it in the supernatural.

While the differences between women and men may seem even insurmountable at times, we are required to step back in order that we may have perspective so that we can understand that the differences are not the problem. They are part of God's ordained solution to the problem of sin. Seen in a different light, differences can allow for equality.

In fact, the economy of salvation relies upon the created differences existing in creation; perhaps the tendency towards sameness is something we should consider avoiding in particular cases, exercising instead our differences so as to experience both radical equality and radical love.

# RESPONSE

# Understanding Difference: A Theological Reflection

### Rev. Dennis J. Billy, C.Ss.R.

*Robert F. Leavitt Distinguished Service, Chair in Theology, St. Mary's Seminary & University, Baltimore, Maryland*

## Introduction

In her essay, "Equality of Difference: Leading to a Most Profound Intimacy and Friendship," Pia de Solenni makes a convincing argument that, in the covenantal bond of marriage, husband and wife can enjoy a very deep and intimate level of virtue friendship. Referring to the creation accounts in Genesis 1-2, the account of the Fall in Genesis 3, sources in the New Testament, and specific texts in Aristotle and Aquinas, she demonstrates that the differences between women and men are ordained by God to reveal something very deep and intimate about the mystery of Christ and his love for the Church. She takes an analogy from Ronald Knox that God designed bread to reveal to us something about the nature of the Sacred Host and applies it to marriage. "[O]ur experience of marriage," she claims, "informs our understanding of the spousal relationship between Christ and his Church." God, in other words, has given us in marriage a concrete sacramental sign of how Christ relates to his Mystical Body, the Church. Such a claim points to the Church's teaching that one of the ends of marriage is that of the *sacramentum*, the idea that marriage reflects a divine-human reality of a God who not only entered our world in the mystery of the Incarnation, but who also enters the hearts of the faithful by imparting his Spirit to them and enabling them to participate as members of his risen and glorified humanity. In this essay, I would like to use de Solenni's insights on the equality of difference as a point of departure for my own reflection on the nature of difference itself and the role it plays in Catholic theology as a whole.

## A God of Variety

When we look at the world around us, we see that it is full of variety. There is not merely one kind of mineral, plant, and animal—but many. According to our belief as Catholic Christians, the doctrine of Creation affirms that the world came into being as a result of God's providential design and executed by his divine command. All that exists does so "drop by drop," *(guttatim)*. God, in other words, created the world, is creating it moment by moment, and will continue to create it. As St. Bonaventure reminds us in his *Itinerarium*, God has left vestiges of himself in his Creation which can be discovered by the careful, discerning mind. What is more, we believe that he created humanity in his image: "God created mankind in his image; in the image of God he created them; male and female he created them" (Gn 1:27, NAB rev. ed).

This variety in creation points to its source and says something about the variety or differences existing within God himself. The doctrine of the Trinity reminds us that God is Three but also One: Father, Son, and Holy Spirit are distinct from each other by virtue of their immanent relations to one another but also intimately bound to one another in an intimate community of love. When seen in this light, variety (or difference) should not be looked upon as something negative but rather as a positive reflection of the roots of the divine reality from which all things flow. The doctrine of the Trinity reminds us that Otherness and Oneness exist in a deep metaphysical harmony within the Godhead.

Moreover, since action flows from being, it follows that the economical actions of the Trinity—Creation, Redemption, and Sanctification—would also display a certain level of diversity. Thus, we see the diversity of things in Creation, the diversity of Christ's redeeming love as shown through his teachings, miracles, and sacrificial death on the cross, and the myriad sanctifying gifts and fruits of the Holy Spirit. Since God's nature and divine actions contain a harmonious blend of diversity and oneness, of difference and unity within themselves, it follows (indeed, it is to be expected) that we would experience similar things in the world he created.

# V. Equality of Difference: Leading to a Most Profound Intimacy

## A Fallen World

In God's creation, variety and oneness, difference and unity, existed in harmony with each other, without tension or discord. As Catholic Christians, however, we believe we live in a fallen world and that the original harmony with God, ourselves, and creation that was given to us as gift has been broken up.

The story of the fall and the doctrine of original sin remind us that the created world, as we now experience it, does not conform to God's original design. Our first parents, disobeyed God's command by eating of the tree of the knowledge of good and evil, an action that affirmed their desire to place themselves at the center of the moral universe rather than God (Gn 3:1-7). Their fall from grace caused a seminal and universal disruption within our human makeup. Because our first parents were a part of God's creation (and the pinnacle of it), their fall from grace had ripple effects throughout the whole of creation.

This original fall from grace had three consequences. Anthropologically, it meant our minds became darkened, our wills weakened, and our passions disordered and out of sync. We now had to work by the sweat of our brow; men and women experienced tensions in their relations with one another; women experienced the pains of child labor; our bodies experienced disease, death, and final decay. Cosmologically, it meant that the universe experienced discord and corruption that manifested itself in it providing an inhospitable environment for humanity as opposed to a hospitable one. Theologically, it meant that the sin of our first parents created discord with God. We no longer lived in fellowship with him but were banished from the Garden and experienced guilt and shame in our relationship with him.

The Fall of Adam and Eve disrupted the tranquil relations that had previously existed between God, humanity, and the cosmos. To heal the wound caused by humanity's fall, God decided to repair it from the inside out by becoming human, entering our world in the person of Jesus Christ, and taking upon himself the sins of all humanity. Through him, the created world, having fallen, was now to become a redeemed world.

## The Gift of Redemption

After the Fall, God had any number of options before him. He could have destroyed what was left of the world and start over; he could have sent an angel to restore to creation its pristine beauty; he could have simply willed it to happen—to name but a few. Instead, he chose to enter our world and repair it himself by sending his Only Begotten Son to assume our human nature and demonstrate the extent of his love for us by dying on the cross for us.

As St. Athanasius of Alexandria reminds us, "God became man so that man might become divine." The relationship between the human and divine in Jesus Christ (the hypostatic union, as we call it) represents yet another instance where God manifests himself by means of unity in diversity. In the person of Jesus, the two natures remain distinct yet also intimately one. Jesus is One Divine Person with two very different natures: one human; the other divine. In our Christological formulation of the mystery of the Incarnation, the two natures exist in a close, hypostatic union, yet it is the one Person of the Incarnate Word who acts. As the Council of Chalcedon teaches, "the distinction between the two natures was never abolished by their union but the character proper to each of the two natures was preserved as they come together in one Person and one hypostasis."[21]

When he redeemed the world, God did not merely restore it to its original harmonious level of existence but elevated it so it could share deeply in his glorified existence. Jesus' glorified humanity represents the first fruits of this new creation. This same unity in diversity manifests itself in his Mystical Body, the Church, which consists of many members, each with a different role to place in the building up of God's kingdom (1 Cor 12:1-26). It also holds true for the sacramental life of the Church. At the Eucharist, for example, when the priest consecrates bread formed from many grains of wheat that have been crushed, watered, kneaded, and baked into a life-sustaining food. He also consecrates wine, which has been formed by the crushing of grapes, extracting juice from them, and giving it time to ferment to produce a drink that warms the heart and fosters fellowship in the human family. Acting in *persona Christi*, the priest extends his hands over these works of human hands, and the Spirit of God transforms them into the Body and Blood of Christ, enabling those who receive it to commune with Jesus. In the Eucharist, God has transformed the many into One Bread and One Body.

The point here is that variety (and therefore difference) exists at the very heart of the Trinitarian, Christological, Ecclesiological, and Sacramental mysteries. It also exists (albeit with varying degrees of integration) in the first Creation, the fallen Creation, and the New Creation. It is little wonder that it exists in humanity's many diverse cultures, languages, races, religions, and ethnic backgrounds. God is a God of variety. Created in his image and likeness, it follows that humanity itself would be one full of variety. Since "grace perfects nature," as Aquinas reminds us in his *Summa theologiae*, it follows that humanity's perfection lies in the mystery of the Triune God, where unity and diversity coexist in an intimate communion of divine love. St. Augustine, the author of the *Confessions* puts it so well: "Thou hast made us for thyself, O Lord, and our heart is restless until it finds its rest in thee."

## Conclusion

All of this brings us back to the original question about the differences between men and women. Although some may object, most people see things very plainly. Men and women are different on physical, psychological (emotional), even spiritual levels. Because of the mystery of the Incarnation, theology and anthropology are now closely related and deeply intertwined. The reality of God becoming man—the Divine Logos taking on human spirit, mind, and flesh—makes this a necessity. An honest assessment of the man-and-woman relationship must be seen in this light. Three different perspectives come to mind: (1) the feminine in man versus the male in the feminine; (2) the image of God planted in each human individual, and (3) the image of God present in the male-female relationship itself, especially in the sacrament of marriage. Let us take each of these levels.

That woman was taken from a rib from Adam's side in the account from Genesis indicates that men have an unconscious feminine side to their psyches. The fact that his rib was taken from him while he was asleep (Gn 2:21-22) indicates that he was unconscious of this feminine side of his personality and that Eve was given to him as a way of getting in touch with it. When seen in this light, women are meant to help men get in touch with their feminine side, while men are called to do just the opposite for women, who need men in order to help them get in touch with their unconscious masculine side. In this sense men and women have an intrinsic need for one another. Each reaches its fulfillment in relationship to the other. Their differences are not opposed but actually complement one another.

On the second level, it is important to recognize that, as individuals, God has created man and woman in his image and likeness in their own right. This image is typically referred to as the image of God imprinted in the threefold powers of the soul: intellect, memory, and will. Although criticized by some as being too individualistic and even inward looking, it carries a great deal of weight within the Christian tradition and should not be easily discarded. The human person *does* reflect God's image: intellect, memory, and will say something about how each human person is created in the image and likeness of God.

On the third level, the key verse in Genesis reads: "God created man in his image; in the divine image he created him; male and female he created them" (Gn 1:27). This verse indicates that God created humanity in both the singular ("he created him") and in the plural ("he created them"). This dual description points to a dual way that God has implanted his image in humanity. He has done so first in the threefold powers of the soul (intellect, will, and memory), but he has also done so in the very relationship between man and woman itself. In some way, the image of the Trinitarian God has been implanted in the very way they relate to one another. Just as Father and Son are bound by the Holy Spirit in an intimate bond of love, so do man and woman enter, at marriage, into a holy covenant of love that reflects the love of God for humanity and of Christ for his Church.

These three levels reveal the extent of God's love for humanity and the task he sets before us during our earthly pilgrimage. He calls all of us to be in communion with the feminine (or masculine) side of our unconscious awareness. He also asks us to get in touch with and polish, by the help of God's grace, the divine image he has planted in our intellect, memory and will. Finally, he wishes us to honor and respect the way he manifests himself in the relationship between the sexes in holy matrimony. As de Solenni righty points out, in marriage, men and women are capable

## V. Equality of Difference: Leading to a Most Profound Intimacy

of "a most profound intimacy and friendship." The extent to which such close, intimate friendships between men and women can exist outside the marriage covenant still needs to be discussed. Although men and women are all on a journey and must employ proper boundaries, as well as prudent and virtuous means in working toward their desired goals, history has shown that holy and chaste friendships between men and woman can exist and be mutually supportive in their vocations of celibacy. Rooted in their love for Christ, the spiritual friendships of St. Francis and St. Clare; St. Francis de Sales and St. Jane Frances de Chantal; and St. John Paul II and St. Teresa of Calcutta offer concrete evidence of the possibility for such relationships. Celibate priests (and other male celibates) need to learn how to develop friendships with women that are spiritual, intimate, and chaste. Developing an intimate friendship with the Blessed Mother and female saints may open up a way to reaching such a goal.

# VI

# Discovering the Gaze of the Virgin: Facing the Impact of Clerical Sexual Abuse on Women's Capacity for Spiritual and Physical Motherhood

### Lisa Lickona

*Assistant Professor of Systematic Theology, Saint Bernard's School of Theology and Ministry, Rochester, New York*

## Introduction

The starting point for my reflections is the very grave wound that is incurred when a member of the clergy abuses a woman. Man dominates woman, reducing her to an object of his gratification. Precisely because sexuality is not simply "skin-deep," this attack goes to the core of her self-understanding, her relationship with her own body, and, most profoundly, her relation to God who is both Creator and Redeemer. Her *dignity* (to use John Paul II's term) is assaulted, and thus her *vocation* as wife and mother, both physical and spiritual, is threatened. Deeply undermined by the man who rejects her as "gift," the woman experiences a diminishment of her capacity to herself become "self-gift" to her future or present husband and children.

In this chapter, I desire to contribute to the healing of this deep wound by providing a meditation on the concept of "virginity." This may seem to be a very strange way into the topic at hand. Yet, I ask you to bear with me as I unfold this idea. What we have before us in this sad situation, it seems to me, are at once *two* vulnerable populations. First are the women who have been deeply wounded. Not only have they suffered a sexual assault, but these women are *in the Church*: they regularly rely on the sacramental system of the Church for their sustenance (found at the altar of the Lord) and their healing (sought in the confessional). After their abuse, though, they find themselves suddenly and dramatically cut off from those sources of strength and consolation. The Church's sacramental system is mediated through the humanity of the man who acts *in persona Christi,* but for these women, the priest is now the face of the abuser. Precisely those things that formerly offered hope and solace now cause pain and traumatic responses.

We are faced with a serious problem. How will such a woman find healing? How will she be able to encounter Christ again? After this violation, how can the Church communicate to her that she is loved, accepted, and indeed cherished?

But on the other side of this encounter are priests, and here I am thinking of all those men who will have to face the wounds inflicted by others and pastorally attend to their victims. We need to think about how so many men "slipped through the cracks" of an ecclesial education intended to prepare them to give their lives in selfless love to the Church. And, perhaps even more importantly, we need to prepare the young would-be priests of today to become the future face of Christ the Bridegroom, that they might be present to the women whom their brother priests have deeply hurt.

A recent conversation suggested a way forward. A priest friend of mine who leads a youth group for seventh and eighth graders was telling me about the activities that he engages in with the young people in anticipation of their participation in the annual March for Life in Washington, D.C. He said that when they discuss the reality of abortion, what it is and what it means, both for themselves and in the wider cultural context, he tells the students that the problem of abortion "always begins with us." "Thinking about how a child comes from the sexual union of a man and woman," Father Roberto told me, "becomes a moment for the young people—especially the eighth-graders—to think about how boys and girls look at each other."

This conversation struck me deeply, as it expressed in simple terms exactly what I would like to present in this chapter. In talking to young people, Father Roberto does not present abortion as an evil that afflicts only children who are killed, or women who are forced into abortion by their circumstances, or even men who lose their chance to be fathers. All of these things about the scourge of abortion are true. But not one of them

# VI. Discovering the Gaze of the Virgin

implicates *me*, my way of life. But, in fact, as Father Roberto points out, we *are all* implicated in sexual sin precisely because each of us is created as either male or female and has within us a power to "look at each other," that is, to look at the other of the opposite sex in a way that either elevates and generates the other or degrades and defiles them. This way of looking, which proceeds from the heart, before any sexual contact between a man and a woman even occurs, is the tragic source of the evils of abortion that are visited on man, woman, and, of course, the child.

In the same way, the problem of clerical abuse of women involves a tragic violation of a woman by a man. And, I would hold, its "solution," the possibility of healing, both for the victims and for the entire Church, lies in a similar encounter, a look of love.

This "way of looking" is what Luigi Giussani refers to when he speaks of "virginity." Following him, I present virginity as a way of looking at and interacting with reality, an expression of a unitive love that is present paradigmatically in Christ. The virginal gaze expresses the way that Christ himself loves. I hope to show, further, that this concept of the virginal gaze is deeply correspondent with the heart of John Paul II's theological anthropology and, as such, should be integrated into our way of educating men and women in the tradition of that Pontiff's thought. Finally, I want to begin to explore what this virginal gaze can mean, how it can be a moment of healing and the beginning of a new and fruitful relationship between man and woman in the Church.

This wider reflection on the virginal gaze draws from the lives of two different saints: Maria Goretti and Mary Magdalene. Maria is a figure of the twentieth century, an eleven-year-old girl who was murdered after an attempted rape and canonized some forty years later as a virgin-martyr. Mary Magdalene is perhaps the main woman of the Gospels (other than the Mother of God), a sufferer from the personal disintegration that is caused by demonic infestation, and who was healed by Christ and, in following him, becomes the first to see him in resurrected form and to announce that fact. Both are figures of womanhood that have fascinated and challenged our notions of gender and sex. But ultimately, both women's lives turn on a fundamental encounter with the man, Jesus Christ. Both encounter and live a different way of looking at reality because Christ has looked at them—and this leads them to live a fulfilled personal integrity, which we call sanctity. In the Christian dispensation, this integrity becomes a gift to us insofar as their subjectivity, the inner dynamisms of their lives, are offered to us as objective points of reflection and, finally, sources of grace for our own lives.

## Maria Goretti

On July 6, 1902, Maria Goretti, the eleven-year-old daughter of Italian peasant farmers, died, a victim of a brutal stabbing and attempted rape.[1] In 1950, Maria was canonized as a virgin martyr: a woman who suffered death rather than yield to an assault on her virginal purity.[2] Yet, while it is true that Maria defended herself from the assault of her attacker, twenty-year-old Alessandro Serenelli, Maria's virtue was not, first of all, one of self-defense.[3] As Alessandro later admitted, in the moment of the attack, Maria's concern was *for him*. As he brandished a butcher knife over her, insisting that she yield to his demand for sex, Maria called out "Don't do it... It is a sin... You will go to hell!" In this moment, Maria's first thought was not for *her* purity, but *his* eternal soul.

The next day, shortly before she succumbed to the fourteen stab-wounds, Maria renewed this profession. Asked by the priest who came to offer her Viaticum whether she forgave Alessandro, Maria gave an answer that it is almost impossible to imagine issuing from the lips of an eleven-year-old girl in severe pain and on the verge of death: "Yes, I forgive him for the love of Jesus... and I want him to come with me to Paradise... I want him at my side... May God forgive him, because I have already forgiven him."

Six years later, Maria made good on these words by "coming" to Alessandro as he languished in prison, serving a thirty-year term; she appeared to him in a dream and offered him her forgiveness. Alessandro's depression lifted, and he became a model prisoner. Upon his release, he visited Maria's mother and asked her for her forgiveness. For the last twenty-four years of his life, he was a lay brother among the Friars Minor Capuchin. He spoke often of Maria as "his little saint" and prayed to her daily, and, perhaps most telling: Alessandro's own testimony was included in the process of Maria's canonization.

# VI. Discovering the Gaze of the Virgin

## What is a "Virgin"?

Since ancient times, Christians have expressed great wonder before the witness of the *virgin martyr*. If a woman will endure death rather than permit herself to be violated by a man, then "virginity" is not all about physical integrity. It must have an eternal value. And indeed, the Church has followed Christ in affirming that virginity has a prophetic dimension: "some have renounced marriage for the sake of the kingdom of heaven" (Matt 19:12). Accordingly, ancient virgin martyrs like Lucy and Agatha insisted on physical purity as a sign of a profession that had been made to Christ, the pledge of their complete belonging. To remain a virgin and to die for it was to die for Christ, the spouse to whom they had united themselves. In doing so, these women gave witness to an eschatological reality, the ultimate destiny of the soul: union with Christ.

In Maria, we are able to see the flowering of the virginal witness as a full participation in Christ's redemptive love that seeks union with us. The virgin is the one who experiences herself as belonging wholly to Christ, and *the fruit of this union is a lived awareness of others in union with him, a lived desire for their happiness and final destiny.*[4] As she is dying, Maria wants Alessandro to join her in heaven. This is the fullest expression of Maria's sanctity: her gaze upon the man who would have raped her, who had mortally wounded her, with the desire that he be drawn with her into eternal communion. And its most outstanding result is just that: Alessandro's complete conversion, his turning toward Christ through Maria, his sister in Christ, who becomes his intercessor.

Maria's story draws both victim and perpetrator into a single drama that revolves around her act of love and forgiveness, a life-giving, generative act at the center of a violent attack. Moreover, this is truly a witness for our time, in which we are becoming more and more aware of sexual violations of women by men.

We should not be surprised. God sends saints to lead us and teach us. The saints are those who bring to life an aspect of the Christian mystery in their own flesh, giving us a way into the mystery, a point of contemplation. The value of Maria's witness is that she suggests to us a new way of living, and through her ongoing intercession, invites us to join her in it.

So, what is it we might learn from Maria?

I would suggest that in the gaze of this young woman threatened with rape and murder we encounter something greater even than the brutal evil of sexual assault. Something else breaks in—or, we might better say, Someone. I would suggest that Maria's gaze is Christ's own gaze upon Alessandro. When Alessandro strikes out in terror it is not merely because sex has been refused to him. It is because in Maria's gaze, he sees Christ. In this way, the virgin martyr is true martyr: she is killed *in odium fidei*, out of hatred for Christ, who has become flesh in the one whom he has taken as spouse.

But how can we understand such a gaze as something that is of value for all of us? How can "virginity" become a useful concept for all persons, not just those who are living this as a form of life? How can it be offered even as a starting point for those eighth graders to whom Father Roberto is speaking? Here we really have to go deeper into what "virginity" could mean.

In the Church's tradition, the virgin or celibate is one who lives a certain path of renunciation. He or she renounces marriage, with all its physical joys and physical fruit, for the sake of the kingdom. Thus, he or she becomes a sign for the "rest of us" of an exclusive love-relationship with Christ that is the destiny of all souls.

Following the tradition, Luigi Giussani teaches that "Those who do not marry because of love for Christ must make this affection transparent in every relationship they live, with everyone. They must be a sign of His presence, a sign that provokes every man."[5] Virginity is the sign of that radical way of loving that has entered the world in Jesus Christ, and the virgin is called to aspire to such love.

In a recent essay, scholar Paolo Prosperi helpfully unfolds Giussani's thought. For Giussani, virginity is "a possession in detachment."[6] As Prosperi explains, by identifying virginity in this way, Giussani is not in any way making unnecessary the sorts of renunciation that characterize the life of the virgin or celibate, but rather he is "highlighting something more important: the end of this detachment and sacrifice. When truly embraced in and for Christ, it is not the annihilation of the impetus of love, but rather a different and fuller form of union with that which one loves."[7]

Virginity understood thus "is a way of relating to reality that allows for a fuller possession, one that is a genuine foretaste of the modality that the

# VI. Discovering the Gaze of the Virgin

blessed will enjoy in their relation with things, and especially with people, in the kingdom of heaven." —a modality that we see unfold in the witness of Maria Goretti.

In keeping with the notion that love is itself a "unitive power" (Thomas Aquinas' *vis unitiva*), Prosperi highlights a second definition of virginity that is prominent in Giussani: virginity is a way of "relating to things according to their truth." He goes on:

> How can one make sense of such a claim? It is important to see, first of all, that the noblest form of possession, at least in the case of human beings, is knowing the truth of something. I can passionately kiss and embrace a glass, but if I do not know it is a glass, I cannot possess it with the same fullness as someone who instead quietly pours some good Brunnello and drinks from it. To possess something in a *human* way means first of all to understand what that thing is and then relate to it in the full respect of that truth. This helps us to understand why Giussani's second definition of virginity, the relating to things according to their truth, only appears to have nothing to do with sex or chastity. As a matter of fact, in order genuinely to appreciate something, which is to say, to understand it, one needs to remain at a certain distance, to maintain a certain detachment.[8]

In this account, detachment is not primarily negative, but positive. Giussani was fond of saying that we cannot appreciate a painting with our nose up against it. In order to love it, we must draw back from it. Thus, the positive function of detachment in the life of the virgin is the creation of the possibility of a contemplative gaze on the world; renunciation makes opens a space of reverence.

Moreover—and this is key for our concerns--for Giussani, such reverence is not limited to the love of those who live virginity in the world. He often insists, with vehemence even, that genuine married love has the same form:

> To truly love a person, you need detachment: does a man adore his woman more when he looks at her from one meter away, in

awe at the being he has before him, almost on his knees, even if he's standing, almost on his knees in front of her; or, when he takes her for himself? No! No, when he takes her for himself, it's over.[9]

Thus, for Giussani, genuine marital love implies a "virginal" relation to one's spouse. It is important to note that in this teaching, Giussani is not laying aside sexual love or trading it in for some sort of spiritualized replacement. Rather, in his teaching on virginity, he is unfolding an integral element of love, *all love*, including the love that involves mutual physical possession, the love of man and woman.[10]

**The Gaze of Love**

We have thus reached an interesting point of intersection with the thought of Pope Saint John Paul II, for such a gaze of wonder is precisely at the heart of his presentation of the first encounter of man and woman "in the beginning." Let us turn to this account to deepen our understanding of virginity as a "way of looking at the other."

As is well known, in his *Theology of the Body*, John Paul II engages the two creation accounts of the book of Genesis. In the first creation account (the "Priestly" account), the human person appears as the final work of God's creation, which occurs over six days (Gen 1:1-2:3).[11] The late pontiff characterizes this first account as "theological," "cosmological," and "metaphysical." It is a more "objective account" corresponding to a definition of who or what the human person is. In it, the human person appears at the pinnacle of creation. He alone is made in God's image and likeness and thus is capable of a unique relationship with God the Creator. In both instantiations, as male and female, the human person is called to fruitfulness and dominion over the earth.[12]

John Paul II then turns to the second "Yahwist" account. An older strand, this account is "psychological" and "mythical," and hence more closely tied to man in his "subjectivity."[13] John Paul II uses this account to unfold the *fundamental interior experiences of man and woman* that correspond to the definition that is given in the first account. What is it to be made "in the image of God"? To be endowed with reason and will? To be male and

## VI. Discovering the Gaze of the Virgin

female? To be called to dominion and fruitfulness? All of these questions are engaged in depth.

In the second account, man (*ha 'adam*) is created from the dust of the earth, enlivened by God's own breath, and set in a garden among the animals. Asked by God to name the animals, man finds "no suitable partner" for himself, an experience that God judges to be "not good" (Gen 2:18-19). God then puts the man to sleep and from his side forms a second human being:

> So the LORD God cast a deep sleep on the man, and while he was asleep, he took out one of his ribs and closed up its place with flesh. The LORD God then built up into a woman the rib that he had taken from the man. When he brought her to the man, the man said: "This one, at last, is bone of my bones and flesh of my flesh; This one shall be called 'woman,'" for out of 'her man' this one has been taken." That is why a man leaves his father and mother and clings to his wife, and the two of them become one body (Gen 2:21-24).

From this account, John Paul II draws out two points that are important for our current concern. First, he argues that everything that happens in this account up to the moment in which the woman is formed from man's side refers to men and women *equally*.[14] Here he defers to the Hebrew text, which uses the generic term *ha 'adam* for "man": "It is not good for the man (*ha 'adam*) to be alone." *Ha 'adam*, John Paul II notes, refers to the human person in a general sense (a point that is totally obscured by the fact that "Adam" then becomes the name of the first male human being). Taken in context, gender differentiation does not appear until the moment when this new human person is formed from "man's" rib. This is signaled by the first use of the gender-specific nouns *'ish* and *ishshah*: "Here at last is bone of my bones and flesh of my flesh: this one shall be called woman (*ishshah*) because she was taken out of her man (*'ish*)."

This analysis makes it possible for John Paul II to discern in the moment before the creation of woman, the moment in which *ha 'adam* is found to be "alone," a fundamental *human* experience, which he calls "original solitude." On the one hand, this solitude is a positive experience in that it reveals to the human person what it is to be made in the image of God. Placed in the garden by God and given the task of naming the animals, he discovers himself to be a creature-in-relation. He alone can realize that he *is* alone, and this self-awareness is clearly the result of a test that God has given him. Thus, the experience of original solitude is one of an "I" in front of a "you": "The created man finds himself from the first moment of his existence *before God* in search of his own being, as it were; one could say, in search of his own definition; today one would say, in search of his own 'identity.'"[15]

In this search, man discovers that he is a self-conscious, self-determining person, endowed with a body that is made to work creatively on the earth. In other words, original solitude is a subjective experience of his unique *dignity*. "Man is 'alone': this is to say that through his own humanity, through what he is, he is at the same time set into a unique, exclusive, and unrepeatable relationship with God himself."[16]

However, *at first*, this human person does not comprehend the goodness of this solitude, signaled by God's observation that "it is *not good* for man to be alone." Not until he wakes from his divinely imposed sleep (what John Paull II calls a "return to non-being") does the human person experience solitude as fundamentally positive. And this happens precisely when *ha 'adam* awakens to find himself *in front of another human being*. Seeing this new person, different from all the other creatures, the man lets out a joyful cry: "Here at last is bone of my bones and flesh of my flesh: this one shall be called woman (*'ishshah*) because she was taken out of her man (*'ish*)" (Gen 2:23-25).

The man cries out in wonder before the woman who is the answer to his loneliness; it is a wonderfully comprehensive vision. In receiving the woman who is "for him," he beholds her as gift, the authentic answer to his solitude. In her reality as gift, he sees the Giver that stands behind her being, the Creator God. In addition, through her goodness, her giftedness, he encounters the full truth of creation itself: *everything* is a gift. Where before the single human person before God was filled with a sense of loneliness, now, as two "I's," as two persons facing each other, man and woman are charged with wonder and awe: how great is every living thing, how precious are all things in the light of this encounter of love!

Moreover, in this moment, man is given an intimate experience of his *own* personal value. In the woman who is "like him," the man can see for the first time the full goodness and value of his very self. He too is created for his own sake, in a unique relation with his Creator, and yet he is, at the same time, called to realize himself through generous self-gift. He is created from love and for love.[17] And the woman's experience is the same: through the man's eyes, as it were, she sees her own divinely willed goodness.

John Paul II emphasizes that, precisely through this experience of "original unity," man and woman recall each other to that original solitude that is "man's original virginal value."[18] In this way, he draws on the idea of virginity as we discussed above: the virgin points to the reality of the person made for communion with God. Yet, can we not see in John Paul II's analysis of this first encounter of man and woman Giussani's idea of a "possession in detachment"? Even as the original unity of the first man and woman is sealed through their physical union--"*That is why* a man leaves his father and mother and clings to his wife, and the two of them become one body"—this experience unfolds *within a gaze of love that contemplates the other in the full truth of their creation.*

**The Abused Woman**

But here, precisely in the context of the "beatifying beginning," we run up against a possible objection to our project of considering virginity as a useful way to approach the profound difficulties in the relations between men and women which are made obvious in the problem of clerical abuse of women. Doesn't all this emphasis on the virginal gaze enshrine a sort of Pollyanna version of man and woman, an almost unimaginable ideal that runs the risk of further marginalizing the women who have suffered abuse? At this point, it becomes critical to go deeper into the experience of the abused woman and the extent to which she is liberated through an encounter that happens in time, in the midst of our *fallen* state.

In *Mulieris Dignitatem*, John Paul II has done just that. In this text, he presents an extended meditation on Christ's culturally ground-breaking approach to women. As the Pontiff emphasizes, over and over in the Gospels, Christ looks with his full human and masculine gaze upon the woman who has been wounded by a man. John Paul II takes the woman caught in adultery as a paradigm.[19] She has sinned, to be sure, but now she is being accused by men who believe themselves to be, by virtue of their position within the Jewish societal structure, free from any guilt. They take refuge in their positions, while the woman has been left out in the open, to face her "punishment," a deadly stoning, alone.

The tenderness with which Christ approaches this woman is specifically linked to how he looks at her. According to the Pope, in this moment, Christ sees her in the context of her original creation, in that original unity willed by God.

> The man was also entrusted by the Creator to the woman—they were *entrusted to each other as persons* made in the image and likeness of God himself. . . . This test is meant for both of them—man and woman—from the "beginning." After original sin, contrary forces are at work in man and woman as a result of the threefold concupiscence, the "stimulus of sin." They act from deep within the human being. Thus Jesus will say in the Sermon on the Mount: *"Every one who looks at a woman lustfully has already committed adultery with her in his heart"* (Mt 5:28). These words, addressed directly to man, show the fundamental truth of his responsibility vis-a-vis woman: her dignity, her motherhood, her vocation.[20]

This is a striking passage because of the way John Paul II characterizes Christ's gaze upon the woman. Christ sees her not just in relation to her husband or the men who would stone her, but rather, in this moment, he looks at her through the eyes of her Creator, who has created woman in relation to man. In the light of the "original unity" that man and woman share, Christ calls *man* to task for the way that he has looked at the woman.

In this context, John Paul II references Christ's teaching on "lust." To our modern ears, this might seem laughable. Whatever place sexual passion had in the scenario is long since past; here we are dealing with violence against a woman. But the choice is not arbitrary, for in his teaching on lust, John Paul II has highlighted the anthropological depth of the relation between man and woman—not just *this* man and *this* woman, but men and women in general. The "look of lust"[21] represents the universal temptation of a man to "look" at a woman in order to dominate her.

## VI. Discovering the Gaze of the Virgin

In the *Theology of the Body*, the late Pontiff unfolds the concept of lust over several addresses. What is important for us here is the way that the lustful look functions as a sort of foil to the virginal gaze. For John Paul II, lust begins in the heart, with a fundamental rejection of God as Creator, as Giver, and therefore of all that is gift: the self, the other, the entirety of creation. The look of lust expresses a precise way of "knowing" that "reduces" the woman. It is a "restriction, as it were, or closure of the horizon of the mind and heart."[22] For the man who succumbs to the temptation of lust, the woman is no longer a human subject with an eternal destiny. Rather, she is formatted as an object, a means to an end that he himself has determined.

Returning to Giussani's notion of virginity within marriage helps us understand what John Paul II means. The mutual "possession" of man and woman requires, at its heart, a reverent beholding, a detachment, to remain true to the other. But lust, driven by concupiscence, seeks to "possess" through a reductive knowledge: the woman is known only insofar as she is something that will satisfy my desires.[23] Hence the "look of lust" is a deformation of the original gaze of man upon woman. It is a "knowing" that seeks to reduce the woman, until she is nothing but an impersonal object.

It is thus not at all surprising that lust can result in violence, as it does with Alessandro and Maria,[24] as it does with the men who intend to stone the woman caught in adultery. Giving into his temptation to dominate the woman who is no longer truly "other," no longer seen as an equal, a helper, man formats her as raw matter upon which he works his schemes—whether for power or sex. Giussani is blunt about this: taking a woman without the appropriate detachment is a sort of violence. "What is immediate binds, enchains, until one is strangled. . . The immediate strangles us."[25]

But what about the impact on the woman who is thus objectified? Although John Paul II does not undertake an analysis of the effect of man's look of lust upon a woman, we can guess at the profound impact that this abuse causes by going even deeper into the way that the man and woman each experience their "I" to be fulfilled through the encounter with the other.

In *Mulieris Dignitatem,* John Paul II expands upon the experience of original unity by showing how the interplay of love and self-discovery, which is apparent in original unity, continues in the conception and birth of a child. The encounter of man and woman through the gift of the child changes both man and woman in relation to each other. Yielding herself to her husband, a woman becomes a mother, setting off a series of biophysical processes that only the woman has access to. Her body is in some ways taken over for the sake of the new life of another human being. But the experience of becoming a mother, if it is embraced by the woman, has the capacity to awaken a deep change within her. When a woman lets this reality change her, she discovers a spiritual vocation, a new way of relating to everything, precisely through the encounter with the child:

> Motherhood involves a special communion with the mystery of life as it develops in the woman's womb. The mother is filled with wonder at this mystery of life and "understands" with unique intuition what is happening inside her. In the light of the "beginning," the mother accepts and loves as a person the child she is carrying in her womb. This unique contact with the new human being developing within her gives rise to an attitude towards human beings—not only toward her own child, but every human being—which profoundly marks the woman's personality.[26]

If the woman discovers herself as mother before the person of the child, man discovers himself as father in front of the woman. Now man must stand back and await *her* initiative, which becomes paramount for his own self-understanding:

> It is commonly thought that women are more capable than men of paying attention to another person, and that motherhood develops this predisposition even more. The man—even with all his sharing in parenthood—always remains "outside" the process of pregnancy and the baby's birth; in many ways he has to learn his own "fatherhood" from the mother.[27]

## VI. Discovering the Gaze of the Virgin

As John Paul II repeatedly emphasized, women's particular *genius* is her capacity to receive the other as other. She points man to the world of persons:

> Perhaps more than men, women *acknowledge the person,* because they see persons with their hearts. They see them independently of various ideological or political systems. They see others in their greatness and limitations; they try to go out to them and *help them.*[28]

In the light of this, we can begin to surmise the depth of damage that sexual abuse can wreak on a woman. Precisely because a woman is more keenly attuned to the person, the woman can be more profoundly wounded in the realm of personal relation, especially by sexual assault which happens within the context of an already established relationship like that between a woman and someone she trusts or looks up to. After the woman has suffered this sort of objectification by a man, the temptation is that she comes to see herself entirely "through his eyes," internalizing the man's reductive gaze. She is undermined in her capacity for relation to God, herself, men, and children.

Is it a stretch to see in many of the sufferings that are exclusive to women the very effects of this objectification and reduction of the woman? An experience of abuse causes a devastating dissolution of the unity of her person, which plays out in self-abusive behaviors.[29] Moreover, the impact of such internalization can create a cycle of abuse, whereby a woman, unable to see herself in any way other than as an object, repeatedly falls in with a man who will hurt her. And, most sadly, the woman who cannot see her own personal value finds it challenging to see the child as a vulnerable other. The child becomes a problem to be erased.

But what John Paul II's analysis makes clear is how the woman's suffering is man's as well. When woman cannot fulfill her task of motherhood, man is shut out from fatherhood. A human future, not to mention the future of the Church's fatherly priesthood, depends on helping both men and women come to see each other in the light of their eternal destiny, the plan that God has had for them since "the beginning."

## Mary Magdalene

But, as John Paul II makes clear, the seeds of this renewal have already been sown in Christ's own gaze upon women. Among them, Mary Magdalene stands out as one who has suffered profound personal damage, and yet has known liberation through her encounter with the One who has seen, known, and loved her. What is it for a woman who has experienced abuse by someone she deeply trusts to come to Christ, to be seen by Christ? And what happens in the sphere of that gaze?

We can begin by asking what it is to be seen by Christ at all. There are many accounts of this in the Gospels. John and Andrew, Zacchaeus, Mary Magdalene, the woman at the well—all of these people meet Jesus and are profoundly converted by the encounter. Their relationship with everything changes. They give away what they have. They forsake family relations. They begin to "follow" him and to tell others about him. It seems that a true encounter with Jesus can do nothing but evoke profound changes in a person.

Yet, in these moments, Christ never wrests anyone's attention. He doesn't argue anyone into submission. In fact, there is little evidence that people are profoundly converted solely by *listening* to Christ's teaching. The Apostles here are the paradigm. John and Andrew follow after him after he invites them to "come and see" the place where he is staying. They spend an afternoon with him. Clearly, they are deeply attracted to him; Andrew cannot help but bring his brother Simon to Jesus (Jn 1:35-42), and when Jesus appears on the beach as they mend their nets and calls them to follow him, they come willingly, leaving their former lives—and presumably wives and children—to stay close to this new Rabbi (Mk 1:16-18).

And yet, the Gospels repeated show how, even after this dramatic detachment from everything they hold dear, the disciples are often perplexed by Christ's teaching (see, for example, Mk 6:52, Lk 18:34). They are less "bowled over" by argument than, we may say, under the sway of a charismatic personality.[30] Jesus attracts these men so powerfully that even when they sin, as Peter does by a threefold denial, they cannot help wanting to be with him, desiring to remain close to him. "You know I love you

Lord," Peter repeats three times, a profession of an affection that persists, despite the sense of sorrow he has for his sin (Jn 21:15-18).

The dramatic changes that we see happening in those that follow Christ draw us to a consideration of Christ himself. How did Christ affect these changes in those who followed him? Here we are at the heart of the concept of virginity, this "possession in detachment," a way of interacting with every person according to his or her destiny.[31]

We know that in each of these encounters, Christ loves first. And his love is of the highest sort. He describes it himself in John 17:26, when he prays to the Father with the Apostles gathered around him: "I made known to them your name and I will make it known, that the love with which you loved me may be in them and I in them." Christ draws each and every man and woman into that same love by which he himself is loved by the Father, the Father who professes at Christ's Baptism: "This is my Beloved Son, with whom I am well-pleased" (Mt 3:17). That is to say that each man and woman that he meets is received by Christ as gift. He sees each one in the truth of their creation: "God saw all things and behold they are good" (Gen 1:31). In this way, Christ's gaze on his followers is truly that of the last Adam on the new Eve, the Church. And as the Bridegroom he is, he desires to lay down his life for us (cf. Eph 5:25-27).

What a man and woman encounter in Christ is precisely the love of the one who comes to do the Father's will, the love of the one who becomes man, lives among us, suffers, and dies for us. It is a love that seeks to serve us, renew us, recreate us. This self-giving, immolating love is intrinsic to Christ's virginal gaze:

> The virgin is the one who, in looking at a human face, is given to pierce through it and perceive the abyssal mystery concealed within... A disinterested love born from looking upon a beautiful creature becomes, in Christ, a generous readiness to lay down one's life for the salvation of each and every creature. Jesus Christ is able to glimpse in even the most disfigured face the radiance of the boundless love that chose and called this face into being. [32]

This is the love that Mary Magdalene encounters. And who *is* Mary Magdalene? She is a woman "out of whom he had driven seven demons"

(Mk 16:9). Simply from this fact, we can infer that Mary has suffered such dramatic abuse at the hands of another—probably many others—that she has become vulnerable to demonic possession, the ultimate form of the dissolution of the "I," the total rejection of the gift that a person is. Mary has known such objectification that her very person has become a platform for demonic manipulation and manifestation. What is left for a woman in this situation? The woman who has been thus reduced turns to "using" her own body herself to make her way in the world, selling her "self" for the sake of survival. Although modern exegetes steer clear of identifying Mary with the unnamed "sinner" who anoints the feet of Jesus, she is certainly a sister-sufferer to that woman.[33]

The Gospels do not recount Christ's healing of Mary nor what her reaction to that was beyond the fact that she was among the women who "accompanied him" (Lk 8:2-3). This following will bring Mary all the way to the foot of the cross (Mk 15:40; Mt 27:56; Jn 19:25; Lk 23:49), and finally to the empty tomb (Jn 20: 1-18). Here, we can see the full measure of Mary's healing:

> Mary stayed outside the tomb weeping. And as she wept, she bent over into the tomb and saw two angels in white sitting there, one at the head and one at the feet where the body of Jesus had been. And they said to her, "Woman, why are you weeping?" She said to them, "They have taken my Lord, and I don't know where they laid him." When she had said this, she turned around and saw Jesus there, but did not know it was Jesus. Jesus said to her, "Woman, why are you weeping? Whom are you looking for?" She thought it was the gardener and said to him, "Sir, if you carried him away, tell me where you laid him, and I will take him." Jesus said to her, "Mary!" She turned and said to him in Hebrew, "Rabbouni," which means Teacher. Jesus said to her, "Stop holding on to me, for I have not yet ascended to the Father. But go to my brothers and tell them, 'I am going to my Father and your Father, to my God and your God.'" Mary of Magdala went and announced to the disciples, "I have seen the Lord," and what he told her (Jn 20:11-18).

## VI. Discovering the Gaze of the Virgin

In a significant way, this passage draws together all that we have been saying. Mary longs for her beloved Lord. She weeps alone in the garden, hoping to find him. And Christ comes to her with astounding tenderness: "Woman, why are you weeping?" When she tells him what she most desires—to find him who is her life and love—he reveals himself to her by calling her by name: "Mary." Full of joy, Mary throws her arms around him, as if to possess him. But even as she does, Christ offers her something unexpected: distance. "Stop holding onto me."

Traditional depictions of this moment tend to present Mary as the former harlot, grasping at the person of Christ, with Christ almost pushing her away, as though defending his physical purity. Yet, in the light of the deeper understanding of virginity we have developed here, we can see how incomplete these images are. In his admonition, "do not hold on to me," Christ is urging Mary to stand back from him, but he is not rebuking her. Rather, he is showing her that he alone can restore the reverent distance that her soul needs—that she might see him, but also that he might see her and love her.

Three indications show that what is at stake in this scene is not merely "purity," that Christ is not simply telling Mary to avoid physical interaction with him.

First of all, Mary's touch of Christ happens after he calls her by name and after and she has "turned," a phrase that John uses to indicate conversion. When Mary touches Christ she is *already* converted in her heart.

Moreover, we know from the other Resurrection appearances that Christ *wants to be touched*. When Jesus appears to the disciples in Luke, they are frightened that he is a ghost. "Why are you troubled? And why do questions arise in your hearts? Look at my hands and my feet, that it is I myself. Touch me and see, because a ghost does not have flesh and bones as you can see I have" (Lk 28:38-39). And when Jesus appears to Thomas, he *tells* Thomas to touch him: "Put your finger here and see my hands, and bring your hand and put it into my side" (Jn 20:27). Thus, the Risen Christ is not someone who does not want to be physically touched.

Finally, Christ himself gives Mary the clearest reason for his admonition: "I have not yet ascended to the Father." Christ points her not away from him, but *toward* a true sort of worship of him as he is and will remain eternally: the Son of God who dwells at the Father's right hand.

In this light, it is clear that what Christ is teaching Mary in this moment is not to not touch him, but rather *how* to touch him—without "holding on." He is teaching her true "possession," which will be the basis of her own personal liberation.

This liberation is revealed in a garden scene that replays the gaze of "the beginning." Here is the man who calls the woman "by name," who in revealing his own "I" as the eternal Son of God at the same reveals her "I." Mary, who has suffered the wounds of being objectified and objectifying herself will now learn to behold that self through his eyes. She discovers her virginal value, her original solitude. And in this moment of her liberation, her vocation begins, her unique form of self-gift. She becomes a witness, a true disciple, the "Apostles of the Apostles" (Thomas Aquinas), the first harbinger of the Resurrection. She who has suffered at the hands of men, *will now go to men* to witness to them. With them she will experience the extraordinary companionship that is the life of the early Church.

In all, we can say that the gaze of Christ restores Mary's capacity to give of herself totally: she is empowered, liberated by Christ to move and act. Through her, he shows all of us that virginal quality that must be the source of our relationship to all things, including him. We are to touch him without "holding on." And this virginity will be a new source of freedom and vocation. This is the sort of liberation that Christ offers every man and woman, the gaze that liberates and frees the "I." "This is what virginity is at its core: the refraction, in and through my eyes, of the eternal Love that wills you to be."[34]

## Conclusion: Through the Eyes of the Virgin

We began with this question: How do men and women look at each other? In the sketches of two saints, we have encountered new possibilities. In Maria Goretti, we see a young woman in the moment of her assault seeing and subsequently freeing her rapist and murderer. In Mary Magdalene, we see an abused woman who is freed by a man's gaze that reintegrates and renews her from within, making possible an extraordinary vocation.

All of this, of course, demands more exploration: what is the pedagogy that helps young men and women to recover the way of viewing each other that was willed by the Creator "from the beginning"? How can this path be taken in our historical moment, in reference to the wounds that real men and women bear?

The lives of the saints suggest fruitful new starting points. At the heart of my proposal is a new view of virginity, not primarily as renunciation, a mere safeguard of physical purity, but as a way of knowing and then acting in relation to reality that promises a deeper freedom. Such a gaze has been part and parcel of the witness of the Church's saints since the beginning and continues unto this day. May this witness and their continued prayers provoke within us the desire to recover and more deeply live it.

## RESPONSE

# The Whole and Holy Priest: *Living Spiritual Fatherhood through the Four Modalities of Mature Masculinity*

### Bill Donaghy

*Senior Lecturer and Content Specialist Theology of the Body Institute, Downingtown, Pennsylvania,* **Adjunct Faculty at Immaculata** *University, East Whiteland Township, Pennsylvania.*

### Introduction

The Fatherhood of God is revealed through the physical. The Heavenly Father is first encountered, engaged, met and mediated through the face, hands, eyes, and voice of the earthly father we encounter in our childhood. At least, this was the pedagogy the Father envisioned for us in the beginning.

The milk of comfort was to be the gift of the mother, her warm breast a resting place. She would nourish, sweeten and strengthen with colostrum, and give succor to the new life being formed. The gift of the father was to be a drink with a little more *kick,* as it were. This is the *tonic of masculinity* meant to be poured out as an elixir of life for new sons and daughters. It would embolden and invite them forth into the wild, into the deep, into the adventure of an unknown and mysterious New World meant to be explored. Fatherhood is meant to call one away from the *mater* and into the *matter* of the world in which we "live, and move and have our being." [35] The mother cradles and cares for the interior world; she connects, makes communion, and anbolises. She is the womb. The father prepares and provokes towards the external world; he extracts, analyzes, and catabolizes. He is the wanderer. He maps out the terrain of the world and then returns as steward, guardian and guide for the family.

Both roles are essential. Both realms are ideally to be present and experienced in the life of each human person. For the flourishing of the person we need "a garden enclosed, a fountain sealed" [36] that holds the wellspring of life, and we need the one who moves *outside;* he whom the Lord "settled... in the garden of Eden, to cultivate and care for it." [37]

But what occurs in the life of the young when the steward, guardian and guide of the father is absent or distant? What if this tonic of masculinity is diluted or worse becomes *toxic?* More particularly for the purposes of this paper, what happens when a man preparing for the priesthood - that penultimate fatherly call to tend the garden of the Church and give meaning and mission to the family of God - has not encountered, engaged and been imbibed with this tonic of masculinity from a young age? What effect does the malnourished priest have on the burgeoning family of God?

Without the whole and holy integration of the masculine and feminine and (specific to this paper) the unique and essential masculine mentorship of the father in his life, the priest can suffer an imbalanced dependence on the feminine to comfort and console. His mother hunger can lead him to become unhealthily attached and enmeshed in the women surrounding his life and work. Conversely, through a deep frustration with his father hunger, he could take on a predator role, misusing his masculine strength to dominate, appropriate and control the feminine present in his life.

This paper will explore the importance of avoiding these and other unhealthy extremes through becoming an integrated man who lives out in his priesthood the four essential modalities of son, brother, spouse and father. These must be embraced and actualized in order for the man of God to realize his identity and his mission as a spiritual father.

**Gifted and Given**

The modalities of son and brother (and comparatively daughter and sister) are essentially received as gratuitous gift. We do not, strictly speaking, create them ourselves. We are gifted with sonship. We are gifted with the experience of being brother by the immediate family or the wider community we discover ourselves maturing within. The modalities of spouse and father (as of spouse and mother) are essentially achieved or actualized through the total gift of self. Here we give back as gift from the wellspring of gift we have received. This reciprocity of gift fuels the human family and has the power to create the dream of a civilization of love and a culture of life. Let's reflect on each modality more precisely.

**Beloved Son**

The prolific author G.K. Chesterton captures the sense of the gift of sonship well in his 1905 essay "On Certain Modern Writers and the Institution of the Family:

> The supreme adventure is being born. There we do walk suddenly into a splendid and startling trap. There we do see something of which we have not dreamed before. Our father and mother do lie in wait for us and leap out on us, like brigands from a bush. Our uncle is a surprise. Our aunt is, in the beautiful common expression, a bolt from the blue. When we step into the family, by the act of being born, we do step into a world which is incalculable, into a world which has its own strange laws, into a world which could do without us, into a world that we have not made.[38]

Imagine the rich soil of the soul of the baby boy brought up in a sacramental marriage, longed for and loved into existence by mother and father. From the warm cradle of their hands, he soon meets and is carried by the priest as *father* in the encounter of Baptism. With his own hands, the priest lays upon the head, hands and chest the matter of the sacraments: water and oil. Father prepares the young life for the fullness of the Heavenly Father's embrace. By sacramental signs and actions, the priest, as spiritual father, reveals the wholeness and holiness of the personal vocation. This beloved son is then taken back into the "natural family... an intimate communion of life and love" and "the primary place of 'humanization' for the person and society"... a "cradle of life and love". [39]

All is gift. The love of God has been poured out, literally, and the newborn is beloved. Not through any merit, work, effort, or accomplishment has this been done. Love for the beloved son is free, unconditional and unwarranted. And "... by being integrated into the spirit the senses receive a new depth and reach into the infinity of the spiritual adventure." [40] The potential for later activation in a vocation is present, but this freely given sonship and restoration to the Family of God is gift.

The modality of being the beloved son is absolutely foundational for the man who is later called to spiritual fatherhood. It is also a well that he must visit daily and allow himself to be refreshed in. Christ is here, as always, the model for all men. In Mark 3:17, the Father speaks from heaven, "This is my beloved Son, with whom I am well pleased." This pleasure of the Father in the Son is not contingent upon the work, efforts, achievements or accomplishments of the Son. In fact, the public ministry of Jesus has not yet begun! Love of the Son is gift. Jesus retains the posture of receptivity to the Father's love throughout his earthly life. Luke 6:12 recounts that "In those days he departed to the mountain to pray, and he spent the night in prayer to God." Christ says in John 15:9, "As the Father has loved me, so have I loved you; abide in my love." The love of the Father is always received and then given.

Pope Benedict XVI sees this modality of the beloved son perpetually receiving love as essential to the very existence and identity of the personal subject. He writes, "From the point of view of the Christian faith, man comes in the profoundest sense to himself not through what he does but through what he accepts. He must wait for the gift of love, and love can only be received as a gift. It cannot be 'made' on one's own, without anyone else; one must wait for it, let it be given to one. And one cannot become wholly man in any other way than by being loved, by letting oneself be loved..." [41]

The priest who allows himself to be loved by such a gracious Father also allows that love to fill in any void from an absentee father from his childhood. This gratuitous love of the Heavenly Father also begins the healing of any abuse suffered by a son from an earthly father: either emotional, spiritual or physical. Benedict XVI continues, "That this most necessary thing is at the same time the freest and the most unenforceable means precisely that for his 'salvation' man is meant to rely on receiving. If he declines to let himself be presented with the gift, then he destroys himself.'"[42]

Receiving the love of the Father as a beloved son is the first key to unlock the power of spiritual fatherhood for the priest.

## Brother

The second modality to be embraced and actualized for the healthy integration of the priest's life and ministry is that of brother. St. John Paul II wrote that "People live not only alongside one another, but also in manifold relationships. They live for each other; relating to one another, they are brothers and sisters…" [43] As with the gift of sonship, brotherhood is also freely given. We awaken to it in a real and certain sense.

Our life begins, in the ideal way, with the free gift of love from a mother and father, then widens into a band of brothers and sisters (either in the immediate family or through the life of our community). Our brothers and/or male friends, like our fathers, are like mirrors into which we gaze for the reflection of what masculinity is and how we live it. Sometimes the reflection is clear and encouraging, sometimes it's distorted, blurred or broken.

In our hyper-sexualized culture, we hear ridiculous words like "bromance" and "man-crush", and we may turn away in fear from a man's fundamental need for friendship with other men. Sadly, for various reasons, we live a more isolated life. The truth is that men need other men from whom we learn the craft of masculinity. We need brothers to journey with to understand the mystery of becoming a man, of our unique work in the world, our vocation, and of our call to care for and cultivate life with our sisters. The seminary is meant to be a place where authentic brotherhood can be experienced, perhaps for the first time or ideally in a more intentional and rarified atmosphere.

Being a brother is about sincerity and faithfulness, not bravado or an unhealthy competitiveness. Brothers are attentive to the people around them. For other men, they build up relationships. Brothers are called to inspire, defend and encourage one another. Brothers are called to cultivate and care for the shared life of their sisters. All the more in the life of the priest. The priest-brother shares in that primordial gaze of the first man who declared upon seeing the woman, "This one, at last, is bone of my bones and flesh of my flesh…" [44] He recognizes that they share a common ancestry. As St. John Paul II wrote in his Theology of the Body, "both to seek the common past as though they descended from the same family circle, as though from infancy they had been united by memories of the common hearth."[45]

The priest who lives authentic brotherhood is able to have confidence that this sister of his is also on the journey. This sister is never an object to be appropriated or seized but rather held in the highest regard and with reverence. Brotherhood is fed by a spirituality of communion for the priest. This spirituality was a main component in the pastoral plan for the third millennium penned by St. John Paul II. "A spirituality of communion indicates above all the heart's contemplation of the mystery of the Trinity dwelling in us, and whose light we must also be able to see shining on the face of the brothers and sisters around us. A spirituality of communion also means an ability to think of our brothers and sisters in faith within the profound unity of the Mystical Body, and therefore as 'those who are a part of me'". [46]

This second modality for living an integrated spiritual fatherhood is again a received reality. It presents itself to the man and brings to mind the countless encounters of the priest with the unique and unrepeatable gifts of women in his ministry and life. Opportunities abound for the priest-brother to allow for the tenderness, insight, and wisdom of woman to enter his sphere of ministry. The heart, however, must remain open to receive this. The perennial challenge remains that of trying to appropriate this feminine gift and mystery. The temptation is present here to move from the gifting that is woman towards the grasping and taking of their unique beauty.

The phrase *toxic masculinity* has been hovering around for decades, but truly inscribed itself into the modern lexicon as a hashtag in connection with the #MeToo movement in late 2017. Sadly, the association of masculinity with toxicity has now led some to desire a kind of annihilation of maleness. In a reductionistic age such as ours, those with the XY marker and higher testosterone levels is by nature violent, aggressive, egocentric, unfeeling and dominating. Therefore, say the modern reconstructionists, man must be emasculated. And in the process, reformulated and reconfigured into something less "offensive." Although the wound inflicted by a toxic masculinity has certainly contaminated our culture, wounded women, and befuddled the development of boys in the past, the answer is not to cast it out entirely. We must work to bring balance.

As St. John Paul II wrote, in "the sphere of what is 'human' - of what is humanly personal- 'masculinity' and 'femininity' are distinct, yet, at the same time, they complete and explain each other." [47] The healthy priest who knows and lives his call to brotherhood can be a model for men and a true balm for the wounded hearts of women.

Again, St. John Paul II in his beautiful and deeply personal *Meditation On Givenness* states:

> "God has given you to me." As is apparent, these words I heard in my youth were not a mere random remark. God does indeed give people to us; he gives us brothers and sisters in our humanity, beginning with our parents. Then, as we grow up, he places more and more new people on our life's path. Every such person, in some way, is a gift for us, and we can say of each: "God has given you to me." This awareness becomes a source of enrichment for each of us. We would be in grave danger were we to be unable to recognize the richness in each human person. Our humanity would be in peril were we to shut ourselves up only in our own selves and reject the broad horizon that opens out to the eyes of our soul as the years go by."[48]

## Spouse

As one's priestly identity is deepened, and the giftedness of life and of the irreplaceable feminine meets the thirst of the human heart for love, the ache intensifies. The integrated priest must not be surprised by this. Man was made for Beauty and "this primordial beauty with which the Creator has endowed man is also a desire for the communion in which the sincere gift of self is manifested. This beauty and this communion are not goods that have been lost irretrievably - they are goods to be redeemed, retrieved. In this sense, every human person is given to every other - every woman is given to every man, and every man is given to every woman." [49]

The priest of God must reach, with the help of God, a sublime and holy indifference. His clear knowledge that he is made for love and Beauty must not be suffocated or smothered out of fear that he may fall into sin or grasp and use the feminine. As the late Msgr. Lorenzo Albacete said,

"We talk about different 'sexual orientations' in human life. But the ultimate orientation of human sexuality is the human heart's yearning for infinity. Human sexuality, therefore, is a sign of eternity." [50]

This is the space where the modalities pivot. He who has been gifted must no longer grasp. He must become a gift himself. The priest is too called to marriage, but not the earthly sign that passes away upon death. He is called "further up and further in." The priest is called to live the spousal meaning of his body just the same as every and any man. In fact, the "... choice of virginity or celibacy for one's whole life, has become in the experience of the disciples and followers of Christ an act of particular response to the love of the Divine Bridegroom, and therefore acquired the meaning of an act of spousal love..." [51]

The integrated priest hears now a call to adventure, to go beyond himself, to commit not to an idea, or a program, but truly to another Person. This Other is his lodestar and ultimate end. This Other is the fulfillment of the original mission where "a man leaves his father and mother and clings to his wife, and the two of them become one body." [52] It is stitched right into the very fabric of the body. We are literally designed for relationship, for self-giving love. And in that self-giving love, where we seem to lose ourselves, is the very place we find ourselves. By loving, we become the man we're meant to be:

> "Man cannot live without love, St. John Paul II penned in his first encyclical to the world. "He remains a being that is incomprehensible for himself, his life is senseless, if love is not revealed to him, if he does not encounter love, if he does not experience it and make it his own..." [53]

With marriage, there's certainly difficulty and suffering at times. Marriage can be an intimidating concept for a lot of men because it truly is a kind of death. Death to ourselves, our independence, our own way. Priesthood is a laying down of the life in order to give life.

Marriage is designed to be a saint-making machine. Marriage turns self-centered boys into selfless men, or it will destroy each spouse with selfishness and ultimately the relationship. This is the same in the sphere of priestly ministry. This marriage to the Church invites the priest to realize his potential and his masculine genius: the call to become a gift.

**Father**

Fatherhood is the watermark behind everything, and everyone. It was the Heavenly Father, after all, Who created the world, spoke the first Word, and the universe unfurled like a beautiful canvas; and He is still creating new wonders every day. This is the Father's love; it is free, it is fruitful, and totally unmerited. This is the plan that the Father is inviting the priest to share in. He takes part in this greatest of projects; the building of a culture of life and a civilization of love. The priest is invited through the modality of spiritual fatherhood to bring the very life of God into the visible world.

From the beginning there has been an enemy of this project of the human family. He attacked it from the very start in the Garden of Eden by first attacking the woman, who was to be "mother of all the living." This was a veiled threat against our masculine call to make love present with the help of the woman, to bring life to the world, to protect her beauty, her femininity, her motherhood and this new life we both have to care for and cultivate.

In one of his final interviews, St. John Paul II reflected on this attack on man which has affected all of history. He said "Original sin attempts... to abolish fatherhood, destroying its rays which permeate the created world, placing in doubt the truth about God who is Love..." [54] The call to a mature spiritual fatherhood; to protect, to serve, to shepherd and to love remains for every priest. Let's recall that the Fatherhood of God is revealed through the physical. The Heavenly Father is also encountered, engaged, met and mediated through the face, hands, eyes, and voice of the priest-father we encounter in our life of faith. At least, this was the pedagogy Christ envisioned for us in establishing the apostles as his ambassadors. "He who hears you, hears me." [55] The "rays which permeate the created world" tumbling down from the Father do truly flow through the hands and eyes and voice and heart of the priest. But priests must allow these rays to pierce first the layers of their own consciousness, their heart, their attitudes, their very wounds. Their toxic masculinity must be refreshed and rejuvenated by the tonic of masculinity.

In an address to men in 2012, Pope Benedict XVI wrote "Man's refusal to make any commitment... means that man remains closed in on himself and keeps his 'I' ultimately for himself, without really rising above it." [56] Do we dare to rise? If priests are to rediscover their identity, to know who they are, they must return and reclaim the story of their origins as beloved sons, attentive brothers, loving spouses and faithful fathers.

## Conclusion

Now more than ever, perhaps more profoundly than at any other time in the history of the human family, holy and happy, integrated men of God must become who they were born to be. As sons they must reconnect with the love of the Father, as brothers they must band together as one, as spouses in communion with the Church Who is the Bride, they must serve and lead in love as a gift of self. Priests must rise and take up the task of the family, pouring themselves out and giving new life to new sons and daughters; this is the divine project that can bring the very life of God into the world through the whole and holy priest.

# VII

## Male-Female Complementarity: Sexuality and the Catholic Priesthood

### Monica Migliorino Miller

*Sacred Heart Major Seminary, Detroit, Michigan*

**Introduction**

In 1976, Pope Paul VI issued the document, called in English, "On the Admission of Women to the Ministerial Priesthood," or *Inter Insignores*.[1] The teaching of the document that women could not be admitted to the priesthood was ratified by Pope John Paul II in his apostolic letter *Ordinatio Sacerdotalis* in 1994.[2] That document stated:

> In order that all doubt may be removed regarding a matter of great importance, a matter which pertains to the Church's divine constitution itself, in virtue of my ministry in confirming the brethren, I declare that the Church has no authority whatsoever to confer priestly ordination on women and that this judgement is to be definitively held by all the Church's faithful."[3]

Now, one would think, that with a statement as clear and unequivocal as this, that the debate within the Church on women's ordination would be ended. However, to borrow a remark made by the great Msgr. George Kelly in his book *The Battle for the American Church*—a remark that typifies those who have difficulty accepting papal decrees: "Rome has spoken—the case is still open."[4]

Anyone paying even the most disinterested attention to the passing of John Paul II and the election of Benedict XVI would have been inundated with media commentary and debate on the trinity of issues: that is—priestly celibacy; divorced and remarried Catholics; and of course women's ordination—as if John Paul II had never declared this a closed case. When the late Holy Father declared that women could not be priests, or conversely, why the ministerial priesthood is reserved to males, he said the issue had to do with "the Church's divine constitution itself." In many ways this chapter is an examination of the divine constitution—or nature—of the Church to which the male priesthood is necessary.

The roots of the continued discussion on the subject of women's ordination can be traced, not only to the stubborn dissent on the part of a whole generation of theologians whose time has not yet completely passed and who continue to stir commotion on issues that are settled, but also from a true lack of understanding and appreciation for why the Church teaches what she teaches. Even many Catholics who are loyal to the Church do not understand why the Church insists on an all-male priesthood, but support the teaching simply based on the fact that the Church teaches it—yet they falter when asked to defend the teaching with systematic reasoning. Thus, much work still needs to be done to move the Church forward and bring her to a time when the nature of the Eucharist and the role of the male priest within the Eucharist are consciously appreciated among the faithful.

The modern challenge to the all-male priesthood is based on two misconceptions. The first has to do with the meaning of authority itself. What indeed is authority? The second is an under-appreciation for the role of symbols within Catholic worship, and of course, most particularly, the symbolic value of male and female sexuality. These misconceptions are widespread enough and deep enough and affect the most important activity of the Church—namely her worship—that we are in the midst of a liturgical and ecclesial crisis. The debate on the all-male priesthood should begin with the primary question: "Is the male gender of Jesus Christ significant to the accomplishment of redemption?" The answer to this question will largely determine whether a person agrees with or disagrees with the all-male priesthood.

## First Misconception: Authority

Let us attend to the first misconception. The liturgical and ecclesial crisis can only be resolved when Christians come to appreciate that real authority is not synonymous with power. The person who possesses authority is not simply or always the strong one within a group who then uses his strength to organize that group around his vision. Someone who has this power can declare himself outside the group and exert a dominant position toward the group in a world in which there is no inherent relation between the leader and the group. Nor is there any real relation among any of the members of the group. In fact, when order is achieved by the imposition of power, this presupposes that the group has no meaning or purpose outside of the leader's will. This is the Nietzschean world without ontological truth or harmony, but this is not the world of God the Father. God has not created a world in which authority is arbitrary and a mere matter of quantifiable strength. In other words, we need to get away from the idea that whoever holds office, whoever has the strength of will, whoever has strength because of size or numbers, is the one who therefore has authority and is deserving of respect. Priests are not respected because they have quantifiable power. Priests are respected because of who they represent—for whom they are a living sacrament. Namely, a priest manifests the authority of Christ, as Jesus is the Eucharistic life-giver to his Church.

The word *authority* comes from the Latin *auctores* meaning to be the author or creator of something. A person has authority precisely by giving life. If God has authority, it is because he is life itself and the creator of all life. When Christians recite the Nicene Creed the first item of faith declared is, "We believe in One God, the Father, the Almighty, the creator of heaven and earth." God is Almighty!—but not in the sense of simply holding power over something in some arbitrary way. Rather "creator of heaven and earth" defines the almighty character of God. He is truly almighty because he can create out of nothing. But the fact that he creates is the essence of God's authority.

Obedience to God allows the human being to live and know the source of life and human freedom. Authority is the power to give life, but equally as important, authority is entirely bound up with the right to exercise responsibility for the life that one has created so that this life may be brought to its fulfillment.

If authority is the power to give life and the responsibility to oversee the good for that life, then it is not too hard to understand Christ's authority in relation to the Church. The first principle of Christ's authority is that it exists within a covenant. Authority is covenantal. Christ is actually in union with the one to whom he exercises authority, namely the Church. There is a love relation between Christ and the one he has authority toward.

**Second Misconception: Role of Symbols in Catholic Worship**

Keeping in mind the true meaning of authority—let us move to the second misconception having to do with the role of symbols in Catholic worship. A current theological trend—and feminist theology is guided by this idea—is that there is no historical language for God. In a sense, God cannot really be spoken of. In the fallen word of time there are no words, there are no signs that can truly speak of God and communicate his essence. Symbols are always partial and temporary, conditioned by culture—useful only as long as there is a human experience to support them. Thus, symbols are purely functional. A symbol for God used two or three thousand years ago may have to be set aside for other symbols that are more relevant to our age. It would seem, that the contemporary awareness of the dignity and equality of women dictates that male-figures and symbols for God within Judeo/Christianity be balanced or replaced with feminine figures and symbols. Ideally, we should dispense with being dependent upon time-bound symbols altogether since God is spirit and no concrete symbol can manifest who God is.

What all this points to is a kind of despair, a pessimism of history, and a pessimism that indeed has the power to undercut the very foundations of Catholicism. The idea that all symbols are partial, fragmentary, and passing means that the created order cannot truly speak of God—we cannot know the will of God definitively as the historical order, rather than disclosing Him—is a barrier to Him. The purely functional role of symbols affects the view of the priesthood. The priesthood is valued, not according to its sacramental meaning but according to its functionality.

Rosemary Radford Ruether, said for example, in her book *Sexism and Godtalk* that Christ is only one model for redeemed humanity. She then proceeds to blame history for the unavailability of a full model: "Fullness of redeemed humanity, as image of God, is something only partially disclosed under the conditions of history. We seek it as a future self and world, still not fully achieved, still not fully revealed."[5] Here is the great flaw. Because Christ is a male, he is only one model of redeemed humanity. In Himself, he cannot sum up what it means to be redeemed. We must therefore cast about for other models, which will always be partial. By such models we are forced to live in a fragmented world, forced to live in a world where "the fullness of redeemed humanity is only partially disclosed."[6] The fragmented partial model is the result of failure to accept that marriage is rooted in a marital covenant between Christ and the Church. There is no alternative model. This *is the* covenant itself.

**What exactly is Redeemed by Christ?**

In answer to the primary question that I asked earlier, it is obvious that the Church concludes that Christ's gender is related to the accomplishment of redemption. But let us ask—What e*xactly is* redeemed by Christ? Salvation in Christ is not simply the salvation of individual souls (I may add, individual souls beyond the body and beyond gender). The salvation of souls occurs within a broader, deeper more complex, and more profound redemption—namely the redemption of the whole created order. What is saved, even perfected, and given its final meaning in the redemption of Christ is what was given in the Beginning—the Good Creation of God. This Good Creation has a beauty, identity, and order in the nuptial mystery of the first man and the first woman. Their conjugal unity provides the world with its meaning and purpose as oriented towards God. The conjugal unity of the man and the woman is, according to Ephesians, the "great mystery" as we see in Eph. 5: 31-32. "For this reason a man shall leave his father and his mother and cling to his wife and the two shall become one flesh. This is a great mystery, for it refers to Christ and the Church."

The "this" in the Pauline passage is the conjugal unity of Adam and Eve. The passage serves as a kind of climax to the drama of salvation history beginning with the Jews who spoke of the covenant between God and His people as a marriage. Forevermore, sexuality cannot be seen as mere biology, mere functionality. No, from the Beginning, male and female gender point to truths beyond themselves, and thus, from the Beginning, male and female sexuality have a sacramental character. The Order of Redemption is related to the Order of Creation. When the Second Person of the Trinity entered human history as a male, it is not only male gender that is affirmed. Christ's male gender, as did Adam's male gender, exists only in relation—namely it exists only in relation to what is feminine.

Thus, it is a huge mistake to conclude that Christ's male gender only honors that which is male and somehow women are just left out—forever relegated to second class citizens. No, the Incarnation honors the nuptial differences of the sexes so that what is taken up in the Incarnation is not human nature flat and generic—but the marital order of the world that was given in the Beginning. The masculinity of Christ exists in relation to the bridal Church, and rather than being a soteriological problem as Ruether would see it, it is the very basis upon which his salvific work is effective. Indeed it is this covenantal, marital truth about the world and God's relation to the world that is celebrated in the Eucharist.

If this is the truth about Christ, then male sexuality is integral to the sacramental worship of the Church by which the grace of the covenant is mediated. Within this covenant, the male priest is the symbol of Christ the head whereby the mysteries of the redemption flowing from the head are dispensed. The apostle, bishop and priest carry a certain responsibility for the faith wherein is contained their authority in relation to the Church. The masculine sex of their office serves as a sign of Christ's unique gift of self - this unique giving of self which reveals the love of the Father. But this responsibility, essential to the New Covenant, does not exhaust the covenant. This authority operates in relation to the feminine authority of the Church exemplified by Christian women. That is of course the subject of another paper.

Men and women, according to the inherent truth, beauty and dignity of their sexuality are symbols taken up into the order of redemption in which the unity between Christ and the Church is sacramentally affected and revealed. All authority then is exercised within a covenant; it is always qualified by the relation, and authority is differentiated according to the way men and women give life. As a result, authority within the Catholic Church is not a quantifiable power exercised as force to accomplish certain ends. Authority is not simply the exercise of leadership wherein the leader, due to some preeminence of personal talent and personality, directs the course of a group of persons subordinate to him. The authority by which redemption is affected in the Catholic Church is the love of God in Christ appropriated liturgically by men and women in their imaging of the covenant as source and cause of life in God. In short, authority in the Church is the power to effect supernatural life, more specifically, the power to appropriate and make effective the covenantal redemption of Christ in the world.

The supernatural life of God is manifested in the world through the relation of the head and the body. Liturgically and ecclesially, Christ, the head, and his Body, the Church, exist according to a mystical unity, but the head and the body are not blurred, and they are not confused. This truth honors one of the most basic Judaic principles that God cannot be confused or collapsed into nature—yet God and nature can and do exist in a harmony.

**What is the Nature of Headship?**

The Church teaches that priests represent Christ as head of the Church. We may ask at this point, what is the nature of headship, and how is the male priest the sign of this headship? In the Pauline epistles headship has two meanings—it means that Christ is Lord to whom everything else is subordinated. However, the term "head" also means *source* or *origin*, and this sense of the term is every bit as important as the first. Paul even refers to Christ as the *arche*—the beginning. Christ is the first (or beginning) of many brethren as in Col. 1:18. Indeed, it is because Christ is the origin, or source or beginning of the Church that he is also her Lord.

There are several Pauline passages, particularly in Colossians and Ephesians that equate headship with source. Time constraints make a detailed exegesis of these passages impossible. However, perhaps the greatest sense of Christ's headship as source is to be found in the very fact that Christ came to "give himself up" and "to make an offering of himself." The death of the head causes life for the body. Christ expressed this idea when he said, "Lest a grain of wheat fall into the ground and die it remains a single grain of wheat, but when it dies it produces much fruit." The death of the one head is the source of the many members.

The Church rests on the fact that Christ himself historically established her worship. He himself is the guarantee that the worship the Church offers to the Father is efficaciously pleasing to him because what the Church offers in the Eucharist is the one sacrifice of Christ, offered on his own authority.

Priestly power is inherently connected to masculine sexuality. Priestly power has to do with engendering and maintaining the divine life of God in the Church. The priest has a delegation from God. His authority is not self-bestowed—or bestowed by the community's fiat. Christ, who is the only true priest has chosen certain men to be his instruments whereby Christ maintains his presence in the Church. To this end Christ passes on to priests what he has received from the Father.

The meaning of priestly authority is bound to male sexuality because of the relation between the headship of Christ and his engendering of the Church. This is the manner, in which Christ exists as *source*. Furthermore, this divine life transmitted via the priesthood is *received* by the Church. Her life is bestowed upon her from the outside. The Church is not her own cause. The male body is related to priestly action because the meaning of masculinity does not rest in itself but derives its meaning by being an expression for what is transcendent as opposed to what is immanent. A priest's authority is not his own. He is a sacrament of the one true priest who is Christ. Ultimately, a priest is not only a sign of Christ. As an effective sign, the sacrament of Holy Orders makes the truth about the fatherhood of God real in the world, insofar as Christ is the icon of the Father.

The feminist restructuring of ecclesial authority must demolish the religious significance of fatherhood. God, as the source of life, has no way to insert himself in the order of creation that signifies his unique power in relation to what he has created. In feminist theology, fatherhood and thus God himself, is not only remote; he is invisible. The masculinity of the priesthood, however, speaks a truth about the authority of God, about how God relates to the world. Fundamentally, when the Church insists on the masculinity of the priesthood, she is preserving the order of God's love for the world, which is inherently marital.

By entrusting his authority to males, Christ preserves a truth about his love in relation to creation. His sacrifice is uniquely his own offered *for the Church*. The particularity of his sacrifice has its historical and eternal expression in the marital order of the New Creation. In marriage, nothing can substitute for the unique gift a husband makes to his wife and the wife to her husband. The gift of self is embodied in a personal word of the man as man and the woman as woman out of which the unity of their "one flesh" is formed. The male priesthood speaks of the uniqueness of Christ's gift of self—a complete personal self-donation that is the source of a unique covenantal response. A bi-sexual priesthood would render Christ's sacrifice unintelligible. The economy of Christian worship would be dissolved and thus the Christian revelation.

The feminist quest for a female priesthood is rooted in the mistaken notion that all words are basically the same, that symbols as such are meaningless, that revelation has no language except what is contrived by an historical relativism. Feminist thinkers tend to view the male and the female body as virtually irrelevant. What counts for them is the *person* and what the person is able "to do" despite their sexual gender. One's sex should not matter when considering whether one is "qualified for the job." However, when the "job" is to image the marital/covenantal structure of God's love and authority in the world, the bodily reality of masculinity and femininity cannot be dispensed. The human body as male or female—indeed the entire person—as male or female serves as a communicator of God's covenantal love.

## What is there about Masculinity that Reveals God that Femininity does not?

We need to explore how, according to the Order of Creation, the male body and sexuality serve as a symbol of God to the world. In other words, it is necessary to understand what there is about masculinity that reveals God which femininity does not. By this investigation we will see that masculinity (as well as femininity) are not arbitrary symbols of the covenant. But by their very nature, they speak a truth about God and the world. Hans Urs von Balthasar explains:

> The redemptive mystery "Christ-Church" is the superabundant fulfillment of the mystery of Creation between man and woman. As Paul affirms very forcefully. So that the fundamental mystery of Creation is called "great" precisely in view of its fulfillment of the mystery of Redemption. The natural sexual difference is charged *as* difference, with a supernatural emphasis, of which it is not itself aware, so that outside of Christian Revelation it is possible to arrive at various deformations of this difference such as, for example, a one-sided matriarchite or patriarchite, an underestimation of woman, or finally, such a leveling of the sexes as to destroy all values of sexuality. It is only from the indestructible difference between Christ and the Church (prepared but not incarnate in the difference between Yahweh and Israel) that there is reflected the decisive light about the real reciprocity between man and woman.[7]

In all of Revelation, both in the Old and the New Covenants, God is the transcendent Other. He is not to be associated with or confused with creation or nature. As God-Creator he stands apart from what he has made. He can look at something outside of himself and call it "very good" (Gen. 1:31). Male sexuality stands as a sign of this type of creative action. To be male means to stand apart, over and against the world. Father Walter Ong, S.J. provided one of the most insightful works on the meaning of male sexuality in his book *Fighting for Life*:

> The adversary relationship with the environment, which has been seen to go back to the biological situation of the male embryo and the fetus in the womb, would appear to serve as one basis for the male's tendency to fight. Human males tend to feel an environment, including other individuals of the species, as a kind of againstness, something to be fought with and altered. Environment is feminine, and women typically find that they can rely on it as it comes to them.[8]

What is pervasive in the world is not masculinity, as Aristotle would have it, but femininity. Nature, creation, and mother are everywhere. For a man to be a man he must claim his identity as apart from and other than this matrix. Ong states, quite contrary to Aristotelian philosophy, "that nature's primary impulse is to make a female."[9] A woman is not a castrated male, a deficient man—rather a male is a female to which something has been added.[10]

The fact that a man must show that he is different has great implications for the meaning of male ecclesial authority. Because his being must be confirmed from the outside, ecclesial authority must be bestowed—ritualistically—officially. This is why male ecclesial authority is that of public office. For him to be different means for him to stand out from the rest in some easily recognizable official capacity lest he fall back into and be absorbed by the feminine, in this case, the Church herself. Male sexuality is signified by representing what is apart in a confirmation of what it is to be male. Von Balthasar expressed clearly the difference between male and female authority:

> While man as a sexual being, only represents what he is not and transmits what he does not actually possess, and so is…at the same time more and less than himself, a woman rests on herself, she is fully what she is, that is, the whole reality of a created being that faces God as a partner, receives his seed and spirit, preserves them, brings them to maturity and educates them. Restored nature would bring to light—within parity of nature and parity of the sexes—above all the fundamental difference, according to which woman does not represent but is, while man has to represent and, therefore, is more and less than what he is.[11]

Ong observes that female authority is not ritualized because a woman has no need to prove herself sexually. Rather it is the man who must prove that he is different from her. A woman, because of her reproductive cycle, is constantly affirmed interiorly that she can give life. The fact that male ecclesial power is conferred externally, ritualistically, is consistent with the difference between male and female sexuality. A woman has no need to "earn" or have her authority conferred.[12] She possesses it in herself because, as Von Balthasar stated, "woman does not represent, but is." [13] Masculinity has to be earned:

> Masculinity for human males...engenders agonistic activity because it is something to be won, achieved "always in a state of being earned" ... not at all simply something one is born with. The genetic determinants of masculinity notably for human beings, establish not so much a state of being as a program. A male finds his masculinity in some way outside of himself, especially in higher animal species and most especially among humans.[14]

Because a man's identity is external, outside of himself, in some sense against the world, he can represent what he is not. Because his identity does not rest in himself (he is less than and more than what he is) a man is transparent—a symbol, a sign of what is beyond and outside of him.[15] Priestly power will then be the result of an official public consecration. He will receive a power outside of himself. A woman's authority has no need for such a ritual.

Male sexuality represents God the Father. God is likened to the masculine because he is a source of life that is "other, different, separated (*kadosh* the Hebrew word translated *sanctus, hagios*, holy, means at root "separated") from all creation, even from human beings, though they are 'made in his image and likeness.'"[16]

It is then easy to see how male sexuality is a sign of this truth about God. A man, even if he is the most caring and tender of all fathers, still remains separate, apart from his children. He cannot know them physically, and thus psychically, with the same intimate bond that profoundly characterizes motherhood. First of all, in the act of procreation the male must deposit his life principle away from himself. Indeed, after the procreative act he can indeed step away from it literally and face what he has done. The creative action of God as described in Genesis Chapter One corresponds to this reality. God creates but can look at his creation that is outside of himself. As if to say God steps back from it, faces it, surveys it, contemplates it, perhaps is even in a kind of wonderment over it, as the text states "God looked at everything he made, and he found it very good" (Gn. 1: 31).

## VII. Male-Female Complementarity: Sexuality and the Catholic Priesthood 219

Whatever effects come from the conjugal act, and particularly the conception of another human being, the man is removed from it in a way that the woman is not. Everything is now the woman's. A man's explicit role in procreation is over with quickly, while the woman will experience its effects for months to come.[17]

There is an essential difference between motherhood and fatherhood. Mothers are inherently attached to their children while fathers are physically detached and distant. Because there are no male umbilical cords, human beings do not have a comparable problem separating themselves from fathers. Nor do we have a problem separating ourselves from God.[18]

We are separated from God as from a father. We have never been physically and physiologically attached to God, yet Hebrew-Christian teaching insists that he loves us—hence he calls us, his children set apart from him, and draws us near to him with love. In this sense, related to the biological sense though not entirely the same, God is male. He is not nature.... Always distinctive of God is that, with all his tenderness and concern and closeness...he is always also other, different, separated, as a father physically is, and not by becoming so but simply by being so.[19]

While a man is a source of life that is apart and other, he is, nonetheless, the initiator of the procreative act and of conception which, in this male sexuality, also images God—who alone actively initiated all of creation. The observation of Aristotle, also taught by Aquinas, that masculinity is active in relation to the feminine is essentially correct. The attribution of superiority to the active was, however, incorrect.[20] Aquinas defined fatherhood as "the relation of being the source of generation in the highest form of life."[21]

Male sexuality, as active and initiating, is a generating principle and stands in this way as an image of God who generates all of creation. The following observation will help us understand in what manner masculinity forms the proper image for God and Christ and in what manner femininity is related to this image:

> Ordained liturgical priesthood is the seedbed of union in, with and through Christ. It is rooted in the generative nature of God. It is from this life-initiating essence [of God] that all life and growth, spiritual *and* material, has its existence... this generative

initiative is the essence of masculine being, as germination is the essence of feminine being... The Eucharist is Christ. It enters us as seed to quicken us, to conceive life in us, to regenerate us. Just so man enters woman to initiate life and growth and new being. Just so, the sperm penetrates the ovum to stimulate life and growth and individuation. If the sperm does not enter the ovum, the female cell remains closed upon itself...[22]

The generative quality of God and the germinative quality of that which he has created forms the covenantal structure of God's relationship to his people. It is a relation that is inherently marital. Christ spoke of his death in terms of a seed dying in relation to the earth which consumes it: "Amen. Amen. I say to you. Lest a grain of wheat fall into the ground and dies, it remains alone. But if it dies, it brings forth much fruit" (Jn. 12:24-25).

The death of Christ is essentially generative and marital in its order. In fact, we may go so far as to say that his death is an essentially masculine death. It is the death of the man for the woman in which isolation is broken and a covenant is formed. By dying, the seed no longer remains alone. And it dies by falling into the feminine earth. The seed of the man will be absorbed into the woman, into her own life-principle. The man will lose himself by being taken into her. As we stated earlier, femininity is pervasive. A man to be truly a man must declare his difference. A woman knows her power. She is the source of both men and woman "the mother of all the living." She can produce a male who is totally dependent upon her "which is more than any male can do for either a male or a female."[23]

A man must show himself worthy of the woman by an external proof of his manhood in a heroic contest against the world in what Ong described as "agonistic" activity.[24] A man will know his identity by what he achieves external to himself. If he fails in achievement, he cannot be consoled by saying to himself, "'I can still become a mother.' In his own mind his underpinnings are very weak, what he does is lonely and therefore heroic, because it is his daring against a cruel world."[25] A woman rests in herself through the bodily interiority of her own powers. But a man must *become* a man. In the lonely, heroic act of himself against the world, the man is finally able to give to the woman something that she cannot give to herself.[26] He can give to her something that is uniquely *his own*. This is the male sacrifice that Christ fulfilled on the cross for his bridal Church. He dies *for* her. Because of this initiatory act neither remains alone. They are one flesh.

It is not an accident that feminist theologians destroy the Eucharist as a sacrifice and even empty the Passion of Christ of any sacrificial meaning. Because there is a connection between Christ's masculinity and his sacrificial act of love, feminists must render both insignificant. As we have seen, Ruether believes Christ's masculinity has no ultimate theological value and his life and death (bound as it is by the limitations of history) is only one model of redemption.[27] Therefore, the Eucharist is not the Body and Blood of Christ given for the Church—the Eucharist is the Church, and she is able to give it to herself.[28] For Ruether, there is nothing unique about Christ, neither his masculinity nor his sacrifice in relation to the Church. There is no need then for any unique sign to represent him, to mark him off from the community and creation—namely a male priesthood. The Church, for the sake of feminine authority or power, must completely absorb Christ. And the absorption is effectively accomplished by a demolition of the nuptial order of redemption. Ironically, by absorbing or denying the meaning of Christ's masculinity, the feminine has truly become pervasive. Christ the male was born from a woman. Christ received his masculine body from a woman. This shows the overwhelming femininity of the Church. Feminism, by making women "priests," will have fulfilled its goal by feminizing everything in the world. Notice, feminist theology never proposes that the Church be thought of in masculine terms. In the end, the goddess will have conquered everything.

Priestly authority is to engender the life of God within the Church and thus within the world. It is an authority that reveals the Father because priests represent Christ who revealed the love of the Father through his sacrifice. The Vatican II decree on the Pastoral Office of Bishops states:

> Having been sent by the Father, [Christ] in turn sent his Apostles whom he sanctified by conferring on them the Holy Spirit so that they might also glorify the Father on earth and procure the salvation of men "for the building up of the body of Christ" (Eph. 4:12) which is the Church.[29]

The "building up of the body" is precisely the role of the head performed in his capacity as the New Adam. The Apostles and their successors have been entrusted with participation in Christ's headship. The Apostles are sent to carry on the salvific work of Christ, which is the work of the head to the body.[30] The divine mission entrusted to the Apostles by Christ was willed by him to "last until the end of the world" (cf. Matt. 28:20). Therefore, *Lumen Gentium* teaches that the Apostles, according to the will of Christ, appointed successors, namely bishops:

> Amongst those various offices which have been exercised in the Church from the earliest times the chief place, according to the witness of tradition, is held by the function of those who, through their appointment to the dignity and responsibility of the bishop, and in virtue consequently of the unbroken succession, going back to the beginning, are regarded as the transmitters of the apostolic line…In the person of the bishops, then to whom the priests render assistance, the Lord Jesus Christ, supreme high priest, is present in the midst of his faithful.[31]

The document goes on to explain that the authority of bishops and priests is sacramental. They share in Christ's consecration and mission. Priests by the sacrament of Orders are "after the image of Christ, the supreme and eternal priest" (Heb. 5:1-10, 7:24, 9:11-28).[32] A priest's authority is of a particular kind. His authority is grounded in a sacramental manifestation of Christ as priest, Christ as shepherd—meaning Christ as cause of the Church by his sacrifice. Priests are life-givers to the body of Christ by sacramentally extending Christ's salvific work. Because they share in the headship of Christ, it is in the celebration of the Eucharist:

> …that they exercise in a supreme degree their sacred functions; there, acting in the person of Christ, and proclaiming his mystery, they unite the votive offerings of the faithful to the sacrifice of Christ their head, and in the sacrifice of the Mass, they make present again and apply, until the coming of the Lord (cf. 1 Cor. 11:26), the unique sacrifice of the New Testament, that

namely of Christ offering himself once for all a spotless victim to the Father (cf. Heb. (9:11-28).[33]

The priest's participation in the headship of Christ exists for the sake of worship—giving himself up for her (Eph. 5:25). Priests sacramentally effect the personal unique love of Christ—the love that is his own, the love of the bridegroom. Henri de Lubac, quoting St. Cyril of Alexandria, expresses the marital nature of the redemption made present in the Eucharist:

> The participation of the Body and Blood of Christ effects nothing short of this, that we pass over unto that which we receive." The head and the members make one single body; the Bridegroom and the Bride are "one flesh." There are not two Christs, one personal and the other "mystical." *And there is certainly no confusion of Head with members; Christians are not the "physical" (or eucharistic) body of Christ, and the Bride is not the Bridegroom.* All the distinctions are there, but they do not add up to discontinuity; the Church is not just *a* body, but *the* body of Christ; man must not separate what God has united—therefore "let him not separate the Church from the Lord."[34] (emphasis added)

The marital structure of the Eucharist preserves what is unique in male and female responsibility. This responsibility is from the beginning of creation in which the man (Adam) is the source of Eve. She confers on him his identity and purpose and is rendered mother of all the living. The worship of the Church is constituted by a marital/covenantal freedom and responsibility:

> This worship, centered on the Eucharistic sacrifice, the *Christus totus* has therefore the structured, the qualified freedom, of the marital relation inherent in the New Covenant, in which the sacrifice offered *in persona Christi* by the priest is not competitive with the Church's sacrifice of praise, but is creative of it, and qualitatively distinct from it. Any ecclesiology which cannot accept

this model of freedom in the Church has substituted an abstraction for the reality.[35]

Vatican II is clear on the nature of the priesthood. The priesthood exists according to the nature and mission of Christ to offer sacrifice and to forgive sin. By this authority, Christ himself "builds up, sanctifies and rules his Body."[36] Vatican II speaks of the "special character" conferred through the sacrament of Ordination by which men are "configured to Christ the priest in such a way that they are able to act in the person of Christ the head.[37]

To act in the person of Christ the head is to stand in his place as *source* of the Church by offering his sacrifice. The offer of Christ's sacrifice is the salvific responsibility of the priesthood. Through the Eucharistic ministry of priests, the whole assembly of the Church is offered to God through Christ, the high priest who offered up himself "that we might be the body of so great a head."[38]

Redemption springs from the truth that the righteous act of Christ (Rm. 5:18) *is his own*. Thus, only Christ could commission the Apostles "to do this in memory of me." The Apostles have received a real authority. Pierre Benoit, O.P. explains that they would never have dared to repeat Christ's action unless they had received authority from Christ to do so. The Last Supper is not a mere commemoration for a dear departed friend "but the renewal of a sacred action by which the sacrifice of the Master still living was made present under the appearance of bread and wine."[39] Because the sacrifice is Christ's *own* to be offered, priests acting *in persona Christi* confirm the goodness of creation in that they sacramentally stand in the place of the New Adam to the New Eve.

Here the meaning of masculinity and femininity knows its value, knows its goodness, because it knows its differentiated responsibility in effecting the New Covenant. The society of Christ and the Church is marital, and it is at one with the Eucharistic sacrifice. The order of redemption is maritally structured, and it is this covenant of the One Flesh that is celebrated in the Eucharist by which the Church herself exists in true worship with her head. The very validity of this worship is attacked if a woman were to stand *in persona Christi*—not simply because Christ is a man—but rather because masculinity and femininity are the symbols by which the New Covenant lives—by which is truth is expressed.

A female priesthood attacks the order of redemption, and thus any Eucharist offered by a woman would be invalid by its very nature because the marital symbols by which the New Covenant lives are themselves violated. Thus, the internal truth by which the covenant lives is not expressed. Some other reality (or idea) is expressed, but not the redemption of the Good Creation known by the One Flesh of Christ and his Church. A woman standing in the place of the head offering his sacrifice does not express the covenant because the covenant exists according to male and female responsibility for redemption. The issue here is not simply that a "woman priest" takes on an authority she does not possess—rather a female priesthood robs women of their own particular authority without which the covenant does not exist.

## Conclusion

The masculine priesthood represents Christ as *source* of the Church, but this authority does not sum up the essence of ecclesial authority or the essence of the Church. We must always keep in mind that we are dealing with a covenant. Christ is a man, but he is only fully so through the womanly essence of the Church. He needs her to be filled with his presence—like a womb full of life to bear him and keep him present in this world. He sees himself reflected in her as she is sprung from his side as he died upon the cross. The words of the first Adam are now those of the Second. In the ancient and eschatological hymn of covenantal love, Jesus in union with the Church cries out, "This one at last is bone of my bones and flesh of my flesh."

# RESPONSE

# Woman in the Life of the Priest according to St. John Paul II

### Rev. Msgr. Piotr Mazurkiewicz

*Professor of the Institute of Political Science, Cardinal Stefan Wyszyński University, Warsaw, Poland*

"*By God's will, I am again among a group of women. I will remember this: whenever a woman comes into your room, always stand up, even if you were the most occupied. Rise, regardless of whether it is Mother Superior, who has entered the room, or Sister Cleophas whose role is to fire the furnace. Remember that she always reminds you of the Handmaid of the Lord, in whose name the Church itself rises. Remember that in this way you pay a debt of honour to the Immaculate Mother, who is more closely linked to this woman than you are. In this manner, you pay a debt to your birth Mother, who served you with her own blood and body... Stand up and do not hesitate, overcome your masculine haughtiness and dominion... Rise, even if the poorest of Magdalenes entered... Only then will you follow your Master, who rose from his Throne at the right hand of the Father to descend to the Handmaid of the Lord... Only then will you follow the Father Creator, who sent Mary to help Eve ... Rise, without delay, it will do you good.*"[40]

### Introduction: Difference and Complementarity

Man and woman are similar and different at the same time. The difference of the sexes is directly related to the different role played by a man and a woman in relation to the conception, birth, and upbringing of a child. It is not necessary to share the Christian faith to see this difference. A little common sense is sufficient. Aristotle writes:

> The friendship between husband and wife appears to be a natural instinct; since man is by nature a pairing creature even more than he is a political creature, inasmuch as the family is an earlier and more fundamental institution than the State, and the

procreation of offspring a more general characteristic of the animal creation. So whereas with the other animals the association of the sexes aims only at continuing the species, human beings cohabit not only for the sake of begetting children but also to provide the needs of life; for with the human race division of labor begins at the outset, and man and woman have different functions; thus they supply each other's wants, putting their special capacities into the common stock. Hence the friendship of man and wife seems to be one of utility and pleasure combined. But it may also be based on virtue, if the partners be of high moral character; for either sex has its special virtue, and this may be the ground of attraction".[41]

God created humankind as male and female (*Genesis* 1:27). The difference is something intended by God and forms an essential element of the mystery of the human. Man and woman are different, but at the same time they are equal in their dignity. These are two different worlds and two complementary ways of being human. The woman is complementary to the man just as the man is the complement of the woman. A woman and a man are mutually complementary not only physically and mentally, but also in ontic terms.[42] As a result, the disparities between them, sometimes observed in the statistics, are not always something negative that calls for their elimination. Saint Catherine of Siena recorded the words of Jesus:

> I place, indifferently, (...) many gifts and graces of virtue, and not only in the case of spiritual things but also of temporal. I use the word temporal for the things necessary to the physical life of man; all these I have given indifferently, and I have not placed them all in one soul, in order that man should, perforce, have material for love of his fellow. I could easily have created men possessed of all that they should need both for body and soul, but I wish that one should have need of the other, and that they should be My ministers to administer the graces and the gifts that they have received from Me. Whether man will or no, he cannot help making an act of love.[43]

Noticeable difference between a man and a woman is also an intellectual challenge, as much for women as it is for men.

The complementarity of women and men in physical and mental terms is relatively easy not only to notice, but also to understand. However, focusing on this dimension, as does Aristotle for example, causes the difference to be recognized mainly in a functional sense. Hence the question is to what extent these "functions" are innate (natural) and to what extent they are learned (socially constructed), and therefore, to what extent they may also be subject to reconstruction. Can a woman replace a man in everything, including in priesthood, or should there be some areas reserved for one sex only? Is the "liberation" of a woman from "coercion" to bear and raise children a prerequisite for her being treated equally with a man?

However, from the point of view of the mystery of man, ontic complementarity is of fundamental importance. The idea of ontic complementarity of the sexes speaks, therefore, of a much deeper relationship between man and woman, because without this relationship it is impossible to be fully human. God says, "It is not good for the man to be alone. I will make a helper suitable for him." (*Genesis* 2:18). It is not only about help in terms of action (after all, much work could have been done by animals) or a good mood (a dog or a cat can also improve our mood), but also about help in the way of existence which is inherent for a human being. "The biblical context" – writes John Paul II – "enables us to understand this in the sense that the woman must "help" the man – and in his turn he must help her – first of all by the very fact of their "being human persons".[44] It is undoubtedly about "help" that goes both ways, about mutual "help" in being human, because only through the integration of what is "masculine" and what is "feminine" is humanity realized in full.[45] To experience his humanity fully, a man lacks something that only a woman possesses. To fully experience her humanity, a woman lacks something that only a man has. A man cannot fully understand himself – and what is meant here is an intellectual act – without trying to understand a woman. He cannot understand who he is, what is his dignity and his calling. A woman cannot fully understand herself either, without trying to understand a man. A question can therefore be asked: had Adam known that he was a man before he saw and marvelled at a creature so similar, yet so different? The "knowledge of man" – writes John Paul II – "passes through masculinity and femininity. These are, as it were, two "incarnations" of the same metaphysical solitude before God and the world."[46] Only looking at a woman, so similar and yet so different at the same time, does a man begin to understand his otherness and his masculine way of being human. Only looking at a man does a woman begin to understand herself and her feminine way of being human. The sex, being subordinated to fertility, is essentially of a relational nature. It never occurs in the singular. "(...) femininity finds itself, in a sense, in the presence of masculinity, while masculinity is confirmed through femininity".[47] A man and a woman perceive themselves as different spiritually, emotionally, mentally, physically and sexually, at the same time being fully aware of their personal dignity and their ability to complement each other, to be a gift to each other (*communio personarum*).[48]

Adam, looking at the woman, begins to understand what it means to be a man. It is similar with Eve, who, looking at the man, begins to understand what it means to be a woman. They start to understand themselves better, while discovering that humanity consists of more than one sex. There also exists the second continent, which calls for being discovered. A person of different sex presents a challenge and carries an inner mystery. Difficulty of mutual understanding in the relation between man and woman was planned by God and helps humans to be themselves more fully: a man to be more fully a man, and a woman to be a woman in a fuller sense. Resigning from an effort to understand a person of the opposite sex, attempting to blur the ontic difference, contributes to a significant impoverishment of the experience of being a human. "In the "unity of the two"" – as John Paul II underlines – "man and woman are called from the beginning not only to exist "side by side" or "together", but they are also called *to exist mutually* "*one for the other.*"[49] "«The woman is 'a helper' for the man, just as the man is 'a helper' for the woman!»: in the encounter of man and woman a unitary conception of the human person is brought about, based not on the logic of self-centredness and self-affirmation, but on that of love and solidarity."[50] A meeting with a person of the opposite sex gives rise to natural curiosity and surprise, and enables self-transcendence, that is, forgetting about oneself because of another person – so similar and yet so different at the same time. From the lips of

Adam spring out words of delight, which can be considered the first love song noted in the Bible.

A human being – as the Vatican Council teaches – "(…) is the only creature on earth which God willed for itself" and at the same time is the creature who "cannot fully find himself except through a sincere gift of himself."[51] Innocence in the state from before original sin allows a man and a woman to enjoy the whole truth about another human being. It allows a visualization of the beauty of the other person, which – although the first delight undoubtedly concerns the corporeality of a woman – transcends the physical dimension. It allows acceptance of another human being as a person. It teaches enjoyment of another as a person whom the Creator willed for himself or herself.

Perhaps the awareness of how radically Christianity transformed the world of pagan antiquity, bringing to it the conviction of equal dignity of men and women, is too weak today. It was manifested, among others, in the prohibition of killing "surplus" girls, a custom common in Roman culture; in the abolition of the father's right to marry his daughter against her will and to kill an adulterous daughter; in calling men to purity, which had previously applied only to women; and, [52] finally, in a departure from the metaphysics of the natural inferiority of women in relation to men, present both in the writings of Plato and of Aristotle.[53]

In Christianity, woman is placed at the side of the man as his other "I", as an interlocutor and suitable help.[54] The principle of reciprocity – in helping each other, but also in mutual submission one to the other in love – is characteristic of all thinking of John Paul II on the subject of relations between man and woman.[55] John Paul II emphasizes:

> (D)omination indicates the disturbance and *loss of the stability* of that *fundamental equality* which the man and the woman possess in the "unity of the two": and this is especially to the disadvantage of the woman, whereas only the equality resulting from their dignity as persons can give to their mutual relationship the character of an authentic *"communio personarum"*. While the violation of this equality, which is both a gift and a right deriving from God the Creator, involves an element to the disadvantage of the woman, at the same time it also diminishes the true dignity of

# VII. Male-Female Complementarity: Sexuality and the Catholic Priesthood

the man".[56] Elsewhere, the Pope writes: "Certainly, the validity of many assertions relating to the position of women in different sectors of society and of the Church cannot be denied. It is equally important to point out that women's new self-awareness also helps men to reconsider their way of looking at things, the way they understand themselves, where they place themselves in history and how they interpret it, and the way they organize social, political, economic, religious and ecclesial life.[57]

## It is not good for the man to be alone

When God creates the world, every day, looking at the work of his hands, he finds it good. Only in the second account of creation, when God looks at Adam, does he utter the opposite opinion: "It is not good for the man to be alone" (*Genesis* 2:18). This assessment is surprising since we find ourselves in the Garden of Eden before original sin. Adam enjoys God's friendship, and it would seem that he should not be lacking anything. He himself – as it seems – does not perceive any dearth. It is God, who notices a "fault" in the work of creation and decides to fix it. Adam begins to fully understand the meaning of God's correction only when he sees Eve by his side. The world without a woman was truly "deficient." This perception is made first by the sense of sight, and only then is intellectually "processed." "(M)an cannot exist "alone" (see: *Genesis* 2:18)" – writes St. John Paul II – "he can exist only as a "unity of the two", and therefore *in relation to another human person*. It is a question here of a mutual relationship: man to woman and woman to man."[58] The word "only" used here needs to be emphasized.

This remark applies to every human being because relationality is inscribed by God in human nature. The Pope also emphasizes a particularly important feature of priestly personality, which is the capacity to relate to others.[59] He writes:

> To be human means to be called to interpersonal communion. The text of Genesis 2:18-25 shows that marriage is the first and, in a sense, the fundamental dimension of this call. But it is not the only one. The whole of human history unfolds within the context of this call. In this history, on the basis of the principle of mutually

being "for" the other, in interpersonal "communion", there develops in humanity itself, in accordance with God's will, the integration of *what is "masculine" and what is "feminine"*.[60]

The Scripture repeatedly reminds of this God-given task. "(I)n the Lord" – writes St. Paul – "woman is not independent of man, nor is man independent of woman. For as woman came from man, so also man is born of woman. But everything comes from God" (1 *Corinthians* 11:11-12). The logical consequence of the observation that the woman is the necessary ontological complement" to the man is to state that neither can she be absent from the life of the priest. Otherwise, he would be threatened with some kind of "existential" disability and mental, and, perhaps, also spiritual, immaturity. A symptom of such immaturity is misogyny, manifested in a general fear of women as inherently "unclean", contempt or patronizing treatment of women, resulting from the belief in a "natural" superiority of men. It happens that a priest thinks that the main task of a woman is to wipe the floor twice with a cloth before he deigns to graciously walk on it.

In the life of a man – writes John Paul II – a woman appears as "a great source of inspiration (...) for the life of piety."[61] It is not sufficient, however, to view the potential relationships in the priestly life in their functional dimension. It is not only that other people, including women, are needed by priests in order for them to be able to properly fulfill their priestly responsibility. In the Apostolic Exhortation *Pastores Dabo Vobis* we read:

> Affective maturity presupposes an awareness that love has a central role in human life. In fact, (...) «Man cannot live without love. He remains a being that is incomprehensible for himself; his life is meaningless, if love is not revealed to him, if he does not encounter love, if he does not experience it and make it his own, if he does not participate intimately in it ». We are speaking of a love that involves the entire person, in all his or her aspects – physical, psychic and spiritual – and which is expressed in the "nuptial meaning" of the human body, thanks to which a person gives oneself to another and takes the other to oneself.[62]

Let us note that these words refer directly to seminary formation. To raise an emotionally mature man – also when he is to be a priest – one must not forget that he "cannot live without love". Hence the necessity, especially in the world marked by the trivialization of sexuality, that "an education for sexuality (...) should be truly and fully personal and therefore should present chastity in a manner that shows appreciation and love for it as a "virtue that develops a person's authentic maturity and makes him or her capable of respecting and fostering the 'nuptial meaning' of the body.""[63] The charism of celibacy – states John Paul II realistically – does not affect one's emotional and instinctive inclinations. In order for the reaction to the encounter with the opposite sex not to be neurotic fear, "candidates to the priesthood need an affective maturity which is prudent, able to renounce anything that is a threat to it, vigilant over both body and spirit, and capable of esteem and respect in interpersonal relationships between men and women."[64]

A woman usually enters a man's life as mother, wife, daughter, or sister. Each of these relationships is associated with a different kind of love. She brings "feminine genius" into his male world. The matter seems simple. However, in dealing with priestly life, the presence of women has a particular character and calls for a specific analysis".[65]

Since women appear in four different roles on the Pope's list, two of which, as directly related to marriage, are in conflict with priestly celibacy, let us dwell a little longer on the role of the woman as mother and sister. "Thus the dimensions of mother and sister" – we read – "*are the two fundamental dimensions* of the relationship between women and priests."[66] Although there is also a woman as a daughter in the context of spiritual fatherhood (see: *1 Thessalonians* 2:11; *Galatians* 4:19), this theme is not specifically worked out by the Pope. The Pope generally refers to the text from the Letter to Timothy (see: *1 Timothy* 5: 1-2).

**Woman as mother**

In every person's life, the mother is the first woman. "Our mother is *the woman to whom we owe our life*. She conceived us in her womb and brought us into the world amid the pains which are part of the experience of every woman who gives birth. Through childbirth, a special and almost *sacred* bond is established between a human being and his mother."[67] But motherhood is not just a biological fact. A woman, who makes a place in herself for a child that she carries under her heart for nine months, nourishes it with her "body", and gives birth to it amidst labour pains is generally linked with her child with such special love that the Bible recognizes such love as coming the closest to God's selfless love for man. "Can a mother forget the baby at her breast and have no compassion on the child she has borne? Though she may forget, I will not forget you!" (*Isaiah* 49:15). A mother teaches us to speak in our mother tongue, teaches us how to pray and love. In the case of priests, she is often the person who stands at the origins of her son's priestly vocation. It is not always as dramatic a story as that of St. Monica and St. Augustine. *"How many of us also owe to our mothers our very vocation to the priesthood!* Experience shows that very often it is the mother who for years nurtures in her own heart a desire for a priestly vocation for her son and *obtains it by praying with persevering trust and deep humility.* Thus, without imposing her own will, she favours with the effectiveness typical of faith the blossoming of an aspiration to the priesthood in the soul of her son, an aspiration which will bear fruit in due season."[68] This also shows a special relation of women towards the sacrament of priesthood. "They do not stand at the altar, but they send to the altar" – said Cardinal Stefan Wyszyński.[69]

At the level of nature, the bond with the mother is undoubtedly the strongest one in a priest's life. We remain children of our parents forever, something that also gives them, for example, the right to paternal or maternal rebuke. When a priest becomes such a serious person that no one dares to make critical comments towards him, there still remain his father and mother, and their love imbued with concern not so much for the earthly welfare of the son, but for his eternal salvation. For motherhood, like fatherhood, first and foremost has a spiritual dimension.[70]

To become a mature man and start adult life, the priest – like Lord Jesus – must say goodbye to his mother and leave the family home. The indication: "a man will leave his father and mother ..." (*Matthew* 19:5) also applies to clergy. One has to stop being a little boy to become an adult son. Here, a model of a proper relationship with a woman is shaped for life. In our priestly life, we are to treat older women as mothers – teaches St. Paul (1 *Timothy* 5:2). This means that a proper attitude towards one's mother is a condition for a proper relationship with women from this group. Without fear stemming from being oversensitive regarding our own independence, but also without letting them mother us too much. For mature women are sometimes tempted to manage the affairs of a priest or even those of a parish as part of "maternal" care. St. Luke describes what happened to Paul and Barnabas in Antioch of Pisidia: "But the Jewish leaders incited the God-fearing women of high standing and the leading men of the city. They stirred up persecution against Paul and Barnabas, and expelled them from their region" (*Acts* 13:50). "God-fearing women of high standing" should have limited influence on the life of a priest.

In my priestly life, my mother appeared also in at least two important roles: firstly, as the person conducting sacramental pre-evangelisation. My mother is a very warm, sociable person, who establishes contacts with people easily, much more easily than I do. She used to talk about God in her workplace, on the bus or on the tram, also approaching random people. And this happened during the times of communism. If it turned out that someone had not had a sacramental wedding, had not baptized a child, or had not been to confession for a long time, she would say, "My son will arrange it for you." And she sent these people to me. Often, indeed, the relation of this or that person with God was actually regulated. I had holy water in abundance. Secondly, when she was quite old and – as she herself put it – she was fulfilling increasingly well the command of Lord Jesus to become like a child. In my life, I have met many vulnerable people in need of help, but it was only when I looked into the eyes of my mother in such a situation that the gestures I made began to express what was happening in my heart. It has changed my attitude towards people who, for example, awkwardly cross the street to the other side or cannot find their purse while standing in front of me in the queue to the cash register.

**Woman as sister**

Following the figure of the mother, the figure of a sister appears in the life of a priest.[71] "Many of us priests have sisters in our families. In any event, every priest from childhood onwards has met girls, if not in his own family, at least in the neighbourhood, in childhood games or at school. A type of mixed community has *enormous importance for the formation of the personalities of boys and girls.*[72] I think that almost all of us priests remember some specific school friends, perhaps also a high school sweetheart. They continued their lives in one way or another, most often getting married. It is understandable that "(t)he vocation to marriage obviously assumes and requires that the environment in which one lives is made up of both men and women".[73] However, according to the Pope, not only the vocation to marriage, but also a vocation to the priesthood and the consecrated life requires living in the human environment composed of men and women. He writes:

> In this setting (...) there arise not only vocations to marriage but also *vocations to the priesthood and the consecrated life.* These do not develop in isolation. Every candidate for the priesthood, when he crosses the threshold of the seminary, has behind him the experience of his own family and of school, where he was able to meet many young people of his own age, of both sexes.[74]

It is not about just "being among" women and men. It is about the experience of meeting peers of the same and opposite sex, learning to see differences and similarities, to understand different ways of perceiving the world, and to approach with respect what is not fully understood.

We are all brothers and sisters in Christ. John Paul II points out that "also a bond such as that of "brotherhood" means something different from "brotherhood according to the flesh" deriving from a common origin from the same set of parents."[75] Firstly, brother and sister signify the relationship between "those who hear the word of God and obey it" (*Luke* 11:28), hence the figure of the "woman-sister" in the pages of the New Testament. St. Paul writes, "Don't we have the right to take a believing women-sister along with us, as do the other apostles and the Lord's brothers and Cephas?" (1 *Corinthians* 9:5).[76] However, he gives his disciple Timothy very specific advice to treat "younger women as sisters, with absolute purity" (1 *Timothy* 5:1-2). The "help" on the part a woman is so essential to a man in his experience of his humanity, and at the same time, how easily it is to be susceptible to abuse in this delicate area. That is why "(i)n order to live as a celibate in a mature and untroubled way it seems particularly important that the priest should develop deep within himself *the image of women as sisters"*, notes John Paul II.⁷⁷

## Selflessness

The word "sister" has multiple meanings in everyday language. In Christian civilization, we use this term in reference to not only our biological sisters or nuns, but also a broad group of women who became sisters in a universal manner, thanks to their sisterly attitude towards those the most in need:

> *A «sister» is a guarantee of selflessness:* in the school, in the hospital, in prison and in other areas of social service. When a woman remains single, in her "gift of self as sister" by means of apostolic commitment or generous dedication to neighbour, she develops a particular *spiritual motherhood*".⁷⁸ A reminder of this is especially important in times when there are so many women-singles, painfully experiencing their singleness. "This selfless gift of femininity "as sister" lights up human existence, evokes the best sentiments of which human beings are capable and always leaves behind gratitude for the good freely offered.⁷⁹

It is a creative way to use one's singleness, even if it was not the first choice in a woman's life.

In my priestly CV, I also have the experience of a brief – only thirteen months' long – work in the Vatican. I left the Holy City with the conviction that life there had only been possible thanks to two groups of people: the hidden saints (which is understandable by itself) and women. Pious women, unlike men, generally do not aim at pursuing a career. They simply do what they read in their lives as God's will. In a somewhat natural way, it is some kind of work of service, even if it brings with it a kind of universal recognition or "fame". Suffice it to mention Mother Teresa of Calcutta. The assumption that women are naturally more prone to selflessness than men is perhaps a kind of idealization, but perhaps to some extent justified by some Gospel texts. When, during the Last Supper, the Lord Jesus takes a bowl and a sheet to wash the Apostles' feet, twice he meets with opposition by Peter. "No," said Peter, "you shall never wash my feet" (*John* 13:8). The gesture that the Lord Jesus teaches his disciples was originally utterly incomprehensible to them. Perhaps it was because Peter sensed what obligation that would entail for him in a moment: "Now that I, your Lord and Teacher, have washed your feet, you also should wash one another's feet. I have set you an example that you should do as I have done for you" (*John* 13:14-15). Meanwhile, the same gesture is performed towards Jesus twice by women, as if anticipating his behaviour. First, we have the forgiven sinful woman (*Luke* 7:36-50) and then Mary, sister of Lazarus (*John* 12:1-8). In both cases, men react negatively to the woman's gesture. While Judas' words are not very surprising, the behaviour of Simon the Pharisee, who invited Jesus to dinner, is puzzling. Jesus says to Simon:

> Do you see this woman? I came into your house. You did not give me any water for my feet, but she wet my feet with her tears and wiped them with her hair. You did not give me a kiss, but this woman, from the time I entered, has not stopped kissing my feet. You did not put oil on my head, but she has poured perfume on my feet" (*Luke* 7:44-46).

Both women, even though for different reasons, spontaneously assume a serving attitude, while men carry out calculations.

### *Purity*

The word "sister" also reminds us of another important dimension of fraternal relationships – purity. "Certainly «woman as sister» represents a *specific manifestation of the spiritual beauty of women;* but it is at the same time a revelation that they are in a certain sense «set apart»".[80] The word "sister" also includes an emotional component. It denotes not so much a female person who wandered randomly around the family home, but the second woman after the mother, who – often also chronologically – appeared in the priest's life before any school friend appeared, and whom our parents taught us to love. Anyone who has experienced the love of a natural sister is perfectly able to capture the difference between the love that this woman, close to his heart, can bestow on him and the exclusivity of her feelings for her husband. Purity in the brother-sister relationship is not limited to the inviolability of the physical realm, but also to not encroaching on the spiritual intimacy reserved for the wife-husband relationship. I have a sister, younger than me, beautiful and wise (and she cooks well). She has recently been widowed. There has never been even a hint of ambiguity in the cordiality shown to each other. Simply put, her body is the body of the sister, and mine – the body of the brother. She has her family and I have my priesthood. Today, we are linked the most by the joint care for our mother. Based on the example of the relations with my sister, I also learned how to properly set up relations with other women. "What you think is inappropriate in relation to your own sister, do not do in relation to any woman", my confessor once told me.

Blood kinship alone does not guarantee absolute protection against emotional or sexual abuse. The Book of Leviticus includes a prohibition of "sexual relations with your sister, either your father's daughter or your mother's daughter, whether she was born in the same home or elsewhere" (*Leviticus* 18:9). We can guess that since such prohibition was established, it means that it was not devoid of purpose. The Biblical story of Amnon, son of David, who fell in love with his sister, tells not only about the bad brother-to-sister relation, but also about a pattern of sexual abuse evidenced to this day (see 2 *Samuel* 13:1-19).

Purity breeds trust. John Paul II emphasizes, "Every priest thus has the great *responsibility of developing an authentic way of relating* to women *as a brother*, a way of relating which does not admit of ambiguity".[81] I once came across a statement by a woman who worked closely with priests: "When I meet with a priest who is my parish priest, my children's catechist, a community moderator or the director of an institution, I have to remember that I am meeting him like I meet with other men, for example a married neighbour or a colleague from work".[82] This is not only about inappropriate conduct, but also about responsibility for inappropriate feelings. It must not be forgotten that a woman not only has a more delicate body (see: 1 *Peter* 3:7) but is generally also more sensitive emotionally. Allowing anyone into a friendship relationship makes us forever responsible for this relationship. "You become responsible, forever, for what you have tamed."[83] The company of women, especially the young ones, should not be regarded as a type of "compensation" to the priest for the fact that he lives in the solitude of celibacy. It is easy for a priest, under the pretext of priestly duties, to gather around a group of female admirers, who are kept in a kind of emotional dependence. On the one hand, young men, potential competitors to the feelings of single girls, usually disappear from the pastoral work. On the other hand, enticing women's emotional attachment, even if not accompanied by the slightest appearance of physical impurity, may in itself be impure, that is, tinged with wrong intention. Each of them has her own vocation: some are to get married, others to enter a convent, and for the rest, God has some other specific plans. John Paul II gives a special criterion for proper conduct in this respect. Women who are treated as a mother or sister in an honest and mature manner "will find no particular difficulties in their contact with priests. For example they will not find difficulties in confessing their faults in the Sacrament of Penance".[84] This does not mean that priests, as a rule, should confess the women with whom they are friends. I think that it is not so much about the psychological aspect as about the internal disposition of the priest, required by canon 977 of the Code of Canon Law.

There are women, shaking whose hand is too much – you feel they do not want to let your hand go; there are also those where a tender greeting in the presence of the husband is completely innocent. There are individual women to whom I have refused confession because in other similar situations I found that I was asked for spiritual direction just in order to enable them to meet with me.

### Fidelity to the Vocation

> If in a relationship with a woman the [priest's] gift and the choice of celibacy should become endangered, the priest cannot but strive earnestly to remain faithful to his own vocation. Such a defence would not mean that marriage in itself is something bad, but that for him the path is a different one. For him to abandon that path would be to break the word he has given to God.[85]

The Pope emphasizes, on the one hand, a special responsibility on the part of the priest, and on the other hand, that "help" is truly a help only when it helps to grow in holiness on the path of the particular person's proper vocation. In the case of a priest, it is the vocation of priesthood, for there is no "third way" between marriage and celibacy. Jesus, in the Gospel list of persons to be abandoned if the relationship with them were to conflict with the love for him, also mentions the sister (see *Matthew* 19:29). "For too little doth he love Thee, who loves any thing with Thee, which he loveth not for Thee."[86] We will not learn to love God while learning not to love people. But St. Augustine, author of the commentary on the First Letter of St. John, teaches us to love man "for" God.

What is the proper measure of the purity of man? Card. Raniero Cantalamessa notes that when St. Paul writes about the "unleavened bread of purity" (1 Corinthians 5:7-8), he uses the Greek word *heilikrineia*, which embraces the notion of sunshine (*heile*) and trial and judgement (*krino*). It therefore means solar transparency; something that has been viewed under the light and found pure.[87] One day we will, therefore, be judged by the Sun. It seems that this purity, in order to be able to pass successfully this exam, is achieved only with time and after the trial, if at all. Even the greatest saints did not immediately manage to find the right balance in this area. Undoubtedly, however – as shown in the example of St. Teresa of Avila - deep prayer is the most effective tool for purifying a person:

> The vision of Christ left behind an impression of His exceeding beauty, and it remains with me to this day. (...) One exceedingly great blessing has resulted therefrom, and it is this,—I had one very grievous fault, which was the source of much evil; namely, whenever I found anybody well disposed towards myself, and I liked him, I used to have such an affection for him as compelled me always to remember and think of him, though I had no intention of offending God: however, I was pleased to see him, to think of him and of his good qualities. All this was so hurtful, that it brought my soul to the very verge of destruction. But ever since I saw the great beauty of our Lord, I never saw any one who in comparison with Him seemed even endurable, or that could occupy my thoughts. For if I but turn mine eyes inwardly for a moment to the contemplation of the image which I have within me, I find myself so free, that from that instant everything I see is loathsome in comparison with the excellences and graces of which

I had a vision in our Lord. Neither is there any sweetness, nor any kind of pleasure, which I can make any account of, compared with that which comes from hearing but one word from His divine mouth. What, then, must it be when I hear so many? I look upon it as impossible—unless our Lord, for my sins, should permit the loss of this remembrance—that I should have the power to occupy myself with anything in such a way as that I should not instantly recover my liberty by thinking of our Lord.[88]

## Mary, Mother of priests[89]

The Blessed Virgin Mary, virgin and mother, according to the tradition of the Church, is the fundamental model of a woman. "The Mother of the Son of God has become the "great inspiration" for individuals and for whole Christian nations. This too, in its own way, *tells us much about the importance of women in human life,* and, in a special way, *in the life of the priest.*"[90]

Marian piety played a very important role in the life of Karol Wojtyła / John Paul II. This fact is sometimes interpreted as an effect of some kind of compensation after the early loss of his mother. It must not be forgotten, however, that Marian devotion is an important element of experiencing the Catholic faith in Poland in general, in the land dotted with Marian shrines. Mary occupied a central place also in the life of Stefan Cardinal Wyszyński, a generation older than Wojtyła, who used to supplement his episcopal call of *Soli Deo!* with the words *per Mariam.* Finally, it should also be remembered that Wojtyła's spiritual master and guide in this field was St. Luis Grignion de Montfort, a man originating from a different cultural tradition.

In *Redemptoris Mater*, we have quite a long reflection on the woman who called out to Jesus from amongst the crowd: "Blessed is the womb that bore you, and the breasts that you sucked!" (*Luke* 11:27). Through his response, the Pope states that Jesus "wishes to divert attention from motherhood understood only as a fleshly bond, in order to direct it towards those mysterious bonds of the spirit which develop from hearing and keeping God's word."[91] He speaks of a new kind of motherhood that comes from listening to God's Word and following it in one's life. Mary is an exemplification of such an attitude. Antonello da Messina in the painting

Annunciata "forgot" to paint the Archangel Gabriel transmitting God's will. The Holy Scriptures and a little wind were enough for Mary to understand the meaning of the Annunciation and "transfer" the Word from the Bible directly to her womb. In her life, "(t)hrough faith Mary continued to hear and to ponder that word [Annunciation], in which there became ever clearer, in a way "which surpasses knowledge" (see: *Ephesians* 3:19). Thus, in a sense, Mary as Mother became the first "disciple" of her Son."[92] And at the foot of the Cross, she became "our mother in the order of grace."[93] The Church does not hesitate to call her the Mother of Christ and the Mother of the people, "having cooperated by charity that faithful might be born in the Church, who are members of that Head."[94] Through Mary's spiritual motherhood, we come to the priest's relationship with a woman, which initially seemed absolutely excluded: the priest and the daughter. For what is excluded in the physical dimension is possible in the spiritual dimension. A priest's task is not only to celebrate the sacraments or to offer spiritual guidance. It is also, by analogy with Mary's attitude, spiritual fatherhood for both men and women.

One of the special dimensions of piety, linking the Mother of God with the priesthood, is her relationship with the Eucharist through the relationship between the human body of Jesus and the Eucharistic body. By offering herself to the Incarnation of God's Word, "(i)n a certain sense Mary lived her *Eucharistic faith* even before the institution of the Eucharist" – we read in the encyclical letter *Ecclesia de Eucharistia*.[95] "At the Annunciation Mary conceived the Son of God in the physical reality of his body and blood, thus anticipating within herself what to some degree happens sacramentally in every believer who receives, under the signs of bread and wine, the Lord's body and blood."[96] In the visitation of her relative, Mary appears as the first tabernacle in history in which St. Elizabeth adores the Son of God. St. John the Apostle, taking her "to himself", at the same time, accepts everything that was written on Golgotha in the heart of the mother of Christ the Redeemer.[97] Mary is discreetly, yet very realistically, present in the sacrament of priesthood.[98] John Paul II writes:

> What must Mary have felt as she heard from the mouth of Peter, John, James and the other Apostles the words spoken at the Last Supper: «This is my body which is given for you» (*Luke* 22:19)?

The body given up for us and made present under sacramental signs was the same body which she had conceived in her womb! For Mary, receiving the Eucharist must have somehow meant welcoming once more into her womb that heart which had beat in unison with hers and reliving what she had experienced at the foot of the Cross.[99]

Our ability to understand the feelings of Mary's heart helps us to live the Eucharist properly:

*For us, as priests, the Last Supper is an especially holy moment.* Christ, who says to the Apostles: "Do this in remembrance of me" (1 Cor 11:24), institutes the Sacrament of Holy Orders. With respect to our lives as priests, this is *an eminently Christocentric moment:* for we receive the priesthood from Christ the Priest, the one Priest of the New Covenant. But as we think of the sacrifice of the Body and Blood, which we offer *in persona Christi, we find it difficult not to recognize therein the presence of the Mother.*[100]

### Friendship that leads to Holiness

On the one hand, it is difficult to imagine a priest who works exclusively with men. On the other hand, as Clive S. Lewis warns, friendship between people of the opposite sex very easily – sometimes within half an hour – turns into erotic love.[101] The concern to keep it pure and non-exclusive is not an easy task. An elderly priest acquaintance of mine used to say, "Next to the male monastery there is a female monastery. Nothing wrong with that. But it can be." We have many good examples of friendship between priests and women, but probably even more examples of those who have suffered a severe defeat. Non-exclusivity can also be understood in the sense that it is not about a priest's relationship with only one woman, but a certain type of friendly relationship that is by nature open to a larger number of people. So, the priest has friends, and they are not only men.

However, books on the mutual relations between priest and woman generally contain not only tips and warnings but also a series of positive examples of male-female friendship that led friends to holiness. This list usually includes the names of St. Benedict and St. Scholastica, St. Francis and St. Clare, Blessed Henry Suso and Sister Elsbeth Stagel, Blessed Jordan of Saxony and Blessed Diana Andalò, St. Francis de Sales and St. Jane Francis de Chantal, St. Brother Albert Chmielowski and Blessed Bernardine Maria Jabłońska. This list can be significantly extended by adding, for example, the names of holy women and their holy confessors. Note that on this "standard" list we have almost only religious sisters, that is, people living in a monastery. A man can learn a lot from a woman, and a woman from a man, also on the path to holiness. Personally, already as a priest, I learned adoration of the Blessed Sacrament from a woman, although I still remain far from holiness.

St. John Paul II, sometime after his election, wrote to his friend from Cracow, Wanda Półtawska: "You have walked step in step alongside with my priesthood, and for so many years you have participated in the discovery of these meanings and these values. You have participated creatively. You cannot say that you do not see a «place» for yourself now."[102] She was the Pope's personal advisor on issues related to *Humanae vitae*. She was by his side when he was lying in the Gemelli Clinic after the assassination attempt. *La Stampa,* due to the personal investigation she carried out in the Vatican regarding the mysterious photos taken of the Pope during his convalescence, called her "agent 007 of John Paul II". The photos revealed that there were serious security gaps since the Pope could be photographed from such a long distance.

"Man cannot live without love. He remains a being that is incomprehensible for himself, his life is senseless, if love is not revealed to him, if he does not encounter love, if he does not experience it and make it his own, if he does not participate intimately in it" – wrote John Paul II in his encyclical letter *Redemptor hominis*. And although this truth also applies to human love, the proper sense of the above sentence applies to Christ's love revealed in the mystery of the Redemption. "How precious must man be in the eyes of the Creator, if he «gained so great a Redeemer», and if God «gave his only Son» in order that man «should not perish but have eternal life»" (see: *John* 3:16). "In reality, the name for that deep amazement at man's worth and dignity is the Gospel, that is to say: the Good News. It is also called Christianity".[103] St. Teresa of Jesus wrote of this Love. Only one whose love led to the discovery of true Love can say along with her: *Sólo Dios basta!*

# VIII

# Sexual Integrity, Spirituality and Priestly Formation

## Patricia Cooney Hathaway

*Professor of Spiritual and Systematic Theology,
Sacred Heart Major Seminary*

**Introduction**

In the introduction to "The Gift of the Priestly Vocation," the new *Ratio Fundamentalis,* prepared by the Congregation for the Clergy in Rome, the bishops emphasize that the seminarian is the "agent" of his own formation: "Even if much of the effectiveness of the training offered depends on the maturity and the strength of personality of those entrusted with formation, one must always keep in mind that the seminarian first—and later the priest—is the *necessary and irreplaceable agent in his own formation* [emphasis mine]."[1] In other words, "agent of his own formation" refers to the responsibility of the seminarian to pursue integrity in all aspects of his life, especially, in relation to the topic of this chapter, the integration of a healthy approach to the sexual and spiritual dimensions of life—one that can only take place through the inspiration and guidance of the Holy Spirit who is the true formator.

The description of sexual integrity which informs this study is found in the writings of Pope John Paul II who states that a person of sexual integrity knows the truth about the meaning of sexuality, can abide by that truth, and joyfully act in accord with that truth.[2] Sexual Integrity involves the practice of being honest and consistent in living out of a certain set of principles and values regarding the role of sexuality in one's live, even in the face of adversity and criticism. Thus, a correct understanding of the meaning that the Church brings to sexuality and spirituality is paramount in the life of a seminarian. I have found that some men, influenced by a culture that is steeped in the subjectivity of human sexuality and the relativism of moral values, arrive at the seminary with a distorted view of sexuality as well as a rather privatized understanding of spirituality. The consequences of such perspectives are described in an article, "Educating Seminarians for Healthy Sexuality," by Brother James Zullo: "Male and female attitudes toward sexuality can either hinder or facilitate our growth toward healthy spiritual lives. One cannot develop a healthy spirituality when one has misguided or misinformed notions about human sexuality."[3]

This chapter explores the relationship between sexual integrity, spirituality and their expression in programs for priestly formation. It begins with a description of sexual integrity, followed by a presentation of the Christian meaning of sexuality and spirituality which needs to be internalized by seminarians. It then examines the most recent guideline for priestly formation, "The Gift of the Priestly Vocation,"[4] regarding the integration of the Church's teaching on sexuality and spirituality in formation programs. This section is followed by a presentation of two formation programs in the United States as examples of the efforts to educate and form seminarians as men of integrity in all areas of their lives, which is followed by the author's reflections on the strengths and limitations of current priestly formation programs drawing on her experience as faculty member of Sacred Heart Major Seminary for many years. The final section addresses how formation programs are responding to the sex abuse crisis.

## Toward a Christian Understanding of Sexuality and Spirituality

Given the confusion about sexuality that permeates our culture, it is important to begin with a clarification of terms. The word, "sex" has a Latin root from the verb *secare*, which means literally to "cut off," "to sever," "to disconnect from the whole."[5] Many people are surprised by the negative connotation, yet does it not express our experience of life? We are pushed out of the warm, nurturing womb of our mothers into a world that will often be experienced, even in the best of circumstances, as arbitrary, inhospitable, or not necessarily committed to our well-being. Feeling incomplete or disconnected, we often search out relationships that will make us feel connected, secure and whole.

## VIII. Sexual Integrity, Spirituality and Priestly Formation

Unfortunately, the term "sexuality" as commonly used today, does not reflect its original meaning. On the contrary, it carries the very narrow connotation of "having sex." A basic understanding of sexuality includes the following: *Sex* refers to the biological difference between male and female determined by their anatomy at birth. *Gender* is a psychological and social term that refers to the meaning a person and/or society gives to the attributes of masculinity and femininity. Today, beliefs about gender are shifting rapidly and radically. We are surrounded by evolving notions of what it means to be a woman or a man and the explosion, connotation and confusion around the meaning and implications of terms (e.g., cisgender, transgender, gender dysphoria, etc.). *Genitality* refers to the physical expression and consummation of our capacity for intimacy and generativity. And finally, chastity is a virtue that enables women and men to be faithful to their commitments and to be respectful of the personhood of others.[6]

Given the fact that in the past, for the most part, Christianity has been influenced by negative and unchristian views of sex, it has not developed a life-giving spirituality of sexuality.[7] Thankfully, in recent years, that has changed. The document, "The Truth and Meaning of Sexuality," from the Pontifical Council for the Family emphasizes that "sexuality is a fundamental component of personality, one of its modes of being, of manifestation, of communicating with others, of feeling, of expressing and of living human love."[8] Contemporary theologians also stress that sexuality refers to an all-encompassing desire within us—a desire planted in us by God—for love, community, friendship, family, affection, wholeness, joy and delight.

In his book, *Intimate Connection: Male Sexuality, Masculine Spirituality*, Dr. James Nelson describes sexuality as the physiological and psychological grounding of our capacity to love. At its undistorted best, our sexuality is that basic *eros* of our humanness—urging, pulling, luring, driving us out of loneliness into communion, out of stagnation into creativity. It is "God's ingenious way of calling us into communion with others through our need to reach out and touch and embrace—emotionally, intellectually and physically."[9] In light of this perspective, I believe it is fair to say that from a Christian perspective the very desire that moves us toward intimacy and communion with one another is the same desire that moves us into a love relationship with God. One could say they are two sides of the same coin. A realistic view of sexuality, however, also recognizes that due to sin, this powerful desire and drive can be misdirected into unhealthy attitudes and harmful behaviors that deeply wound, hurt, misuse and abuse others. That is why one of the fundamental tasks of spirituality is to help us understand and channel our sexuality correctly.

Unfortunately, many Catholics today, and that includes men coming into the seminary, live out of a narrow, privatized approach to spirituality—one that centers around the interior life of prayer, devotions, and the sacramental life of the Church. While that is true, a contemporary approach to spirituality broadens that understanding to include the bodily, social, political and secular dimensions of life. Christian spirituality, then, refers to a manner of living in which we respond to God's initiative in Christ, through the power of the Holy Spirit within the context of one's daily life, celebrated in community and dedicated to bringing about God's kingdom of love, mercy, and forgiveness in our world. Encountering God within the context of our daily lives includes our sexuality; that is, it affirms the presence of God and the sacred in our sexual desires, feelings, and expressions of love and affection toward others.

The importance of the integration of these two areas of our lives is expressed well in the writings of Pope John Paul II and Pope Benedict XVI. Seminarians listen carefully to the authoritative teaching of a pope, so their perspective plays a key role in the seminarian's formation. A few of the central principles of Pope John Paul's "Theology of the Body" include,

- God created man and woman in His image and likeness. We are created different yet equal. (Genesis 1:26-27)
- From the beginning, human beings have had a special relationship of love and intimacy with God that is unlike any other creature.
- Sexuality is a "good" created by God.
- In creating us male and female, our very embodiment is central to who we are and to our relationship with God; we are not souls that happen to be attached to bodies; rather we are body person.

- The consequence of sin is disunity which results in a strained relationship between humanity and God, but also among human beings and between spirit and flesh within each of us.
- The Word made Flesh in Jesus is the source of our redemption. "Through Jesus, the body entered theology...through the main door...for it is the body, and it alone, that is capable of making visible what is invisible"[10] the spiritual and the divine.
- The lynch pin of John Paul's teaching resides in the nuptial meaning of the body; that is our capacity for self-giving love.[11]

Building on John Paul II's Theology of the Body, Pope Benedict XVI's contribution to a positive approach to the integration of human and spiritual development is found in his teaching on the relationship between *eros* and *agape* in his encyclical *Deus Caritas Est*:

- He questions the Enlightenment critique that Christianity destroyed *eros*.
- He maintains that Christianity has not destroyed *eros* but rather has declared war on the cultural distortion of *eros* as lust—that is, as a kind of intoxication that overpowers reason and strips *eros* of its dignity and dehumanizes it.
- He emphasizes that only when *eros* is joined to agape, a self-giving love that seeks only the flourishing and well-being of another person, does the human person attain his or her full stature.
- He affirms Jesus as a model of a healthy integration of *eros* and *agape*.[12]

This overview of the meaning our Christian tradition sheds light on sexual integrity; sexuality and spirituality provide a framework for evaluating the guidelines provided by the latest document on priestly formation from the Congregation of the Clergy, "The Gift of the Priestly Vocation,"[13] to which we will now turn.

## Guidelines for Seminarian Formation: The Gift of the Priestly Vocation

The Congregation for the Clergy began preparing the first draft of the present *Ratio Fundamentalis* in 2014. From its beginning through 2015, it was sent to a number of Dicasteries of the Roman Curia, numerous conferences of Bishops, Apostolic Nunciatures, among others for their input. The Congregation for the Clergy also organized an International Conference held in November 2015 during which Cardinals, Bishops, professors, formators and experts offered their valuable contributions to the discussion of the formation of candidates for Holy Orders. At the end of this consultation process, and in light of the suggestions received, a definitive text was brought to Pope Francis for his approval.[14]

In December 2016, the Vatican brought forth this new set of guidelines for the formation of seminarians to ordained priesthood. All seminarian formation programs must now be based on this edition which builds on several previously written documents on priestly formation, particularly Pope John Paul II's ground-breaking post-Synodal Apostolic Exhortation, *Pastores Dabo Vobis* (25 March 1992). Most significant, this document was promulgated in response to recognizing that there was a need for a new *Ratio Fundamentalis*. Why the need? As we know, there have been many changes in the Church and the world since the last *Ratio* was written in 1970, so it is crucial that there is a document that reflects what seminarian formation looks like today. Certainly, the sexual abuse crisis and the growing secularization of culture raised concerns about the adequacy and effectiveness of existing seminary formation programs.

This new *Ratio Fundamentalis*, "The Gift of the Priestly Vocation," presents formation as consisting of two phases: *initial and ongoing*. As the focus of this chapter is on initial formation, I will concentrate on areas within initial formation which the *Ratio* outlines. The first includes priestly identity, which acknowledges that the seminarian must gradually come to see himself configured to Christ who is head, shepherd, servant and spouse:[15]

> The priest is, therefore, called to form himself so that his heart and his life are conformed to the Lord Jesus, in this way becoming a

sign of the love God has for each person. By being intimately united to Christ, he will be able to preach the Gospel and become an instrument of the mercy of God…. while also responding to the demands and the deep questions of our time.[16]

The second area of emphasis consists of four stages whose characteristics are as follows:

1. **The Propaedeutic or Preparatory period.** This stage is now considered mandatory. It follows the primary discernment of a vocation and the first vocational accompaniment outside the seminary. The document states that the experience of recent decades has revealed the need to dedicate a period of time to preparation of an introductory nature. Its principal objective is to provide a solid basis for the spiritual life and to nurture a greater awareness for personal growth.[17]

2. **The Stage of Discipleship, the period of philosophical studies.** Pursuant to the focus of this chapter, this stage places special attention on the human dimension of formation, particularly areas of physical, psycho-affective, and sexual growth toward a mature, balanced personality required of a future priest:

    > For priestly formation, the importance of human formation cannot be sufficiently emphasized. Indeed, the holiness of the priest is built upon it and depends, in large part, upon the authenticity and maturity of his humanity. The lack of a well-structured and balanced personality is a serious and objective hindrance to the continuation of formation for priesthood.[18]

3. **The Stage of Theological Studies (or Configuration)** focuses on the spirituality of the seminarian: i.e., the absolute necessity of developing a deep, personal relationship with Jesus Christ and the internalization of his disposition and values. Most important is the seminarian's pursuit of this configuration with interior freedom

and joy, without any imposition from without. The document states:

> The content of this stage is demanding and requires a great deal of commitment. It asks for a constant responsibility in living the cardinal and theological virtues and the evangelical counsels. It demands a docility to the action of God through the promptings of the Holy Spirit, according to an authentically priestly and missionary mindset.[19]

4. **The Pastoral Stage (or Vocational Synthesis)** begins with the Order of Diaconate wherein the seminarian leaves the seminary and begins his pastoral life. The stage has a twofold purpose: on the one hand it is about being inducted into the pastoral life, with a gradual assumption of responsibilities in a spirit of service; on the other hand, it is about making a suitable preparation, with the help of a specific accompaniment, in view of the priesthood. Most important, during this stage the candidate is asked to declare freely, consciously and definitively his intention to be a priest, having received diaconal ordination.[20]

As we have seen in this overview, this section of the *Ratio* emphasizes that the intellectual life is not to be the only factor to be considered in evaluating the progress made by the seminarian at each stage. On the contrary, only those seminarians will pass on to the next stage, who, in addition to having passed the necessary exams, will have reached the level of human and vocational maturity required for each stage.[21]

In addition to the four stages of formation, the new *Ratio* updated the language around the fundamental guidelines for priestly formation. Drawing on the work of Pope John Paul II in *Pastores Dabo Vobis*, where he describes the fundamental guidelines of priestly formation as four pillars: human, spiritual, intellectual, and pastoral, this updated *Ratio* changed "pillars" to "dimensions" and revised the content and goal of each. This change was made out of concern that the term "pillars" can be interpreted as static compartmentalization of each area, whereas "dimen-

## VIII. Sexual Integrity, Spirituality and Priestly Formation

sions" emphasize the dynamic interpenetration and interdependence of each with the others and within the seminarian.[22]

### Human Dimension

The section on the human dimension of formation begins by stating that the divine call engages and involves the "concrete" human person. It emphasizes that a "correct and harmonious spiritual life demands a well-structured humanity; indeed, as St. Thomas Aquinas reminds us, *grace builds upon nature*, it does not supplant nature, but perfects it."[23] So that this training is fruitful, the document insists that every seminarian be aware of his family history—its strengths, possible dysfunctions, and the wounds he may carry due to his upbringing. It stresses the importance of his sharing this history with his formators so that he does not bring these issues into the service of the Christian community. It stresses the importance of a well–integrated sexuality, although it does not spell out what that integration includes—thus, the importance of the first section of this chapter which describes the meaning of sexuality and spirituality within the Christian tradition.[24] Finally, it promotes the integral growth of the person and encourages the integration of all its dimensions, each interpenetrating the others.

### Spiritual Dimension

The area of spiritual formation focuses on: establishing a deep, personal relationship with God, nourished by prolonged and silent prayer; reflection on the Word of God through the practice of Lectio Divina; and devout participation in the sacraments, liturgy and community life, with special emphasis on the sacraments of the Eucharist and Penance. The evangelical counsels have an important role in the spirituality of the priest, following Jesus in faith, simplicity and freedom of heart. Over time, the seminarian must come to recognize and welcome celibacy in a spirit of interior freedom and joy as a special gift of God. As such:

> With a proper emotional formation, understood as a journey toward the fullness of love, priestly celibacy must not be viewed

so much as something that has to be given up for God as a gift received from his mercy. The one who enters upon this state of life must be aware that he is not assuming a burden but receiving, above all, a liberating grace.[25]

The document also states that it would be gravely imprudent to admit to the sacrament of Orders a seminarian who does not enjoy free and serene affective maturity.[26]

## The Intellectual Dimension

The area of intellectual formation aims to deepen the faith of the seminarian through achieving a solid competence in philosophy and theology, along with a more general educational preparation. This competence is essential so that the seminarian may proclaim the Gospel message to the people of our own day with credibility, thus enabling them to enter into dialogue with the contemporary world.[27]

## The Pastoral Dimension

Since a goal of formation is to prepare seminarians to be shepherds in the image of Christ for the service of the people of God, priestly formation must be permeated by a pastoral spirit. This includes compassion, generosity, love for all, especially the poor, and zeal for the Kingdom of God which characterized the public ministry of Jesus Christ. In a particular way, seminarians must be duly prepared to work together with permanent deacons and with the laity, appreciating their particular contributions. Formation also should prepare them to be experts in the art of pastoral discernment, that is to say, able to listen deeply to real situations and capable of good judgment in making choices and decisions.[28] A sound pastoral formation should include apostolic experiences as well as a study of pastoral theology which includes the contribution of the human sciences, especially of psychology, pedagogy and sociology.[29]

In conclusion, the *Ratio Fundamentalis* stresses that these four dimensions give shape and structure to the identity of the seminarian and the priest and make him capable of that "gift of self" to the Church which is the essence of pastoral charity. It further states that the entire journey of formation must never be reduced to a single aspect to the detriment of others, but it must always be an integrated journey of the disciple called to priesthood.[30]

### *Ratio Nationalis:* Shaping Men of Integrity

Considering new understandings of the dynamics of the human person, the *Ratio Fundamentalis* states that each conference of bishops is required to prepare its own *Ratio Nationalis*.[31] Each should include:

- A summary description of the particular social, cultural, and ecclesial context in which a future priest will find themselves exercising ministry.
- A description of the stages of formation, placed in the context of the particular situation of the country.
- A description of the means to be adopted to provide for the dimensions of formation (human, spiritual, intellectual, and pastoral).[32]

I have chosen two examples of formation programs that have adopted the directives and guidelines from "The Gift of the Priestly Vocation": Sacred Heart Major Seminary located in Detroit, Michigan, and the Institute for Priestly Formation's Summer Program (IPF) for Diocesan Seminarians based at Creighton University, Omaha, Nebraska. Each has developed a positive, realistic and substantial formation program regarding the internalization and integration of the sexual and spiritual components of life. The goal of each is to form men of integrity—in relation to the focus of this chapter—who have internalized the principles and values of the Church's teaching regarding the integration of the sexual and spiritual dimensions of life.

### *Sacred Heart Major Seminary (SHMS): Program in Chaste Celibacy*

Several years ago, the Rector of Sacred Heart Major Seminary formed a committee which was charged with reviewing our celibacy formation program; and making suggestions for a renewed program. The committee concluded that our students would be best served by a program that would cover the basic content areas across the three levels of Sacred Heart's formation: College, Philosophy and Theology. The committee designed a program so that a student would cover ten basic components throughout his formation period, taking care that what was presented would be deepened at each level of formation. The content areas, which are covered over a six-year period, were developed according to the three levels. The ten content areas, each with guiding questions are described as follows:

- **Key documents:** A study of the magisterial documents on priestly celibacy; documents from the Universal Magisterium; documents from the USCCB and documents of local bishops. Guiding question: What does the wisdom of the Church teach me about living as a celibate?
- **Scriptural Foundations**: A study of the New Testament texts that refer to celibacy and to the priesthood. Guiding question: What texts give wisdom or edification for celibate living?
- **History of the celibate priesthood:** Presentation and discussion of the differing interpretations of the history of celibate priesthood in the Church; the exemplary celibate priests in our history. Guiding questions: What does the Holy Spirit teach me about my celibacy through the Church's experience of priestly celibacy? What are the pitfalls I can avoid when I look at the history?
- **Age Appropriate Psychosexual Development; Counseling Others**: A study of the stages of psychosexual development for men and women. The moral dimension of our psychosexual development will be discussed. Discussion of pastoral counseling directed at assisting parishioners to deal with the gift of their sexuality. Guiding questions: What desires and behaviors are normal? When should I get special help with my psychosexual development? What are the "bottom lines" regarding psychosexual development and being a seminarian? A priest?
- **Prayer; Relationship with God:** A practical study of prayer forms of our Catholic tradition. Discussion of developing a pattern of prayer to sustain one's relationships as a priest. Guiding

## VIII. Sexual Integrity, Spirituality and Priestly Formation

questions: What does it mean to say that the Lord is my "other"? What do I need to be healthy and generous in my celibacy?

- **Celibacy and the Evangelical Counsels:** Study and discussion of the life of celibacy in the context of a life of simplicity and ecclesial obedience. Guiding questions: How does celibacy fit in with the call to radical discipleship? What other dimensions of discipleship can help me be chaste and generous?
- **Celibacy and Priesthood:** Study and discussion of the life of celibacy in the context of ordained priesthood. Theological and practical reflection on the life of the celibate priest. Guiding questions: What about celibacy fits in with our beliefs about the priesthood and the Eucharist? How does celibacy help a priest in his ministry?
- **Capacity for Intimacy in Human Friendships**: Fraternity study and discussion of the capacity/need for intimacy as a gift. Guiding questions: How does friendship figure into the life of a priest? What commitments are involved in being a member of the seminary community or the fraternity of priests? What is the difference between friendship and fraternity? What does one do when one falls in love?
- **Discerning a Call to Celibacy:** Study of the discernment of God's will according to St. Ignatius of Loyola. A discussion of celibacy as service and spousal celibacy. Guiding questions: What kind of confirmation of a call should I look for? What kind of confirmation is unrealistic?
- **Strategies for Living Celibacy and Purity**: A study and discussion of practical ways of living a healthy celibate lifestyle. A discussion of the temptations to unchaste behaviors such as masturbation, use of pornography, and sexual activity with others. Guiding questions: What are long-term strategies for chaste living? What do I do with sexual desire? What should be done if one falls in love as a seminarian? As a priest?[33]

These ten topics should be continually reassessed by the faculty and formation team. Are they attending to the real issues newly ordained priests will confront? Are they too focused on the seminarian's personal integration and not enough on ministerial issues such as: the ability to work in a productive way with women; boundary issues; ability to work with members of the laity in positions of authority; and the cultural confusion about gender issues and the meaning of masculinity and femininity? Finally, is the academic faculty adequately involved in the assessment of what constitutes the content of these ten topics, sharing the insights which come out of their training and life experience?

## *The Institute for Priestly Formation's Summer Program for Diocesan Seminarians*

Seminarians from around the country, including many from Sacred Heart Major Seminary, have benefited from the summer formation course, "Growing into Authentic Manhood with Christ the Priest," located at Creighton University, Omaha, Nebraska. The vision of the course is to foster the integration of the human and spiritual dimensions of the seminarian's life so that he can faithfully exercise Christ's own pastoral charity in his future ministry. Relying on the *Ratio Fundamentalis*, published by the Vatican, the course promotes the integration of the whole man in relationship with Jesus Christ with the intent that seminarians will acquire the understanding and the tools to equip them to choose the steps that will facilitate the joyful, generous living out of their vocation. The topics cover many areas vital to the integration of a healthy sexuality with a robust spiritual life:

- **Rules for the Discernment of Spirits**: The seminarian learns to apply the various Rules for the Discernment of Spirits to deepen his awareness and understanding of the integration of his humanity and his spirituality to be able to choose fidelity to Christ in his daily living.
- **Authentic Manhood in Christ:** The ideal of Christian manhood is found in the characteristics of Jesus Christ, in his words/teaching, his actions and his relationships. Jesus understands himself first and foremost to be Son of the Father, and he lives every part of his life in reference to this foundational relation-ship

with the Father. The seminarian will understand that friendship with Jesus leads to authentic manhood.

- **Authentic Manhood in Christ—Growing into Maturity:** Given the confusion around masculine identity in our culture, this topic explores competing images of manhood prevalent in our culture and challenges the seminarian to exercise discernment regarding what kind of man he wants to become. The seminarian will gain an understanding of a vision of manhood in Christ in contrast to the view of contemporary culture.
- **Authentic Masculinity:** Becoming a Man of Communion. The mature man is one who is capable of falling in love, who is interiorly free to exercise self-giving love. The authentic man in Christ is always one who seeks communion. The seminarian will become aware of the importance of growing in *affective maturity*.
- **Man of Communion—Living in Healthy Relationships**: The experience of being loved deeply by the Lord ignites an impulse to move toward others. Though the contemporary world tends to see celibacy as a life of isolation and loneliness, the priest has to maintain close relationships with people who know him well, in whom he can confide, and with whom he can share friendship. The seminarian needs to learn how to distinguish between healthy and unhealthy boundaries within his own life.
- **Healing and Integration:** A seminarian needs to recognize the importance of healing on the path to increased personal integration and expanding availability for loving relationships. Healing is a normal aspect of ongoing development. The seminarian will discover how human vulnerability can become a place of encounter with God.
- **Moving from Anger and Resentment to Forgiveness**: The man of communion cannot be dependent on other people's reaction to him for his self-worth or as a precondition of his compassion toward them. The mature Christian invites Jesus to exercise his own love, mercy, compassion and forgiveness from the cross in his heart toward anyone who has caused him pain. The seminarian will grow in awareness of the dynamics of hidden pain often underlying experiences of anger and resentment. He will be

able to enter into genuine forgiveness and its indispensable role in healing.

- **The Gift of Human Sexuality**: Having looked at relationship with Jesus as the source of authentic manhood and having developed a picture of a man of communion, this section of the course examines chaste celibacy as a generative gift. The goal of this session is that the seminarian grows in understanding and appreciation of the gift of his sexuality.

- **Maintaining Chastity**: Living authentic masculinity involves confronting challenge related to sexual integration and maturity. The holy gift of sexuality can be distorted through temptation and sexual struggles. Specifically, the man learns to bring struggle and failure into relationship with Jesus so that the urge to escape into fantasy is replaced by a real, personal intimacy. The seminarian will reject as an illusion that masturbation satisfies loneliness and accept Christ's invitation to intimacy.

- **Same Sex Attraction**: The necessity to understand the moral and spiritual dynamics of same sex attraction and the importance of compassionate pastoral accompaniment of those who experience same sex attraction to support them in chaste living. The seminarian will grow in understanding the interior dynamics underlying same sex attraction.

- **Addressing pornography and addictions**: The prevalence of pornography today and the exposure of young people to pornographic material at an early age presents an especially significant area for healing and maturation in preparation for priestly ordination as well as an urgent problem in future pastoral care. A seminarian must confront any dependence on pornography or other addictive behaviors.

- **The History and Meaning of Priestly Celibacy:** This course culminates in the portrayal of a joyful, peaceful commitment to priestly celibacy in a life rooted in contemplative prayer and generous pastoral service. It includes the passage from the *Ratio Fundamentalis* which states that those who prepare for priesthood ought to recognize and welcome celibacy as a special gift of God, and priestly celibacy should not be viewed as something that has to be given up for God, but rather as a *gift received from his mercy*.[34]

## Personal reflections and Observations as a Faculty Member of SHMS

Anyone who has a position on a seminary faculty today asks themselves repeatedly, if not daily, what have we done, and what are we doing to make sure the men who graduate from our seminary and become priests, are men of integrity, that is, men who have integrated the human, intellectual, spiritual and pastoral dimensions of life in such a way that their ministry will be life-giving, not spiritually death-dealing. In particular, in light of the continuing scandal of the sexual abuse of priests exploiting children, adolescents, vulnerable adults, this chapter has explored not only the Christian understanding of terms such as sexuality, spirituality and sexual integrity, but those documents that lay the foundations and provide the guidelines for the integration which is essential for future priests so that the horror of sexual abuse does not continue.

The reflections that follow do not represent the perspectives of all members of Sacred Heart Major Seminary. Rather, they represent the particular perspective of a woman who is wife, mother, theologian, spiritual director, and faculty member of Sacred Heart Major Seminary since 1988.

### *Mold or Garden: Two Models of Development*

One of the courses I teach at the Seminary is on human and spiritual development. In this course, seminarians and lay students are taught the different stages of development in a person's life, both on a psychological and spiritual level. One of the main texts of the course is *Spiritual Passages: The Psychology of Spiritual Development*, by Fr. Benedict Groeschel, Catholic priest, retreat master and psychologist, in which he describes two models of development.[35]

He states that, until very recently, many religious young people, especially those who entered the seminary or religious life, were fitted into the model of the mold—a static and basically uncreated psychological frame of reference. He points out that a high level of maturity was expected as soon as a habit or collar was put on. [36] There were no admissions requirements that included a psychological profile, or any inquiry into family background, dynamics, health or dysfunction. Seminaries and religious houses were full; one was expected to conform to a precise model of behavior. I think it is fair to say that such a model of formation describes the years between 1940 until Vatican II—the years when the sexual abuse by priests of children, adolescents and vulnerable adults was at its highest.

The second model, the garden, refers to the more creative, developmental approach which recognizes that human beings are in a constant process of becoming. When we are moving or becoming in an appropriate way, we are growing. When we cease to grow, when we are stagnant or regress, we are in the process of decline.[37]

The latest *Ratio Fundamentalis* favors the dynamic approach to human and spiritual development. We have seen this put into practice in the two formation programs explored in this chapter as both take their lead from the *Ratio*. These programs use language that emphasizes growth and maturation: "stages" "dimensions" "ongoing" "becoming" "journey." In a garden there are a variety of flowers, each unique and in need of trimming, cultivating, and the cutting off of dead branches so as to foster new growth. So too, each formation program described above recognizes that each man who comes to the seminary to discern a personal call to priesthood is a unique individual who does not fit into a mold but has a unique story, a developmental history which must be understood and integrated into what the *Ratio* identifies as a "harmonious maturity."[38]

### *Espoused versus Operative Theology*

An exercise I offer in a course on spiritual direction, asks students to identify their espoused theology and their operative theology. Sister Janet Ruffing describes the distinction: our espoused theology is what we think and what we believe. Our operative theology is the beliefs out of which we actually live and minister.[39] Over the years I have noted how important it is for faculty and formation personnel to help seminarians identify the "script" they internalized as a child regarding sexuality. Psychologists tell us that more learning goes on in the first six years of life than at any other time in development. And, most importantly, the messages we receive from our parents in those years are the *most emotionally laden* because they have been given to us by those who have loved us into life.[40]

I have found that some seminarians have unconsciously internalized a negative message regarding sexuality from their families and/or early exposure to negative messages from Church or culture. Unless they have opportunities to identify and bring such distortions into the light, those negative perceptions go underground and emerge later in ways that are unhealthy for themselves a priest and for their parishioners. "The Gift of the Priestly Vocation" stresses the importance of transparency in all areas of the seminarian's life:

> In order for this training to be fruitful, it is important that every seminarian be aware of his own life history and be ready to share it with his formators. This would include especially his experience of childhood and adolescence, the influence that his family and relatives have exercised upon him, his ability to establish mature and well-balanced interpersonal relationships or his lack thereof.[41]

## *A Formation Faculty versus an Academic Faculty*

When Sacred Heart Major Seminary opened its doors in 1988, Cardinal Edmund Szoka, recognizing the faculty's vital role in the formation of seminarians, insisted that the whole faculty was a formation faculty. There was to be no division between the academic and formation faculty. Various components of the seminarian evaluation process included lay faculty members. It was a wonderful experience under the Holy Spirit's guidance to participate in the consensus-building among faculty regarding a seminarian's suitability for the priesthood.

Unfortunately, that changed after the Apostolic Visitation of 2008. The seminary administration received a communication from the Congregation for Catholic Education that mandated lay faculty no longer be included in the evaluation and voting process on candidates for priesthood. Lay members of the faculty, including myself, were deeply hurt and offended that the Vatican did not trust us to vote on candidates who would eventually serve us in parishes. We became exactly what Cardinal Szoka did not want—an academic faculty separate from the formation personnel.

Having experienced the contribution that lay members of the faculty brought to the evaluation process, the Administration found ways to continue to receive feedback from the faculty who were not formation personnel. But it was not the same. Lost were many opportunities for lay faculty to directly interact with seminarians, bringing the fruit of their own life experience into the seminarian's discernment process. Furthermore, seminarians realized that the faculty's role was not purely academic; that we were as vitally concerned and involved in the human, spiritual and pastoral dimensions of their growth and development as the priests. The perception of sacred priests/secular laity was put to rest—for the time being. Ideally, a formation team composed of priests and members of the laity would better serve the seminarians. Such a team moves the evaluation process out of the priestly culture's realm into the realm of the whole people of God for whose service the seminarian is being ordained.

## The Need for a Ministerial Year

At the insistence of Cardinal Szoka, the Sacred Heart curriculum committee designed a five-year program for the education and formation of seminarians with a ministerial year after Second Theology.[42] This year was a blessing for seminarians in a variety of ways. It got them out of an all-male environment and the demands of academic life, and into a parish setting with opportunities to share the fruits of their studies as well as experience first-hand what parish life was like. They had occasions to interact with a variety of people of all ages, experience the rhythm of pastoral life and the style of leadership provided by the pastor and staff. The seminarian accompanied the pastor and witnessed firsthand the life of a priest in a parish. Through a variety of settings with different groups of people, they learned the importance of setting appropriate boundaries between themselves and members of the staff and parish. Having come from a very structured seminary environment, they had to learn how to self-regulate prayer time, leisure, hobbies, visits with family, the aloneness of rectory life, as well as the responsibilities and demands of parish life. The formation team was particularly interested in how they handled evaluation, not only by the pastor, but by the parish staff made up of lay women and men. Subtle and not so subtle expressions of clericalism were recognized and addressed. Many grew in self-knowledge: personality quirks were discovered; gifts confirmed; and an inability to relate well to women or men or for any group for that matter within the parish, was brought to light and addressed.

The year was always a very maturing experience for the seminarians, and they came back to the seminary different—in particular, they took their studies more seriously, having been in situations where members of the laity expected them to answer questions on a variety of church related topics.

Most importantly, many seminarians found their call to priesthood confirmed: "I loved every minute of it!" Others did not. A few shared with me their reasons for leaving formation: "I'm not returning because I realized that I don't like doing all the things priests do"; "I'm not returning because I was not prepared to deal with the loneliness of the priest's life"; "I'm not returning because I found that I miss women too much." The upside of these realizations is the seminarians came to them *before*, not *after* ordination.

In 1990, the ministerial year was eliminated for the purpose of adding an additional year of philosophy to a program that could not exceed six years. Since then, noting many of the issues the newly ordained have to deal with in parish life, the faculty and administration have requested a return to a ministerial year for all seminarians. A few bishops from other dioceses who send their men to Sacred Heart for their education and formation have insisted their men take such a year after either First or Second Theology. A return to this requirement is currently under consideration by the Detroit Diocese as well. In many ways, the strength of a ministerial year is similar to what psychologist Erik Erikson describes as a "psychological moratorium"—it gives the seminarian a break from the structured life of the seminary to grow in self-knowledge and maturity through experiencing himself psychologically, sexually, spiritually and socially in a pastoral setting.

## *Sanctuary versus Service*

In my experience as a long-standing faculty member, I have had the privilege of walking with many seminarians throughout their formation, which includes helping them discern a genuine call to the priesthood. A key area for discernment in general is *motivation*. Over the years, many faculty members and formators have become increasingly aware that, despite a rigorous pre-admission policy, some men enter the seminary for the wrong reasons. They are looking for a sanctuary—a place of refuge, a haven, a hiding place. And they fly—as one formator observed— "under the radar." Some want to be taken care of. Some are afraid they can't make it in the "real" world. Some have a homosexual orientation and look for companionship. Some have a fragile sense of self and want the overlay of priesthood to settle their lack of a solid identity. Others are leery about the role of women in their lives and come to the seminary with ambivalence toward and often discomfort around women. And many others, if not most, come for all the right reasons, namely, a life oriented towards the service of God's people, having experienced a call from the Lord to give their lives to God in authentic discipleship. The *Ratio Fundamentalis* is clear: "Their initial admissions to Seminary should be preceded by a spiritual and ecclesial programme, in which a serious discernment of the *motivations* in responding to a vocation can be undertaken."[43]

Given the priesthood shortage, I am often asked if Sacred Heart accepts every candidate who applies. I have assured inquirers that we do not. Seminary personnel have designed a very thorough "Pre-Admission Checklist" which painstakingly investigates every aspect of an applicant's life. It includes psychological assessment, criminal background checks, Virtus training, discernment weekends, opportunities for men to meet consistently over a period of time with a vocation director and other members of the formation team, and much more.

The intense summer program offered by the IPF offers the seminarian another opportunity to assess his ability to integrate his sexuality with celibacy in an affectively mature, life giving, and generative way. Their focus on "authentic manhood" in a time of confusion around the meaning of masculinity in our culture has been particularly helpful to the men who participate in this program. Reinstituting a ministerial year would help a seminarian discern his true motivation for living a celibate life and working with the people in the parish would give them different perspectives on the many ways people respond to God's call (e.g., marriage, single life, etc.).

## The Role of Women in the Formation of Seminarians

When I first began teaching as a member of the Sacred Heart Faculty, many seminarians were resistant to a woman teaching theology. Some exhibited the disease of clericalism, considering themselves special, set apart and above everyone—including a woman in the position of authority over them. We have come a long way. Now, seminarians, for the most part, appreciate women on the faculty, although there are always a few who would like to return to an all-male environment with "the guys"; that is, themselves and priest faculty. One of the strengths of having men and women on the faculty is that the seminarians have the opportunity to observe healthy, positive relationships and collaboration between female and male faculty members. Regarding the role of women on seminary faculty, "The Gift of the Priestly Vocation" is very positive:

> The presence of women in the Seminary journey of formation has its own formative significance. They can be found as specialists, on the teaching staff, within the apostolate, within families, and in service to the community. Their presence also helps to instill a recognition of how men and women complement each other. Often, women are numerically greater among those whom the priest will serve, and with whom he will work in the pastoral ministry. They offer an edifying example of humanity, generosity and selfless service.[44]

In any given semester at Sacred Heart Seminary, two hundred to three hundred lay women and men pursue degrees in theology for the purpose of serving the church through a variety of ministries. Seminarians and lay students are together for some courses; others are separate due to specific requirements for priesthood. Within this setting, most revelatory is the seminarian's interaction with, or lack thereof with women in some of their classes. Some seminarians recognize there are women who are as bright or brighter than themselves: insightful, prayerful and deeply committed to the Church. While female students appreciate seminarians who are friendly, respectful and genuinely at home in their presence, some report feeling invisible in classes where other seminarians ignore or just don't or won't engage them.

Being attuned to seminarians' interaction, or lack thereof, with women students is revelatory of their future ability to collaborate in a parish setting where most members of their teams will be women. Again in very positive terms, "The Gift of Priestly Vocation" states: "This understanding and this familiarity with the feminine, so present in parishes and many ecclesial contexts are beneficial and essential to the human and spiritual formation of seminarians and should always be seen in a positive light."[45] In my own experience, I can tell that something is amiss if a seminarian will not look me in the eye, or won't return a greeting when walking down a hall. The way that seminarians interact with members of the opposite sex reveals a lot about their self-confidence, their maturity, and their ability to maintain healthy boundaries.

While both formation programs described in this chapter acknowledge the importance of seminarians' ability to interact in a positive way with the laity, neither specifically address the seminarian's attitude toward and ability to work well with women. This is a major area of concern for many women, who working in a parish setting, have experienced some priests as condescending, aloof, arrogant, dismissive and overall uncomfortable in their presence. In truth, most seminaries have no concrete ways to determine a seminarian's attitude toward and ability to work with women in a healthy, productive way.

**Evolution of the four dimensions of a formation program: human, spiritual, intellectual, pastoral.**

The initial program of formation at Sacred Heart Seminary and, I presume, most seminaries in the 1980s, emphasized the intellectual and spiritual dimensions of a seminarian's life. Daily life revolved around a demanding academic schedule and specific disciplines aimed to help the seminarian grow in his spiritual life. The human dimension of formation was not emphasized as some members of the formation team and faculty viewed the social sciences, particularly psychology, with suspicion. Seminarians picked up on that perspective as they viewed any

## VIII. Sexual Integrity, Spirituality and Priestly Formation

recommendation for counseling by the formation team (a rare occurrence) as a form of punishment.

Due to new understandings of psychological and social development, that perspective gradually changed over a period of time. The first and most important factor was *Pastores Dabo Vobis*. It stated that the formation of future priests must address the whole person which consisted of four pillars as we have explored: the human, spiritual, intellectual and pastoral. The Pope placed special emphasis human formation, stating "In order that his ministry may be humanly as credible and acceptable as possible, it is important that the priest should mold his human personality in such a way that it becomes bridge and not an obstacle for others in their meeting with Jesus Christ the Redeemer of humanity."[46]

A second factor during this time were studies that highlighted the importance of a healthy relationship between psychological development and religious growth, pointing out that certain psychological theories provided insight into the nature within which grace works. This recognition was affirmed in the 2016 *Ratio Fundamentalis*:

> The contribution of the psychological sciences has generally shown to be of considerable help to formators, as they are responsible for vocational discernment. This scientific contribution allows the character and personality of the candidates to be known better and it enables formation to be adapted more fittingly to the needs of the individual.[47]

A third factor was the recognition that men interested in priesthood are enormously influenced and challenged by cultural developments such as: increasing secularization, consumerism, and individualism; distortions of human sexuality as expressed in pornography and the hook up culture; the growing acceptance of homosexual lifestyles and trial marriages; and the breakdown of family life and the wounds and brokenness that followed in its wake. They each come to the seminary deeply influenced by these cultural factors, in need of a deep immersion into the human, spiritual and intellectual values of the Christian tradition which will enable them to put on the mind and heart of Jesus in a free and mature decision to pursue discernment for priesthood.

As if these areas did not present significant challenges to the wholistic development and flourishing of the seminarian, the horrific revelation of priest sexual abuse of children, adolescents and vulnerable adults which occurred, not only in the United States, but all over the world, called into question, not only the integrity of the priesthood, but also sowed the seeds of mistrust and lack of confidence in their moral authority—a reality that each seminarian has to contend with. Surely one of the main reasons for this new *Ratio Fundamentalis* is the recognition that this tragic crisis revealed the absolute failure of priestly formation programs all over the world.

It is quite telling that in the midst of this scandal, for the first time, the term "maturity of affections" or "affective maturity" was inserted into the fifth edition of the *Program of Priestly Formation*. This document states:

> Human formation comes together in a particular way in the domain of human sexuality, and this is especially true for those who are preparing for a life of celibacy. The various dimensions of being a human person—the physical, the psychological and the spiritual—converge in affective maturity, which includes human sexuality."[48] This document also describes affective maturity as a person "whose life of feeling is in balance and integrated into thought and values; in other words, a man of feelings who is not driven by them but freely lives his life enriched by them.[49]

**Sexual Abuse Crisis: Approaches in Seminarian Formation**
*Benchmarks for Policies Related to Sexual Abuse.*

Given the focus of this volume on the sexual abuse crisis, it is vitally important to include in this chapter the work-in-progress of the McGrath Institute of Notre Dame in collaboration with the Center for Applied Research in the Apostolate (CARA), entitled, "Benchmarks for Policies Related to Sexual Abuse."

This project involves an ongoing committee comprised of bishops, rectors, priests, and lay collaborators of which the rector of Sacred Heart Major Seminary, Monsignor Todd Lajiness, has been a member. The purpose of this working group has been to develop benchmarks that provide workable and reasonable protocols which can be tailored to fit

VIII. Sexual Integrity, Spirituality and Priestly Formation        273

each seminary community to ensure healthy and safe environments for our seminarians. The benchmarks formed by the working group are:

1. Systematic training of seminarians, faculty, and staff regarding harassment policies;
2. Internal and external reporting and investigations procedures;
3. Victim support;
4. Periodic assessment of internal policies; consistency and portability to suit local conditions.
5. Strategies for integrating these benchmarks into everyday life.[50]

How each formation program handles its education/formation in the area of sexual abuse must be woven together into the whole area of sexual maturity and formation in celibate chastity as presented in "The Gift of Priestly Vocation" and the two formation programs described in this chapter. In relation to the program I know best, Sacred Heart Major Seminary has specific formation sessions devoted to celibate chastity, emotional maturity, relationships with women, and maintaining healthy boundaries. It also provides training sessions on the Dallas Charter, instituted by the US Catholic Bishops in 2002, which focuses on the protection of Children and Young People, and promises to ordain those who share the commitment to protecting children.[51]

In a thought provoking article entitled, "Clergy Sex Abuse: Why Do We Still Need to Talk About This," three psychotherapists recommend that all seminarians and pastors receive training in sexual abuse dynamics, power differentials, the role of transference in clergy/parishioner relationships and the long-term effects of traumatic sexual abuse.[52] The working group, described above, is a step in the right direction to ensure, not only a healthy and safe environment for our seminarians, but also for their training in the recognition of the signs of sexual abuse and reporting procedures so that this tragedy will never occur again.

## Conclusion

One of the main purposes of this new *Ratio Fundamentalis* is to address the realization that, due to a number of factors, previous formation programs had failed and needed to be revised and updated. In truth, the laity deserve better service from the formation process. Thus, "The Gift of the Priestly Vocation" assures the Christian community that it has provided guidelines and directives for the formation of men of integrity who have internalized and live out of an interiorly free, healthy, wholesome and authentic configuration to the Jesus Christ, becoming a sign of God's love, and dedicated to serve the lay faithful entrusted to them. The programs at Sacred Heart Major Seminary and the Institute for Priestly Formation are dedicated to the implementation of these goals. Based upon this assurance, these programs should serve as a source of hope to the Christian community that the tragedy and scandal of the sexual abuse crisis ...

## RESPONSE

# Christian Anthropology and the Vocation to Chastity

## Eduardo J. Echeverria

*Professor of Philosophy and Theology, Sacred Heart Major Seminary, Detroit, Michigan*

Introduction

I am grateful to Pat Cooney-Hathaway for her detailed outline, "Sexual Integrity, Spirituality and Priestly Formation," which provided some orientation as to what themes must be addressed in a Christian anthropology which informs our reflections on human sexuality.

Normative Anthropology

*Creation*

The *Catechism of the Catholic Church* (hereafter *CCC*) defines the vocation to chastity as follows:

> Chastity means the successful integration of sexuality within the person and thus the inner unity of man in his bodily and spiritual being. Sexuality, in which man's belonging to the bodily and biological world is expressed, becomes personal and truly human when it is integrated into the relationship of one person to another, in the complete and lifelong mutual gift of a man and a woman. The virtue of chastity therefore involves the *integrity of the person* and the *integrality of the gift* (§2337; emphasis added).

In this passage from *CCC*, it is clear that the normative anthropological and hence creational starting point for reflecting on the vocation to chastity, the corresponding integrity of the person and the integrality of the self, is the fundamental assertion of Genesis 1: 27: "God created man in his own image . . . male and female he created them." In other words, the sexual difference between male and female is a creational given. Thus, humanity is bound to this binary structure of creation, such that there is no spectrum of normative manifestations of man beyond male and female, in between male and female. It is also a creational given that, simultaneously, humanity is one and a bi-unity, male and female, that is, a unity-in-two, created together. Furthermore, the Word of God also asserts in Genesis 2:18: "It is not good that the man should be alone; I will make him a helper fit for him." This means that God "willed each for the other" (*CCC,* 371). *CCC,* 372 explains the implications of this sexually differentiated reality: "Man and woman were made 'for each other' - not that God left them half-made and incomplete: he created them to be a communion of persons, in which each can be 'helpmate' to the other, for they are equal as persons ('bone of my bones. . .') and complementary as masculine and feminine."

Moreover, we are created in God's image as male and female human beings rather than as generic human beings. John Paul explains:

> Let us enter into the setting of the biblical "beginning" [order of creation]. In it the revealed truth concerning man as "the image and likeness" of God constitutes the immutable *basis of all Christian anthropology.* "God created man in his own image, in the image of God he created him; male and female he created them" (Gen 1: 27).

Furthermore, adds John Paul:

> This concise passage [Genesis 1:27] contains the fundamental anthropological truths: man is the highpoint of the whole order of creation in the visible world; the human race, which takes its origin from the calling into existence of man and woman, crowns the whole work of creation; *both man and woman are human beings to an equal degree,* both are created *in God's image.*[53]

According to *CCC,* "The human person, created in the image of God, is at once corporeal and spiritual. . . Man, whole and entire, is therefore willed by God" (362). This anthropological unity means that the meaning of male and female includes both biological sex and all of what is now included in the term gender.⁵⁴ Therefore, "We cannot treat a person's subjectively experienced gender as a fact of their existence independent of their biological sex. We cannot claim that a person's true identity resides in their subjective sense of self, as distinct from the body with which they were born."⁵⁵ Contrary, then, to the anthropological dualism of soul and body that undergirds "gender ideology,"⁵⁶ the Catholic tradition affirms that the body is intrinsic to selfhood because the human person *is* bodily (*CCC*, 362-368).⁵⁷ John Paul II explains that the body is intrinsic to self-identity: "Man is a subject not only by his self-consciousness and by self-determination, but also based on his own body. *The structure of this body is such that it permits him to be the author of genuinely human activity*. In this activity, the body expresses the person" (See *MWTB 7.2*).⁵⁸ Consequently, argues *CCC,* 365, "the unity of soul and body is so profound that one has to consider the soul to be the 'form' of the body: i.e., it is because of its spiritual soul that the body made of matter becomes a living, human body; spirit and matter, in man, are not two natures united, but rather their union forms a single nature." The body is intrinsic to one's own self and, indeed, it "shares in the dignity of 'the image of God'" (*CCC* §364).⁵⁹

## *Fallen Human Nature*

The integrity of the person refers to the self's personal and bodily unity. Original sin, and hence the person's fallen nature, has fractured the self as bodily and personal. This fracture is such that it renders the person unable to act as an integrated bodily being, alienating him from his own body or another person's body, an alienation that results in a choice to use his own body, or another person's body, as simply an object of pleasure. This choice unavoidably violates the basic human good of self-integration, damaging the body's capacity to function as an integral part of oneself in an act of self-giving, and hence to realize a one-flesh communion of bodily persons. John Paul II explains:

> [There is] a certain constitutive fracture in the human person's interior, *a breakup, as it were, of man's original spiritual and somatic unity.*

> He realizes for the first time that his body has ceased drawing on the power of the spirit, which raised him to the level of the image of God... The body is not subject to the spirit as in the state of original innocence, but carries within itself a constant hotbed of resistance against the spirit and threatens in some way man's unity as a person, that is, the unity of the moral nature that plunges its roots firmly into the very constitution of the person. The concupiscence of the body is a specific threat to the structure of self-possession and self-dominion, through which the human person forms itself (*MWTB* 28.3).

The loss of self-integration, and hence self-possession and self-dominion, undermines the integrality of the gift of self. John Paul adds that this loss

> deprives man, one could say, of the dignity of the gift, which is expressed by his body through femininity and masculinity, and in some sense 'depersonalizes' man, making him as an object 'for the other'. Instead of being 'together with the other'—a subject in unity... man becomes an object for man, the female for the male and vice versa" (*MWTB* 32.4).

Indeed, the man of concupiscence is no longer integrated within himself; his body does not express his reality as a person, something that is fundamental to the meaning of the acting person *qua person*. Consequently, because he is no longer in integral self-possession and self-dominion, he has difficulty, not only identifying himself with his own body, or better, his own personal subjectivity, but also he is unable to relate to the subjectivity of the other human being in conformity with God's original plan of creation, and hence his very humanity is threatened.

Still, the normativity of God's good creation "in some measure continue[s] to permeate and shape the love born in the human heart. The spousal meaning of the body has not become totally foreign to that heart; *it has not been totally suffocated in it by concupiscence, but only habitually threatened.*" The Pope adds: "That *reciprocal communion in humanity itself through the body and through its masculinity and femininity, which had such a strong echo* in the earlier passage of the Yahwist narrative (see Gen 2: 23-25), *is overturned* at this moment, as if the body in its masculinity and femininity ceased to be 'free from suspicion' as the substratum of the communion of persons, as if its original function were 'called into doubt' in the consciousness of the man and the woman'" (*MWTB*, 29.2; see also 29.4 and 32.1). Eloquently, the Pope expresses his conviction that "The 'heart' has become a battlefield between love and concupiscence. The more concupiscence dominates the heart, the less the heart experiences the spousal meaning of the body, and the less sensitive it becomes to the gift of the person that expresses precisely this meaning in the reciprocal relations of man and woman" (*MWTB*, 32.3).

## *Redemption*

Now, we come to the last point regarding the relation between nature, sin and grace, as well as the key idea that grace restores or renews nature. Central to nature's restoration or renewal, says John Paul, is that "Man must rediscover the lost fullness of his humanity" (*MWTB*, 44.1). "In the Sermon on the Mount," the Pope adds,

> Christ does not invite man to return to the state of original innocence, because humanity has left it irrevocably behind, but *he calls him to find*—on the foundation of the perennial and, one might say, indestructible meanings of what is 'human'—the *living forms of the 'new man'*. In this way a connection is formed, even continuity, between the 'beginning' and the perspective of redemption. In the ethos of the redemption of the body, the original ethos of creation was to be taken up anew (*MWTB*, 49.4).

The Redemption of life is accomplished through the mystery of the Incarnation and Christ's finished work—His life, passion, death, resurrection, and ascension—abrogates the antithesis between sin and creation.

Put differently, the Incarnation, Passion, and Resurrection in Jesus Christ means that his grace restores an original good creation. God's original thesis is reasserted and reestablished, but also, as John Paul II asserts in the above quote, it is enriched, fulfilled, and perfected. This Redemption restores the very heart of human nature, causing the rebirth of the human self in Christ (Colossians 2:13; 2 Corinthians 5:17). "Christ alone, through his humanity, reveals the totality of the mystery of man ... The key to his self-understanding lies in contemplating the divine Prototype, the Word made flesh, the eternal Son of the Father."[60] "Without the Gospel," John Paul adds, "man remains a dramatic question with no adequate answer. The correct response to the question about man is Christ, *Redemptor Hominis*."[61] This rebirth manifests itself in the integral redemption of the whole man in Christ through the fellowship of the Father, Son and Holy Spirit, and with one another in them, which has been given to us in grace (Romans 5:5). Indeed, says the Pope, Paul sees the "redemption of the body" (Rom 8: 23) "in *an anthropological*, and simultaneously *a cosmic, dimension*" MWTB, 86.1). "The whole visible creation," in the Pope's words, "the whole cosmos, carries the effects of man's sin" (*MWTB*, 86.1).

## Conclusion

Christ refers us to the normative order of creation. Hence the redemption of man "must consist in *retrieving [man's] dignity*, in which the true meaning of the human body, its meaning as personal and 'of communion',", namely, the spousal meaning of the body, of the reciprocal self-gift of the persons-in-communion, is found fully unfolding the hermeneutics of the integrality of the gift in the conjugal act of marriage.[62]

# IX

# Affective Maturity and its Importance for Seminary Formation

### Rev. Msgr. Michael K. Magee and Suzanne Mulrain

*Dean, School of Theological Studies, Chair of Systematic Theology Department & Professor of Systematic Theology and Sacred Scripture, Saint Charles Borromeo Seminary, Wynnewood, Pennsylvania*

*and*

*Coordinator, School of Theological Studies, Saint Charles Borromeo Seminary, Wynnewood, Pennsylvania*

## Introduction

On October 3, 1979, Pope John Paul II visited St. Charles Borromeo Seminary in Philadelphia, Pennsylvania and encouraged the seminarians to be disciplined, to embrace celibate chastity, to seek intellectual formation in human sciences and sacred sciences, to thrive in human formation, and to prepare for a life of consecrated service in the image of Christ, and self-mastery through human formation to foster solid maturity of personality and traits of character. [1]

It was an ideal that many generations of seminarians had shared, but every generation has unique challenges to face in achieving this goal. The present generation cannot fail to consider the ways that priestly formation may effectively respond to the terrible challenge of clerical sexual abuse in recent decades. When one surveys the wreckage caused by the scandals, a question that naturally arises is: "What signs might have been missed during this man's seminary formation that might have presaged the eventual disasters of his later abusive behavior? What kind of problem should be seen as the ticking time-bomb to be rooted out?" Many clerical perpetrators of sexual abuse seem in fact to have been able throughout their formation to "jump through all hoops" and attain ordination while never having flagrantly violated any rules during their seminary years.

It seems, in the end, that the landscape is more likely to be changed for the better. This will come about not so much by reacting to specific disqualifications as by pursuing more positively the necessary attainment in individual candidates of a concept — perhaps initially elusive but in the process of being fleshed out in current years — mentioned prominently by Saint John Paul II in *Pastores Dabo Vobis*, namely <u>affective maturity</u>. Certainly not all men who have been ordained sufficiently possess the qualities that this notion entails—especially when viewed in retrospect. On the other hand, the painful experience of recent years seems to show that deficits in the attainment of affective maturity *are* prominently evident in retrospect whenever such tragic events later emerge. This essay will therefore seek to examine what is really meant by "affective maturity" and emphasize the importance of using it as a guide for the healing of the present wounds felt within the Church because of clerical sexual misconduct.

The needed healing must involve the concrete application of what the recent *Ratio Fundamentalis* for priestly formation, "The Gift of the Priestly Vocation," requires when it states that the candidate's suitability "must be clearly demonstrated" with "*positive arguments*" that "give moral certainty of the suitability of the candidate" and "not simply the absence of problematic situations."[2] To express this ideal of priestly formation in terms recently articulated by Pope Francis: "It means guarding and fostering vocations, that they may bear mature fruit. They are 'uncut diamonds', to be formed both patiently and carefully, respecting the conscience of the individual, so that they may shine among the People of God."[3]

## The Benefits and Limitations of Psychological Evaluations

A psychological evaluation and assessment tests the intellectual, emotional, and psychological functioning of the applicant to seminary through the use of psychometric measures. It is the mental equivalent of a physical examination. Psychologist Peter Kleponis reviewed the new Guidelines and offered a professional assessment of them. He is a practicing psychologist with extensive experience in counseling, subject interviews, testing formats, counseling session structures, implementing tests, reviewing completed tests and interpreting the psychological assessment for dioceses, rectors and formation teams of seminaries.[4] Overall, Kleponis expressed contentment with the new Guidelines and said that he welcomed them, adding that they would assist professionals in standardizing the evaluative process and ensuring more effective evaluations of seminarians.

At the same time, Kleponis did express some reservations concerning the subsequent use of evaluation reports after they would be handed over to a seminary team or diocese, cautioning that the assistance of a trained and experienced psychologist would be crucial not only for testing the applicants but for reviewing and interpreting the results, drafting the evaluation and recommendation reports, and presenting them confidentially to a diocese, rector, and formation team. Otherwise, it might happen (and indeed, Kleponis claimed that he had observed such) that healthy men of promise who had sometimes presented themselves as candidates for seminary formation were denied access even while unhealthy men had sometimes passed through into admission thus leading to disruptive problems in the seminary community and the priesthood overall.[5]

Even so, the main limitation of psychological testing in ascertaining the eventual suitability of candidates for Holy Orders lies in the importance of affective maturity which, as will be outlined below, cannot be defined exclusively in psychological terms but involves the other dimensions of priestly formation as well, including the candidate's spiritual development, academic integrity, insight, and pastoral zeal for souls, as well as many other criteria which must be considered in an integrative way. Psychological evaluations may help to distinguish relatively promising from less promising candidates in terms of the prospect of such eventual integration, but only long-term verification within a residential context can verify true suitability for Ordination.

## Affective Maturity as the Key Factor in Formation

Reverend Frederick Miller described the elements of sound human formation as many in number, while asserting also that its demands may vary for different individuals.[6] He also described Pope John Paul II's early promotion of the good of human formation and affective maturity in seminaries as early as 1979. Later in his pontificate, Pope John Paul II would make a substantial impact to the field of formation by highlighting the importance of affective maturity and human formation in general within seminarian formation as well as ongoing clergy formation. In this context, he enumerated for seminary formators the most important areas of focus: the balanced development of the human faculties (intelligence, will, passions, feelings); the capacity for human relationships; affective maturity; and the development of a moral conscience.[7] It is through the normal day-to-day interactions with his peers and others on an informal basis, in fact, that a seminarian can expect to develop these necessary human qualities. In addition to the formators, faculty guidance, feedback from peers and self-reflection assist the seminarian in gaining personal insight into growth and the areas of his personality which need further development.[8]

Miller mentions that he attended seminary during the 1960's. He had committed his life to God and the Church. He learned about the abundant grace of celibacy and how it is recognized not only in the desire to imitate Christ, but also in a deep longing for the exclusive, definitive, and total choice of the unique and supreme love of Jesus Christ (Paul VI, *Sacerdotalis Caelibatus*, no. 14). He was taught that the *norm* of celibacy was established by Jesus Christ himself through his choice of a celibate lifestyle. This is stated clearly in the *Directory for the Life and Ministry of Priests*, which says that the example [of celibacy] is Christ, who in going against what could be considered the dominant culture of his time, freely choose to live in celibacy. In following him, the disciples left "everything" to fulfill the mission entrusted to them (Lk 18:28–30).[9]

For this reason, the Church, from apostolic times, has wished to conserve the gift of perpetual continence of the clergy and choose the candidates for Holy Orders from among the celibate faithful (cf. 2 Thess 2:15; 1 Cor 7:5, 9:5; 1 Tim 3:2–12, 5:9; Tit 1:6–8). Miller understands well

## IX. Affective Maturity & its Importance for Seminary Formation

how the grace of celibacy opens the priest to a deep life of communion with Christ in prayer, a prayer that is infused by the Holy Spirit, also called contemplative prayer. He encourages seminarians and priests to explore the intimate relationship that must exist between celibacy and contemplation in the life of the priest. The driving force of celibacy is a friendship with Christ that propels the celibate in the direction of pastoral service of the Church. The grace of celibacy is recognized in the desire for this exclusive friendship and also in the desire to do the works of Christ in the Church. In the charism of priestly celibacy, there is the coalescence of the desire to be all Christ's and to be Christ, the Good Shepherd, in the Church.[10]

The Church discerns whether a man is capable of practicing lifelong continence for the sake of the Kingdom of God. The Church also must discern if the man possesses the affective maturity to love the Church with Christ's own nuptial love, and all the members of the Church as his brothers and sisters, as his sons and daughters in Christ. Finally, the Church discerns whether the candidate shares Christ's desire to be united with all people and is capable to be a living instrument of Christ, the Priest. In his article, Fr. Miller notes it was a difficult period to see so many priests and seminarians questioning the reality and the beauty of celibacy. He stresses that the grace of celibacy is recognized not only in the desire to imitate Christ, but also in a deep longing for the *exclusive, definitive, and total choice of the unique and supreme love of Jesus Christ* (Paul VI, *Sacerdotalis Caelibatus*, no. 14).[11]

Fr. Miller describes how the grace of celibacy opens the priest to a deep life of communion with Christ in prayer, including contemplative prayer, which is infused by the Holy Spirit. Fr. Miller acknowledges that it is imperative that seminarians and priests explore the intimate relationship that must exist between celibacy and contemplation in the life of the priest.

An essential resource on the importance of seminary formation in affective maturity can be found in the United States Conference of Catholic Bishops' *Program of Priestly Formation*, succinctly referenced as the PPF.[12]

Affective maturity is referenced numerous times, including this statement:

A person of affective maturity: someone whose life of feelings is in balance and integrated into thought and values; in other words, a man of feelings who is not driven by them but freely lives his life enriched by them; this might be especially evident in his ability to live well with authority, in his ability to take direction from another, and in his ability to exercise authority well among his peers, as well as an ability to deal productively with conflict and stress.[13]

The current Sixth Edition of the Program of Priestly Formation of the United States Conference of Catholic Bishops (USCCB) was approved by the bishops in November 2019 and confirmed by the Congregation for the Clergy on March 22, 2022, which is set to enter into effect on August 4, 2023. Prior to implementation of the PPF, each new edition (which itself is a local adaptation of the norms of the Roman *Ratio Fundamentalis Institutionis Sacerdotalis*) must always receive the "*confirmatio*" from the Vatican Congregation for the Clergy before the latest edition can be published and implemented. "The updated Sixth Edition approved in 2019 retains and builds upon the aspects of the Fifth Edition which have proven to be the most effective," stated Cardinal Joseph W. Tobin.[14]

The subject of affective maturity in the PPF harmonizes with Pope John Paul II's Post-Synodal Apostolic Exhortation *Pastores dabo vobis* (I Will Give You Shepherds: On the Formation of Priests in the Circumstances of the Present Day, 1992). John Paul II's exhortation provides a rich resource to organize and integrate the program of priestly formation.[15]

Human formation comes together in a particular way in the domain of human sexuality, and this is especially true for those who are preparing for a life of celibacy. The various dimensions of being a human person—the physical, the psychological, and the spiritual—converge in affective maturity, includes human sexuality. Education is necessary for understanding sexuality and living chastely. Those preparing to live out a celibate commitment face particular challenges, especially in today's cultural context of permissiveness.[16]

One change made to the Sixth Edition in 2019 was how a seminarian's progress to ordination is tracked. What had been a seminary college or "pre-theology" program followed by graduate studies – known as the theologate – was complemented by new terms: the "propaedeutic stage" with preparatory and introductory teaching lasting one to two years; and a "discipleship stage," which is to last at least two years. The Program for Priestly Formation [PPF] consistently accounts for developments in the Church and society in recent years, such as contemporary problems: "Weaknesses of ethical standards and a moral relativism have a corrosive effect on American public life as seen, for example, in marriage and family life, in business and in politics."[17]

Additionally, the PPF firmly states:

> Within the church, clericalism and abuse of power have had a corrosive effect. The scandalous and criminal behavior of some clergy who have abused minors and engaged in sexual misconduct with adults, including seminarians, has caused great suffering for the victims and damaged the church's witness in society. This scandal has resulted in a loss of credibility for the church and an overall lack of respect for religion. Both the nation and the Church are summoned to renewal and to a real integrity of life.[18]

The PPF also contains strict instructions for action: "Any seminarian found to have pathological sexual attraction to minors is to be dismissed from the seminary with no possibility for readmission to the same or another seminary."[19]

Sulpician priest, Andrzej Szablewski, addresses the importance of affective maturity as essential in seminary formation in his article "Human Formation and Fraternity."[20] He says he gained insight into human formation and affective maturity by his experience in directing human formation at a seminary in Canada and reading Pope Saint John Paul II's Apostolic Exhortation *Pastores dabo vobis*. Szablewski offers a description of new seminarians as predominantly focused on the long-term goal of ordination through years of obedient and studious commitments while balancing spiritual and pastoral responsibilities. He points out that human formation requires a much more organic process for the integration of intricate intrapersonal and interpersonal dimensions.

Szablewski believes that the approach offered by *Pastores dabo vobis* has successfully found its proper place in both seminary formation and in the ongoing formation of priests. The Apostolic Exhortation *Pastores dabo vobis* articulates the contemporary body of work on priestly formation. Nevertheless—and in direct relation to this chapter—there emerges an obvious lack of critical attention in priestly formation to the affective dimension of the human person.[21] On the basis of his own experience, Szablewski notes that many candidates seem hindered by human limitation or a lack of freedom even while trying realistically and conscientiously to respond to God's priestly call and to live the call in a mature or Christ-like manner. Szablewski presents the findings of Luigi M. Rulla (et al., along with similar studies by Baars and Terruwe, or Kennedy and Heckler, with comparable results),[22] which invite seminary formation teams to consider the great number of seminarians who in different ways seem to be driven by internal affective habits governed by subconscious needs: habits maintained either to defend themselves from these needs or to satisfy them. Sometimes this subconscious factor might have even been a consideredation in the decision to enter religious life and persevere in a vocation.[23] Such unknown or perhaps ignored motivations might even clash with their formally expressed personal or institutional self-transcendent values. They might also be inconsistent with the call of Christ to love and to be loved or dissonant with the call to be a "man of communion" (cf. Luigi M. Rulla et al., *Anthropology of the Christian Vocation*, Rome, Gregorian University Press, 2 vols.,1989).[24]

According to Szablewski, merely choosing to implement suggestions into better practices in formation would be far from sufficient. He proposes instead that seminary formators follow the lead of Saint John Paul II in seeking to promote, in a positive way, a deep and penetrating spirituality of communion as the guiding principle of education in all situations of Christian formation. This applies to the formation of ministers of the altar, consecrated persons, pastoral workers, or those who will be builders or promoters of families. This is what John Paul II recommended in 2001 in *Novo millenio ineunte* (no. 43).[25]

In particular, as Szablewski notes, John Paul II warns against a mentality of activism, which is functionally prevalent in the secular world. John Paul II instead encourages people to grow in freedom and to choose and "to be" rather than "to do," and to fix their eyes on Christ and grow in holiness as He is holy, by choosing "what we ought to be" and not "what we are." We also must choose "what is intrinsically good" rather than "what is good for me."[26] At issue here is not a question of psychopathology, but rather a question of lesser or greater degrees of social and psychological immaturity that constitute the difference between the "ideal self" and how one actually lives and strives for objective holiness (Rulla et al., 1989).[27]

Szablewski cites *Pastores dabo vobis* no. 44 which emphasizes that human maturity, especially affective maturity, requires a clear and strong training in freedom. This must be authentic freedom, which expresses itself in convinced and heartfelt obedience to the "truth" of one's own being, to the "meaning" of one's own existence, that is to the "sincere gift of self." Affective maturity presupposes an awareness that love has a central role in human life. We are speaking of a love "that involves the entire person, in all his or her aspects – physical, psychic and spiritual – and which is expressed in the 'nuptial meaning' of the human body, thanks to which a person gives oneself to another and takes the other to oneself."[28]

For his own part, Szablewski observes that many current psychological studies today focus on the "filial" dimension of our existence, such as how a child's early experiences might influence personality formation and the style one will adopt in living one's priesthood or marriage:

> On the anthropological and theological levels, we often find the priesthood described in unidirectional accents on "filial-fraternal" dimension, in disequilibrium with coexistent "spousal-paternal" dimensions. This often results in apostolic partiality or even incompetence or ineffectiveness.
>
> Therefore, each dimension: filial, fraternal, spousal, and paternal, has to find its expression in the life of the candidate in training as well as in priestly ministry and life. From our filial relationship with God, flows also our filial relationship with our bishop, our spiritual director, as well as the "fraternal" relationships with other seminarians and members of the presbyterium, particularly with the seminary formation team. In Christ's "spousal" relationship with the Church is rooted our "spousal" relationship with all Christ's members, in all its faithfulness, unity, exclusivity or totality.

> And finally, in the priestly "nuptial self-offering of love" one expresses the "paternal" dimension of his vocation. Even if this is in the supernatural order, it still has all its psychological richness and relational aspect. God has loved us first (1 Jn 4:10) and upon this Love (Jesus Christ) is built the circular dialectic of love: to love and to be loved.[29]

Human formation begins with attention to such issues as affective maturity, celibacy and friendship. The initial formation process serves to confirm or disconfirm one's vocation and establish some healthy paths for a mature and healthy life and ministry. Szablewski sees Saint John Paul II's desire for mature and true friendship throughout formation as a foundation to support a man's subsequent priestly life:

> In view of the commitment to celibacy, affective maturity should bring to human relationships of serene friendship and deep brotherliness a strong, lively and personal love for Jesus Christ.... A precious help can be given by a suitable education to true friendship, following the image of the bonds of fraternal affection which Christ himself lived on earth (cf. Jn 11:5). [30]

Pope John Paul II has helped seminaries understand the critical importance of affective maturity and celibacy as essential elements of the personality of today's priest.[31]

## Affective Maturity Described

Affective formation emerges as a vital dimension in the development of a seminarian's human formation, which must encompass the heart as well as the mind. It is within the context of the seminary community of formation, as established by the Church, that this formation normally occurs:

> To be admitted to the seminary the Church requires that the candidate possess the physical and psychological health to dedicate himself permanently to the sacred ministry. He is to cultivate the virtues which are highly valued in human relationships so that

there is a harmony between the human and supernatural values of Christian life. The specific aim of affective formation is to foster the development of both the seminarian's affective life and its role in his personal and pastoral relationships.[32]

The emphasis on affective formation in the formation of the priest arises from the fact that he, modeled after the pattern of Jesus Christ, is called to lay down his entire life for others. The Second Vatican Council's Decree on the Ministry and Life of Priests, *Presbyterorum Ordinis* makes clear that through the act of ordination, as well as according to his mission, the priest is incorporated into the service of Christ as teacher, priest, and king. Through this threefold service priests share in Christ's ministry to build up God's people by preaching God's Word, interceding for the people, and guiding them to the fullness of Christian maturity. The priest is chosen for this life-long ministry from among his Christian brothers to lay down his life in self-sacrifice to serve God and others and act on their behalf before God, The priest offers sacrifices and intercedes for them.[33]

In 1975, The Sacred Congregation for the Doctrine of the Faith described further the distinctive role of sexuality in the life of every person when it stated: "The human person is so profoundly affected by sexuality that it must be considered as one of the factors which give to each individual's life the principal traits that distinguish it."[34] Indeed, the mystery of human sexuality permeates every moment of human existence. To understand and accept oneself as a sexual person and to learn to relate comfortably with others are ongoing developmental tasks which will always be present in a person's life. A seminarian is encouraged to discuss this area of his growth honestly with his formation director and spiritual director. Pope John Paul II did not underestimate the difficulty in achieving affective maturity in our contemporary society. He proposed a concrete and realistic strategy:

> Since the charism of celibacy, even when it is genuine and has proved itself, leaves man's affectations and his instinctive impulses intact, candidates to the priesthood need an affective maturity which is prudent, able to renounce anything that is a threat to it, vigilant over body and spirit, and capable of esteem and respect in

> interpersonal relationships between men and women. A precious help can be given by a suitable education to true friendship, following the image of the bonds of fraternal affection which Christ himself lived on earth.[35]

In *Pastores dabo vobis*, Pope John Paul II strongly emphasized that the basis of all priestly formation is a sound human formation. The Holy Father wrote:

> The priest should seek to reflect in himself, as far as possible, the human perfection which shines forth in the Incarnate Son of God. This is called for not only by the dignity of the priestly vocation but also by the demands of priestly ministry itself which needs a humanity that will be a bridge, not an obstacle, between men and women and Christ. Therefore, the seminarian should cultivate those human qualities and virtues which are needed to be a balanced person, "strong and free, capable of bearing the weight of pastoral responsibilities.

Priest psychologist Kevin McClone has extensively studied healthy affective maturity in seminarians and priests with a focus on intimacy. He observes, in fact, that many of these individuals do not understand how to define, nor recognize, nor live healthy intimacy and affective maturity. He has explained that the word intimacy is related to two Latin words: *intimus* which refers to that which is innermost; and the word *intimare* which means to announce, publish or make known. Combining these two meanings leads one to see the process of intimacy as "making known that which is innermost." McClone cites Thomas Malone's book, *The Art of Intimacy*, which describes the outstanding quality of the intimate experience is the "sense of being in touch with our real selves."[36] This description aligns well with the "man of communion" who is comfortable and in touch with himself and others. McClone notes that taking the risk to self-disclose oneself presupposes a certain self-awareness and self-intimacy that allows one to share who that person is. He adds:

Affective maturity involves having the relational skills to more effectively identify, understand and express my real feelings with the diversity of persons that make up the contemporary church while having a growing capacity to listen, understand, and empathize with their experiences.[37]

McClone poses questions to probe how to understand affective maturity: How well do I know myself with a balanced sense of my strengths and weaknesses? Do I know myself well enough to share my authentic self with others? Do I like the person that I am becoming? Do I esteem myself? Do I have close friends with whom I can deeply share? Am I comfortable being alone with myself as well as being with others? How am I growing in my intimacy with God? How do I relate to women? Am I comfortable with my own sexuality? How do I relate to men? How can I be more of my real self while relating to other persons? How comfortable am I relating to those in authority? This last question regarding relating to those in authority obviously has particular relevance in the case of priestly formation. Challenging authority, especially in the seminarian community, though not widespread, has emerged as a possible concern in seminarian formation programs and with some clergy. When this occurs, it may be due not only to underlying ecclesiological issues, but very likely reveals concern relating to affective maturity.

McClone identifies several criteria for healthy intimacy and affective maturity, beginning with the candidate's capacity for healthy relationships. To be an effective pastoral minister in the diverse church of today, one must be skilled in relationality and unencumbered by internal obstacles in relating to others. McClone suggests that being mindful of being relational in dialogue with others will help the seminarian and priest relate in more honest and conscious ways with oneself, with others, and with God. As he expresses it:

> These various relational dimensions are interconnected and influence each other's growth. For example, to the degree that I become more in touch with my true self, I grow to be more authentic in my relationships with others and my intimacy with God deepens. In sum, intimacy demands a more active engage-

ment in taking the necessary risks to grow in self-intimacy, interpersonal intimacy and intimacy with God. The formator may inquire: to what degree does this candidate demonstrate a growing capacity to relate to a wide diversity of persons that make up the contemporary church in a way that builds deeper connection, tolerance for diversity and support?[38]

McClone points to other skills needed for healthy relating and affective maturity as well as adequate growth capacity for deepening self-awareness. The formator must know how to evaluate the person in his totality, not forgetting the gradual nature of psychosexual development. The formator must see the candidate's strong and weak points and address them promptly – providing commendations as well as recommendations – as well as taking note of the level of awareness that the candidate has of his own family of origin history and its impact on his life. Healthy intimacy indeed presupposes certain reflective self-awareness.[39]

A recent dissertation, *Affectivity: A Way Forward for Seminary Formation* by Bernard L. Gordon combines the application of the teaching of Saint Thomas Aquinas to the affective formation of men preparing to be Catholic priests.[40] Gordon describes Thomistic teaching as most helpful in understanding affective maturity and its integral importance for a truly Christian and priestly life in the service of God and others, flowing as it does from a theological anthropology which recognizes proper affective growth as an essential dimension of human life and interpersonal relationships.[41]

Gordon highlights affective maturity as important for all persons but especially for seminarians and the universal Church. Growth in affective maturity should be observable throughout one's seminary formation, and we suggest, into one's priesthood. Furthermore, the effective pursuit of affective maturity in candidates can effectively change the landscape of the recent crises in the Church, since the identification and fostering of necessary indicators of affective maturity in candidates being advanced would appear of itself to diminish greatly the likelihood of candidates being ordained who exhibit some of the psychological and moral deficits witnessed in past cases of clerical sexual abuse. Such a development promises to be of great benefit to the universal Church and the faithful who could thereby hope to be served by affectively mature and well-balanced priests capable of relating well with others and fulfilling their commitments in a mature and virtuous way.

Gordon expounds Saint Thomas' teaching on the passions of love, hope and anger as principles to be presented to the seminarian in order for him to reflect upon his experiences with the passions and articulate his affective experiences so that he may be understood and guided by his formators. The author argues, for example, that Thomas' teaching on the cardinal and theological virtues can be applied as principles of affective formation. The gifts and fruits of the Holy Spirit are also presented specifically as principles of affective development, providing a blueprint by which affective maturity may be recognized and assessed. Gordon then explains how Saint Thomas' teaching on the capital vices, such as pride and vainglory, can help the seminarian to respond to affections that may be disordered. In general terms, Gordon demonstrates how Saint Thomas' teaching on infused virtue may be applied by the seminarian as a principle of affective growth so as to order his desires and affections to the good.

As a test case, he examines chastity as a virtue enabling the priest properly to form his sexuality in relation to others and to love and care for others responsibly as a pastor. A key contribution of this particular study may be found in its emphasis on the principle that affective maturity must be given a proper theological and Christological foundation. Only in this way can the seminarian become a man and a priest who reflects the life of Christ the Good Shepherd to those entrusted to his pastoral care.[42] Gordon also affirms that the theological virtues perfect the human affectivity.[43]

**Recent Studies on the Use of Psychological Evaluation in Seminary Formation**

One very helpful contribution in the definition of affective maturity from both a psychological and an ecclesial perspective is provided by a dissertation at the Institute of Psychological Sciences defended in 2017 by Charles Russell.[44] This work first seeks to define the concept of affective maturity while situating it in the contemporary life of the Church. It explores affective maturity's foundation in an anthropology firmly rooted in sound reason and Christian revelation. More specifically, diagnostic and potentially therapeutic is the author's subsequent attempt to relate the issue of affective maturity to the notion of attachment theory, taking note of the specific problems in the former and the complications in the latter. He then attempts to integrate these concepts and apply them in the presentation and examination of several concrete cases, which are imaginary composites of realistic situations involving candidates for formation and priestly ordination.

Russell notes the term" affective maturity" is a relatively new concept dating only from the time of Pope Saint John Paul II and only a few ecclesiastical documents mention it explicitly.[45] Furthermore, even though the same Pope in his Apostolic Exhortation *Pastores dabo vobis* had specifically mentioned affective maturity, designating it as "a significant and decisive factor in the formation of candidates for the priesthood," he had not in fact provided any concise definition of the concept.[46] Russell himself defines it as:

> the radical integration of the human faculties such that those faculties become ordered to self-gift," an integration that he characterizes as "the fruit of authentic encounter with others in which the dynamic truth that each person is an end in himself and cannot be used as a means to an end radically integrates the human faculties, ordering them to self-gift.[47]

In fleshing out this definition, he cites the work of Karol Wojtyla before his election as Pope John Paul II, *Love and Responsibility*, noting that affective maturity presupposes a steady identity out of which one operates, "allow[ing] one to recognize, accept, and embody the truth that he exists as being made for self-gift."[48] In order to live in a way that accords with such a purpose, one must have a proper ordering of desires and emotions, being able to forego proximate satisfactions for the sake of more distant ones, in keeping with the truth of oneself and of the situation being encountered.[49]

Obviously crucial to Russell's distillation of the concept of affective maturity from recent papal and other ecclesial documents is the more widely mentioned notion of the "man of communion," which provides

Russell's title. Pope John Paul in fact compiles a rather formidable list of qualities implied by such a designation:

> Of special importance is the capacity to relate to others.... This demands that the priest not be arrogant, or quarrelsome, but affable, hospitable, sincere in his words and heart, prudent and discreet, generous, and ready to serve, capable of opening himself to clear and brotherly relationships and of encouraging the same in others, and quick to understand, forgive and console (125) (cf. 1 Tm. 3:1-5; Ti. 1:7-9).[50]

In an appendix at the end of his study, Russell fills out the list further, providing a composite description of an affectively mature candidate that will no doubt prove helpful to formators. Among such qualities are: ability to tolerate ambiguity; healthy curiosity about the world; ability to look upon sinners with compassion; trust in the Church's judgement; recognizing that his own motives can be mixed and that he is capable of either good or evil; solid moral judgment while maintaining tranquility about others' contrary decisions; comfort with and genuine, but not fastidious, care over his own body; comfort with silence even when he might prefer the company of others; ability to grieve; appreciation of women as his intellectual and moral though not necessarily physical equals; avoidance of black and white thinking; concrete and demonstrated boundaries with the ability to say yes or no freely; ability to recognize when he is not feeling completely himself; and capacity for delayed gratification.[51]

It is in regard to this characterization of the affectively mature candidate as a "man of communion" that it becomes evident that the description at issue is not merely a psychological profile but is governed also by theological considerations. He draws upon the *Catechism of the Catholic Church*, which adds in n. 357: "that being made in God's image and likeness means that man, 'is capable of self-knowledge, of self-possession, and of freely giving himself and entering into communion with other persons." Such a concept, of course, is drawn equally from Sacred Scripture in its affirmation that "God is love" (1 John 4:8), and therefore that "the human person exists for the purpose of love because he is made in God's image and likeness."[52]

Even so, this spiritual profile finds its criterion in every aspect of the man's concrete composite as a physical and spiritual being. Indeed, the dimensions of the emotions and of sexuality, far from being excluded from such a calculus, is in fact central to it.

On the one hand, Russell is careful to caution against the reduction of the qualification "affective" to the merely *emotional* level. He cautions that the term "affective maturity" might "suggest to psychologists that it means 'emotional maturity,' which it does not."[53] Rather than being reducible to purely psychological terms, in other words, the notion of affective maturity as it is brought to bear upon priestly formation "requires then an explicit reading of and competency in philosophy, theology, and the Magisterial documents related to this topic."[54] It is not merely the "affections" that are at issue, but the whole complex of the *affectus* — i.e., of one's appetites and desires including the *rational* appetite: that is, the will, tamed by right reason.[55]

When affective maturity is either stunted or permanently impeded, according to Russell, behaviors may arise as maladaptive coping mechanisms which are detrimental to the candidate's healthy relationality. These may include repression: abuse of alcohol or other addictive substances; or various forms of unchaste behaviors.[56] Thus, while it may be tempting to consider such maladaptive coping mechanisms in isolation as a principal problem of priestly formation, they are quite likely instead to be symptomatic of a more generalized problem in the development of affective maturity.

Even while not considering affective maturity to be reducible to either affectivity or sexuality, however, Russell draws upon the norms for sexual education provided by the Congregation for Catholic Education in 1983 to assert that:

> The Church's understanding of affective formation gives pride of place to sexuality because a man's biological generativity exercises a compelling, though hardly deterministic, influence over him when it is unintentionally formed. Without a truly human formation of sexuality, there can be no complete maturity of affections because a man will not be fully capable of saying "Yes" and "No" in freedom. Therefore, according to the Church, formation of

sexuality is critical for the formation of affectivity and the general maturity of the human person, and it always results in chastity.[57]

It is for this reason, says Russell, that:

> Chastity is the Church's primary and most basic measure of affective maturity (cf. John Paul II, 1992). In addition to being the measure for affective maturity, chastity also brings about the maturity of the affections (Congregation for the Clergy, 2016). While the mature person is able to govern more than the outward expression of his sexuality, embodied in chastity, governing that outward expression works to mature a man's appetite, which begins to mold his affectivity, as well.[58]

A candidate's difficulties with chastity, then, will not be the only possible red flag in indicating roadblocks in the development of affective maturity, but they will certainly be among such indications. These include: "strong affective dependencies; notable lack of freedom in relations; excessive rigidity of character; [and] lack of loyalty," as well as uncertainties regarding sexual identity and deep-seated homosexual tendencies may be similarly indicative.[59]

Accordingly, the ability or inability to live chastely, while not the most important, is nevertheless in many ways the most conspicuous category of data indicative of a candidate's affective maturity. There are long-standing traditional means long proposed by the Church for the mastery of sexual urges, which should prove successful in the absence of psychological impediments. The process of such mastery is part and parcel of a *natural* maturation continuum, and it is not unlikely that different young men will be found at various points along this continuum over the course of their journey of formation. On the other hand, as cited from the above guidance of the Congregation for Catholic Education, "if a man has a history of unchastity, and methods proposed by the Church are not working to bring about maturity, then it is inferred there is some psychological impediment that must be overcome in order to live a chaste life."[60] As long as such an impediment manifests itself, this alone is sufficient to suggest that he should be barred from advancement to Sacred Orders. As Russell expresses it:

> While such a policy may seem overly harsh, the man who has the habit of unchastity uses his body in a manner that abuses (that is, misuses) the meaning for which it exists. In failing to live the truth about himself, it is likely impossible for him to value other people as true ends in themselves, as persons who cannot be used or thrown away. Even if the act is not physical, when a man uses another person's body in the context of his own fantasy, he makes that person a means to an end (cf. Matthew 5:28).[61]

The study by Russell does mention certain connections between forms of deviant sexual behavior that have produced such a recent crisis in the Church, on the one hand, and deficient or impeded development in affective maturity, on the other. But his analysis is very careful in avoiding a clumsy muddying of the waters that could be criticized for drawing an undue causal connection between specific tendencies or behaviors. As he puts it, "... it would be a grave error to equate affective immaturity and homosexuality or pedophilia, as some within the Church have done. That kind of simplistic and reductionistic heuristic is incompatible with Christian epistemology."[62]

In fact, as he points out, the suggestion that homosexuality somehow causes pedophilia would be as misguided as the affirmation that celibacy somehow makes it more likely. Rather, as Russell puts it, the Church "does not conflate homosexuality and pedophilia. The Church does, however, find in them a common root, as it were."[63]

Russell helpfully points out that, the ascertainment of an incapacity to manifest affective maturity, either because of failures in chastity, or because of the absence of or deficiency in the positive qualities mentioned as indications of such maturity, has more to do with the *timetable* of a man's advancement than with any absolute disqualification. Whether such a disqualification is permanent or not constitutes a separate discernment. What is clear, however, is that one should not remain within the normal framework of the program of formation if "the time needed to make progress exceeded the Church's ability to keep him in seminary while he targeted these issues."⁶⁴ Depending on his own circumstances he might be either assigned a parish where he could exercise supervised ministerial work, or he might be advised to seek private employment and support himself while remaining in contact with the Seminary, being provided an approved spiritual director and perhaps even assisted with psychological counseling. But he should not be advanced merely because of having completed the academic or other benchmarks of the journey of formation without having manifested sufficient indications of affective maturity.

**Some General Principles**

One of the great benefits of drawing the close connection between problems in the development of affective maturity and the kinds of problematic behaviors that have produced great scandal in the Church is that affective maturity itself can be defined, described, and fostered in quite positive ways, while *problems* become manifest not only in disasters that bring great human cost, but much earlier along the journey, in the simple fact that affective maturity is evidently not being ascertained in the candidate. Meanwhile, the focus of the accompaniment of seminarians can be on the positive values being sought in the candidates on their way to the priesthood. Indeed, it is only sufficient affective maturity which will enable the candidate to display aptitude for a ministry of service and self-sacrifice rooted in authentic love.

*Vastness of Love - VAST*

One way of mapping the journey toward affective maturity is effectively displayed in a day-long workshop presented to the seminarians of Saint Charles Borromeo Seminary in the Fall of 2020 by Father Keith Chylinski, a graduate of the Institute of Psychological Sciences which has since evolved into Divine Mercy University and, since July 1, 2022, Rector of the same Seminary. His presentation was entitled "The Vastness of Love: Human Foundational Principles." In it he contrasted the values noted above with the contrary temptations afforded by contemporary culture, especially in America: namely as "Pelagian" or predominantly task-oriented approach in contrast to a work of love; self-reliance as opposed to self-gift; and in spirituality, an objectification of God and others in contrast to authentic interpersonal reciprocity. At issue is not first a question of learning to *give* love, but of allowing oneself to *be loved by God* so as to learn from him to pass that love to others, as outlined in 1 John 4:19 — "We love because he first loved us."

The title "Vastness of Love" stems from four coordinates forming the mnemonic acronym V-A-S-T, namely vulnerability, acceptance, surrender, and trust. Father Chylinski is a priest well into his second decade of ministry, as well as being trained in psychology. He draws insights in the presentation not only from both of these disciplines of study, but from concrete experiences in assisting others in both human and spiritual growth. Having studied both fields, he notes that the same basic issues tend to arise in psychological and spiritual contexts.

**Vulnerability** entails an ability to tolerate the uncertainty and risk of emotional exposure. It is the alternative to the masks of self-reliance and self-justification that hide the true self of the one who is fearful of being unlovable. On the other hand, one who experiences the certitude of God's love is willing to relate authentically with others despite a healthy awareness of one's own limitations and imperfections. Militating against this vulnerability is a temptation to rely on one's own perceived or pretended strengths, a tendency described eloquently by James Keating:

> To rely on the self contradicts all that is revealed about God's love for us, and our deep vulnerability before the circumstances of life. Our nature defines us as limited and tending toward sin. God loves us, not because we are perfect, but because he is good. He loves us always, and not simply when we are "scrubbed up" and ready for public display. We can at times believe, wrongly, that everything will be "okay" in our lives once we are perfect or invincible. This is a lie. We will never be perfect; and staying in this lie undermines what God wants to share most deeply with us: his own compassion in the sight of our weakness.[65]

Such vulnerability means that a candidate can share his own needs with those upon whom he appropriately trusts as his own confidants, always within proper boundaries given the nature of each relationship.[66] He is able to resist the pressures of the standards of success set by contemporary culture and rely instead on the appeal to perfection specifically as it is taught by Jesus.[67]

Indeed, vulnerability before others as described here is not nearly so important as real vulnerability before God. Ultimately, it means being able to deflect the focus away from the fragile success of one's own attempts at perfection toward the childlike trust of one who is confident that seeking the Father's will is the true measure of love. On this point, Chylinski cites Keating again: "To meditate upon Christ's act of self-donation upon the Cross as a direct result of his obedience, as a result of his listening to the Father's heart, becomes the model of our own vulnerability before God."

**Acceptance** is a second coordinate of affective maturity as outlined in Father Chylinski's presentation. It is founded in *acceptance* of the truth of oneself before God, including the acceptance not only one's own fragility and sin, but also of the suffering that the struggle of the Christian life necessarily entails.[68] The importance of such acceptance for human thriving, as well as the acknowledgement of the struggle that doing so can sometimes entail, is attested by the beginning of the familiar "Serenity Prayer": "God grant me the serenity *to accept the things I cannot change....*" As Jacques Philippe so aptly expresses it, "What often blocks the action of God's grace in our lives is less our sins and failings, than it is our failure to accept our own weakness."[69] In priestly formation, the lack of such acceptance will inevitably lead to a lack of self-knowledge or of transparency, or both, that stifles the candidate's progress toward affective maturity. It also thwarts one's capacity to receive divine assistance, since one would rather pretend to be self-reliant rather than hearing together with Saint Paul the divine promise that "My grace is sufficient for you, for my power is made perfect in weakness…" (2 Cor 12:9-10).

Chylinski observes that the difficulty of the challenge to accept one's suffering — ranging from daily minor faults of self and others and minor inconveniences all the way to wholesale denial of major trauma and outright rationalization of grave sin — is evident in the sequence of the grieving process, in which acceptance comes only *after* having passed through the stages of denial, anger, bargaining and depression. When a candidate fails to accept suffering in his life, as Philippe notes: "The worst pain in suffering lies in rejecting it."[70]

One finds a model here in Saint Francis' radical acceptance of his own poverty before God, while the wise words of numerous Saints corroborate the connection between such acceptance and spiritual growth, as for example Saint John Vianney's discovery that "Peaceful suffering is no longer suffering," and Padre Pio's enigmatic but mysteriously cogent claim that "I suffer only when I don't suffer." Chylinski invites the seminar participants to reflect specifically on what invitations to suffer they may be consciously or unconsciously rejecting, and to embrace consciously the Cross of Jesus as the quintessential transformation of suffering into love. Helpful in this respect are the far less familiar closing words of the Serenity Prayer as it comes to us from Reinhold Niebuhr:

> Living one day at a time; Enjoying one moment at a time; Accepting hardships as the pathway to peace; Taking, as He did, this sinful world as it is, not as I would have it; Trusting that He will make all things right if I surrender to His Will. That I may be reasonably happy in this life and supremely happy with Him forever in the next. Amen.

**Surrender** should follow acceptance of one's own poverty and consequent radical need for God. Such surrender is intimately connected with acceptance because in the call to "die to self;" it is precisely the falsely constructed self that must be surrendered. Besides a serene acquiescence to the divine will, such surrender also entails letting go of the need to be perfect and an attempt to control or "impress" God, as if one could really hide one's weaknesses from Him. The very attempt to do so, in fact, will lead to frustration, resentments, and a judgmental stance toward others as well.

The lack of surrender and the pretension of self-reliance will likely manifest itself in tendencies such as intellectualization (i.e., an attempt to control by means of one's understanding) or spiritualization (the attempt to deny the emotions while controlling through religious observance). The *Catechism of the Catholic Church*, in fact (n. 1866), is quite lucid in highlighting the corrosive spiritual effect of such a failure to surrender in the context of its description of the *sin of pride*: "Pride is undue self-esteem or self-love, which seeks attention and honor and sets oneself *in competition with God*."

Ironically, then, it is the rejection of one's spiritual childhood before God that stunts progress toward true affective and spiritual maturity. Consequently, it would also hamper a priest's pastoral aptitude by leading him to treat: divine truth as a commodity to be wielded as a weapon rather than gratefully received and joyfully shared; liturgical performance as a criterion of measurable perfection rather than the surrender of one's subjectivity to the divine majesty; and pastoral performance as a compulsion to "figure out" every situation rather than to place it trustingly before God with confidence in the discernment that only He can bestow as a gift. And, with potentially tragic outcomes, the gift of chastity will likely elude one who seeks to grasp it by means of white-knuckled repression or control rather by the *surrender* of one's desires in chaste love.

In the conversation with the seminarian, it is necessary to invite him to identify very specifically and concretely those things that he may be afraid to surrender — whether it may be some form of power or control that seems to afford security, or work projects, relationships, financial arrangements, interests or hobbies, vices or habits that might be incompatible with his authentically discerned vocation. A prayer that exemplifies this coordinate of growth toward affective and spiritual maturity is Saint Ignatius of Loyola's *Suscipe* prayer: "Take, Lord, receive all my liberty...."

**Trust** is the fourth coordinate of Chylinski's presentation. It illustrates most clearly the beautiful paradox of the fact that that affective and spiritual maturity really depend on the successful integration into one's thinking, feeling and acting of the injunction of Jesus (Matt 18:3) to "become *like children.*" One is able to grow affectively and spiritually — to transcend one's limitations and past sins — not so much by cementing and relying upon one's own skills, strengths or reputation, but by a childlike trust in *God's*: goodness and power; His mercy and love; His nearness and providence; and His desire to be present to us. In exemplification of such trust, Chylinski cites the diary of Saint Faustina Kowalska, as she recounts what she hears Jesus saying to her:

> My child, life on earth is a struggle indeed; a great struggle for my kingdom. But fear not, because you are not alone. I am always supporting you, so lean on Me as you struggle, fearing nothing.

Take the vessel of trust and draw from the fountain of life – for yourself, but also for other souls, especially such as are distrustful of My goodness.[71]

**Specific challenges are discernible.** Charles Russell's dissertation, presented above, illustrates the strong relationship that exists between family-of-origin issues, defense mechanisms, and affective maturity. His particular framing of the relationship builds upon research connected with psychological theories of attachment. Regardless of whether this is the most or the only valid way of framing the issue, the experience of formators in seminaries strongly corroborates the affirmation that a seminarian's family of origin is a powerful indicator — even if not in a deterministic way — of the challenges he is likely to encounter along the journey toward affective maturity. Many of the defense mechanisms that he develops in order to survive amid family turmoil, while they may be rational and even ingenious devices to serve him well there, may take on a life of their own and predispose him to relate to others in a manner that becomes dysfunctional in a seminary environment, not to mention in pastoral ministry later on.

Such a correlation should never be used to screen out applicants from troubled family backgrounds, because many such applicants have also manifest gifts of resiliency and empathy as well as a profound understanding of human suffering. The solution lies instead in the encouragement of transparency, fueled by a climate of mutual trust between the seminarian and formators and assisted by carefully chosen experts in the psychological sciences. These experts will assist the candidate to recognize dysfunctional patterns of reaction and behavior to develop wholesome and appropriate skills of relationship with proper boundaries and well-placed trust in order not only to function in community and ministry in accordance with the ideals exemplified by vulnerability, acceptance, surrender and trust, as described above.

For this reason, the Formation Advisor's regular meetings with advisees should focus frequently on informal conversations regarding the candidate's family of origin. Even when he does not mention them spontaneously, the candidate is not infrequently burdened by concerns and tensions arising from his home life and may not readily recognize how profoundly they impact his present behavior and interactions with others, especially those in authority. Bringing such concerns to concrete expression will almost always be beneficial, even if it must be left to professional counselors to assist the candidate to make conscious connections with his present challenges, which may include perfectionism, fear of criticism, codependency, over-responsibility, anxieties, or any number of other challenges that he has not yet integrated into the framework of vulnerability, acceptance, surrender, and trust described above.

**Addiction** is one of the most prevalent of the dysfunctional coping mechanisms connected with stunted development of affective maturity, whether involving substances or addictive behavior, especially in the use of pornography which has become ubiquitous. It might seem scandalous to some but the typical class of new seminarians in any given year is now comprised of young men of whom very few will not have been exposed already to pornography, often at very young ages. In formation, this calls for a delicate balance of clarity in highlighting the absolute unacceptability of such an exploitation and desecration for human sexuality. Additionally, it calls for understanding and willingness to assist the seminarian in overcoming habits of its use in a non-judgmental and compassionate way with the help of tools such as accountability software, support groups, counseling, etc. Similar approaches are warranted, with solutions appropriate to the specific stage of formation, in the case of alcohol or drug use. Any such problems must, of course, be clearly mastered for a significant period of time prior to advancement to the Diaconate.

Obviously, the candidate's freedom to the anonymity of the internal forum is a time-tested value in the Church's pastoral wisdom developed over the centuries. At the same time, recent experience seems to show that when addictive patterns of behavior are being experienced, an adequate degree of transparency in the external forum is crucial to the mastery over addictive behavior which will be needed for advancement to Sacred Orders. To that end, formators themselves will need to be updated frequently and well-informed about best practices and available resources, and it will be crucial to maintain an awareness that the necessary sobriety (in terms of all forms of addictive behavior and not only substance abuse) is best viewed as the goal of a journey which may coincide with the time a candidate spends in the Seminary, provided that: there is transparency; real progress is being made; and that each decision of advancement, to Candidacy or to specific ministries along the way, is being evaluated in terms of a realistic prospect of readiness for Sacred Orders within the shortening time frame that is implied with each successive advancement. Furthermore, since matters of conscience can only be brought freely by the candidate into the external forum, internal-forum advisors such as counselors and spiritual directors will need to be part of the conversation with other formators regarding general expectations of this nature, so as to be able to assist the candidate himself in deciding whether to petition for a given step or ministry.

The issue regarding **same-sex attraction** is related to affective maturity. In evaluating the suitability for Sacred Orders of men reporting or exhibiting same-sex attraction, the Congregation for Catholic Education's in its 2005 *Instruction Concerning the Criteria for the Discernment of Vocations with regard to Persons with Homosexual Tendencies in view of their Admission to the Seminary and to Holy Orders* actually begins its treatment of the question by a discussion of affective maturity, stating that:

> The candidate to the ordained ministry, therefore, must reach affective maturity. Such maturity will allow him to relate correctly to both men and women, developing in him a true sense of spiritual fatherhood towards the Church community that will be entrusted to him.[72]

After distinguishing further between homosexual *acts* and homosexual *tendencies*, the Congregation lays down the norm that "the Church, while profoundly respecting the persons in question, cannot admit to the seminary or to holy orders those who practice homosexuality, present deep-seated homosexual tendencies or support the so-called 'gay culture.'" Clearly to be distinguished from such a "deep-seated" tendency, according to the same document, is to be considered "the case in which one were dealing with homosexual tendencies that were only the expression of a transitory problem—for example, that of an adolescence not yet superseded."[73]

## IX. Affective Maturity & its Importance for Seminary Formation

It is neither necessary nor within the scope of this essay to analyze the Congregation's rationale for this distinction, nor for the relevant norms being laid down in its regard. What is clear from the foregoing, however, is that whenever a candidate reporting or exhibiting a tendency to same-sex attraction may nevertheless be considered a viable candidate, it is precisely and only due to the fact that in his case, such a tendency is not to be considered a constitutional and ineradicable element of his personal identity, but rather as a "transitory" and more superficial phenomenon of his experience along his journey toward affective maturity.

The fostering of a high degree of mutual trust between seminarians and their formators will be crucial to addressing this issue appropriately, avoiding the phenomenon, on the one hand, of the "submarine" seminarian who hides deep-seated tendencies and proceeds to Ordination only to act out later; and, on the one hand, of the virtuous but scrupulous seminarian who struggles with tendencies of a more superficial and transitory nature which should not rightly be regarded as incapacitating for Ordination. Extremely helpful to this analysis is the contribution of Doctors Peter Kleponis and Richard Fitzgibbons on the distinction between "deep-seated" and "transitory" same-sex attraction.[74] In particular, it provides criteria for the discernment of a likely "transitory" condition based not simply on the passage of time, but on the "ego-dystonic" nature of the same-sex attraction which in itself applies the ability to change. As they describe it:

> Candidates with transitory same-sex attractions do not base their masculine identity upon their sexual attractions….[They] do not believe they were born with them and greatly desire to overcome them. Usually, they have not had a history of homosexual acting out. They accept the Church's teaching on sexual morality and want to live and teach it. They do not subscribe to current societal views on homosexuality and same-sex unions.[75]

Experience in recent years does seem to corroborate the thesis that candidates matching Kleponis and Fitzgibbons' description of "ego-dystonic" same-sex attraction can be encouraged to seek and benefit from professional counseling, since their struggles are often related to deficits of male confidence rooted in family-of-origin issues and related to problems in the development of close male friendships, poor body image, and other difficulties that may be confronted, often with marked success. Even so, the Congregation's *monitum* in the above-mentioned document is also crucial; namely, the candidate must have manifested freedom from any acting out or other dysfunctional behaviors associated with such tendencies for a minimum of three years prior to Ordination to the Diaconate.

**The Development of Affective Maturity in Seminary Formation**

It is crucial that a candidate for Ordination demonstrate real affective maturity rather than merely intellectual competency or ministerial skills. As a result, the formation of priests requires a residential setting in which formators and candidates interact on a daily basis not only formally but informally. Often enough, a candidate may demonstrate a high degree of mastery in theology, Sacred Scripture, moral theology, canon law, and liturgical ministry while struggling in emotional intelligence and in the formation of solid peer relationships. Sometimes he may relate well to authority figures but not to peers, or vice versa. He may even earn high marks during limited periods during summers or once per week apostolates, but only in the context of a full-time residential community— where the greater part of each year is spent for several years— is it really feasible for him — in dialogue with his formators and peers — to discern his readiness not for a momentary performance but for a way of life calling for true affective maturity.

Also important for such discernment is the opportunity for input on the part of lay faculty, especially including women, with whom his interactions are revelatory of the presence or absence of affective maturity in ways that never surface between peers or with priests. Also revelatory are strategically timed peer evaluations solicited from his classmates generally. Sometimes these surface concerns that will not have been observed in conversations with formators, but they may at least reveal that a young man is considerably more skilled and outgoing in everyday life than his more guarded interactions with authority figures might have suggested.

A particular challenge today for priestly formation in the United States is the phenomenon of a population of seminarians drawn from different ethnic and cultural backgrounds. It may be tempting to formators, for example, to consider a man as lacking in initiative or unduly passive when his demeanor is actually influenced by a culture that may not be so inviting of unsolicited communication with superiors. Or again, one may mistakenly find a candidate to be negligent of norms when perhaps his perception of such norms might be affected by the manner in which such norms are conveyed. For example, seminarians from an Anglo-Saxon background might be readily responsive to norms conveyed by a message on a bulletin board, while in some other cultures, such a communication would fail to signal effectively the real expectations of authorities. Clearly, then, the assessment of affective maturity in a multicultural context requires sensitivity for the interpretation from one language and culture to another, not merely of words but of other means of conveying intentions and expectations. This is especially so as regards standards of academic integrity and responsibility. It is certainly not illegitimate to expect originality of work and respect for the intellectual property of others as an important indicator of personal maturity and integrity, as well as to expect that someone from another cultural background learn to respect the norms of the culture in which he resides, even temporarily. But it would be unrealistic to suppose that everyone, regardless of his cultural background, starts out from the same vantage point or arrives at this goal by the same path as any other.

**Conclusion**

In most cases, the journey toward affective maturity is observably underway throughout the candidate's time in priestly formation. It is a requirement not only of justice but of realism to affirm that some particular deficits in affective maturity, which would be prohibitive if observed a month before his petition for Ordination to the Diaconate, are far less debilitating when they are encountered earlier on in the process. Advancement to the Ministry of Lector, for example, should not be taken to indicate that the same candidate is already deemed suitable for the Diaconate.

Even so, some of the more insightful candidates, even without actually calling into question their discernment of their vocation in a broader sense, feel a need to step away temporarily from formation rather than simply remaining "on the conveyor belt" to be advanced to the same steps and ministries being attained by others in the same class. Precisely because it involves a journey toward an appropriate level of affective maturity, the journey toward sacred Orders cannot always occur on a uniform timeline. And if more time is required, discernment needs to be made with (or sometimes for) the candidate between a supervised pastoral year in a parish, on the one hand, and on the other, an indefinite period of withdrawal altogether from residential and supervised formation. In fact, if the candidate has been observed to be lacking in the necessary foundations of personal care and/or if he is excessively motivated by the approval of others rather than by duly internalized values relevant to affective maturity and priestly formation, the latter course may clearly be advisable. In this case, any resumption of the seminary process should come only after re-admission, probably with the assistance of further psychological screening, taking account of the specific issues that surfaced previously in his formation.

Throughout his formation, the candidate has been monitored and has also monitored his own progress in terms of the four dimensions of priestly formation including the human, spiritual, intellectual, and pastoral. Affective maturity is relevant not only to the human dimension, but to all four of these. But as the candidate finally approaches the moment of petitioning and being approved for priestly Ordination, a key indicator of the effective suitability for lifetime ministry will be seen in the fact that these dimensions are no longer so clearly distinct from one another but are inextricably united. If a Deacon were prematurely or misguidedly advanced to that ministry, a deficit in his human, academic or spiritual formation would hamper his pastoral performance as well. Conversely, by this time, an inability to engage pastoral situations effectively or to apply himself in a disciplined way to his studies or to prayer would probably long since have revealed a deficit or even an incapacity in human formation. Precisely in view of this ultimate of all dimensions in the development of an affectively mature and competent priest, the process of formation requires an integrated team of formators who, though each focused on a distinct aspect of the formative process, nevertheless meet frequently in common discussion of the seminarian's progress in all of the various dimensions.

IX. Affective Maturity & its Importance for Seminary Formation 313

Indeed, since affective maturity is verified in a context of a demonstrated capacity for healthy relationships across a broad spectrum of persons, formators can effectively assist the candidate toward this end. These formators should assist not as a disjointed array of experts in different departments but as a team able to enter constantly into an ongoing conversation with the candidate, in addition to a healthy and respectful collaboration with one another.

## RESPONSE

# Affective Maturity in Relation to the Spiritual Life and the Virtues

## Carmina Chapp and Robert L. Fastiggi

*Adjunct Professor of Theology, St. Bernard's School of Theology and Ministry, Rochester, New York*

*and*

*Professor of Dogmatic Theology, Sacred Heart Major Seminary, Detroit, Michigan*

### Introduction

In their chapter, Monsignor Michael Magee and Professor Suzanne Mulrain highlight the importance of affective maturity in seminary formation. In this essay, we would like to build upon their important insights with an emphasis on the connection between affective maturity, the spiritual life, and the cultivation of the virtues. In a special way, we will explain how affective maturity requires more than human effort. It requires the transforming power of divine grace. St. Thomas Aquinas (c.1225-1274) provided a classic articulation of the relation between nature and grace when he said: "grace does not take away nature but perfects it": *gratia non tollit naturam sed perficit*.[76] Thus, supernatural grace elevates and perfects human nature, building upon the natural, human virtues already present.

### What is affective maturity?

According to Fr. John Hardon, S.J., affections refer to:
a broad variety of human sentiments that are distinguished from strictly mental or cognitive experiences. Affections pertain to the will, desires, and feelings, i.e. the outgoing activities. In the spiritual

life they are identified with those movements of the soul that reach out to God and with the invisible world of angels and saints.[77] The *Catechism of the Catholic Church* examines the affections when discussing the passions and offers the following key points:

> The term "passions" refers to the affections or the feelings. By his emotions man intuits the good and suspects evil.
>
> The principal passions are love and hatred, desire and fear, joy, sadness, and anger.
>
> In the passions, as movements of the sensitive appetite, there is neither moral good nor evil. But insofar as they engage reason and will, there is moral good or evil in them.
>
> Emotions and feelings can be taken up in the virtues or perverted by the vices.
>
> The perfection of the moral good consists in man's being moved to the good not only by his will but also by his "heart."[78]

The affections, emotions, or passions are expressions of who we are as human beings. We should not be ashamed to have emotions such as love and hatred, desire and fear, joy, sadness, and anger. Because "emotions and feelings can be taken up in the virtues or perverted by the vices", affective maturity requires cultivating the virtues and overcoming vices. Both the human and theological virtues must be cultivated to achieve affective maturity, which leads to proper control of the passions. Growth in affective maturity, therefore, involves human effort, divine grace, and the cultivation of the virtues.

**Cultivating Virtues and Avoiding Vices**

The *Catechism* defines virtue as "a habitual and firm disposition to do good" (no. 1833). It also recognizes that there are human virtues and theological virtues. The human virtues "are stable dispositions of the intellect and the will that govern our acts, order our passions, and guide our conduct in accordance with reason and faith" (no. 1834). The human virtues are traditionally grouped according to the four cardinal (or pivotal) virtues of prudence, justice, fortitude, and temperance. These cardinal virtues are described in this way:

> Prudence disposes the practical reason to discern, in every circumstance, our true good and to choose the right means for achieving it.
>
> Justice consists in the firm and constant will to give God and neighbor their due.
>
> Fortitude ensures firmness in difficulties and constancy in the pursuit of the good.
>
> Temperance moderates the attraction of the pleasures of the senses and provides balance in the use of created goods.[79]

The four cardinal virtues are called human virtues because they can be perfected by natural means such as "education, deliberate acts, and perseverance in struggle."[80] Human effort and disciple can perfect the cardinal virtues, but divine grace is needed to purify and elevate them.[81]

In addition to the four cardinal virtues, there are the three theological virtues of faith, hope, and charity. These theological virtues "adapt man's faculties for participation in the divine nature."[82] They "are infused by God into the souls of the faithful to make them capable of acting as his children and of meriting eternal life."[83] When souls grow in humility, they come to realize more deeply that these virtues are divine gifts. They come to understand that God is the source of all graces, and they must willingly give consent so that "Our Lord might work these graces in [the soul]."[84]

The three theological virtues of faith, hope, and charity "have God for their origin, their motive, and their object - God known by faith, God hoped in and loved for his own sake."[85] Affective maturity is intimately linked to spiritual maturity because growth in faith, hope, and charity requires a life of prayer rooted in the Eucharist and authentic devotion to the Blessed Virgin Mary, the angels, and the saints. Affective maturity is essential for every state of life. Those called to the sacrament of matrimony must cultivate the four cardinal virtues as well the theological virtues in order to form "a partnership of the whole of life" that is "ordered toward the good of the spouses and the procreation and education of children."[86] Those called to the single life or to consecrated celibacy "must walk unhesitatingly ... in the path of living faith, which arouses hope and works through charity."[87]

Priests who freely embrace the gift of celibacy must achieve affective maturity if they are to be effective ministers to the faithful. Priests who are centered on themselves or controlled by disordered passions will not be able to manifest the chaste love of Christ. They will become a cause for scandal and harm if they fail to achieve self-control, sobriety, and chastity. Priestly celibacy, when lived out properly, configures the priest in a radical way to Christ, who offered himself for the sake of his Bride, the Church. Cardinal Robert Sarah sees priestly celibacy as a means to live in deep intimacy with Jesus. He writes:

> The priest is truly the friend of Jesus. He offers himself to God. He offers himself to the whole Church and to each of the faithful to whom he is sent. The priest learns the logic of his celibacy in the Eucharist. "Acting in the person of Christ, the priest unites himself most intimately with the offering, and places on the altar his entire life, which bears the marks of the holocaust." He learns in the Eucharistic sacrifice what the total gift of self means.[88]

The desire for love is natural, but loving others in a chaste manner requires supernatural help. Vatican II's Decree on Priestly Formation—*Optatam Totius* (1965) offers these wise reflections:

> Students who follow the venerable tradition of celibacy ... embrace the Lord with an undivided love, ... bear witness to the resurrection of the world to come (cf. Luke 20:36), and obtain a most suitable aid for the continual exercise of that perfect charity whereby they can become all things to all men in their priestly ministry. ...
>
> They are to be warned of the dangers that threaten their chastity especially in present-day society. Aided by suitable safeguards, both divine and human, let them learn to integrate their renunciation of marriage in such a way that they ... acquire a deeper mastery of soul and body and a fuller maturity, and more perfectly receive the blessedness spoken of in the Gospel.[89]

*Optatam Totius* goes on to explain how proper seminary training cultivates human maturity, which "will be made especially evident in stability of mind, in an ability to make weighty decisions, and in a sound evaluation of men and events."[90] As such, seminarians:

> are to be formed in strength of character, and, in general, they are to learn to esteem those virtues which are held in high regard by men and which recommend a minister of Christ. Such virtues are sincerity of mind, a constant concern for justice, fidelity to one's promises, refinement in manners, modesty in speech coupled with charity.[91]

Affective maturity is absolutely essential, if priests are to treat women with dignity and respect and avoid any form of physical, spiritual, or psychological abuse. Priests who sexually exploit women not only sin grievously, but they also cause enormous emotional harm. They wound the Body of Christ and cause scandal. Those involved in priestly formation must help future priests become men of virtue and charity.

Affective maturity cannot be achieved by seminary formation alone. Seminarians and priests must develop a genuine relationship of love with God. They need to be nourished by Eucharistic adoration and genuine devotion to the Blessed Virgin Mary and the saints. Priests need good spiritual direction and ongoing formation even after ordination. Some priests go through a mid-life crisis and face self-doubts and temptations. The Church must find ways to help priests who experience such difficulties. Affective maturity requires growth in the virtues, especially faith, hope, and charity.

**Formation in Affective Maturity, the Virtues, and Holiness**

In his 1992 apostolic exhortation, *Pastores Dabo Vobis* John Paul II identifies four areas of priestly formation: the human, the spiritual, the intellectual, and the pastoral. All four of these areas—sometimes called the four pillars of priestly formation—are essential to affective maturity. In a special way, though, John Paul II highlights the importance of human and spiritual formation for the cultivation of affective maturity. In speaking of human formation, he links affective maturity to love, and he provides some insights that are well worth citing:

> Affective maturity presupposes an awareness that love has a central role in human life. ... We are speaking of a love that involves the entire person, in all his or her aspects - physical, psychic and spiritual - and which is expressed in the "nuptial meaning" of the human body, thanks to which a person gives oneself to another and takes the other to oneself. ... Sometimes the very family situations in which priestly vocations arise will display not a few weaknesses and at times even serious failings.
>
> In such a context, an education for sexuality becomes more difficult but also more urgent. It should be truly and fully personal and therefore should present chastity in a manner that shows appreciation and love for it as a "virtue that develops a person's authentic maturity and makes him or her capable of respecting and fostering the 'nuptial meaning' of the body."[92]

While affective maturity is necessary for all men and women, it is especially important for priests. John Paul II believes that the call to priestly celibacy requires a man to make a free offering of self with the grace of the Holy Spirit. This necessarily involves affective maturity, which "should bring to human relationships of serene friendship and deep brotherliness a strong, lively and personal love for Jesus Christ."[93] The commitment to priestly celibacy, though, requires vigilance because human affections still remain in the man committed to continence. As John Paul II writes:

> Since the charism of celibacy, even when it is genuine and has proved itself, leaves one's affections and instinctive impulses intact, candidates to the priesthood need an affective maturity which is prudent, able to renounce anything that is a threat to it, vigilant over both body and spirit, and capable of esteem and respect in interpersonal relationships between men and women. A precious help can be given by a suitable education to true friendship, following the image of the bonds of fraternal affection which Christ himself lived on earth (cf. Jn. 11:5).[94]

The vigilance over body and spirit requires the cultivation of the human virtues, especially prudence and temperance. It also requires divine grace, which is sustained and deepened by a life of prayer. The life of prayer is not simply one of external observance. It is a personal encounter with the living God. John Paul II explains the life of prayer in terms of a loving bond with the Holy Spirit and the Lord Jesus:

> The Spirit, by consecrating the priest and configuring him to Jesus Christ, head and shepherd, creates a bond which, located in the priest's very being, demands to be assimilated and lived out in a personal, free and conscious way through an ever richer communion of life and love and an ever broader and more radical sharing in the feelings and attitudes of Jesus Christ. In this bond between the Lord Jesus and the priest, an ontological and psychological bond, a sacramental and moral bond, is the foundation and likewise the power for that "life according to the Spirit" and that "radicalism of the Gospel" to which every priest is called today and which is fostered by ongoing formation in its spiritual aspect. This formation proves necessary also for the priestly ministry to be genuine and spiritually fruitful.[95]

Here we see how affective maturity must be sustained by a life of prayer and intimacy with Christ in the power of the Holy Spirit.

On December 8, 2016, the Congregation for the Clergy issued an updated *Ratio Fundamentalis Institutionis Sacerdotalis*, which in English is entitled *The Gift of the Priestly Formation*. This document builds upon *Pastores Dabo Vobis* and reaffirms the need for future priests to be formed in the virtues under the power of divine grace.[96] The hope is that future priests will grow in affective maturity and embrace the gift of priestly celibacy with serenity and peace. The evangelical counsel of chastity "develops the maturity of the person making him able to live the reality of his own body and affectivity within the logic of gift."[97] Well-formed priests who embrace celibacy as a gift are able to love and minister to others with the love of Christ. They are able to enter into chaste friendships with men and women with an affective maturity sustained by the virtues of prudence and temperance. The grace of Christ supplies the supernatural assistance needed to overcome any disordered affections.

## Conclusion

The development of affective maturity requires discipline, prayer, and the cultivation of both the human and theological virtues. Revelations of clerical sexual misconduct could be indications that changes are needed in priestly formation. The documents of the Church on priestly formation that we have mentioned—*Optatam Totius*, *Pastores Dabo Vobis*, and *The Gift of the Priestly Vocation*—all provide beautiful insights on the need for affective maturity sustained by the virtues, prayer, and the life of grace. Failures to apply these insights can and do occur, and sometimes those entrusted with priestly formation are themselves lacking in affective maturity. All this shows how important it is for bishops to appoint spiritually mature priests; male and female religious; as well as male and female laypersons to serve as seminary professors and formation personnel. Seminarians and priests are human, and many today carry emotional wounds from childhood and bad family experiences. God, though, can heal these wounds, and his grace can build on nature to form priests of affective maturity who serve the people of God with the love of Christ.

# FOOTNOTES

## Introduction

¹Congregation for the Doctrine of the Faith (CDF), *Letter to Bishops of the Catholic Church on the Collaboration of Men and Women in the Church and the World* (hereinafter "Letter to Bishops"), May 31, 2004, no. 1, https://vatican.va/roman_curia/congregations/cfaith/documents/rc_con_cfaith_doc_20040731_collaboration_en.html (last accessed March 21, 2022).

² Ibid.

³ Ibid., no. 8.

⁴ Ibid., no. 13.

⁵ Ibid.

⁶ Ibid.

⁷ Pope John Paul II, Apostolic Letter, *Mulieris Dignitatem* (On the Dignity and Vocation on the Occasion of the Marian Year) August 15, 1988, at 21-22, https://vatican.va/content/john-paul-ii/en/apost_letters/1988/documents/hf_jp-ii_apl_19880815_mulieris-dignitatem.html (last accessed March 26, 2022).

⁸ See *Letter to Bishops, supra*.

⁹ Pope John Paul II, *Letter to Women*, June 29, 1995, https://vatican.va/content/john-paul-ii/en/letters/1995/documents/hf_jp-ii_let_29061995_women.html (last accessed March 26, 2022).

¹⁰ Pope Benedict XVI, *Address to the Participants in the International Convention on the Theme 'Woman and Man,' the Humanum in its Entirety* (hereinafter "2008 Address") February 9, 2008, https://vatican.va/content/benedict-xvi/en/speeches/2008/february/documents/hf_ben-xvi_spe_20080209_donna-uomo.pdf (last accessed March 26, 2022).

¹¹ Ibid.

¹² Pope Benedict XVI, *Apostolic Journey to Brazil on the Occasion of the Fifth General Conference of Bishops of Latin America and the Caribbean* (May 9-14, 2007) May 13, 2007, https://vatican.va/content/benedict-xvi/en/travels/2007/outside/documents/brasile.html (last accessed March 26, 2022).

¹³ Pope Benedict, *General Audiences*, September 1, 2010 to April 6, 2011, https://vatican.va/content/benedict-xvi/en/audiences/ 2010.index.html and https://vatican.va/content/benedict-xvi/en/audiences/2011.index.html, respectively (last accessed March 26, 2022).

¹⁴ See *2008 Address, supra.*

¹⁵ Pope John Paul II, Encyclical Letter *Dominum et Vivificantem* (On the Holy Spirit in the Life of the Church and the World) May 18, 1986, nos. 39, 48, https://vatican.va/content/john-paul-ii/en/encyclicals/documents/hf_jp-ii_enc_18051986_dominum-et-vivificantem.html#-3C (last accessed March 26, 2022).

¹⁶ Pope Francis, *Address at the End of the Eucharist Concelebration, Meeting the Protection of Minors in the Church (February 21-24, 2019)*, February 24, 2019, https://vatican.va/content/francesco/en/speeches/2019/february/documents/papa-francesco_20190224_incontro-protezioneminori-chiusura.html (last accessed March 22, 2022).

¹⁷ Ibid.

¹⁸ For canon law norms, revisions, and modifications see: *The Abuse of Minors: The Church's Response*, https://vatican.va/resources/index_en.htm (last accessed March 19. 2022).

¹⁹ The book reviews are available on the website of the *International Catholic Jurists Forum.* Click on the book entitled Jane F. Adolphe, Ronald J. Rychlak, eds., *Clerical Sexual Misconduct: An Interdisciplinary Analysis* (Cluny: 2020) https://icjurist.org/clerical-sexual-misconduct/ (last accessed March 17, 2022).

²⁰ Jane F. Adolphe, Ronald J. Rychlak, xi.

²¹ Ibid.

²² Ibid.

²³ See, e.g., Salvatore Cernuzio, *Il velo del silenzio. abusi, violenze, frustrazioni nella vita religiosa femminile* (San Paolo Edizioni: 2021); See an article about the book by Claire Giangravé, "New Book Shines Light on Abuse and Racist Discrimination of Catholic Nuns," *Religion News Service*, ( November 29, 2021) https://religionnews.com/2021/11/29/new-book-shines-light-on-abuse-and-racist-discrimination-of-catholic-nuns/ (last accessed March 20, 2022), wherein one "abused nun [wa]s transferred, accused of seducing the priest, and the priest stay[ed] at his place, continuing his predatory activity undisturbed," while other reports of sexual abuse were not taken seriously; See also Saji Thomas, "Sisters Record Testimony in trial of Indian Bishop accused of Raping Nun," *Global Sisters Report: A Project of National Catholic Report,* February 2021, https://globalsistersreport.org/news/news/news/sisters-record-testimony-trial-indian-bishop-accused-raping-nun (last accessed March 21, 2022); See also Doris Wagner, "Sexual Abuse of Nuns - Facts and Questions," *Voices of Faith,* February 26, 2019 available

at https://voicesoffaith.org/conversations-1/2019/2/25/sexual-abuse-of-nuns-facts-and-questions-by-doris-wagner (last accessed March 21, 2022).

[24] See, e.g., Marie-Lucile Kubacki, "The (nearly) Free Work of Sisters," Woman Church World, in *Osservatore Romano* (March: 2018) (not available online); See also an article about the publication by Nicole Winfield, "Vatican Magazine Denounces Nun's Servitude," *Associated Press,* March 1, 2018, https://apnews.com/article/vatican-city-ap-top-news-newspapers-international-news-europe-b224527fd8de462c81eee69ca8d11bbb (last accessed, March 20, 2022) wherein it is admitted that cases of female religious-on-female religious sexual violence are rare, but abuses of power within certain religious congregations are problems.

[25] Regarding the February 2019 edition of "Woman Church World," the supplement to *Osservatore Romano* (not available online), see Tucker Reals, "Pope Francis Confirms Priests' Abuse of Nuns included 'Sexual Slavery,'" *CBS News*, February 19, 2019, https://cbsnews.com/news/pope-francis-priests-nuns-sexual-slavery-abuse-saint-jean-order-france/ (last accessed March 21, 2022).

[26] Pope Francis, Apostolic Journey to the United Arab Emirates, *Press Conference on the return flight from Abu Dhabi to Rome*, February 5, 2019**,** https://vatican.va/content/francesco/en/speeches/2019/february/documents/papa-francesco_20190205_emiratiarabi-voloritorno.html (last accessed March221, 2022).

[27] Ibid.; See also "Pope Francis, "Priests Nuns Sexual Slavery Abuse Saint Jean Order France," *CBS News*, https://cbsnews.com/news/pope-francis-priests-nuns-sexual-slavery-abuse-saint-jean-order-france/ (last accessed March 21, 2022).

[28] "Women's Magazine Bosses Quit over 'Climate of Distrust,'" *CBS News/AP*, March 26, 2019, https://cbsnews.com/news/vatican-womens-magazine-women-church-world-editors-quit-climate-distrust/ (last accessed March 22, 2022).

[29] Ibid.

[30] Nicole Winfield, "Women Relaunches Magazine Team after Resignations," *ABC News,* April 30, 2019, available at https://abcnews.go.com/International/wireStory/vatican-relaunches-womens-magazine-team-resignations-62723285 (last accessed March 21, 2022).

[31] Jane F. Adolphe, "The Movement to Appoint more Women to Vatican Posts: Who Benefits?" *Inside the Vatican*, May 1, 2021, https://insidethevatican.com/magazine/culture/the-movement-to-appoint-more-women-to-vatican-posts-who-benefits/ (last accessed

March 21, 2020); See also an overview regarding the role of law males and woman: "Pope Francis Promulgates Apostolic Constitution on Roman Curia *'Praedicate Evangelium,'" Vatican News*, March 19, 2022, https://vaticannews.va/en/pope/news/2022-03/pope-francis-promulgates-constitution-praedicate-evangelium.html (last access March 22, 2022) wherein the following excerpt quote from *Praedicate Evangelium* has been translated from Italian into English: "*Every Christian, by virtue of Baptism, is a missionary disciple to the extent that he or she has encountered the love of God in Christ Jesus. One cannot fail to take this into account in the updating of the Curia, whose reform, therefore, must provide for the involvement of laymen and women, even in roles of government and responsibility;*" cf. Italian version of the "Apostolic Constitution *Praedicate Evangelium* on the Roman Curia and its service to the Church and to the World," March 19, 2022, https://press.vatican.va/content/salastampa/it/bollettino/pubblico/2022/03/19/0189/00404.html (last accessed March 2, 2022).

[32] Ibid.

[33] See the Comments of Cardinal João Braz de Aviz, Congregation for Institutes of Consecrate Life, and Societies of Apostolic Life, in "Woman Church World" (February: 2020) supplement to *Osservatore Romano* discussed in "Former Prostitutes among Ex-nuns at Vatican Shelter: Cardinal," *Matters India*, January 25, 2020 https://mattersindia.com/2020/01/former-prostitutes-among-ex-nuns-at-vatican-shelter-cardinal/ (last accessed March 20, 2021); See also Rev. Giovanni Cucci, SJ "Authority and Abuse Issues Among Religious," *Civilta Cattolica*, August 1, 2020, updated November, 10, 2020) https://laciviltacattolica.com/authority-and-abuse-issues-among-women-religious/ (March 21, 2022).

[34] See *2008 Address*.

[35] Hannah Brockhaus, "Involve more women in seminary formation, urges Vatican cardinal" *Catholic News Agency* (April 24, 2020) https://catholicnewsagency.com/news/44314/involve-more-women-in-seminary-formation-urges-vatican-cardinal (accessed February 16, 2022)

[36] Ibid.

[37] "Press Conference to present the International Theological Symposium 'For a Fundamental Theology of Priesthood,' organized by the Congregation for Bishops (Rome, 17-19 February 2022)," *Holy See Press Office*, December 04, 2021, https://press.vatican.va/content/salastampa/en/bollettino/pubblico/2021/04/12/210412c.html (last accessed March 26, 2022).

[38] Ibid.
[39] Ibid.
[40] Ibid.

⁴¹ Full Text of Pope Francis' Letter to the Church in Chile," *Catholic News Agency*, June 5, 2018, https://catholicnewsagency.com/news/38567/full-text-of-pope-francis-letter-to-the-church-in-chile (last accessed March 26, 2022):, wherein it states: "Let us allow ourselves to be helped and to help create a society where the culture of abuse does not find the space to perpetuate itself. I exhort all Christians and especially those responsible for centers of higher education, formal or informal, healthcare centers, institutes of formation and universities, to join together with the dioceses and with all of civil society to lucidly and strategically promote a culture of care and protection. Let each of these spaces promote a new mentality."

⁴² Jesse O'Neil, "Missouri Congresswoman Criticized for Using term 'birthing people,'" *NY Post*, May 08, 2021, at https://nypost.com/2021/05/08/missouri-congresswoman-under-fire-for-calling-women-birthing-people (last accessed March 26, 2021); See also "462-ranked Biological Man becomes Woman's Swimming Champion," *EU Times*, March 20, 2022, https://eutimes.net/2022/03/462-ranked-biological-man-becomes-womens-swimming-champion (last accessed March 26, 2022); Tyler O'Neil, Ketanji Brown Jackson, "Biden's Supreme Court Pick, Refuses to Define the word 'Woman'," *Foxnews.com*, March 23, 2022, https://foxnews.com/politics/ketanji-brown-jackson-bidens-supreme-court-pick-refuses-to-define-the-word-woman (last accessed March 25, 2022).

⁴³ See *2008 Address*.

# Chapter 1

¹ See Lea Karen Kiv, "#ChurchToo: How can we prevent the abuse of women by the clergy?" *America* (Nov.16, 2019) https://america-magazine.org/faith/2018/11/16/churchtoo-how-can-we-prevent-abuse-women-clergy (accessed Dec. 1, 2020).

² See Kathleen McPhillips, "The Catholic Church is headed for another sex abuse scandal as #NunsToo speak up" *The Conversation* (Feb. 16, 2019) https://theconversation.com/the-catholic-church-is-headed-for-another-sex-abuse-scandal-as-nunstoo-speak-up-111539 (accessed Dec. 1, 2020).

³ See Michel Martin (host) "I Just froze: former nun talks about experiences of sexual and spiritual abuse," transcript of *NPR: All Things Considered* (Feb. 16, 2019) https://npr.org/2019/02/09/693062479/former-nun-talks-about-experiences-of-abuse-in-germany (accessed Dec. 1, 2020).

⁴ 1983 Code of Canon Law (CIC), can. 277§1.

[5] Unless there is laicization and a dispensation from celibacy.

[6] See Patti Maguire Armstrong, "Clerical Abuse Survivor: Faith is a 'Powerful Tool to Heal'," *National Catholic Register* (Nov. 21, 2020), available at: https://ncregister.com/interview/clerical-abuse-survivor-faith-is-a-powerful-tool-to-heal (accessed Dec. 1, 2020).

[7] See *Catechism of the Catholic Church* (CCC), 405.

[8] CCC,1866.

[9] Pius XI, encyclical *Ad Catholici Sacerdotii* (Dec. 20, 1935), no. 39, http://vatican.va/content/pius-xi/en/encyclicals/documents/hf_p-xi_enc_19351220_ad-catholici-sacerdotii.html (accessed Feb. 22, 2021).

[10] Ibid., no. 40.

[11] Pope Pius XII, Encyclical, *Sacra Virginitas* (March 25, 1954) at no. 64, http://vatican.va/content/pius-xii/en/encyclicals/documents/hf_p-xii_enc_25031954_sacra-virginitas.html (accessed Feb. 24, 2021).

[12] Vatican II, *Decree on the Ministry and Life of Priests, Presbyterorum Ordinis*, (Dec. 11, 1965), no. 18. All translations of Vatican II are taken from *The Documents of Vatican II: Vatican Translation* (Staten Island, NY: St Pauls Publications, 2013).

[13] Vatican II, *Decree on Priestly Training, Optatam Totius* (Oct. 28, 1965), no. 8.

[14] See Pope Benedict XVI, Apostolic Letter *motu proprio*, *Ministrorum Institutio* (Jan. 16, 2013) art. 7.

[15] The text of this letter can be found in Italian on the Vatican website in the documents of the Congregation for Catholic Education. An English translation is available on the website of the United States Conference of Catholic Bishops under the committee for Clergy, Consecrated Life, and Vocations: https://usccb.org/beliefs-and-teachings/vocations/priesthood/priestly-formation/upload/spiritual.pdf (last accessed March 29, 2022).

[16] Congregation for Catholic Education, *The Virgin Mary in Intellectual and Spiritual Formation* (March 25, 1988), no. 1 as found in Marianne Trouvé, FSP, *Mother of Christ, Mother of the Church: Documents on the Blessed Virgin Mary* (Boston: Pauline Books & Media, 2001) p. 340.

[17] Ibid., no. 28, p. 353.

[18] Ibid., no. 34; p. 356.

[19] St. Louis de Montfort, *True Devotion to the Blessed Virgin*, trans. Montfort Fathers (Bay Shore, NY: Montfort Publications, 1996) no. 55, p. 25.

[20] Ibid., no. 266, p, 137; a variation of *totus tuus* is directed to Jesus through Mary. It is found in *True Devotion* no. 233, which provides this short prayer of consecration: "I am all yours, and all that I have is yours, O dear Jesus, through Mary, your holy Mother." See ibid., p. 120.

²¹ Pope John Paul II, Encyclical, *Redemptoris Mater* (March 25, 1987) no. 48; Trouvé, p. 307.

²² Pope John Paul II, Apostolic Exhortation, *Pastores Dabo Vobis* (March 25, 1992) no. 82 http://vatican.va/content/john-paul-ii/en/apost_exhortations/documents/hf_jp-ii_exh_25031992_pastores-dabo-vobis.html (accessed Feb. 24, 2021).

²³ Pope Francis, *Address to the International Theological Commission* (December 5, 2014) http://vatican.va/content/francesco/en/speeches/2014/december/documents/papa-francesco_20141205_commissione-teologica-internazionale.html (accessed Feb. 24, 2021).

²⁴ Pope, John Paul II, Apostolic Letter, *Mulieris dignitatem* (On the Dignity and Vocation of Woman), (August 15, 1988), no. 3, http://vatican.va/content/john-paul-ii/en/apost_letters/1988/documents/hf_jp-ii_apl_19880815_mulieris-dignitatem.html (accessed December 10, 2020).

²⁵ *True Devotion*, no. 63; p.28.

²⁶ Mother Teresa, *Where There is Love, There is God*, edited and with an introduction by Brian Kolodiejchuk, MC (New York: Doubleday, 2010), 37.

²⁷ See Pius IX, *Ineffabilis Deus* (Dec. 8, 1854) in Heinrich Denzinger and Peter Hünermann, *Compendium of Creeds, Definitions, and Declarations on Matters of Faith and Morals* [henceforth D-H] (San Francisco: Ignatius Press, 2012) no. 2800; see also Vatican II, *Lumen Gentium*, 61.

²⁸ D-H 3274; see St. Thomas Aquinas, *Summa theologiae* III q. 30 a. 1.

²⁹ St. Thomas Aquinas, *Summa theologiae* III q. 30 a. 1.

³⁰ Pope Francis, *Homily for the Solemnity of Mary, Mother of God* (Jan. 1, 2021) https://vatican.va/content/francesco/en/homilies/2021/documents/papa-francesco_20210101_omelia-madredidio-pace.html (last accessed March 29, 2021).

³¹ Vatican II, *Lumen Gentium* (Nov. 21, 1964), no. 56, https://vatican.va/archive/hist_councils/ii_vatican_council/documents/vat-ii_const_19641121_lumen-gentium_en.html (last accessed March 29, 2021).

³² Pope Francis, *Homily for the Solemnity of Mary, Mother of God* (Jan. 1, 2020), http://vatican.va/content/francesco/en/homilies/2020/documents/papa-francesco_20200101_omelia-madredidio-pace.html (accessed Feb. 24, 2021).

³³ Pope Francis, *Press conference on the flight returning from Rio de Janeiro* (July 28, 2013) http://vatican.va/content/francesco/en/speeches/2013/july/documents/papa-francesco_20130728_gmg-conferenza-stampa.html (accessed Feb. 24, 2021).

³⁴ CCC, 2339 (emphasis in original).

35 See Gal 5:22–23 (Vulg.) and CCC, 1832.

36 *True Devotion*, no. 37.

37 Pope Benedict XVI, *Homily for the canonization of Frei Antônio de Sant'Ana Galvão at Campo de Marte, São Paulo* (May 11, 2007) no. 5, http://vatican.va/content/benedict-xvi/it/speeches/2007/may/documents/hf_ben-xvi_spe_20070511_bishops-brazil.html (last accessed Feb. 26, 2021).

38 See Gloria Falcão Dodd, *The Virgin Mary, Mediatrix of All Grace: History and Theology of the Movement for a Dogmatic Definition from 1896 to 1964* (New Bedford, MA: Academy of the Immaculate, 2012).

39 Fr. Emile Neubert, S.M., *Mary and the Priestly Ministry* (New Bedford, MA: Academy of the Immaculate, 2009), 124.

40 Ibid., 123–124.

41 Ibid., 127.

42 Ibid., 129.

43 Pope John Paul II, Apostolic Exhortation, *Redemptoris Custos* (Guardian of the Redeemer), (August 15, 1989), no. 20; Trouvé, p.463. The 2020–2021 Year of St. Joseph is a great reminder of the example of the most chaste spouse of the Blessed Virgin Mary.

44 See William Thompson, editor, *Bérulle and the French School: Selected Writings*, translated by Lowell Glendon, S.S. (New York: Paulist Press, 1989), especially 47–54.

45 See *Oeuvres completes de saint Jean Eudes* (Paris: P. Lethielleux, 1905) Tome 12, pages 160–166. The French title of this spiritual marriage or alliance is *"Contrat d'une sainte alliance avec la très sacrée Vierge Marie, Mère de Dieu"* [Contract of a holy marriage with the most holy Virgin Mary, Mother of God]. This 'holy marriage" is a type of intimate consecration to the Virgin Mary.

46 See Tom Casey, S.J. "Mary—how she made a new man of Ignatius" on the website, "In All Things", available here: https://jesuit.ie/blog/tom-casey-sj/may-mary-made-new-man-ignatius/ (accessed Feb. 24, 2021).

47 John Paul II, apostolic letter, *Rosarium Virginis Mariae* (Oct. 16, 2002), no. 16, available at: http://vatican.va/content/john-paul-ii/en/apost_letters/2002/documents/hf_jp-ii_apl_20021016_rosarium-virginis-mariae.html (accessed Feb. 27, 2021).

48 See "Full Text of Benedict XVI Essay, 'The Church and the Scandal of Sexual Abuse,'" III.2, *Catholic News Agency*, April 10, 2019, https://catholicnewsagency.com/news/full-text-of-benedict-xvi-the-church-and-the-scandal-of-sexual-abuse-59639 (accessed Dec. 5, 2020).

49 See Paul Gondreau, "The Maleness of Christ," *Clerical Sexual Misconduct: An Interdisciplinary Analysis*, eds. Jane F. Adolphe and Ronald J. Rychlak (Providence, RI: Cluny Media, 2020), 347-63; See also Paul

Gondreau, "Aquinas on Christ's Male Sexuality as Integral to His Full Humanity: Anti-Docetism in the Common Doctor," *Thomas Aquinas and the Crisis of Christology*, eds. Michael Dauphinais, Andrew Hofer, O.P., and Roger Nutt (Ave Maria, FL: Sapientia Press, 2021).

[50] Pope John Paul II, Apostolic Letter *Mulieris Dignitatem* (On the Dignity and Vocation of Women), (August 15, 1988), no. 26, http://vatican.va/content/john-paul-ii/en/apost_letters/1988/documents/hf_jp-ii_apl_19880815_mulieris-dignitatem.html (last accessed March 30, 2022), wherein the Polish pontiff reiterates the Congregation for the Doctrine of the Faith's 1976 Declaration *Inter Insigniores* (On the Question of the Admission of Women to the Ministerial Priesthood), no. 2: "If he [Jesus] acted in this way [by choosing only male apostles], it was not in order to conform to the customs of his time, for his attitude towards women was quite different from that of his milieu, and he deliberately and courageously broke with it." https://vatican.va/roman_curia/congregations/cfaith/documents/rc_con_cfaith_doc_19761015_inter-insigniores_en.html (last accessed on Jan. 15, 2021).

[51] The prayer, the full version of which expresses gratitude to God for not being made a gentile, a woman, or a slave/ignoramus, found in b. Menachot 43b:17, and online at Sefaria sefaria.org/Menachot.43b?lang=bi. (last accessed October 4, 2020). For a tracing of the history of this (and other) Jewish prayers, see Yoel Kahn, *The Three Blessings: Boundaries, Censorship, and Identity in Jewish Liturgy* (Oxford: Oxford University Press, 2011).

[52] "From the third day [after sexual relations] until the fortieth, one should pray that it [the fetus] will be male" (b. Berakhot 60a:13, https://sefaria.org/Berakhot.60a?lang=bi (last accessed Oct. 4, 2020).

[53] The citation is from b. Kiddushin 80b:5, https://sefaria.org/Kiddushin.80b?lang=bi (last accessed Oct. 11, 2020).

[54] B. Pesachim 62b:9, https://sefaria.org/Pesachim.62b?lang=bi (last accessed Nov. 25, 2020).

[55] Commenting on Deuteronomy 11:19 ("And you shall teach them [the ordinances and commandments of the Lord] to your children"), the Talmud clarifies that "your children" should be taken to mean "your sons, but not your daughters" (b. Kiddushin 30a:6, https://sefaria.org/Kiddushin.30a?lang=bi (last accessed Oct. 9, 2020). The Mishnah makes this a disputed point, however; see, e.g., b. Sotah 3:4 for teaching Torah to daughters, https://sefaria.org/Mishnah_Sotah.3.4?lang=bi&with=all&lang2=en (last accessed Oct. 9, 2020).

[56] This passage comes from b. Berakhot 17a:14, https://sefaria.org/Berakhot.17a?lang=bi (last accessed Oct. 10, 2020).

57 "Women are a people unto themselves" is found in b. Shabbat 62a:11, https://sefaria.org/Shabbat.62a?lang=bi (last accessed Oct. 10, 2020). The ancient Temple layout is detailed in the Mishnah, b. Middot 2:5-6, https://sefaria.org/Mishnah_Middot.2.5?lang=bi (last accessed Oct. 9, 2020).

58 B. Berakhot 24a:17, https://sefaria.org/Berakhot.24a?lang=bi (last accessed Oct. 10, 2020).

59 See, for instance, b. Shabbat 13a:4-10 and 13b:1, https://sefaria.org/Shabbat.13a?lang=bi (last accessed Oct. 10, 2020); and b. Kiddushin 80b:4-7, https://sefaria.org/Kiddushin.80b?lang=bi (last accessed Oct. 10, 2020). For more on this in the Talmud, see Rabbi Nisan Dovid Dubov, *The Laws of Yichud: Permissibility and Prohibition Regarding the Seclusion of a Man and Woman* (Brooklyn, NY: Sichos in English, 2006).

60 Thus, b. Ketubot 72a:10 and 19: "And who is considered a woman who violates the precepts of Jewish women? One who, for example, goes out of her house, and her head, i.e., her hair, is uncovered; or she spins wool in the public marketplace; or she speaks with every man she encounters. . . The prohibition against a woman going out with her head uncovered is not merely a custom of Jewish women. Rather, it is by Torah law, as it is written [in Numbers 5:18]," https://sefaria.org/Ketubot.72a?lang=bi (last accessed Oct. 17, 2020).

61 In the Mishnah, the School of Hillel states that a man may divorce his wife "even due to a minor issue, e.g., because she burned or over-salted his dish, as it is stated: 'Because he has found some unseemly matter in her' [Deut 24:1]," while Rabbi Akiva adds, "He may divorce her even if he found another woman who is better looking than her and wishes to marry her, as it is stated in that verse: 'And if it comes to pass, if she finds no favor in his eyes' [Deut 24:1]" (b. Gittin 90a:3-4, https://sefaria.org/Gittin.90a?lang=bi (last accessed Oct. 5, 2020).

62 This comes from b. Menachot 43b:18-44a:1, https://sefaria.org/Menachot.43b?lang=bi (last accessed on Oct. 4, 2020). It is Rabbi Jacob's own son who identifies women with slaves, for which reason the son finds it redundant to express gratitude to God for not being made a slave after having voiced gratitude for not being made a woman.

63 Thus, *Inter Insignores*, no. 4: "An examination of the Gospels shows . . . that Jesus broke with the prejudices of his time, by widely contravening the discriminations practiced with regard to women."

64 *Mulieris Dignitatem*, no. 13 (emphasis in the original).

65 Joseph Ratzinger/Pope Benedict XVI, *Jesus of Nazareth*, vol. 1, *From the Baptism in the Jordan to the Transfiguration*, trans. Adrien J. Walker (New York: Image, 2007), 183. John Paul II compiles these words and works nearly exhaustively in Part Five of *Mulieris Dignitatem*, nos. 12-16. One also

finds a quite cursory sketch of them in Sara Butler, "Embodied Ecclesiology: Church Teaching on the Priesthood," in *Women, Sex, and the Church: A Case for Catholic Teaching*, ed. Erika Bachiochi (Boston: Pauline Books & Media, 2010), 143-59, at 148.

⁶⁶ Thus, *Inter Insigniores*, no. 2: "He [Jesus] does not hesitate to depart from the Mosaic Law in order to affirm the equality of the rights and duties of men and women with regard to the marriage bond."

⁶⁷ Thomas Aquinas, *Summa contra gentiles*, III.123; see Aristotle, *Nicomachean Ethics*, 8.8 (1159b).

⁶⁸ Ratzinger/Benedict XVI, *Jesus of Nazareth*, 1:183.

⁶⁹ For a good example of this view, see Haye Van der Meer, *Women Priests in the Catholic Church? A Theological-Historical Investigation*, trans. Arlene and Leonard Swidler (Philadelphia: Temple University Press, 1973), 14.

⁷⁰ For a deeper anthropological look at the complementary differences between the sexes without implying inequality in personal dignity, see Laura L. Garcia, "Authentic Freedom and Equality in Difference," in *Women, Sex, and the Church*, ed. Erika Bachiochi, 15-33.

⁷¹ Ratzinger/Benedict, 1:181.

⁷² Sara Butler, *The Catholic Priesthood and Women: A Guide to the Teaching of the Church* (Chicago: Hillenbrand Books, 2007), 13.

⁷³ Ben Witherington III, *Women in the Ministry of Jesus. A Study of Jesus' Attitudes to Women and Their Roles as Reflected in His Earthly Life* (Cambridge: Cambridge University Press, 1984), 195, n. 233. For her part, Sara Bulter writes, "If Jesus did not share the prejudices of his contemporaries, it would appear that he 'could have' entrusted the apostolic charge to women if he had wished to, but freely chose to do otherwise" (*The Catholic Priesthood*, 67).

⁷⁴ For much more on all this, see my essay, "Jesus and Paul on the Meaning and Purpose of Human Sexuality," *Nova et Vetera* (English), 18.2 (2020), 461-503, at 464-75.

⁷⁵ Aquinas, *Summa theologiae* (hereafter *ST*), I-II, q. 91, a. 5; see also I-II, q. 107, a. 2; and q. 108, a. 3. For Peter Lombard, see *Sentences* III, d. 40.

⁷⁶ *ST* III, q. 15, aa. 1 and 2.

⁷⁷ Constantinople II, twelfth anathema (Tanner, *Decrees of the Ecumenical Councils*, 2, 1:119); for more on this, see Paul Gondreau, *The Passions of Christ's Soul in the Theology of St. Thomas Aquinas* (Münster: Aschendorff, 2002; reprinted, Providence, RI: Cluny Media, 2018), 340-49.

⁷⁸ For an overview of these findings, see Paul Gondreau, "Thomas Aquinas on Sexual Difference: The Metaphysical Biology and Moral Significance of Human Sexuality," *Pro Ecclesia* 30, no. 3 (2021), forthcoming; neurobiological differences between the sexes are also covered in Paul Gondreau, "Aquinas on Christ's Male Sexuality." In brief,

the male brain owns more extensive testosterone circuits, the hormone that mediates male aggression and the male sexual drive, whereas the female brain engages more the cerebral cortex and has more extensive oxytocin circuits, the so-called bonding hormone, hardwiring women neurobiologically in a particular way for relationships. As a result, women experience optimal sexual pleasure within the context of a committed relationship, more so than for men, given the orientation of the male sex drive to physical attraction and pleasure. The physician and psychologist Leonard Sax puts it this way: "Women's sexual experience is 'happening' more in the cerebral cortex and is therefore more connected with the rest of what's going on in their mind. The sexual experience in men is less connected with the cortex, less connected with the outside world. . . . 'For women, an important goal of sex is intimacy; the best context for pleasurable sex is a committed relationship. This is less true for men.'" *Why Gender Matters. What Parents and Teachers Need to Know about the Emerging Science of Sex Differences*, second ed. (New York: Harmony, 2017), 122-3 (see also 228-9); the citation is from the psychologist Leitita Anne Peplau, "Human Sexuality: How Do Men and Women Differ?" *Current Directions in Psychological Science*, vol. 12 (2003), 37-44.

[79] For men showing greater propensity to engage in casual sex, see the classic study by Russell D. Clark and Elaine Hatfield, "Gender Differences in Receptivity to Sexual Offers," *Journal of Psychology and Human Sexuality* 2, no. 1 (1989), 39-55, with the opening abstract stating: "In [our] experiments . . . male and female confederates of average attractiveness approached potential partners with one of three requests: 'Would you go out tonight?' 'Will you come over to my apartment?' or 'Would you go to bed with me?' The great majority of men were willing to have a sexual liaison with the women who approached them. Women were not. Not one woman agreed to a sexual liaison." This study, with some modifications, was repeated several years later, with similar results; see Mercedes Tappé, Lisamarie Bensman, Kentaro Hayashi, and Elaine Hatfield, "Gender Differences in Receptivity to Sexual Offers: A New Research Prototype," *Interpersona: An International Journal on Personal Relationships* 7, no. 2 (2013); accessed November 14, 2019, https://interpersona.psychopen.eu/article/view/121/html. See also R. F. Baumeister, K. R. Catanese, and K. D. Vohs, "Is There a Gender Difference in Sex Drive? Theoretical Views, Conceptual Distinctions, and a Review of Relevant Evidence," *Personality and Social Psychology Review* 5 (2001), 242-73.

[80] This according to the psychologist Paul Vitz in his paper, "Men and Women: The Psychology of Their Differences and Their Complementarity," delivered at the annual symposium of the Catholic Women's Forum of the Ethics and Public Policy Center, Washington, D.C., June 26, 2019.

See also Samantha J. Dawson, Brittany A. Bannerman, and Martin Lalumière, "Paraphilic Interests: An Examination of Sex Differences in a Nonclinical Sample," *Sexual Abuse: A Journal of Research and Treatment* 28, no. 1 (2016), 20-45; accessed November 9, 2019, https://journals.sagepub.com/doi/pdf/10.1177/1079063214525645; see in particular its conclusion: "Our results suggest a reliable and substantial sex difference in paraphilic [i.e., sexually deviant] interests, such that men report less repulsion to a variety of paraphilic acts than do women, and more men than women report being actually aroused by particular paraphilic activities," 37. The study also observes: "Sex drive appears to provide the best explanation for the sex difference in paraphilic interests. . . . Sex drive, comprised of measures assessing sexual compulsivity and hypersexuality, was found to significantly and fully mediate the sex difference in overall paraphilic scores," 34-5.

[81] For the citations from Aquinas, see *ST* I, q. 98, a. 2; and III, q. 15, a. 1.

[82] *In IV Sent.*, d. 26, q. 1, a. 3 (trans. Mortensen [Green Bay, WI: Aquinas Institute, 2018], 8-9). The heresy that Thomas is referring to is of course Albigensianism, even if not named.

[83] For Aquinas on the passions or emotions being morally neutral in themselves, see *ST* I-II, q. 24, aa. 1-2; q. 59, a. 5 ad 2; and *In Ethic.*, Bk. II, lect. 3. See also Mark Jordan, "Aquinas's Construction of a Moral Account of the Passions," *Freiburger Zeitschrift für Philosophie und Theologie* 33 (1986), 71-97.

[84] "Moral virtue perfects the appetitive part of the soul by directing [the passions or emotions] to the good defined by reason," writes Thomas, as, indeed, passion or emotion constitutes the "proper matter" of the moral virtues. *ST* I-II, q. 59, aa. 4-5) See Aristotle, *Nicomachean Ethics*, Bk. II, ch. 6 (1106b15-16). For much more on this, see my own "The Passions and the Moral Life: Appreciating the Originality of Aquinas," *Thomist* 71 (2007), 419-50. As for chastity, the moral theologian Servais Pinckaers observes that sexuality "is realized in man in a different and far richer way than in animals" since it gets "integrated in the totality of human nature" through the virtue of chastity. *The Sources of Christian Ethics*, trans. Mary Thomas Noble (Washington, D.C.: Catholic University of America Press, 1995), 438. For how a much deeper examination of how this traces out, see Paul Gondreau "Thomas Aquinas on Sexual Difference," section III.

[85] Chalcedon (451) figures prominently here, attesting that "Christ is consubstantial [*homoousios*] with us as regards his humanity," and that Christ's two natures, human and divine, "undergo no confusion, no change, no division, no separation." See Tanner, *Decrees of the Ecumenical Councils*, 1:86.

⁸⁶ *In III Sent.*, d. 12, q. 3, a. 1, qa. 1, sol. 1. The title of the query is *Utrum Christus debuerit sexum aliquem*, Whether Christ had to assume any particular sex. For much more on all this, see my "The Maleness of Christ," 348-52.

⁸⁷ The expression "Christ's action is our instruction" occurs seventeen times in Aquinas's works (see, e.g., *ST* III, q. 40, a. 1 ad 3). For more on this, see Richard Schenk, "*Omnis Christi actio nostra est instructio*. The Deeds and Sayings of Jesus as Revelation in the View of Thomas Aquinas," *La doctrine de la révélation divine de saint Thomas d'Aquin*, ed. L. Elders (Vatican City: Libreria Editrice Vaticana, 1990) 103-31.

⁸⁸ Pope John Paul II, Apostolic Exhortation *Familiaris Consortio* (On the Role of the Christian Family in the Modern World), (Nov. 22, 1981), no. 24, http://vatican.va/content/john-paul-ii/en/apost_exhortations/documents/hf_jp-ii_exh_19811122_familiaris-consortio.html (last accessed Feb. 5, 2021).

⁸⁹ Council of Trent, Session 22 on the holy sacrifice of the Mass, chapter 1, affirms that the apostles' priestly "ordination" occurred during the Last Supper, as does Canon 2 of the same session: "If anyone says that by the words, *Do this in remembrance of* me, Christ did not make the apostles priests . . . let him be anathema" (Tanner, *Decrees of the Ecumenical Councils*, 2:733 and 735). Benedict XVI observes how, beyond the actions at the Last Supper, the fact that Jesus "made twelve" (the literal language of Mk 3:14, though the more common translation is "he appointed twelve") shows that the apostolic office was marked from its inception for priestly ministry: "These words of the Evangelist [in Mk 3:14] take up the Old Testament terminology for appointment to the priesthood (cf. 1 Kings 12:31; 13:33) and thus characterize the apostolic office as a priestly ministry." *Jesus of Nazareth*, 1:171.

⁹⁰ Ratzinger/Benedict, 1:178.

⁹¹ Ibid.

⁹² Dominic Legge, O.P., "Cleansing the Church of Clerical Sacrilege," *First Things*, Aug. 16, 2018; https://firstthings.com/web-exclusives/2018/08/cleansing-the-church-of-clerical-sacrilege (accessed Dec. 5, 2020).

⁹³ See the reporting of this by David Hemmer, "Archbishop 'infuriated' by Pearl River priest's actions, says altar has been burned," *WWLTV com*, Oct. 9, 2020, https://wwltv.com/article/news/ investigations/david-hammer/archbishop-infuriated-by-pearl-river-priests-actions-says-altar-has-been-burned/289-0d9d4b3c-706f-4334-9d8e-0451278da4a7 (last accessed March 29, 2022).

⁹⁴ *ST* II-II, q. 152, a. 1, corp. and ad 4; see also a. 4.

⁹⁵ Pope Benedict XVI, *Address to Members of the Roman Curia* (December 21, 2012) *Vatican Information Service*, visnews-en.blogspot.com/2012/12/family-dialogue-new-evangelisation.html (last accessed March 29,

2022). Even in 1930, Pope Pius XI denounced the "new and utterly perverse morality" of his day in his Encyclical Letter *Casti Connubii* (On Christian Marriage), (December 31, 1930), no. 3, https://vatican.va/content/pius-xi/en/encyclicals/documents/hf_p-xi_enc_19301231_casti-connubii.html (last accessed March 29, 2022).

## Chapter 2

[1] Previous versions of portions of this paper have been published previously as more research has led to developments in the theory. See "Redeeming Masculinity: Adam's Sin and the Fall of Man," *Institute for Priestly Formation,* (Summer 2021), publication pending; "Woman and Man: Identity, Genius, and Mission," *The Complementarity of Men and Women,* ed. Paul Vitz (Washington, D.C.: Catholic University Press, 2021), 89-131. See also "Redeeming Woman: A Response to the 'Second Sex' Issue from within the Tradition of Catholic Scriptural Exegesis," *Religions,* Special Issue: *Feminism from the Perspective of Catholic Theology,* ed. Tracey Rowland, (August 2020). The research presented here appeared originally in "The Nature of Woman in Relation to Man: Genesis 1 and 2 Through the Lens of the Metaphysical Anthropology of Aquinas," *Logos: A Journal of Catholic Thought and Culture,* (Winter 2014). The research into the masculine genius was originally published in an essay entitled "The Genius of Man," *Promise and Challenge: Catholic Women Reflect on Feminism, Complementarity, and the Church,* ed. Mary Hasson (Huntington: Our Sunday Visitor, 2015). Both of those essays were initial forays into the subject matter. The account I offer here (and in the three more recent essays mentioned at the beginning of this note) reflect some important refinements of the general theory under investigation. No doubt additional refinements will be made in the course of further research.

[2] "Original Sin," *New Advent Catholic Encyclopedia,* https://newadvent.org/cathen/11312a.htm (last accessed March 29. 2022).

[3] See especially Joseph F. Sagues, S.J., "On God the Creator and Sanctifier; On Sins," *Sacrae Theologiae Summa,* Volume IIB, Book V, *Biblioteca de Autores Christianos,* trans. Kenneth Baker, S.J (Saddle River: Keep the Faith Publications, Inc., 2014).

[4] Catholic Church, *Compendium of the Social Teaching of the Church* (Washington, D.C.: United States Conference of Catholic Bishops, 2006), 147. Quoting John Paul II, *Letter to Women* (Washington, D.C.: United States Conference of Catholic Bishops, 1995), 8. After creating man male and female, God says to both: *"Fill the earth and subdue it"* (Gen 1:28). Not

only does he give them the power to procreate as a means of perpetuating the human species throughout time, *he also gives them the earth, charging them with the responsible use of its resources.* As a rational and free being, man is called to transform the face of the earth. In this task, which is essentially that of culture, *man and woman alike* share equal responsibility from the start. In their fruitful relationship as husband and wife, in their common task of exercising dominion over the earth, woman and man are marked neither by a static and undifferentiated equality nor by an irreconcilable and inexorably conflictual difference. Their most natural relationship, which corresponds to the plan of God, is the "unity of the two", a relational "uni-duality", which enables each to experience their interpersonal and reciprocal relationship as a gift which enriches and which confers responsibility." Italics in original.

[5] For a more complete account of the sexual revolution and its impact, as well as the consequences of the widespread rejection of *Humanae Vitae*, see Mary Eberstadt, "The Prophetic Power of *Humanae Vitae*," *First Things*, April 2018, https://firstthings.com/article/2018/04/the-prophetic-power-of-humanae-vitae (last accessed March 29, 2022); Deborah Savage, "Rethinking *Humanae Vitae*," *Why Humanae Vitae is Still Right*, ed. Janet Smith (San Francisco: Ignatius Press, 2018). A somewhat shorter version of that essay entitled "Reflections on the Revolution" can be found here: https://firstthings.com/article/2018/10/reflections-on-the-revolution (last accessed March 29, 2022).

[6] Pope John Paul II, Apostolic Letter, *Mulieris Dignitatem* (August 15, 1988), https://vaticana.va/content/john-paul-ii/en/apost_letters/1988/documents/hf_jp-ii_apl_19880815_mulieris-dignitatem.html (last accessed March 30, 2022).

[7] Pope John Paul II, Apostolic Exhortation, *Christifideles laici* (December 30, 1988), 50. https://vaticana.va/content/john-paul-ii/en/apost_exhortations/documents/hf_jp-ii_exh_30121988_christifideles-laici.html (last accessed March 30, 2022).

[8] John Paul II, *Man and Woman He Created Them: The Theology of the Body (TOB)*, ed. Michael Waldstein, (Boston: Pauline Books & Media, 2006), 2:4.5, 136-137.

[9] Ibid.

[10] Ibid., 137.

[11] Ibid., 3:2.1, 138–39. These two categories, "being and existence" and "personal subjectivity," are foundational to the thought of Karol Wojtyla/John Paul II. Throughout his writings, this philosopher pope frequently contrasts the philosophy of being (metaphysics) and the philosophy of consciousness (phenomenology) and seeks ways to reconcile and synthesize their claims. His own anthropology is a creative completion

of the Aristotelian-Thomistic account of man in which he synthesizes the metaphysical anthropology of the Thomist tradition with a more phenomenological analysis of human experience. He is concerned to correct what he perceives to be an inadequacy in the received tradition on the meaning of the person. The tradition has relied on the Boethian definition of the person as an "individual substance of a rational nature" which, he argues, though it provides the necessary "metaphysical terrain" in the dimension of being and paves the way for the realization of personal human subjectivity, leaves out an adequate investigation of lived human experience and thus lacks an essential component of what it means to be an actual living person. The thrust of his effort is to capture the meaning of human personhood in light of both the objective nature of the person and his lived experience as the subject of his own acts. See Karol Wojtyla, "Subjectivity and the Irreducible in the Human Being," *Person and Community: Selected Essays*, (New York: Peter Lang, 1993), 209-217.

[12] TOB, 7:1-2.

[13] This constitutes a major refinement to the theory I have proposed in previous iterations. Those earlier attempts were limited to a strictly philosophical analysis of the texts in question. I have had to conclude that interpreting Genesis 1 and 2 through the lens of scholastic philosophical categories bears the risk of ascribing meaning to the text that it really doesn't have. For example, the Semitic worldview does not contain the notion of "substantial form" or the distinction between "substance and accident." These terms were introduced into the tradition by Aristotle in particular and subsequently leveraged by Aquinas. They are categories essential to the metaphysical lens employed here. But before we can employ that lens, we must account for the more properly Hebraic anthropology at work in Genesis 1 and 2. However, we will see that the validity of John Paul's claim actually is even more apparent once we take that step. I am forever in debt to Dr. Joseph Atkinson for pointing this out to me and for his help in identifying the key principles at work.

[14] For a fuller account, please see Deborah Savage, "Redeeming Masculinity: Adam's Sin and the Fall of Man," *Institute for Priestly Formation*, (Summer 2021), publication pending; "Woman and Man: Identity, Genius, and Mission," *The Complementarity of Men and Women*, ed. Paul Vitz (Washington, D.C.: Catholic University Press, 2021), 89-131. See also "Redeeming Woman: A Response to the 'Second Sex' Issue from within the Tradition of Catholic Scriptural Exegesis," *Religions*, Special Issue: *Feminism from the Perspective of Catholic Theology*, ed. Tracey Rowland, (August 2020). The research presented here appeared originally in "The Nature of Woman in Relation to Man: Genesis 1 and 2 Through the Lens of the Metaphysical Anthropology of Aquinas," *Logos: A Journal of Catholic Thought*

*and Culture*, (Winter 2014). The research into the masculine genius was originally published in an essay entitled "The Genius of Man," *Promise and Challenge: Catholic Women Reflect on Feminism, Complementarity, and the Church*, ed. Mary Hasson, (Huntington: Our Sunday Visitor, 2015). Both of those essays were initial forays into the subject matter. The account I offer here (and in the three more recent essays mentioned at the beginning of this note) reflect some important refinements of the general theory under investigation. No doubt additional refinements will be made in the course of further research.

[15] As I am not a scripture scholar, I am indebted to several scholars who are in translating and interpreting these passages. First, Monsignor Michael Magee, chair of the Systematic Theology Department and professor of Sacred Scripture at St. Charles Borromeo Seminary in Philadelphia, who helped with the meaning of the original Hebrew texts and affirmed my hypothesis. Dr. Joseph Atkinson, Professor of Scripture at the John Paul II Institute in Washington, D.C. has also confirmed my interpretation and helped me to extend it. Dr. Michael Waldstein, editor of the definitive text of John Paul II's *Theology of the Body* and Professor of Theology at the University of Steubenville has been extremely helpful in assisting me to refine that interpretation.

[16] Dr. Atkinson argues that the idea of the "corporate personality" is the most promising principle for grasping the anthropology at work in the Old Testament. See Joseph Atkinson, *Biblical and Theological Foundations of the Family* (Washington D.C.: Catholic University Press, 2014), 163. I am immeasurably indebted to Dr. Atkinson for both his work and his guidance in this area. For a thorough treatment of the meaning of the Hebraic principle of corporate personality and a comprehensive review of the literature on the topic, see Chapter 6, p. 161-192. The definitive text on this topic is a manuscript by H. Wheeler Robinson, *Corporate Personality in Ancient Israel* (Philadelphia: Fortress Press, 1967).

[17] Dr. Atkinson offers an analysis of the evidence from Scripture in Chapter 6. Atkinson, *Biblical and Theological Foundations*, 170-173.

[18] Ibid., 164.

[19] Ibid., 164. Here quoting Robinson.

[20] Ibid.

[21] Ibid., 168.

[22] Ibid., 166-7. Dr. Atkinson is citing Jean de Fraine, *Adam and the Family of Man* (Staten Island: Alba House, 1965), 14-15. The original quote is from A.M. Dubarle in *Melange Lebreton*, RSR 39 (1951/53), I, 59.

[23] It is important to note that, though we have always thought of the main characters in these first two chapters of Genesis as Adam and Eve,

only Eve is ever actually named – and even then, not until after the Fall. The reference here is most certainly NOT to "Adam," the husband of Eve.

[24] Though "*'adam*" **can** be used to designate the individual man so called, and also another individual man, what is meant in a particular passage would be clear either from the context or from the use of the definite article with it: viz., if the reference is to *hâ'adam*, it would refer back to some man already indicated from the context. In Gen 1:27, the "man" already indicated from the context is precisely the individual man who also stands for the collective: the word "*'adam*" mentioned in v. 26 is without the definite article and therefore can be said to indicate man *as such*. Thus, '*adam* is a reference to man *per se*, not to an individual or particular human being. A different word – either *hâ'adam* or *'ish* – would have been used (both these terms are used in both the first and second creation accounts) if the intention was to refer to the individual man or that particular man the tradition has come to refer to as Adam, the husband of Eve. So, it is really not going too far to say that if there were a reference to the notion of man *qua* man in Hebrew it would be *'adam*.

[25] *Otho* is a contraction of the untranslatable object marker (*oth*) and the masculine pronoun (*o*). *Otham* is the object marker contracted with the masculine plural pronoun (*am*). The grammatical gender is masculine, which is the "default" gender for a mixed group of males and females.

[26] *Biblical and Theological Foundations*, 171. Dr. Atkinson is here referring specifically to Genesis 2, but, given (as we will see) that similar terms are used, this can also be applied to Genesis 1.

[27] The word *'ish*, on the other hand, designates specifically the male, the concrete individual man, because the word *zâchâr* is the one used in an adjectival sense for "male" (it is related to the word for "remember," perhaps because of the computation of genealogy through the male line). Sometimes *'ish* is also used in the sense of "each one, each man." The word *'ish* is not used at all until Gn 2:23, right after the woman is created and Adam is naming her *ishshâh* - while saying this is because she is taken from the *'ish*. To avoid any illegitimate leaps in interpretation, the best way to maximize care and precision would be to say that, of all the terms available in Hebrew, the one that would have to be adopted to designate what later philosophy would refer to as man in the abstract would have to be *'adam*. It is this word that stands for "man" as the English language has traditionally and collectively used the word; it corresponds to the Greek *anthrôpos*, the Latin *homo*, the German *mensch*, or the Polish *człowiek*.

[28] *Biblical and Theological Foundations*, 170.

[29] This is a somewhat different interpretation of this passage from that of other scholars, in particular that of John Paul II in his *Theology of the Body*. There he argues that the reference to man at 2:7 is a reference to man in

the abstract or collective sense. But my reading of the text and its use of *ha-adam* to refer to "man" in that passage leads to the conclusion that it is a reference to a specific "human being," in this case a man. As stated previously, in the Hebrew, *adam* without the definitive article *ha,* can refer to man in the collective sense (see Gen 1:26). But when the definitive article is used, it is a reference to a specific "human being," and, in this case, according to the narrative that follows, one who is male. And indeed, the narrative goes on to reveal that it is from the man's (*ha'adam*) rib that the woman (*ishshah*) is created. It seems clear from the passage that the reference is to the man, that is, the concrete person of the *ha-adam*, while a specific individual, is at the same time representative and as it were 'contains' the whole of humanity, an interpretation that is very much in accord with Semitic thinking. However, it is essential to affirm as well that John Paul II is absolutely correct to point out that it is only with the creation of *isshah* (the concretely existing woman we have come to refer to as Eve) that *'ish* (the concretely existing man we have come to refer to as Adam) appears. There is no *'ish* without *isshah*. Some scripture scholars want to argue that Genesis 2 must be interpreted in light of Genesis 1's reference to *adam* and that woman and man are created simultaneously from *adam* in both accounts. Along with Brevard Childs, I dispute this interpretation. The Hebrew text is clear and direct in this instance. Gen 2:22-23 states that the matter from which the woman (*ishshah*) is formed is from the *ha-adam* and that the woman (*ishshah*) was taken out of the *'ish*. See Brevard S. Childs, *Old Testament Theology in a Canonical Context* (Philadelphia: Fortress Press, 1985), 189-194. A careful reading of both the text and the narrative reveals the clear meaning of Genesis 2. The author is indebted to her colleague, Dr. Mary Lemmons, for suggesting that this point be clarified and to both Monsignor Michael Magee and Dr. Joseph Atkinson for their expertise in helping to confirm this interpretation.

[30] In the creation account found in Genesis 2, we are no longer speaking of man in the abstract (*adam*) but individual persons. The Hebrew text includes reference to both *ha-adam* ("the human being" which, in Genesis 2, is a reference to a male at the level of the species, and *ish* and *isshah,* which refer to a concretely existing man and woman). At this point, matter (dust, man's rib) enters the picture. And, as Aquinas states, thus we enter the realm of accident. Aquinas explains gender as a type of (inseparable) accident. See Thomas Aquinas, *De Ente et Essentia,* trans. Armand Maurer (Rome: Pontifical Council for Medieval Studies: Medieval Studies in Translation, 2nd ed), 6, 5, p. 68. But since this type of accident is said to be something attributable to the species, the categories of male and female, while certainly inseparable from the essence of the person, cannot be attributed to the species *per se*. To be "male" and "female" is a

special kind of inseparable accident, perhaps even in a category all its own. See John Finley, "The Metaphysics of Gender: A Thomistic Approach," *The Thomist: A Speculative Quarterly Review* 79, no. 4 (2015): 585-614.

[31] Aquinas, *Summa Contra Gentiles*, II, 81, 8. The author is indebted to Sister Prudence Allen and Monsignor John Wippel for pointing out this passage. Though it does not deal directly with the distinction between genders but with the individuation of the human soul and its continuing individuation after it is separated from the body at death. It is here that Aquinas introduces the notion of the commensuration of each soul to each body. Commensuration is a term that means literally to have the same measure. Aquinas means here that each body is adapted or accommodated, even interpenetrated in an equal measure by the soul intended for it. See also Aquinas, *De veritate*, Q 5, 10 where Aquinas states: "the soul when joined to a body imitates the composition of that body."

[32] Though it will not be possible to include it here, it should also be noted at the outset that scientific research regarding what distinguishes men and women supports many of the conclusions found in the work of John Paul II as well as in this paper. See Steven E. Rhoades, *Taking Sex Differences Seriously* (San Francisco: Encounter Books, 2004), 22-26; Anne Moir and David Jessel, *Brain Sex: The Real Difference Between Men and Women* (New York: Dell Publishing, 1991), 68-112. For additional sources and a critique of brain organization theory as a whole, see Rebecca Jordan-Young, *Brainstorm* (Cambridge: Harvard University Press, 2010). The author's general argument is that there are risks associated with attributing sex differences to hormones and that brain organization theory (found in these other sources) cannot account for all of them. See also Paul Vitz, "Their Differences and Their Complementarity: Evidence from Psychology and Neuroscience," *The Complementarity of Women and Men*, ed. Paul Vitz (Washington D.C.: Catholic University of America Press, 2021), 182-215.

[33] The lineage of the "second sex" assumption, at least in the Western intellectual tradition, is buried deep in its history. It can be traced as far back as the pre-Socratic philosophers, finally finding its earliest concrete expression in a claim most have either dismissed, forgotten, or never heard Aristotle's argument that women are merely "malformed males" and are therefore "inferior to man." On this account, man (*qua* male) represents the prime analogue of what it is to be human. Aristotle's claim that woman is merely a "malformed male" gained powerful traction through the introduction of an arguably flawed historical interpretation of Genesis 2:18-23, traceable in particular to the Hellenistic Jewish philosopher, Philo (BC 13-AD 54).

³⁴ Aristotle, *The Generation of Animals*, 765a, 20; Cited also by Sr. Prudence Allen, *The Concept of Woman, Vol I: The Aristotelian Revolution* (Grand Rapids: Wm. B. Eerdmans Publishing Co, 1985), 87-99, 193. See also Philo, *Supplement I: Questions and Answers on Genesis* (Cambridge and London: Harvard University Press and William Heinemann, Ltd., 1929-62), Bk I, Ch. 27, 16. Philo's theory reflects the same conclusion, viz., that woman is not equal to man. But Philo was also an important first century theologian who interpreted the creation of woman in Genesis 2 through the lens of his philosophical conclusions. Philo's account merged with Aristotle's theory, adding a theological thrust to his influence on the development of the concept of woman in Christian thought.

³⁵ The word *ezer* is translated in many different ways: a "suitable helper," "suitable partner." Perhaps the best is found in the Jewish Tanakh – a "fitting helper."

³⁶ Though the word *tsela* is traditionally translated as "rib," it is not at all clear that this is correct. The basic meaning of the word in Hebrew is ambiguous and there are quite a few possibilities, including "plank," "side," and references to geographical and architectural terms. There have been many hypotheses concerning the word but the only thing that is really clear is that, if it does mean "rib," it does so only in this one passage. Several possible interpretations have particular appeal: if it is taken to mean "side" or "plank," it could be thought to be the source of the expression that woman is man's "better half"; or, given its proximity to the heart, it has been taken to stand for human interiority. Perhaps the most satisfying possibility is that it is a reference to sacral architecture since in some contexts *tsela* refers to the side portions of the sanctuary that are necessary for its stability and function. The conclusion can be drawn that the Yawhist author of the passage used terminology "designed to evoke associations with the construction of the sanctuary" to suggest that human beings "come to fulfillment for which they are destined by creation only as man and wife and as God's temple." See *Theological Dictionary of the Old Testament*, ed., G. Johannes Botterweck, Helmer Ringgren, and Heinz-Josef Fabry (Grand Rapids: Eerdmans, 2003).

³⁷ This interpretation is supported by Brevard Childs who states that "the creation of the woman, which is sequential in time, fors a climax to the creation which resounds with joy at the close of the chapter." See Childs, *Old Testament Theology in a Canonical Context*, 191.

³⁸ As St. Thomas himself argues, woman is as necessary to creation as the male of the species (*Summa Theolgiae*, I, 92, *sed contra*). Thus, woman cannot be thought of as a creature whose place in that order is subservient or somehow less in stature than that of man.

39 This point is also made by Cardinal Joseph Ratzinger in his 2004 "Letter to the Bishops of the Catholic Church on the Collaboration of Men and Women in the Church and in the World," when he points out that "the term here does not refer to an inferior, but to a vital helper." See in particular footnote 5. I am using the word "servant" here as it is usually meant – as someone who occupies a lower rung on the ladder in any particular context. A different interpretation of the word servant is associated with being a follower of Christ, which, at this point in salvation history, cannot be invoked. But I do not mean to imply that woman is not to serve man. As St. Paul says in Ephesians 5, both men and women are to submit to one another out of reverence for Christ. The question of the headship of the man in the family is not under scrutiny here and is a topic for further research.

40 Excellent examples can be found in the Psalms: e.g., Psalm 30:11b, "The LORD will be **a helper** (*'ezer*) to me", or Psalm 121:1, "I will lift up my eyes to the mountains, whence comes **my help** (*'ezrî*)." The name of the great scribe "Ezra" of the restoration of Israel under the Persians, namesake of the biblical book, seems to be the Aramaic masculine form of the same word.

41 In his very fine translation of these texts, Robert Alter *ezer negdo* as "sustainer" rather than helper, a word with a much closer meaning to that intended by the sacred author in my opinion. The author refers here to "helper" since that is the more traditional term used in most translations and makes my dispute with the usual interpretation more precise.

42 Following text is from the Woman and Man essay.

43 As is well known, John Paul II introduces the term "feminine genius" into the tradition. It appears for the first time in *Mulieris Dignitatem*, no. 31. I would argue that the word "charism" is more apt since its meaning is more recognizable and consistent with the tradition. The other curious thing is that he says nothing about the existence of a "masculine genius." This is a lacuna in his project which I have sought to correct. Clearly there is one.

44 Properly speaking, the Hebrew word here is *banah* and actually means "building."

45 *Summa Theologiae* I, Q. 94, a. 3. And though it is from an entirely different tradition, I find it so interesting to consider that one of Lao-Tze's more famous aphorisms is: "The beginning of wisdom is to call things by their right names."

46 Indeed, St. Thomas Aquinas argues that Adam received an additional preternatural gift, infused knowledge, in order to be able to name all the animals brought before him. *Summa Theologiae* I, Q. 94, a. 3. And though it is from an entirely different tradition, I find it so interesting to consider

that one of Lao-Tze's more famous aphorisms is: "The beginning of wisdom is to call things by their right names."

[47] Anthony Esolen, "Finding the Masculine Genius," interview by Zenit, A Zenit Daily Dispatch, ZENIT, 2007, https://ewtn.com/catholicism/library/finding-the-masculine-genius-4020 (last accessed March 20, 2022). Though Professor Esolen admits he doesn't exactly have a theory, his thinking is very helpful.

[48] See Rhoades, *Taking Sex Differences Seriously*, 22-26; Moir and Jessel, *Brain Sex*, 68-112. Though I am unable to incorporate it here, Father Walter Ong, S.J., demonstrates in his text *Fighting for Life: Contest, Sexuality, and Consciousness*, that man knows instinctively that he is the "expendable sex"; in an almost primordial way, he recognizes that his direct role in the propagation of the species is only momentary and that, once that is accomplished, his task is to protect and defend mother and child, even to the point of death. For a superb analysis of Ong's contribution to our understanding of the masculine genius, please see Fr. Christian Raab, "In Search of the Masculine Genius: The Contribution of Walter Ong," *Logos* 1, no. 21 (Winter 2018): 83-177, https://muse.jhu.edu/article/680908/pdf (last accessed March 29, 2022).

[49] For a fuller account of this reality, please see my paper "The Metaphysics of Creation as the Foundation of Environmental Stewardship and Economic Prosperity," *Nova et Vetera* 12 (Winter 2012): 233–52.

[50] Even a well-known mainstream feminist seems to agree with this point. See Camille Paglia, "It's a Man's World, and It Always Will Be," *Time Magazine*, December 16, 2013, http://ideas.time.com/2013/12/16/its-a-mans-world-and-it-always-will-be/ (last accessed March 29, 2022). For a different and very disturbing proposal concerning the role men have played and are destined to play in human history, see Melvin Konner, M.D., *Women After All: Sex, Evolution, and the End of Male Supremacy* (New York: W.W. Norton and Company, 2015). Konner's analysis will have to be reckoned with and will be the subject of future research. But for additional reflection on this very question, please see my essay "Adam's Gift: Man in the Order of Creation," *Humanum: Issues in Family, Culture, and Science* 3, (2016) https://humanumreview.com/articles/adams-gift-man-in-the-order-of-creation (last accessed March 29, 2022).

[51] Mieczyslaw A. Krapiec, *I-Man* (New Britain: Mariel Publications, 1983), 29-38. Father Krapiec points to the fact that of all the creatures on earth, man is actually a kind of alien in his environment. He does not possess fangs or a pointed snout that permits him to smell out and tear apart his food. He does not have fur to protect him from the harshness of his surroundings. This analysis is also reflected by Aquinas, *ST* I.76. a.5. In short, as John Paul II illuminates so beautifully in the introduction to his

encyclical *On Human Work*: "Man is made to be in the visible universe an image and likeness of God himself, and he is placed in it in order to subdue the earth. From the beginning therefore he is *called to work*. *Work is one of the characteristics that distinguish* man from the rest of creatures, whose activity for sustaining their lives cannot be called work. Only man is capable of work, and only man works, at the same time by work occupying his existence on earth."

[52] There is an interesting connection to be made and explored between this aspect of the genius of man and Cardinal Angelo Scola's argument that the father introduces the child to the "law of exchange (work) as the law of growth in life." See Angelo Scola, *The Nuptial Mystery* (Grand Rapids Michigan: Eerdmans Publishing Company, 2005), 242.

[53] Congregation for the Doctrine of the Faith, *Letter to the Bishops on the Collaboration of Men and Women in the Church and in the World* (March 31, 2004), no. 8, https://vatican.va/roman_curia/congregations/cfaith/documents/rc_con_cfaith_doc_20040731_collaboration_en.html (last accessed March 30, 2022).

[54] *Mulieris Dignitatem*, 4 and 29. However, grounded as it is in the undeniable fact that all women have the potential to be mothers, his work is vulnerable to the criticism that it risks a kind of biological determinism regarding the role that women can and ought to play in human society. See for example Elizabeth A. Johnson, "Imaging God, Embodying Christ: Women as a Sign of the Times," *The Church Women Want*, ed. Elizabeth A. Johnson (New York: Crossroad, 2002). Obviously, this was neither his meaning nor his intention. I am arguing that there is actually a prior point of departure for an account of the feminine genius, one unencumbered by the risk of such criticisms.

[55] And, as revealed at the foot of the cross, God has entrusted all of humanity to Mary's - and therefore to woman's – care. See *Mulieris Dignitatem*, 14.

[56] Cardinal Angelo Scola argues that the father introduces the child to the "law of exchange [work] as the law of growth in life," while the mother introduces her to the "law of gratuity [love]." See Scola, *The Nuptial Mystery*, 242.

[57] Rhoades, *Taking Sex Differences Seriously*, 134 and 193. Indeed, the entire book is full of scientific evidence and real-life examples in support of this conclusion.

[58] Genesis 3:16-19

[59] Again, the interpretation of the fall on offer here is markedly different from the historical development of Original Sin. I do dispute certain aspects of the traditional understanding of Original Sin as inconsistent with the more robust anthropology I have attempted to

provide as well as with the narrative of Genesis 3. I am starting from a different account of woman and man and so this is not surprising. But I do think my interpretation conforms more precisely to the original text and is particularly suited to our concerns in this paper. Further research is needed into how my analysis both leverages and distinguishes itself from the traditional teaching.

[60] In this section, I will be relying primarily on a text from the older Jesuit tradition, compiled by Joseph F. Sagues, S.J., *Sacra Theologiae Summa IIB: On God the Creator and Sanctifier.* 2014. This text provides a definitive summary of the received tradition. Very little in the way of scholarship into the meaning of Genesis 3 was pursued in the period between Trent and the Second Vatican Council, until the writings of Pope St. John Paul II. John Paul was the next scholar to take up the question in any meaningful way; his thinking on the subject is found in *Theology of the Body.*

[61] Sagues, *Sacra Theologiae,* Thesis 40, #908, 511.

[62] Ibid., #903-905 and 908, 507-508, 511.

[63] Catechism of the Catholic Church (CCC), 2nd ed., (1997), no. 397.

[64] Sagues, *Sacra Theologiae,* Thesis 40, #915, Scholium 3, 515-517.

[65] Ibid., #915, 515-516.

[66] Sagues, *Sacra Theologiae,* Thesis 40, #915-2, 516.

[67] Sagues, *Sacra Theologiae,* Thesis 40, #914-2-c., 514.

[68] CCC, 405.

[69] Sagues, *Sacra Theologiae,* Thesis 41, #921, 520-521.

[70] Ibid., #914-2-d., 514. See also Aquinas, *Summa Theologiae* II, II: "the woman was used as an instrument of temptation to bring down the man."

[71] Ibid., #915-2, 516.

[72] Ibid.

[73] Ibid., #916, Scholium 4, 517-518.

[74] More research is called for into the obvious connections between this more properly theological account and the results of psychology's investigations of the ways in which men and women manifest their particular woundedness.

[75] *Mulieris Dignitatem,* no. 30.

[76] Is that not so even today? Though many of us will deny it, women are in very great need of protection now – they have lost their way in large measure, not because they seek to fulfill their own creative potential through work outside the home, but because they insist on doing that within a social and economic context that reduces their natural capacity to bear life to an inconvenience and their natural orientation toward persons to an unnecessary complication. The evidence is all around us that both men and women have lost their orientation in the cosmic scheme.

⁷⁷ See especially Mary Eberstadt, *Adam and Eve after the Pill: Paradoxes of the Sexual Revolution* (San Francisco: Ignatius Press, 2012).

⁷⁸ For an extensive and well cited summary of the statistics on domestic violence and its frequency and impact on women, see: https://ncadv.org/STATISTICS. According to the United Nations' *Global Report on Trafficking in Persons,* women and girls make up 70% of all victims of trafficking world-wide. Full report available at: http://unodc.org/documents/data-and-analysis/glotip/GLOTIP_2014_full_report.pdf (Last accessed March 29, 2022). And according to most recently available census figures (2013) 36% of those living below the poverty level in American are women. 31% of households headed by single women were living below the poverty line. This is more than five times the poverty rate for families headed by a married couple (5.8%). It also contrasts with the 15.9% of male headed households living in poverty during the same period. See "Income and Poverty in the United States (2013)," *United States Census Bureau,* September 16, 2014, at 16, https://census.gov/library/publications/2014/demo/p60-249.html (last accessed March 29, 2022). For evidence that fatherlessness is a predictor of poverty, see Sara McLanahan "Family Structure and the Reproduction of Poverty," *American Journal of Sociology* 90, no. 4 (January 1985): 873-901. For more recent data supporting this claim, see "The Consequences of Fatherlessness," http://fathers.com/statistics-and-research/the-consequences-of-fatherlessness/ (last accessed March 29, 2022).

⁷⁹ See Carol Garhart Mooney, *Theories of Attachment: An Introduction to Bowlby, Ainsworth, Gerber, Brazelton, Kennell, and Klause* (St. Paul: Redleaf Press, 2010). An analysis of the particular personality disorders described by the DSM-5 and found more frequently in women include "instability in interpersonal relationships, seriously unstable affects, fear of abandonment" and others. For a more complete account, please see Dr. Paul Vitz, *Men-Women Complementarity, supra.*

⁸⁰ One wonders if this has anything to do with the frequent report that, in general, men seem reluctant to listen to women, their wives in particular. It is funny, but sadly true. And it can be said to be the reason why women, we must admit, do tend to become rather shrill at times. Perhaps if men listened better, women would not feel they needed to raise their voices in order to be heard.

⁸¹ Pope John Paul II, *Evangelium Vitae* (March 25, 1995), no. 99, https://vatican.va/content/john-paul-ii/en/encyclicals/documents/hf_jp-ii_enc_25031995_evangelium-vitae.html (last accessed March 30, 2022).

⁸² Pope Pius XII, *Address to Members of Various Catholic Women's Associations on Women's Duties in Social and Political Life* (October 22, 1945)

http://catholictradition.org/Encyclicals/questa1.htm (last accessed March 29, 2022).

[83] Catholic Church, *Compendium of the Catechism* (CCC), 295, (*Libreria Editrice Vaticana*: 2005), https://vatican.va/archive/compendium_ccc/documents/archive_2005_compendium-ccc_en.html (last accessed March 29, 2020).

[84] Ibid., 147, quoting Pope John Paul II, *Letter to Women*, (June 29, 1995), no. 8., https://vatican.va/content/john-paul-ii/en/letters/1995/documents/hf_jp-ii_let_29061995_women.html (last accessed March 29, 2022).

## Chapter 3

[1] Mathew 25:34- 36.

[2] Dietrich von Hildebrand, *In Defense of Purity* (Steubenville: Hildebrand Press, 2017).

[3] Ibid., 3.

[4] Ibid.

[5] Karol Wojtyla, *Love and Responsibility* (Boston: Pauline Books and Media, 2013), 82.

[6.] Joseph Ratzinger, trans. Joseph Bolin, "On the Question of the Indissolubility of Marriage," *Paths of Love.com*, Translated by Joseph Bolin, March 25, 2011, https://pathsoflove.com/texts/ratzinger-indissolubility-marriage/ (last accessed March 29, 2022).

[7] Von Hildebrand, 131–132.

[8] Ibid., 132–133.

[9] Ibid., 134–135.

[10] Aurel Kolnai, *Sexual Ethics: The Meaning and Foundations of Sexual Morality*, Translated and edited by Francis Dunlop. Preface by Roger Scuton (Aldershot, Hampshire: Ashgate, 2005), 15.

[11] Von Hildebrand, 17.

[12] Ibid., 15–16.

[13] Ibid.

[1] T. S. Eliot, "East Coker" in *Four Quartets* (New York: Harcourt Brace and Company, 1943), 125-126.

[2] See Thomas Aquinas, *Summa Theologica* trans. Fathers of the English Dominican Province (New York: Benzinger Bros. 1948) Part I-II, Question 5, Article 4 ad 4 and Part I, Question 76.

[3] See, for instance, Luigi Giussani, Stefano Alberto, Javier Paredes, *Generating Traces in the History of the World: New Traces of the Christian Experience* (Montreal: McGill-Queens University Press, 2010), 86ff.

⁴ I will here often be summarizing arguments I have made at greater length elsewhere: "Exigent Relations: Philosophical Reflections on the Centrality of Fatherhood and Sonship," in *Spiritual Fathers, Spiritual Husbands*, eds. Bishop Felipe J. Estevez and Bishop Andrew H. Cozzens (St. Louis, MO: Enroute, 2020) 85-106. "Reciprocal Generativity: Reason, Intimacy, and Sexual Difference, *Logos*, Vol. 24, No. 1 (Winter 2021), 88-123.

⁵ By using the term "natural" I in no way intend to deny the supernatural character of sacramental marriage and the transcendent trajectory of natural marriage.

⁶ I mean in no way to imply that this integration does not imply asceticism and disciplining of the passions.

⁷ See Thomas Aquinas, *Summa Theologica* trans. Fathers of the English Dominican Province (New York: Benzinger Bros. 1948) I-II, q. 93, a. 1.

⁸ T.S. Eliot, "East Coker," 1.

⁹ *ST* I-II, q. 94, a.1.

¹⁰ See Lawrence Dewan, "Natural Law and the First Act of Freedom: Maritain Revisited," in *Wisdom, Law, and Virtue* (New York: Fordham University Press, 2007), 238.

¹¹ See *ST* II-II, q. 152, a. 2, and Fortin, "Exigent Relations," 92ff.

¹² See Aristotle, *Politics*, trans. B. Jowett, in *The Basic Works of Aristotle*, ed. Richard McKeon (New York: Random House, 1941), 1252a 26-28.

¹³ This point came to my attention in the work of Fr. Stephen Brock: Stephen L. Brock, *The Philosophy of Saint Thomas Aquinas: A Sketch* (Eugene Oregon: Cascade Books, 2015), 28. See also *ST* I, q. 93, a. 3.

¹⁴ See John Paul II, *Man and Woman He Created Them: A Theology of the Body*, trans., Michael Waldstein (Boston: Pauline Books and Media, 2006), 13:3-17:6. For an expanded discussion see: Timothy Fortin, "Reciprocal Generativity," 114-117.

¹⁵ See Fabrice Hadjadj, *Qu'est-ce qu'une famille? Suivi de La Transcendance en culottes* (Paris: Salvator, 2014), 57-60. And, Fortin, "Reciprocal Generativity," 110-114.

¹⁶ Emmanuel Levinas, *Time and the Other*, trans. Richard A. Cohen (Pittsburgh: Duquesne University Press, 1987), 86.

¹⁷ Clearly, this is a point to be further developed. Yet, we know that, in His human nature, Jesus was like us in all things but sin. The ordering of man to his end by the natural law is not a matter of sin. Thus, it seems reasonable to say that, in perfectly possessing human nature, our Lord would be subject to the inclinations of the natural law. And, as we have just seen, the most fundamental of those inclinations order man to generativity in the natural order and thereby to espousal. St. Thomas is clear, however, that not every *individual* man is bound by the natural law to procreation;

some may forego natural fatherhood, for the sake of the spiritual good of the community; they can forego natural fatherhood for spiritual fatherhood. See *ST* II-II, q. 152, a. 2.

[18] Timothy Fortin, "Exigent Relations," 99-100.

[19] Christopher West, *At the Heart of the Gospel: Reclaiming the Body for the New Evangelization* (New York: Image Books, 2012), 119-123.

[20] Fulton Sheen, *Through the Year with Fulton Sheen,* compiler Henry Dieterich (San Francisco: Ignatius Press, 1985), 60.

[21] Christopher West, *Theology of the Body for Beginners* (North Palm Beach, FL: Beacon Publishing, 2018), 100-102.

## Chapter 4

[1] Peter C. Kleponis, *Integrity Restored: Helping Catholic Families Win the Battle Against Pornography* (Revised and Expanded Edition) Amazon Kindle Edition, November 6, 2019); *Revealed: Exposing the truth about pornography* (Elizabethtown, PA: Integrity Restored, 2018); *Integrity Starts here! A Catholic Approach to Restoring Sexual integrity* (Denver, CO: Outskirts Press, 2016); *The Relationship between Narcissism and Spiritual Well-being in Roman Catholic Seminarians* (doctoral dissertation), Minneapolis, MN: Capella University, 2010).

[2] Jacobellis v. Ohio, 378 U.S. 184, 197 (1964) (Stewart, J., concurring), (emphasis added).

[3] Kleponis, 2018.

[4] John Paul II, *The Theology of the Body: Human Love in the Divine Plan* (Boston: Pauline Books & Media, 1997); Brenda Báez, *John Paul II on Love and Responsibility (New York:* Love and Responsibility Foundation, Summer 2000 edition) https://academia.edu/40282983/JP2_on_Love-Responsibility (last accessed April 9, 2022).

[5] Bishop Robert W. Finn, *Blessed are the pure in heart: A Pastoral Letter on the Dignity of the Human Person and the Dangers of Pornography* (February 21, 2007) (Diocese of Kansas City -St. Joseph, 2007) 15, https://kofc.org/uns/en/resources/cis/cis323.pdf (last accessed April 9, 2022).

[6] Bishop Paul S. Loverde, *Love Undefiled: A Pastoral Letter on the Evils of Pornography* (Arlington, VA: Diocese of Arlington, 2006); See also Bishop Paul S. Loverde, *Bought with a Price: Every Man's Duty to Protect Himself and his Family from a Pornographic Culture* (March 19, 2014) https://www.arlingtondiocese.org/find-support/anti-pornography/ (last accessed March 9, 2022).

[7] Pope John Paul II, *Theology of the Body: Human Love in the Divine Plan (*Boston: Pauline Books & Media, 1997).

⁸ Mark Laaser, *Healing the Wounds of Sexual Addiction* (Grand Rapids, MI: Zondervan, 2004).

⁹ Kevin Skinner, *Treating Pornography Addiction: the Essential Tools for Recovery*. (Provo, UT: Growth Climate, Inc., 2005).

¹⁰ Ibid.

¹¹ Adapted from David L. Delmonico, *Internet Sex Screening Test* (David L. Delmonico, PhD, NCC, Duquesne University, Pittsburgh, PA, 2000).

¹² Paul Tennant, "Ex-pastor accused of taking $83K from parish," *Eagle Tribune* (November 7, 2010), https://bishop-accountability.org/news2010/11_12/2010_11_07_Tennant_ExPastorAccused.htm (last accessed April 9, 2022).

¹³ LynnAnne M, Joiner, *Congregants' Responses to Clergy Pornography addiction*, Dissertation in Marriage and Therapy, Doctor in Philosophy (Lubbock, TX: Texas Tech University, 2008 ) https://researchgate.net/publication/251375027_Congregants'_Responses_to_Clergy_Pornography_Addiction (last accessed April 9, 2022).

¹⁴ Peter C. Kelponis, *Integrity Restored: Helping Catholic Families Win the Battle Against Pornography* (revised and expanded edition) Amazon Kindle Edition, November 6, 2019, https://amazon.com/Integrity-Restored-Catholic-Families-Pornography-ebook/dp/B0815VZYLK (last accessed April 9, 2022).

¹⁵ Ibid.

¹⁶ Ibid.

¹⁷ Ibid.

¹⁸ Ibid.

¹⁹ Kleponis, 2010.

²⁰ Paula Hall, *Understanding and Treating Sex and Pornography Addiction* (New York: Routledge, 2019).

²¹ Patrick Carnes, *Facing the Shadow: Starting Sexual and Relationship Recovery*, 3rd edition (Carefree, AZ: Gentle Path Press, 2015).

²² Todd Bowman, *Sex Addiction Treatment Professionals Recovery Program* (Olathe, MN: MidAmerica Nazarene University, 2018).

²³ Kleponis, 2016.

²⁴ Michael J. Rounds Why is honesty so important in recovery? *Psychology Today,* July 26, 2020, https://psychologytoday.com/intl/blog/10000-days-sober/202007/why-is-honesty-so-important-in-recovery (last accessed April 10, 2022).

²⁵ *Importance of Accountability in Recovery*, (Van Wert, OH: New Beginnings in Recovery, 2018).

²⁶ *The Role of Counsellor in Addiction Recovery*, Wake Forest University Blog.

[27] M. Hull, Five benefits of Spirituality in Recovery (Umatilla, FL: The Recovery Village, 2021), https://therecoveryvillage.com/recovery/wellness/benefits-spirituality-in-recovery/ (last accessed April 10, 2022).

[28] Tim Powers, *Life skills Education in Recovery: Helping You Get Your Life Back on Track, SoberNation* (2016), https://sobernation.com/life-skills-education-in-recovery-helping-you-get-your-life-back-on-track/ (last accessed April 10, 2022).

[29] *Papa Francesco, Discorso a Seminaristi e Sacerdoti che Studiano a Roma*, Ottobre 24, 2022, https://vatican.va/content/francesco/it/speeches/2022/october/documents/20221024-seminaristi-sacerdoti.html (last accessed November 28, 2022). Translated with the assistance of DeepL.com/translator (free version).

[30] "German Priest Contradicts Pope and Backs Pornography as a Sexual Relief for Celibates," *CNA*, November 16, 2022, https://catholicnewsagency.com/news/252833/german-priest-contradicts-pope-and-backs-pornography-as-sexual-relief-for-celibates (last accessed November 28, 2022).

[31] Mary Eberstadt, Mary Anne Layden, *The Social Costs of Pornography: A Statement of Findings and Recommendations* (Princeton, N.J.: The Witherspoon Institute: 2010) ("The Statement"), at 10. For resources created by the Catholic Church see, for example: Pontifical Council for Social Communications, *PORNOGRAPHY AND Violence in the Communications Media: A Pastoral Response,* https://vatican.va/roman_curia/pontifical_councils/pccs/documents/rc_pc_pccs_doc_07051989_pornography_en.html (last accessed March 17, 2022); Pontifical Council for the Family, *The Truth and Meaning of Human Sexuality: Guidelines for Education in the Church,* December 8, 1995, https://vatican.va/roman_curia/pontifical_councils/family/documents/rc_pc_family_doc_08121995_human-sexuality_en.html (last accessed March 17, 2022); United States Conference of Catholic Bishops, *Create in Me a Clean Heart: A Pastoral Response to Pornography,* https://usccb.org/issues-and-action/human-life-and-dignity/create-in-me-a-clean-heart (last accessed March 17, 2022).

[32] Ibid.

[33] Ibid. and James R. Stoner, Donna M. Hughes, eds., *The Social Costs of Pornography: A Collection of Papers* (Princeton, N.J.: The Witherspoon Institute: 2010); *The Social Costs of Pornography: A Consultation* (Princeton, N.J.: The Witherspoon Institute: 2010) http://socialcostsofpornography.com/videos.php (last accessed March 13, 2022).

[34] Patrick Hough, "The Social Costs of Pornography," *Public Discourse*, March 23, 2010, available at https://thepublicdiscourse.com/2010/03/1215/ (last accessed February 28, 2002).

35 *The Statement, supra,* 13.
36 Ibid.
37 *The Statement, supra,* 8, 17.
38 Ibid., Executive Summary.
39 Ibid.
40 Joel Currier, "Catholic Supply Suspect Admits Deadly Attack, Gets Life Imprisonment without Parole," October 23, 2021 available at https://stltoday.com/news/local/crime-and-courts/catholic-supply-suspect-admits-deadly-attack-gets-life-in-prison-without-parole/article_fa24c829-2241-50ae-bf16-ae76384270e2.html (last accessed March 14, 2022).
41 Ibid.
42 Candice Kim, "From Fantasy to Reality: The Link between Viewing Child Pornography and Molesting Children," *American Prosecutors Research Institute, Child Sexual Exploitation Program Update,* Vol. 1, Number 3, 2004. available at https://ndaa.org/wp-content/uploads/Update_gr_vol1_no3.pdf (last accessed March 15, 2022).
43 See Rev. Sean P. Kilcawley, "Compulsive Sexual Behavior and Seminary Formation: The Root of the Crisis," in Jane F. Adolphe, Ronald J. Rychlak, eds., *Clerical Sexual Misconduct: An Interdisciplinary Analysis* (Cluny: 2020), 29-47.
44 Hanna Brockhaus, "Pope Francis Warns Priests Against Living a Double Life," *National Catholic Register,* September 17, 2008, https://ncregister.com/news/pope-francis-warns-priests-against-living-a-double-life (last accessed March 13, 2022).
45 Pope John Paul II, Apostolic Exhortation, *Pastores Dabo Vobis* (March 25, 1992), no. 44, https://vatican.va/content/john-paul-ii/en/apost_exhortations/documents/hf_jp-ii_exh_25031992_pastores-dabo-vobis.html (last accessed March 2, 2022).
46 See Rev. Sean P. Kilcawley, *supra.*
47 See Dale O'Leary, "Shattering Myths and Lies," in Jane F. Adolphe, Ronald J. Rychlak, eds., *Clerical Sexual Misconduct: An Interdisciplinary Analysis* (Cluny: 2020), 65-67.
48 Kilcawley, *supra* note 16, at 36.
49 John Paul II, Apostolic Exhortation, *Pastores Dabo Vobis,* (March 25, 1992), no. 44, https://vatican.va/content/john-paul-ii/en/apost_exhortations/documents/hf_jp-ii_exh_25031992_pastores-dabo-vobis.html (last accessed March 2, 2022).
50 Ibid.
51 Ibid.
52 Susan Selner-Wright, Janet E. Smith, Deborah Savage, Theresa Farnan, and Suzanne Mulrain, "Sharing a Spirit of Discernment:

Recommendations from Women Faculty at American Seminaries to Presidents of Episcopal Conferences and the Bishops of the United States," in Jane F. Adolphe, Ronald J. Rychlak, eds. *Clerical Sexual Misconduct: An Interdisciplinary Analysis* (Cluny: 2020), at 395.

[53] Ibid.; See also the chapter by Dr. Patricia Cooney Hathaway in this volume.

[54] Pope Benedict XVI, Post-Synodal Apostolic Exhortation, *Sacramentum Caritatis*, February 22, 2007 available at https://vatican.va/content/benedict-xvi/en/apost_exhortations/documents/hf_ben-xvi_exh_20070222_sacramentum-caritatis.html (last accessed, March 12, 2022).

[55] Patti Maguire Armstrong, US Exorcists: Demonic Activity on the Rise, *National Catholic Register*, March 11, 2017, https://ncregister.com/news/us-exorcists-demonic-activity-on-the-rise (last accessed March 10, 2022).

[56] Ibid.

[57] Ibid.

[58] Ibid.

[59] Fr. Chad Ripperger's 2019, Conference on Exorcism, *Sensum Fidelium*, Youtube Channel, available at https://youtu.be/Ffe_p6kKXqw (last accessed March 19, 2022).

[60] Gabriele Amorth, *An Exorcist Tells His Story*, translated by Nicollett V. MacKenzie (Ignatius Press: 1994) 61.

[61] Ibid., 60-61.

# Chapter 5

[1] Smith, Ray A., "The Struggle to Grow a Beard Is Real. So Men Are Faking It," *Wall Street Journal*, November 4, 2019. https://wsj.com/articles/the-struggle-to-grow-a-beard-is-real-so-men-are-faking-it-11572887063?mod=trending_now_5.

[2] St. John Paul II, General Audience of January 16, 1980, available at: https://vatican.va/content/john-paul-ii/en/audiences/1980/documents/hf_jp-ii_aud_19800116.html (accessed April 1, 2022).

[3] Cf. Genesis 1 and 2.

[4] Cf. Genesis 3.

[5] Cf. Scott Hahn, *First Comes Love* (New York: Doubleday Image, 2002) Chapter 6, pp.187-190.

[6] Genesis 3:12.

[7] Ibid.

[8]Aristotle, *Nichomachean Ethics*, 1162a 15-29. Emphasis added. See *Nichomachean Ethics* in *Introduction to Aristotle*, edited by Richard McKeon (New York: The Modern Library of Random House, 1947) p. 490.

[9] Aristotle, *Nichomachean Ethics*, 1661a 20-25; McKeon, 488.

[10] de Solenni, Pia, *A Hermeneutic of Aquinas' Mens through a Sexually Differentiated Epistemology: Towards an Understanding of Woman as Imago Dei*, in the series *Dissertationes*, Pontifical University of the Holy Cross, 2000, pp 27-30.

[11] See Michael Nolan, "What Aquinas Never Said About Women." *First Things*. 1998. http://firstthings.com/article/2009/03/003-what-aquinas-never-said-about-women-38. (accessed April 1, 2022).

[12] Cf. *Summa theologiae*, I, q.92, a.1.

[13] In the *Summa theologiae* [ST] I, q. 92, a. 2, St. Thomas states that God created man as male and female not only for generation. In the ST I, q. 93, a. 4, ad 1, St. Thomas makes it clear that the image of God, characterized by the rational nature, is found in both men and women. The end of men and women—endowed with a rational nature—is to know God as their ultimate end and supreme happiness; see ST I-II, q. 2, a. 8.

[14] de Solenni, *A Hermeneutic of Aquinas' Mens*, 125.

[15] *Summa Contra Gentiles* II.124, 2972- 3.

[16] John 15, 12-13.

[17] For Aquinas, the Incarnation establishes a bond of friendship between human beings and God based on a common human nature, which God has assumed by becoming man. The angels are pure spirits so they cannot have friendship with God in their souls as human can; see ST II-II, q. 23, a. 2.

[18] *The Holy Bible*, Revised Standard Version, Ignatius Press 2006.

[19] *The Old Testament in English*, Volume Two, Translated by Ronald Knox, Sheed & Ward, 1952.

[20] Ronald Knox, *Window in the Wall:* Reflections on the Holy Eucharist (London: Sheed & Ward, 1956), 80.

[21] Council of Chalcedon, Session 5 (October 22, 451); Denzinger-Hünermann, no. 302.

## Chapter 6

[1] Sources on Maria's life on the internet are numerous. For this account, I have relied particularly on "Maria Goretti," *Newsletter of Saint Joseph de Clairval Abbey*, August 15, 2002, https://clairval.com/index.php/en/letter/?id=2140802 as well as the account in Ann Ball's *Modern Saints* (Rockford, IL: Tan Books, 1983), 163-73.

² Pope Pius XII in his canonization homily said that "with splendid courage [Maria] surrendered herself to God and his grace and so gave her life to protect her virginity." He canonized her as a martyr *in defensum castitatis*, "in the defense of chastity." What this might mean can be found in Pope John Paul II's *Message to the Bishop of Albano for the Centenary of the Death of St. Maria Goretti* (Jule 6, 2002) http://vatican.va/content/john-paul-ii/en/speeches/2002/july/documents/hf_jp-ii_spe_20020708_santa-maria-goretti.html) (last accessed March 29, 2022). In this address, John Paul cites the above quote from Pius XII and then goes on to say that Maria's witness expresses the Church's need to "champion the value of sexuality as a factor that involves every aspect of the person and must therefore be lived with an interior attitude of freedom and reciprocal respect, in the light of God's original plan." In the great tradition of papal interpretation, John Paul takes the words of a previous pontiff and then interprets them by offering his own theological-anthropological deepening of "virginity" and "in the defense of chastity." I offer this paper in much the same spirit. (And I would be more forgiving toward John Paul II than this anonymous commentator: "Preserved Whole and Entire: Saint Maria Goretti and Her Successors in Martyrdom," *Hwaet I Meant to Say* (blog), February 15, 2021, https://mrshwaetsit.wordpress.com/2021/02/15/preserved-whole-and-entire-st-maria-goretti-and-her-successors-in-martyrdom/.

³ It may well be, as Mollie Wilson O'Reilly argues in *Commonweal* that "for too long the church has been fixated on women's virginity as an end in itself, as if chastity were a possession a girl can lose for good, rather than a virtue to be cultivated. This view reduces women to objects that men can possessor or spoil and makes men—all men—a threat to be deflected." ("Her, Too: Stop Making Victims of Sexual Assault into Martyrs for Virginity," September 17, 2018, https://commonwealmagazine.org/her-too). However, I would suggest that the recovery of virginity for both men and women must pass through Maria Goretti's witness and not around it. Maria's witness—as martyrs' witnesses always do— puts a point on the most outstanding feature of her life, which I take to be Maria's *virginal gaze*. And while we can and should get clear on exactly how this gaze is expressed in her martyrdom (I would say that she was killed by Alessandro because of the way she looked at him, which he experienced as a rebuke) and how this spiritual quality is expressed in her desire to retain her physical integrity (her virginal body being for her the sign of a deeper, spiritual commitment), I would want to insist, nevertheless, that Maria's witness expresses a spiritual poverty and detachment that is, in fact, very much needed by all of us, male and female alike.

⁴ And here Maria's witness completes that of the earlier virgin martyrs, whose stories, dramatic as they are, never really plumb the depths of the integral personal unity that they were living.

⁵ Luigi Guissani, *Conversazione sul matrimonio*. In Antonio Maria Sicari, *Breve catechesi sul matrimonio*, (Milan: Jaca Book, 1990), 91-109 (unofficial translation).

⁶ Paulo Prosperi, "Do Not Hold Me: Ascending the Ladder of Love" *Communio* 45 (Summer 2018), 211. See Giussani's discussion in *Is It Possible to Live this Way? Vol 3*, Charity (Montreal: McGill-Queens, 2009), 100-12.

⁷ Prosperi., 211-12.

⁸ Ibid., 212.

⁹ Luigi Giussani, *Is It Possible to Live This Way?: Vol. 3, Charity* (Montreal: McGill-Queens, 2009), 107.

¹⁰ Here, the reflection of Antonio Sicari on the "virginal" sensibility at the heart of the very happy and physically fruitful marriage of Saints Louis and Zelie Martin, the parents of Saint Thérèse of Lisieux, is instructive: "The truth is that we are dealing here with an exemplary experience, in which some aspects of marital life, which for many couples remain and will continue to remain obscure, come to light in an amazing way. Yet, due to its remaining in the dark, many families continue to suffer, without ever knowing this amazing truth. What is it? Well, it all begins or should begin—during the years of youth—with the discovery that the human heart is made for the Absolute, and that nothing will ever satisfy that heart except God; that in the end there is always a solitude in the human soul that can never be filled or healed by creatures, not even the most loved creature, another human being. And this is the original 'vocation to virginity,' which everyone, sooner or later, must come to feel, or risk the pain of an eternal wandering around on the surface of his or her own existence. Anyone who then comes to know and love the Son of God made human comes to intuit with plenty of effort that this primary virginity has to concentrate itself lovingly and concretely on Him: only then is the true Christian born." Antonio Sicari, "Blessed Zelie and Louis Martin, the Parents of St. Thérèse of Lisieux," http://louisandzeliemartin.org/sicari (last accessed March 29, 2022). In the same vein, Giussani speaks of a pedagogical approach to the formation of a young man and woman who intend marriage that opens the path to virginity. Cf. *Conversazione sul matrimonio*. In Antonio Maria Sicari, *Breve catechesi sul matrimonio*, 91-109. (Milan: Jaca Book, 1990).

¹¹ Then God said: "Let us make man in our image, after our likeness. Let them have dominion over the fish of the sea, the birds of the air, and the cattle, and over all the wild animals and all the creatures that crawl on the ground." God created man in his image; in the divine image he created him; male and female he created them. God blessed them, saying: "Be

fertile and multiply; fill the earth and subdue it. Have dominion over the fish of the sea, the birds of the air, and all the living things that move on the earth" (Gen 1:26-28).

[12] St. John Paul II, *Man and Woman He Created Them: The Theology of the Body* (henceforth *TOB*), (Boston: St. Paul Media, 2006), 2:3-5.

[13] *TOB*, 3:1.

[14] I follow here John Paul II's analysis. I would also draw the reader's attention to Deborah Savage's insightful exploration of the second creation account through the lens of Hebraic anthropology and Thomistic metaphysics. See "Man, Woman, and the Redemption of the World," [citation to the present text needs to be added].

[15] *TOB* 4:5.

[16] *TOB*, 6:2.

[17] *TOB*, 14:4.

[18] *TOB*, 10:2.

[19] Pope John Paul II, Apostolic Letter, *Mulieris Dignitatem* (August 15, 1988) http://vatican.va/content/john-paul-ii/en/apost_letters/1988/documents/hf_jp-ii_apl_19880815_mulieris-dignitatem.html (last accessed March 29, 2022) 14: "Jesus enters *into the concrete and historical situation of women,* a situation which is *weighed down by the inheritance of sin.* One of the ways in which this inheritance is expressed is habitual discrimination against women in favor of men. This inheritance is rooted within women too. From this point of view the episode of the woman 'caught in adultery' (cf. Jn 8:3-11) is particularly eloquent. In the end Jesus says to her: *'Do not sin again,'* but first he *evokes an awareness* of sin in the men who accuse her in order to stone her, thereby revealing his profound capacity to see human consciences and actions in their true light. Jesus seems to say to the accusers: Is not this woman, for all her sin, above all a confirmation of your own transgressions, of your 'male' injustice, your misdeeds?"

[20] Ibid.

[21] In his translation of *TOB*, Michael Waldstein prefers "desire" to "lust"—hence "concupiscent desire" or "lustful desire." Following the earlier translation of the *Theology of the Body* as well as that of *Mulieris Dignitatem*, I stick with "lust." See *TOB*, 225, translator's note.

[22] *TOB*, 40:5: "A look (or rather looking) is itself a cognitive act."

[23] We can see a true picture of lust in Alessandro Serenelli's own testimony. After his death in 1970, a personal witness in the form of an open letter to the world was found among his belongings in which he describes what led up to the moment when he attacked Maria. He details his own gradual corruption by "printed magazines, immoral shows, and bad examples in the media." "I was blinded by a brute impulse that pushed me down the wrong way of living," he concludes. Alessandro Serenelli,

*Letter* (May 5, 1961) living," he concludes. Alessandro Serenelli, "Spiritual Testament" (May 5, 1961) http://santamariagoretti.it/wp/alessandro-serenelli-2/#testamento.

[24] Rape, it is often insisted, is an act of violence and not an act of passion.

[25] Luigi Giussani, *Is it Possible to Live This Way?*, 107.

[26] *Mulieris Dignitatem*, 18.

[27] Ibid.

[28] Pope John Paul II, *Letter to Women* (June 29, 1995) 12, http://vatican.va/content/john-paul-ii/en/letters/1995/documents/hf_jp-ii_let_29061995_women.html.

[29] See, for example, the connection between morbid obesity and childhood sexual abuse in Bessel van der Kolk, The Body Keeps the Score: Brain, Mind, and Body (New York: Penguin Press, 2014), 144.

[30] Luigi Giussani, *Christ, God's Companionship with Man* (Montreal: McGill-Queens, 2015), 97: wherein it states: "How beautiful it is, going through the Gospel, to discover that the first ones, men like us, who followed Jesus, reached the point of not realizing that this man was God, but of saying, repeating what he claimed about Himself. This is their profession of faith. This was because the apostles did not discover that Jesus was God, but being with Him they got a big impression, so great that they 'had to' say: if we are not to believe in this man, we are not to believe even our own eyes. It is because of this evidence that, even without understanding well, they repeated His words, which were to shape history and hearts."

[31] *Is It Possible to Live This Way?*, *supra*, 108, wherein it states: "The truth in the method of knowing, which Christ possessed, astonished those who watched Him: they were awestruck. That man over there, who did not touch them—he touched the eyes of the blind, the mouths of the mute, he touched the ears of the deaf, to cure them, only that—when they arrived within twenty metres of Him, they were nevertheless pieced by that Presence inside Him, a Presence that remained with them for days, that required an effort to shake off!"

[32] Prosperi, 219.

[33] When Pope Francis elevated the celebration of Mary Magdalene to the rank of feast in 2016, he emphasized that she was a "witness of Divine Mercy." The official decree carefully avoided any sense that Mary Magdalene was a prostitute or even a sinner (Congregation of Divine Worship, "Apostle of the Apostles," June 3, 2016, http://vatican.va/roman_curia/congregations/ccdds/documents/articolo-roche-maddalena_en.pdf . However, a long tradition in the West, beginning at least as early as Pope Saint Gregory the Great in the sixth century, identifies

Mary Magdalene with both the unnamed woman, "a sinner," who anoints Jesus feet in Luke 7:37 and Mary of Bethany, sister to Martha and Lazarus, who anoints Jesus' head before his passion and death (Lk 10: 38-42 and Jn 11). A vast medieval iconography grew up around this interpretation of Mary as a former-prostitute-turned-penitent-and-contemplative. It seems to me that if we look squarely at the sort of abuse Mary Magdalene must have suffered to open her up to severe demonic infestation, we can comfortably, if not neatly, accept the older tradition as revealing a deep insight into the experience of mercy that is hers.

[34] Prosperi, 218.

[35] Acts 17:28, NABRE.

[36] Song of Songs 4:12, NABRE.

[37] Genesis 2:15, NABRE.

[38] G.K. Chesterton, "On Certain Modern Writers and the Institution of the Family," *Heretics*, (Dover Publications: 2006) first published in 1905.

[39] Pope Benedict XVI, *World Day of Peace Message* (January 1, 2008) https://vatican.va/content/benedict-xvi/en/messages/peace/documents/hf_ben-xvi_mes_20071208_xli-world-day-peace.html (last accessed March 29, 2022); Cf. Pope John Paul II, Apostolic Exhortation, *Christifideles Laici* (December 30, 1988) no. 40. https://vatican.va/content/john-paul-ii/en/apost_exhortations/documents/hf_jp-ii_exh_30121988_christifideles-laici.html (last accessed March 29, 2022).

[40] Pope Benedict XVI, *A New Song for the Lord*, (The Crossroad Publishing Company; Reprint edition, 1996).

[41] Benedict XVI, *Introduction to Christianity* (San Francisco: Ignatius Press, 2004).

[42] Ibid.

[43] Pope John Paul II, *Meditation on Givenness*, AAS, 98, no. 8, August 2006, https://communio-icr.com/files/jpii41-4.pdf (last accessed March 29, 2022).

[44] Genesis 2:23

[45] Pope John Paul II, *Man and Woman He Created Them: A Theology of the Body* (TOB) Translation, Introduction and Index by Michael Waldstein (Pauline Books and Media: 2006).

[46] Pope John Paul II, *Novo Millennio Ineunte* (January 2, 2001) 43, https://vatican.va/content/john-paul-ii/en/apost_letters/2001/documents/hf_jp-ii_apl_20010106_novo-millennio-ineunte.html (last accessed March 29, 2022).

[47] Pope John Paul II, Apostolic Letter, *Mulieris Dignitatem*, (August 15, 1988) no. 25 https://vatican.va/content/john-paul-ii/en/apost_letters/

1988/documents/hf_jp-ii_apl_19880815_mulieris-dignitatem.html (last accessed March 29, 2022).
⁴⁸ *Meditation on Givenness*, no. 8.
⁴⁹ Ibid., no. 98.
⁵⁰ Lorenzo Albacete, *God at the Ritz: Attraction to Infinity* (Crossroad. Publishing Company: 2007).
⁵¹ *TOB,* 80:1.
⁵² Genesis 2:24, NABRE.
⁵³ Pope John Paul II, *Redemptor Hominis,* (March 4, 1979), no. 10. https://vatican.va/content/john-paul-ii/en/encyclicals/documents/hf_jp-ii_enc_04031979_redemptor-hominis.html (last accessed March 30, 2022).
⁵⁴ Pope John Paul II, *Crossing the Threshold of Hope* (Knopf:1995).
⁵⁵ Luke 10:16, NABRE.
⁵⁶ Pope Benedict XVI, *Christmas Greetings to the Roman Curia*, (Libreria Editrice Vaticana, 2012).

# Chapter 7

¹ Pope Paul VI, Declaration *Inter Insignores,* (October 15, 1976), https://vatican.va/roman_curia/congregations/cfaith/documents/rc_con_cfaith_doc_19761015_inter-insigniores_en.html (last accessed March 30, 2022).
² Pope Paul II, Apostolic Letter *Ordinatio Sacerdotalis* (May 22, 1994), https://vatican.va/content/john-paul-ii/en/apost_letters/1994/documents/hf_jp-ii_apl_19940522_ordinatio-sacerdotalis.html (last accessed March 30, 2022).
³ Ibid.
⁴ George Kelly, *The Battle for the American Church* (Garden City New York: Image Books, 1981, © 1979).
⁵ Rosemary Radford Ruether, *Sexism and God-Talk-Toward a Feminist Theology*, (Boston: Beacon Press, 1983) 114.
⁶ Ibid.
⁷ Han Urs von Balthasar, "The Uninterrupted Tradition of the Church," *L'Osservatore Romano*, February 24, 977) 6.
⁸ Walter Ong. S.J., *Fighting for Life* (London: Cornell University Press, 1981) 77.
⁹ Ibid., 113; see also 65.
¹⁰ Ibid.
¹¹ Von Balthasar, 7.

[12] George Gilder, *Sexual Suicide* (Guadrangle/New York: Times Book Co., 1973) 16-20.

[13] Von Balthasar, 7.

[14] Ong, 62.

[15] Ibid., 98.

[16] Ibid., 174-175.

[17] Paul Quay, S.J., *The Christian Meaning of Human Sexuality*, (San Francisco: Ignatius Press, 1985), 26 and Stephen B. Clark, *Man and Woman in Christ* (Ann Arbor: Servant Press, 1980), 388.

[18] Ong, 175.

[19] Ibid.,175-176.

[20] Prudence Allen, *The Concept of Woman: The Aristotelian Revolution 750BC-AD 1250* (Eden Press: 1985), 89-92.

[21] Thomas Aquinas, *Summa Theologica* I, Q 28, a. 4, Edmund Hill, *Blackfriars*, Vol. 6 (New York: McGraw-Hill; London: Eyre and Spottoswoode, 1964), 37.

[22] Marie P. Brown, "The Fallacy of the Fempriest," *Homiletic and Pastoral Review* (October 1981) 20-21.

[23] Ong, 113.

[24] James C. Neely, *Gender: The Myth of Equality* (New York: Simon and Schuster: 1981), 52.

[25] Ibid.

[26] Ong, 113 and Margaret Mead, *Male and Female* (New York: Dell, 1949)104-105. Mead states:

> In every known human society, the male's need for achievement can be recognized. ... The recurrent problem of civilization is to define the male role satisfactorily enough---whether it be to build gardens or raise cattle, kill game or kill enemies, build bridges or handle bank-shares—so that the male in the course of his life reaches a solid sense of irreversible achievement, of which his childhood knowledge of the satisfactions of childbearing have given him a glimpse. In the case of women, it is only necessary that they be permitted by the given social arrangements to fulfill their biological role, to attain this sense of irreversible achievement. Mead's anthropological observations fully support the theological conclusions of Von Balthasar quoted earlier. A man must earn his masculinity by outward achievement while a woman rests in herself.

[27] Ruether, 114-115.

[28] Ibid., 208-209.

[29] *Christus Dominus (Decree on the Pastoral Office of Bishops in the Church)* 1, *Documents of Vatican II*, ed. by Austin Flannery, O.P. (Collegeville, MN: The Liturgical Press, 1975) 564.

³⁰ *Lumen Gentium* (The Dogmatic Constitution on the Church), no.18, *Documents of Vatican II*, ed. by Austin Flannery, O.P. (Collegeville, MN: The Liturgical Press, 1975), 370.
³¹ Ibid., no. 20, pp. 371-372.
³² Ibid., no. 28, p. 384.
³³ Ibid., no. 28, pp. 384-385.
³⁴ Henri de Lubac, *The Splendour of the Church* (Glen Rock, NJ: Paulist Press, 1956) 91-92.
³⁵ Archdiocese of Toronto, Canada, Emmet Cardinal Carter, *Do This in Memory of Me: Pastoral Letter on the Sacrament of the Priesthood* (December 8, 1983) 41.
³⁶ *Presbyterorum Ordinis* (Decree on the Ministry and Life of Priests), no. 2, *Documents of Vatican II*, ed. by Austin Flannery, O.P. (Collegeville, MN: The Liturgical Press, 1975), 864-865.
³⁷ Ibid., no. 12, p. 885.
³⁸ Ibid.
³⁹ Pierre Beniot, O.P., "The Accounts of the Institution and What They Imply," *The Eucharist in the New Testament* (Baltimore and Dublin: Helicon Press, 1965), 82.
⁴⁰ Stefan Cardinal Wyszyński, *Zapiski więzienne* (Paris: Éditions du Dialogue, 1982) 214.
⁴¹ Aristotle, *Nicomachean Ethics*, trans. Harris Rackham (New York: G. P. Putnam's sons, 1934) 1162a, http://perseus.tufts.edu/hopper/text.jsp?doc=Perseus%3Atext%3A1999.01.0054%3Abekker+page%3D1162a%3Abekker+line%3D1 (last accessed March 30, 2022).
⁴² See John Paul II, Apostolic Letter *Mulieris dignitatem* (August 15, 1988) no. 7, http://vatican.va/content/john-paul-ii/en/apost_letters/1988/documents/hf_jp-ii_apl_19880815_mulieris-dignitatem.html (last accessed March 30, 2022). The idea of radical independence causes that in gender feminism we are dealing with a general aversion to the vision of a human as a social being who needs others for leading a good life (see: Marguerite A. Peeters, *Le gender, une norme mondiale?* (Paris: MAME, 2013), 51).
⁴³ Saint Catherine of Siena, *The Dialogue of the Seraphic Virgin Catherine of Siena*, trans. Algar Thorold (London: Kegan Paul, Trench, Trubner and Co. Ltd., 1907) 22, http://ntslibrary.com/PDF%20Books/Dialogue-of-St-Catherine.pdf (last accessed March 30, 2022).
⁴⁴ *Mulieris dignitatem*, no. 7.
⁴⁵ Ibid; See Pope John Paul II, *Letter to Women* (June 29, 1995), no. 7, http://vatican.va/content/john-paul-ii/en/letters/1995/documents/hf_jp-ii_let_29061995_women.html (last accessed March 30, 2022).

⁴⁶ Pope John Paul II, *General Audience* (November 21, 1979), no. 1, http://vatican.va/content/john-paul-ii/en/audiences/1979/documents/hf_jp-ii_aud_19791121.html (last accessed March 30, 2022).
⁴⁷ Ibid.
⁴⁸ See Yves Semen, *La préparation au mariage selon Jean-Paul II et la théologie du corps* (Paris: Presses de la Renaissance, 2013), 114.
⁴⁹ *Mulieris dignitatem*, no. 7.
⁵⁰ Pontifical Council for Justice and Peace, *Compendium of the Social Doctrine of the Church*, 2004, no. 147, http://vatican.va/roman_curia/pontifical_councils/justpeace/documents/rc_pc_justpeace_doc_20060526_compendio-dott-soc_en.html (last accessed March 2022).
⁵¹ Second Vatican Council, *Pastoral Constitution on the Church in the Modern World, Gaudium et spes*, 1965, n. 24, https://vatican.va/archive/hist_councils/ii_vatican_council/documents/vat-ii_cons_19651207_gaudium-et-spes_en.html (last accessed March 30, 2022); John Paul II always spoke not about "sincere", but about "selfless" gift of himself.
⁵² See Mary Geach, "Marriage: Arguing to a First Principle in Sexual Ethics." in *Moral Truth and Moral Tradition*, edited by Luke Gormally, (Portland: Four Courts Press, 1994), 178; Jacques Ellul, *Histoire des institutions, Tome 1-2, L'Antiquité* (Paris: Presses Universitaires de France, 1992), 578; "All experts in Roman law – writes Régine Pernoud – "point to the so-called "unnatural disappearance of younger sisters". Indeed, while the father was obligated to keep the male newborns alive (apart from the handicapped and too frail) for the sake of the army, he generally left only one daughter alive, the eldest one; a mention of a Roman family having two daughters is among the exceptions. (…) Only at the end of the 4th century, around the year 390, will civil legislation deprive the father of this right to decide about the life and death of his children. With the spread of the Gospel, the first and most decisive argument for gender-based discrimination disappeared: girls were given the right to life on an equal footing with boys" (Régine Pernoud, *Kobieta w czasach katedr* (*Woman in the Times of the Cathedrals*) (Warszawa: Książnica, 1990), 21–26). The 2012 report entitled "Gendercide: the Missing Women?" developed by the European Parliament, shows that this problem does not belong to the past in places, where there is no reference to Christian anthropology (see: European Parliament. *Report on Gendercide: the Missing Women?*, 2012/2273(INI), https://europarl.europa.eu/doceo/document/A-7-2013-0245_EN.html (last accessed March 30, 2022). See also Adam Jones, "Gendercide: Examining Gender-based Crimes against Women and Men", *Clinics in Dermatology*, Vol. 31, Issue 2, March-April 2013, 226-229.
⁵³ In Plato, we find two mutually contradictory visions of the relationship between a man and a woman. The first humans, according to

*Timaeus*, were creatures of only one sex. The appearance of women was a result of degradation of some of the souls, originally inhabiting male bodies. Men, who "proved themselves cowardly and spent their lives in wrong-doing were transformed" in the second coming into the world (Plato, *Timaeus,* trans. Robert Gregg Bury (Cambridge, Mass: Harvard University Press, 1929), 90e, http://perseus.tufts.edu/hopper/text?doc=Perseus%3Atext%3A1999.01.0180%3Atext%3DTim.%3Apage%3D90 (last accessed March 30, 2022); See Ibid: 42c, http://perseus.tufts.edu/hopper/text?doc=Perseus%3Atext%3A1999.01.0180%3Atext%3DTim.%3Apage%3D42 (last accessed March 2022)). Hence the "natural" inferiority of women in relation to men. However, in *The Republic* Plato states that, "…many women are in many things superior to many men, (…) And if so (…) there is no special faculty of administration in a state which a woman has because she is a woman, or which a man has by virtue of his sex, but the gifts of nature are alike diffused in both; all the pursuits of men are the pursuits of women also, but in all of them a woman is inferior to a man" (Ibid., *The Republic*, edited by Paul Shorey (Cambridge, Mass: Harvard University Press, 1935), 455d-e, https://faculty.mtsac.edu/cmcgruder/cmcgruder/sabbatical_aesthetics/republic.pdf (last accessed March 30, 2022)). It is worth remembering, however, that the consequence of the recognition that, apart from physical strength, there is no difference between a woman and a man, is the liquidation of the institution of marriage and the family, the common property of women (there is no common property of men!) and eugenics policy. Due to a false draw, sexual intercourse takes place in accordance with the principles of eugenics: "the principle has been already laid down that the best of either sex should be united with the best as often, and the inferior with the inferior, as seldom as possible; and that they should rear the offspring of the one sort of union, but not of the other, if the flock is to be maintained in first-rate condition. Now these goings on must be a secret which the rulers only know, or there will be a further danger of our herd, as the guardians may be termed, breaking out into rebellion" (Ibid., 459e-460a, https://faculty.mtsac.edu/cmcgruder/cmcgruder/sabbatical_ aesthetics/republic.pdf (last accessed March 30, 2022)). Children, deprived of the possibility of knowing their biological origin, are taken over by the state for upbringing. It seems no coincidence that this model of the state was considered by Karl Popper to be the prototype of a totalitarian system (even though this statement is completely a-historical). In Plato, therefore, we have "two anthropologies" with all the consequences of the fact: the theory of sex polarity in *Timaeus* and the theory of sex unity in *The Republic*. (See Prudence Allen, *The Concept of Woman. Aristotelian Revolution, 750 BC – AD 1250* (Grand Rapids, Michigan: William B. Eerdmans Publishing, 1997), 57–63). According to

Aristotle, a woman is an incompletely formed man. She is as if an "infertile male" (Aristotle, *On the Generation of Animals*, trans. Arthur Platt, 1912, 728a, https://archive.org/stream/generationofanim00arisuoft/generationof-anim00arisuoft_djvu.txt (last accessed March 30, 2022)), a male lacking certain parts (Ibid., 737a), and the "female state" is a "deformity, though one which occurs in the ordinary course of nature." (Ibid., 775a, https://archive.org/stream/generationofanim00arisuoft/generationofanim00arisuoft_djvu.txt (last accessed March 30, 2022). According to Aristotle, women's inferiority is based on a relationship with reason that differs from that of men. Due to this criterion, he places women somewhat between a man, and a child and a slave. "For the free rules the slave, the male the female, and the man the child in a different way. (...) [F]or the slave has not got the deliberative part at all, and the female has it, but without full authority, while the child has it, but in an undeveloped form" (Aristotle, *Politics*, trans. Harris Rackham (Cambridge, Mass: Harvard University Press, 1944), 1260a, http://perseus.tufts.edu/ hopper/ text?doc=Perseus%3Atext%3A1999.01.0058%3Abook%3D1%3Asection %3D1260a (last accessed March 30, 2022). A woman, lacking the ability to fully control her emotions, as a rule, is not capable of acting in accordance with the virtue of practical wisdom (see: Fred D. Miller, "Naturalism." in *The Cambridge History of Greek and Roman Political Thought*, edited by Christopher Rowe and Malcolm Schofield (Cambridge: Cambridge University Press, 2000), 338). In order to ensure the rationality of a woman's actions, she should be guided by a man. "(...) for the male is by nature better fitted to command than the female (except in some cases where their union has been formed contrary to nature) and the older and fully developed person than the younger and immature" (Aristotle, *Politics*, 1259a–b, http://perseus.tufts.edu/hopper/ text?doc=Perseus%3Atext% 3A1999.01.0058%3Abook%3D1%3Asection%3D1259b__(last accessed March 30, 2022)). Wives and children should be ruled in the same way as the free men are ruled over. "The relation of husband to wife seems to be in the nature of an aristocracy: the husband rules in virtue of fitness, and in matters that belong to a man's sphere; matters suited to a woman he hands over to his wife." (Aristotle. *Nicomachean Ethics*, 1160b, http://perseus.tufts.edu/hopper/text?doc=Perseus%3Atext%3A1999.01. 0054%3Abekker%20page%3D1160b%3Abekker%20line%3D20) (last accessed March 30, 2022)) "(T)he friendship of man and wife is one of utility, a partnership" (Ibid., *Ethica Eudemia*, trans. Harris Rackham (Cambridge, Mass: Harvard University Press, 1935), 1242a, http://perseus.tufts.edu/hopper/text?doc=Perseus%3Atext%3A1999.

01.0050%3Abook%3D7%3Asection%3D1242a) (last accessed March 30, 2022)).

Women, who "are a half of the free population" (id. *Politics*, 1260b, http://perseus.tufts.edu/hopper/text?doc=Perseus%3Atext%3A1999.01.0058%3Abook%3D1%3Asection%3D1260b), should – like men – excercise virtue. "The object of both the individual and of the community should be to secure the existence of each of these qualities in both men and women; for all those States in which the character of women is unsatisfactory, as in Lacedaemon (http://www.perseus.tufts.edu/hopper/entityvote?doc=Perseus:text:1999.01.0060:bekker%20page=1361a&auth=tgn,7011065&n=1&type=place), may be considered only half-happy." (Ibid., *Rhetoric*, trans. John Henry Freese (London: W. Heinemann, 1926), 1361a, http://perseus.tufts.edu/hopper/text?doc=Perseus%3Atext%3A1999.01.0060%3Abekker+page%3D1361a (last accessed March 30, 2022)). Women, however, are granted a subordinate form of virtues, and the proper area of their activity is the household rather than political life. This is one of the reasons why Aristotle opposed the common ownership of women among the ruling elites. "But again, if Socrates intends to make the Farmers have their wives in common but their property private, who is to manage the household in the way in which the women's husbands will carry on the work of the farms?" (Ibid ; *Politics*, 1264b, http://perseus.tufts.edu/hopper/text?doc=Perseus%3Atext%3A1999.01.0058%3Abook%3D2%3Asection%3D1264b (last accessed March 30, 2022)). The second reason is of a much more fundamental nature. Eric Voegelin, in his commentary on Aristotle, notes that, according to the Stagirite, *polis* is a network of diversified relations of friendship. "When the normal relations between men and women, parents and children, are interrupted through a communal organization of sex relations, then the human qualities that ordinarily are invested in such relations have no range of actualization. The concreteness of personal relations will disappear and the very substance of community life will evaporate" (Eric Voegelin, *The Collected Works of Eric Voegelin*, Volume 16 *Order and History* – Vol. III *Plato and Aristotle*, edited by Dante Germino (Columbia and London: University of Missouri Press, 2000), 375-376; https://portalconservador.com/livros/Eric-Voegelin-Order-and-History-Vol.III.pdf (last accessed March 30, 2022). "For there are two things that most cause men to care for and to love each other, the sense of ownership and the sense of preciousness; and neither motive can be present with the citizens of a state so constituted" (Aristotle, *Politics*, 1262b, http://perseus.tufts.edu/hopper/text?doc=Perseus%3Atext%3A1999.01.0058%3Abook%3D2%3Asection%3D1262b) (last accessed March 30, 2022)).The Stagirite presents the emotional nature of women as follows: "Wherefore women are more compassionate and more readily made to weep, more jealous and querulous, more fond of railing, and more contentious. The female also is more subject to depression of spirits and despair than the male. She is also more shameless and false, more readily deceived, and more mindful of injury, more watchful, more idle, and on the whole less excitable than the male" (Aristotle, *History of Animals*, trans. Richard Cresswell (London: George Bell & Sons, 1887), 608b, http://gutenberg.org/files/59058/59058-h/59058-h.htm (last accessed March 30, 2022). For this reason, also in tragedies, a woman may appear as a noble person, but it is not appropriate for her to play the role of an overly valiant or learned person. (See Ibid., *Poetics*, trans. William Rhys Roberts (London: W. Heinemann, 1927), 1454a, http://perseus.tufts.edu/hopper/text?doc=Perseus%3Atext%3A1999.01.0056%3Asection%3D1454a (last accessed March 30, 2022)). The dissemination of Aristotelianism in the Middle Ages was to cause – according to Prudence Allen – an unfavourable change in the perception of women (*defective man*) and, consequently, the exclusion of women from the group of students of the University of Paris in 1231. It did not come to be without the fault of the university reformer, Queen Blanche of Castile. Women, however, could still study at universities in the South of Europe (see: Prudence Allen, *The Concept of Woman*, 416-417 and 443). In Poland on the other hand, in 1400, it was a woman, Queen St. Jadwiga (Hedvig), who renewed the Kraków Academy. Jean Bethke Elshtain argues that the influence of the Stagirite on Western culture was so serious that even American suffragettes fighting for the right to vote still unconsciously viewed themselves, as well as politics as such, through the lens of Aristotelian patterns (see: Jean Bethke Elshtain, "Moral Woman and Immoral Man: Consideration of the Public – Private Split and its Political Ramifications." in *Contemporary Political Philosophy. An Anthology*, edited by Robert E. Goodin and Philip Pettit (Oxford: Blackwell Publishers, 1997), 605-617).

[54] St. Paul writes, "For all of you who were baptized into Christ have clothed yourselves with Christ. There is neither Jew nor Gentile, neither slave nor free, nor is there male and female, for you are all one in Christ Jesus" (*Galatians*, 3:27-28). Reconciling the idea of unquestionable equality in dignity with the different roles in the family and in social life was a real challenge for Christians, including an intellectual one, an example of which was left by St. Augustine. In *De diversis questionibus octoginta tribus*, he places women on the same side as children. "(...) not only are the Old Testament people to be compared to women and children, but also the New Testament people who do not endure to the attaining of perfect manhood due to either lack of strength or fickleness of mind" (*mulieribus et pueris comparandi sunt*) (Saint Augustine, *Eighty-three Different Questions* (Washington:

54(cont.) Catholic University of America Press, 2002), 122). The reasons for putting the women and children on the same side of the stage are different. Children's imperfection consists of a tendency to make mistakes and love of playing. Female imperfection is weakness in acting (*infirmitas*) and lack of perseverance (*privatione perseverantiae*) (ibid.). Augustine also states that, "(...) mankind's deliverance had to be evidenced among both sexes. Therfore, since it was needful to become a man, which is the more honorable sex [*qui sexus honorabilior est*], it reasonably followed that the deliverance of the female sex be seen by that man's birth from a woman" (ibid, p. 42). In *De Trinitate*, however, he poses a rhetorical question: "(...) by putting on the new man, [we] certainly put on Christ through faith. Who is there, then, who will hold women to be alien from this fellowship, whereas they are fellow-heirs of grace with us?" (Saint Augustine, "On the Trinity", XII, VII, 12, in Saint Augustine. *The Doctrinal Treateses*, trans. Arthur West Haddan, et al. (Altenmünster: Jazzbee Verlag - Jurgen Beck, 2017), 165). Then he also wonders whether a woman loses her bodily sex through baptism. Ultimately, he concludes that the equality and identity described by St. Paul is about reason and its ability to study spiritual matters. "But because they are there renewed after the image of God, where there is no sex; man is there made after the image of God, where there is no sex, that is, in the spirit of his mind. (...) so that the image of God may remain on that side of the mind of man on which it cleaves to the beholding and consulting of the eternal reasons of things; and this, it is clear, not men only, but also women have" (ibid., 165).

55 In Genesis, a woman is called a "suitable helper" (Hebr. *ezer kenegdo*) twice (*Gen.*, 2:18-20). Numerous commentaries underline that, altogether, *ezer* is used 21 times in the Old Testament: in addition to the above reference to woman, it is used 3 times in relation to nations, from which Israel expected help, and 16 times referring to God as the helper of Israel (e.g. *Deuteronomy* 33:29; *Psalm* 10:14; *Psalm* 30:10; *Psalm* 54:4; *Psalm* 70:5; *Psalm* 72:12; *Psalm* 121:2). In neither of these texts does it refer to someone who is of inferior status or subordinated. *Kenegdo* literally means "suitable" or "face to face". So, the entire phrase indicates the planned equality and harmony in the relations between a man and a woman.

56 *Mulieris dignitatem*, no. 10. It is worth quoting a passage on this subject from the 11th century treatise on *Spiritual Friendship*: "Indeed divine power fashioned this helper not from similar or even from the same material. But as a more specific motivation for charity and friendship, this power created a woman from the very substance of the man. In a beautiful way, then, from the side of the first human a second was produced, so that nature might teach that all are equal or, as it were, collateral, and that among human beings – and this is a property of friendship there exists neither

superior nor inferior" (Aelred of Rievaulx, *Spiritual Friendship*, I, 57, trans. Lawrence C. Braceland SJ, (Collegeville, MN: Cistercian Publications. Liturgical Press, 2010), 66).

[57] Pope John Paul II, Apostolic Exhortation *Vita Consecrata* (March 25, 1996), no. 57, http://vatican.va/content/john-paul-ii/en/apost_exhortations/documents/hf_jp-ii_exh_25031996_vita-consecrata.html (last accessed March 30, 2022).

[58] *Mulieris dignitatem*, n. 7.

[59] Pope John Paul II, Apostolic Exhortation *Pastores dabo vobis*, (March 25, 1992), no. 43, http://vatican.va/content/john-paul-ii/en/apost_exhortations/documents/hf_jp-ii_exh_25031992_pastores-dabo-vobis.html (last accessed March 30, 2022).

[60] *Mulieris dignitatem*, no. 7.

[61] *Letter to Priests,* no. 2.

[62] *Pastores dabo vobis*, no. 44.

[63] Ibid., no. 44.

[64] Ibid.

[65] *Letter to Priests,* no. 2.

[66] Ibid., no. 5.

[67] Ibid., no. 1.

[68] Ibid., no. 1.

[69] Stefan Cardinal Wyszyński, *Kobieta w Polsce współczesnej (A Woman in Contemporary Poland)* (Poznań-Warsaw: Wydawnictwo Pallottinum, 1978), 15.

[70] See Pope John Paul II, Encyclical Letter *Redemptoris Mater* (March 25, 1987) no. 20-24, http://vatican.va/content/john-paul-ii/en/encyclicals/documents/hf_jp-ii_enc_25031987_redemptoris-mater.html (last accessed March 30, 2022).

[71] *Letter to Priests*, no. 4.

[72] Ibid.

[73] Ibid.

[74] Ibid.

[75] *Redemptoris Mater*, no. 20.

[76] μὴ οὐκ ἔχομεν ἐξουσίαν ἀδελφὴν γυναῖκα περιάγειν, ὡς καὶ οἱ λοιποὶ ἀπόστολοι καὶ οἱ ἀδελφοὶ τοῦ κυρίου καὶ Κηφᾶς. A correct translation of this phrase poses some difficulties. Sometimes it is believed that it relates to believing women helping the apostles, and other times that – because we know that St. Peter was married – to believing it is about wives of the apostles. Certainly, the word "ἀδελφὴν" ("sister") means here that it is about a woman – a Christian.

[77] *Letter to Priests*, no. 4.

78 Ibid. no. 5.
79 Ibid.
80 Ibid.
81 Ibid.
82 Agata Rusak, "Bez niejasności w relacjach" (Without ambiguity in relations), *Pastores* 86 (1) 2020, 71.
83 Antoine de Saint-Exupéry, *The Little Prince* (New York: Hartcourt, 2000), 64.
84 *Letter to Priests*, no. 5.
85 Ibid.
86 Saint Augustine, *The Confessions*, X, 29, trans. E. B. Pusey (Edward Bouverie), release Date: June, 2002 [EBook #3296]; The actual date this file first posted: March 209, 2001; last updated: May 16, 2013, https://gutenberg.org/files/3296/3296-h/3296-h.htm (last accessed March 30, 2022).
87 See Raniero Cantalamessa, *Czystego serca* (Warszawa: Wydawnictwo Sióstr Loretanek, 2008), 56 (Italian original: *Verginità* Milan: Editrice Ancora, 1988).
88 Saint Teresa of Avila, *The Book of Life*, 1904, XXXVII. 4-5, https://ccel.org/ccel/teresa/life.viii.xxxviii.html (last accessed March 30, 2022).
89 *Letter to Priests*, no. 8.
90 Ibid., no. 2.
91 *Redemptoris Mater*, no. 20.
92 Second Vatican Council, *Dogmatic Constitution on the Church, Lumen gentium*, (November 21, 1964), no. 61, http://vatican.va/archive/hist_councils/ii_vatican_council/documents/vat-ii_const_19641121_lumen-gentium_en.html (last accessed March 30, 2022).
93 Ibid., no. 61.
94 Ibid., no. 53-54.
95 John Paul II, Encyclical Letter *Ecclesia de Eucharistia*, (April 17, 2003) no. 55, http://vatican.va/holy_father/special_features/encyclicals/documents/hf_jp-ii_enc_20030417_ecclesia_eucharistia_en.html (last accessed March 30, 2022).

96 Ibid., no. 55.
97 See *Letter to Priests,* no. 3.
98 Ibid., no. 3.
99 *Ecclesia de Eucharistia*, no. 56.
100 *Letter to Priests*, no. 3.

¹⁰¹ Clive S. Lewis, *Four Loves* (London: Geoffrey Bles, 1960), 98, https://archive.org/details/the-four-loves/page/n1/mode/2up?q=first+half (last accessed March 30, 2022).

¹⁰² Wanda Półtawska, *Beskidzkie rekolekcje. Dzieje przyjaźni księdza Karola Wojtyły z rodziną Półtawskich (Beskid Mountains recollections. The history of Father Karol Wojtyła's friendship with the Półtawski family)* (Częstochowa: Edycja Świętego Pawła, 2009), 387. Dr. Wanda Półtawska, a former prisoner of the German concentration camp in Ravensbrück, together with her husband, Andrzej, a professor of philosophy, were among the closest friends of Card. Wojtyła in Cracow.

¹⁰³ *Redemptor hominis*, no. 10.

# Chapter 8

¹ Gift, 53.

² Janet Smith, as quoted in *Sex and the Spiritual Life: Reclaiming Integrity, Wholeness and Intimacy*, ed. Patricia Cooney Hathaway (Notre Dame, Indiana: Ave Maria Press, 2020), 3.

³James Zullo, "Educating Seminarians for Healthy Sexuality." *Seminary Journal*, no. 2(Fall 1995): 31.

⁴Congregation for the Clergy, "The Gift of the Priestly Vocation: *Ratio Fundamentalis Institutionis Sacerdotalis*," L'Osservatore Romano, Vatican City, 8 December 2016. In this chapter, I will be referring to this document in two ways: The Gift of the Priestly Vocation, and the *Ratio Fundamentalis*, as the two terms are interchangeable. In my footnotes, my short reference to this document will be Gift, followed by section number.

⁵ Ronald Rolheiser, OMI, *The Holy Longing. The Search for a Christian Spirituality* (Holy Longing), (New York: Image, 2009), 31.

⁶ CCC, 2337; See also Congregation for Catholic Education, *Male and Female He Created Them: Towards a Path of Dialogue on the Question of Gender Theory in Education* (Vatican City, 2019), http://educatio.va/content/dam/cec/Documenti/19_0997_INGLESE.pdf (last accessed March 30, 2022).

⁷A negative view of Christian Spirituality was influenced by such heresies as Neo-Platonism, Manicheism, Gnosticism, see *Holy Longing*, 195.

⁸ Pontifical Council for the Family, *The Truth and Meaning of Sexuality; Guidelines for Education within the Family*, (December 8, 1995), no. 10, https://vatican.va/roman_curia/pontifical_councils/family/documents/rc_pc_family_doc_08121995_human-sexuality_en.html (last accessed March 30, 2022).

⁹ James Nelson. *Intimate Connection: Male Sexuality, Masculine Spirituality* (Philadelphia: Westminster Press, 1988), 26.

¹⁰ John Paul II, *The Theology of the Body: Human Love in the Divine Plan* (St. Louis, MO: Pauline Books, 1997), 88-89.

¹¹ Pope John Paul II's *Theology of the Body* was presented in a series of weekly addresses between 1979 and 1984. These addresses have been collected and published as *The Theology of the Body: Human Love in the Divine Plan* (St. Louis, MO: Pauline Books, 1997).

¹² Pope Benedict XVI, Encyclical *Deus Caritas Est* (God is Love), (December 25, 2005), https://vatican.va/content/benedict-xvi/en/encyclicals/documents/hf_ben-xvi_enc_20051225_deus-caritas-est.html (last accessed March 30, 2022).

¹³ Gift, 1- 2.
¹⁴ Ibid., 2.
¹⁵ Ibid., 35.
¹⁶Ibid., 40.
¹⁷Ibid., 59.
¹⁸ Ibid., 63.
¹⁹ Ibid., 69.
²⁰ Ibid., 74.
²¹ Ibid., 3.

²² Pope John Paul II, Apostolic Exhortation *Pastores Dabo Vobis* (March 15, 1992), https://vatican.va/content/john-paul-ii/en/apost_exhortations/documents/hf_jp-ii_exh_25031992_pastores-dabo-vobis.html (last accessed March 30 2022).

²³ Gift, 93.
²⁴ Ibid., 94.
²⁵ Gift, 110.
²⁶ Ibid.
²⁷ Ibid., 116.
²⁸ Gift, 120.
²⁹ Ibid., 122.
³⁰ Ibid., 3.

³¹ Each conference of bishops has to create a local*Ratio Nationalis*, which is the application of the overarching document, *Ratio Fundamentalis*, created in 2016. The two programs I outline are examples of how formation personal created a new *Ratio Nationalis* for the United States context.

³² Gift, 7.

³³ Sacred Heart Major Seminary is a Catholic Seminary in Detroit, Michigan associated with the Archdiocese of Detroit. For additional information on priestly formation within the diocese, see the website of

Sacred Heart Major Seminary at https://shms.edu/priestlyformation (last accessed March 30, 3022).

34 The Institute for Priestly Formation (IPF) was founded to assist Bishops in the spiritual formation of diocesan seminarians and priests in the Roman Catholic Church. For additional information on IPF programs, see also the website of Creighton University, creighton.edu (last accessed March 30, 2022).

35 Benedict J. Groeschel, CFR, *Spiritual Passages: The Psychology of Spiritual Development* (New York: Crossroad, 2007), 30- 40.

36 Ibid, 41- 43.

37 Ibid., 40.

38 Gift, 28.

39 Janet Ruffing, *Spiritual Direction: Beyond the Beginnings* (New York: Paulist Press, 2000), 59- 60.

40 See Ana Maria Rizzuto, M.D., *The Birth of the Living God: A Psychoanalytic Study* (Chicago: Chicago University Press, 1979), 3-11.

41 Gift, 94.

42 See the website of Sacred Heart Major Seminary on Priestly Formation, shms.edu/priestlyformation (last accessed March 30, 2022).

43 Gift, 24.

44 Gift, 151.

45 Gift, 95.

46 *Pastores Dabo Vobis*, no. 43.

47 Gift, 192.

48 United States Conference of Catholic Bishops (USCCB) approved the fifth edition of the *Program of Priestly Formation*, June 16, 2005. This document stands as the *Ratio Fundamentalis Institutionis* for the formation of priests in Catholic seminaries in the United States, 77.

49 Program for Priestly Formation, 76.

50 Todd Lajiness, "Sacred Heart Rector Part of Working Group Setting Safe Environment Benchmarks for Seminaries," *Mosaic Online Magazine*, November 9, 2020, https://mosaic.shms.edu/sacred-heart-rector-part-of-working-group-setting-safe-environment-benchmarks-for-seminaries (last accessed March 30, 2022).

51 For additional information on the Dallas Charter and what it seeks to accomplish, see the USCCB website: https://usccb.org/offices/child-and-youth-protection/charter-protection-children-and-young-people (last accessed March 30, 2022).

52 ShashaKleinsorge, Therese Cirner, and Karen Klein Villa, "Clergy SexAbuse: Why Do We Still Need to Talk About This?" *Homiletic & PastoralReview* (January 14, 2021), 1-12.https://hprweb.com/2021/01/

clergy-sex-abuse-why-do-we-still-need-to-talk-about-this/ (last accessed March 30, 2022).

[53] Pope John Paul II, Apostolic Letter *Mulieris Dignitatem*, (On the Dignity and Vocation of Women), (August 15, 1988), no. 6, https://vatican.va/content/john-paul-ii/en/apost_letters/1988/documents/hf_jp-ii_apl_19880815_mulieris-dignitatem.html (last accessed March 30, 2022); See also, *CCC*, 369.

[54] Congregation for Education, *"Male and Female He Created Them": Towards a Path of Dialogue on the Question of Gender Theory in Education* (2019), no. 12.

[55] 175-page report to the Christian Reformed Church (CRC) Synod 2021 from the *Committee to Articulate a Foundation-Laying Biblical Theology of Human Sexuality*, 75. My article review of this Report is published in *Homiletic & Pastoral Review*, December 23, 2020, "Male and Female He Created Them: Ecumenical Reflections."
Online: https://hprweb.com/2020/12/male-and-female-he-created-them-ecumenical-reflections/ (last accessed March 30, 20220.

[56] On gender ideology, see *"Male and Female He Created Them": Towards a Path of Dialogue on the Question of Gender Theory in Education,* Congregation for Catholic Education, (Vatican City, 2019), https://hprweb.com/2020/12/male-and-female-he-created-them-ecumenical-reflections/ (last accessed March 30, 2022).

[57] In John Paul II's 1993 Encyclical *Veritatis Splendor*, (August 6, 1993), nos. 48-49, http://vatican.va/content/john-paul-ii/en/encyclicals/documents/hf_jp-ii_enc_06081993_veritatis-splendor.html (last accessed March 30, 2022), wherein he underscores "the Church's teachings *on the unity of the human person,* whose rational soul is *per se et essentialiter* the form of his body. . . . The spiritual and immortal soul is the principle of unity of the human being, whereby it exists as a whole — *corpore et anima unus*—as a person. . . . *The person, including the body, is completely entrusted to himself, and it is in the unity of body and soul that the person is the subject of his own moral act. . . A doctrine which dissociates the moral act from the bodily dimensions of its exercise is contrary to the teaching of Scripture and Tradition".*

[58] *Man and Woman He Created Them: A Theology of the Body*, trans. Michael Waldstein (Boston: Pauline Media, 2006 [1986]). Subsequent references to this work will be cited parenthetically in the text, *MWTB.*

[59] Pope Francis counters the "autonomous will," particularly in respect of "an ideology of gender 'that denies the difference and reciprocity in nature of a man and a woman and envisages a society without sexual differences, thereby eliminating the anthropological basis of the family', by stressing that "We are creatures, and not omnipotent. Creation is prior to us and must be received as a gift" (*Amoris Laetitia* §56). Elsewhere, he adds,

"Learning to accept our body, to care for it and to respect its fullest meaning, is an essential element of any genuine human ecology. Also, valuing one's own body in its femininity or masculinity is necessary if I am going to be able to recognize myself in an encounter with someone who is different.... It is not a healthy attitude which would seek 'to cancel out sexual difference because it no longer knows how to confront it'" (*Laudato Si'* §155).

[60] Pope John Paul II, *Memory & Identity: Conversations at the Dawn of a Millennium* (New York: Rizzoli, 2005), 110.

[61] Ibid., 114.

[62] Portions of this section are from my book, *"In the Beginning . . ." A Theology of the Body* (Eugene, OR: Pickwick Publications, 2010), 228- 29, 234-35.

# Chapter 9

[1] Cf. Pope John Paul II, *Homily at Saint Charles Borromeo Seminary*, Philadelphia, Pennsylvania, discussed in Tom Cooney, "The Last Papal Visit to Philadelphia: John Paul II in 1979," *The Philadelphia Inquirer*, July 25, 2014. https://inquirer.com/philly/news/pope/The_last_papal_visit_to_Philadelphia_John_Paul_II_in_1979.html. See Video of homily, https://youtu.be/5mHv284D3Pk (last accessed March 30, 2020).

[2] Congregation for the Clergy. *Ratio Fundamentalis. The Gift of the Priestly Vocation*. 2017. No. 206.

[3] Pope Francis, *Address to the Plenary of the Congregation for Clergy* (3 October 2014): *L'Osservatore Romano*, 226 (4 October 2014), 8.

[4] Peter Kleponis, Review of the 2015 edition of the *Guidelines for the Use of Psychology in Seminary Admissions* issued by the United States Conference of Catholic Bishops, Committee on Clergy, Consecrated Life and Vocations, Washington, D.C.: the Linacre. Volume 83. May 2016. pp 217-222.

[5] Kleponis, Review of the 2015 edition of the *Guidelines for the Use of Psychology in Seminary Admissions*.

[6] Frederick Miller, "The Charism of Priestly Celibacy," *Homiletic & Pastoral Review*, March 20, 2020, https://hprweb.com/2020/03/the-charism-of-priestly-celibacy/ (last accessed March 20, 2022).

[7] Eilers, Brian, Video Interview, *Human Dimension of Formation*, St. Mary's Seminary, Director of Formation, https://smseminary.org/human-formation (last accessed March 30, 2020), citing *Pastores Dabo Vobis* no. 43.

[8] Miller, "The Charism of Priestly Celibacy".

[9] Ibid.

¹⁰ Ibid.
¹¹ Ibid.
¹² United States Conference of Catholic Bishops, *Program of Priestly Formation,* Sixth Edition (2022). Hereafter cited as PPF.
¹³ PPF, no. 183e.
¹⁴ Mark Pattison, Mark. "Bishops OK New Edition of Program of Priestly Formation," November 13, 2019, http://iobserve.org/2019/11/13/bishops-ok-new-edition-of-program-of-priestly-formation/ (last accessed March 30, 2022).
¹⁵ Pope John Paul II, Apostolic Exhortation *Pastores dabo vobis,* On the Formation of Priests in the Circumstances of the Present Day, https://vatican.va/content/john-paul-ii/en/apost_exhortations/documents/hf_jp-ii_exh_25031992_pastores-dabo-vobis.html (last accessed March 30, 2022), no. 44.
¹⁶ PPF, no. 20, b-e.
¹⁷ Ibid., no. 20d.
¹⁸ Ibid., no. 21j.
¹⁹ PPF, no. 215.
²⁰ Szablewski, Andrzej, p.s.s. *Human Formation and Fraternity* (September 26, 2010) https://sulpc.org/wp-content/uploads/2020/09/Human_Formation_and_Fraternity.pdf (accessed February 20, 2022).
²¹ Ibid., Cf. *Pastores dabo vobis,* n. 23.
²² Szablewski, Andrzej. *Human Maturity and Relationships in Priestly Formation Today.* https://sulpc.org/wp-content/uploads/2020/09/Human_maturityrelationships.pdf (accessed February 20, 2022).
²³ Ibid.
²⁴ Ibid.
²⁵ Ibid.
²⁶ Ibid.
²⁷ Ibid..
²⁸ Ibid.; cf. *Pastores Dabo Vobis,* 44.
²⁹ Ibid.
³⁰ Pope John Paul II, *Pastores dabo vobis,* no. 44.
³¹ Szablewski, *Human Maturity and Relationships.*
³² Gordon, Bernard L. *St Thomas Aquinas on Affectivity: A Way Forward for Seminary Formation.* Dissertation. December 2019. https://researchonline.nd.edu.au/theses/242/, p. 20 (accessed September 10, 2022).
³³ Second Vatican Council, Decree *Presbyterorum ordinis* (On the Ministry and Life of Priests), December 7, 1965, https://vatican.va/archive/hist_councils/ii_vatican_council/documents/vat-

ii_decree_19651207_presbyterorum-ordinis_en.html (accessed March 30, 2020).

34 Sacred Congregation for the Doctrine of the Faith, Declaration *Persona humana* (On Certain Questions Concerning Sexual Ethics), December 29, 1975, no. 1, https://vatican.va/roman_curia/congregations/cfaith/documents/rc_con_cfaith_doc_19751229_persona-humana_en.html (accessed March 30, 2022).

35 Pope John Paul II, *Pastores dabo vobis,* no. 44.

36 Cf. Kevin P. McClone, "Intimacy and Healthy Affective Maturity Guidelines for Formation, Intimacy and Healthy Affective Maturity Guidelines for Formation," *Human Development*, Vol. 30, No. 4, Winter 2009, 5-6 https://drmcclone.com/wp-content/uploads/2020/05/McClone-Human-Development-2009-Intimacy-and-Healthy-Affective-Maturity-Guidelines-for-Formation.pdf (accessed March 30, 2022).

37 Ibid., 6.

38 Ibid.

39 Ibid.

40 Cf. Gordon, *St Thomas Aquinas on Affectivity*, 3.

41 Ibid.

42 Ibid.

43 Ibid., 244-245: "St Thomas reasons that just as we are directed to human happiness by certain virtues and their appropriate acts, we also need virtues that help us to attain our supernatural beatitude. The logic of Christ as the Shepherd of the People of God requires the seminarian to exercise the cardinal and theological virtues."

44 Charles Russell, *Men of Communion: A Theoretical, Inter-disciplinary Study and Attachment in Roman Catholic Seminarians* (Dissertation: Arlington, VA: Institute for Psychological Studies, 2017).

45 Russell, *Men of Communion*, 39.

46 Pope John Paul II, *Pastores dabo vobis*, no. 43.

47 Russel, *Men of Communion*, 17.

48 Karol Wojtyla, *Love and Responsibility* (San Francisco: Ignatius Press, 1983), the Polish-language original *Miłość i Odpowiedzialność*, of which the English title is an exact rendering, first appeared in 1960.

49 Russell, "Men of Communion," 18- 19.

50 Pope John Paul II, *Pastores dabo vobis*, no. 43.

51 Russel, *Men of Communion*, 160ff.

52 Ibid., 29.

53 Ibid., 10, wherein Russell cites Gerard J. McGlone and Len Sperry, *The Inner Life of Priests* (Collegeville, MN: Liturgical Press, 2012,) (no page is given).

⁵⁴ Ibid., wherein Russell points out in 39-41, the word *affectus* in Latin is much richer than "affect[ivity] in English. Drawing again from the Catechism n. 1766, he points out that "Affectivity is the capacity for communion "[...] Affections have their source in this first movement of the human heart toward the good."

⁵⁵ Ibid., 47.

⁵⁶ Ibid., 86ff. Russell's treatment of the matter at this point is unfolding within a discussion of the relationship between affective maturity and specific forms of problematic developments in attachment, designated by him as anxious-preoccupied, dismissive-avoidant, and fearful-avoidant, which are beyond the scope of the present paper but may be quite useful in concrete situations, especially to psychological counselors engaged in assisting candidates and formators.

⁵⁷ Ibid., 56-57 (Cf. Congregation for Catholic Education, *Educational Guidance in human love: Outlines for Sex Education,* (November 1, 1983), https://vatican.va/roman_curia/congregations/ccatheduc/documents/rc_con_ccatheduc_doc_19831101_sexual-education_en.html (accessed March 30, 2022).

⁵⁸ Ibid., 57.

⁵⁹ Ibid., 10.

⁶⁰ Ibid., 59.

⁶¹ Ibid., 62.

⁶² Ibid., 13.

⁶³ Ibid., 10.

⁶⁴ Ibid., 124. This characterization is given in the context of a hypothetical case description but is one that is quite familiar to anyone involved in priestly formation.

⁶⁵ Deacon James Keating, "Vulnerability as a Place of Divine Encounter," *Homiletic and Pastoral Review,* December 14, 015, https://hprweb.com/2015/12/vulnerability-as-a-place-of-divine-encounter/ (last accessed March 30, 2022).

⁶⁶ Chylinski relies here on the work of (among others) Brené Brown, *Daring Greatly: How the Courage to be Vulnerable Transforms the Way We Live, Love, Parent and Lead* (Avery: 2015), whose TED talk on vulnerability has become one of the top such talks in the world with over 50 million views; and also on the description of interpersonal relationality as a basic premise of Christian anthropology from P.C. Vitz, William J. Nordling, Craig Steven Titus, *A Catholic Christian Meta-Model of the Person* (Sterling, VA: Divine Mercy University Press, 2020).

⁶⁷ Here he cites Jacques Philippe, *Interior Freedom* (New York: Scepter Publishers, 2002) 38- 39.

⁶⁸ One resource Chylinski cites is Stephen Hayes, *Acceptance and Commitment Therapy: The Process and Practice of Mindful Change,* Second Edition (Guilford Press: 2016).

⁶⁹ Philippe, *Interior Freedom,* 33.

⁷⁰ Ibid., p. 46.

⁷¹ Diary of St. Maria Faustina Kowalska: *Divine Mercy in my Soul:* Notebook 5, v.1488.

⁷² Congregation for Catholic Education, *Instruction Concerning the Criteria for the Discernment of Vocations with regard to Persons with Homosexual Tendencies in view of their Admission to the Seminary and to Holy Orders,* (August 31, 2005) no.1, http://vatican.va/roman_curia/congregations/ccatheduc/documents/rc_con_ccatheduc_doc_20051104_istruzione_en.html (last accessed March 30, 2022).

⁷³ Ibid., no. 2.

⁷⁴ Peter Kleponis and Richard Fitzgibbons, "The Distinction between Deep-Seated Homosexual Tendencies and Transitory Same-Sex Attractions in Candidates for Seminary and Religious Life," in *Linacre Quarterly* 78:3 (2011) 355-362. Consultation of this contribution in its entirety is to be highly recommended for formators, since the useful insights that it offers cannot be fully expounded here.

⁷⁵ Ibid., 357.

⁷⁶ St. Thomas Aquinas, *Summa theologiae* I, q. 1 a. 8, ad 2.

⁷⁷ Fr. John A, Hardon, S.J., *Modern Catholic Dictionary* (Bardstown, KY: Eternal Life, 2001) 15.

⁷⁸ *Catechism of the Catholic Church,* 2nd. ed (1997) [henceforth CCC], 1771–1775.

⁷⁹ Ibid., 1835– 1838.

⁸⁰ Ibid., 1839.

⁸¹ See CCC, 1810 and 1839.

⁸² See CCC, 1812 and 2 Peter 1: 4.

⁸³ CCC, 1813.

⁸⁴ Fr. Augustin Poulain, SJ, *The Graces of Interior Prayer* (Gilbert, AZ: Caritas Publishing, 2016), 146– 147 (with reference to Teresa of Avila's *Life* chap. xvii, 4).

⁸⁵ CCC, 1840.

⁸⁶ Ibid., 1601.

⁸⁷ Vatican II, *Lumen Gentium* (Nov. 21, 1964), no. 41, https://vatican.va/archive/hist_councils/ii_vatican_council/documents/vat-ii_const_19641121_lumen-gentium_en.html (last accessed March 30, 2022).

⁸⁸ Robert Cardinal Sarah, "Loving to the End: An Ecclesiological and Pastoral Look at Priestly Celibacy" in Benedict XVI and Robert Cardinal

Sarah, *From the Depths of Our Hearts: Priesthood, Celibacy, and the Crisis of the Catholic Church* trans. Michael J. Miller (San Francisco: Ignatius Press, 2020), 114–115 with a reference to St. Paul VI's 1967 Encyclical *Sacerdotalis Caelibatus*, no. 29.

[89] Vatican II, *Optatam Totius* (October 28, 1965), no.10, https://vatican.va/archive/hist_councils/ii_vatican_council/documents/vat-ii_decree_19651028_optatam-totius_en.html (last accessed March 30, 2022).

[90] Ibid., no. 11.

[91] Ibid.

[92] Pope John Paul II, Apostolic Exhortation, *Pastoris Dabo Vobis* (March 25, 1992), no. 44. https://vatican.va/content/john-paul-ii/en/apost_exhortations/documents/hf_jp-ii_exh_25031992_pastores-dabo-vobis.html (last accessed March 30, 20220).

[93] Ibid.

[94] Ibid.

[95] Ibid., no. 72.

[96] See especially nos. 63 and 64 of *The Gift of The Priestly Vocation*.

[97] Congregation for the Clergy, *The Gift of the Priestly Vocation* (December 8, 2016), no. 110.

www.ingramcontent.com/pod-product-compliance
Lightning Source LLC
Chambersburg PA
CBHW052042220426
43663CB00012B/2415